Secondary Action Heroes
of Golden Age Comics

Also by Lou Mougin

*Secondary Superheroes
of Golden Age Comics* (McFarland, 2020)

Secondary Action Heroes of Golden Age Comics

Lou Mougin

McFarland & Company, Inc., Publishers
Jefferson, North Carolina

Unless otherwise noted, comics covers shown are from those comics determined to be in the public domain by the Digital Comic Museum (digitalcomicmuseum.com).

Library of Congress Cataloguing-in-Publication Data

Names: Mougin, Lou, author.
Title: Secondary action heroes of Golden Age comics / Lou Mougin.
Description: Jefferson, North Carolina : McFarland & Company, Inc., Publishers, 2023. | Includes bibliographical references and index.
Identifiers: LCCN 2023036700 | ISBN 9781476691527 (paperback : acid free paper) ∞
ISBN 9781476649900 (ebook)
Subjects: LCSH: Superheroes in comics. | Comic books, strips, etc.—History and criticism. | LCGFT: Comics criticism.
Classification: LCC PN6714 .M688 2020 | DDC 741.5/9—dc23/eng/20230901
LC record available at https://lccn.loc.gov/2023036700

British Library cataloguing data are available

ISBN (print) 978-1-4766-9152-7
ISBN (ebook) 978-1-4766-4990-0

© 2023 The Estate of Lou Mougin. All rights reserved

No part of this book may be reproduced or transmitted in any form or by any means, electronic or mechanical, including photocopying or recording, or by any information storage and retrieval system, without permission in writing from the publisher.

On the front: Cover illustration from *Sheena, Queen of the Jungle*, Number 15, Spring 1952 (Fiction House)

Printed in the United States of America

McFarland & Company, Inc., Publishers
Box 611, Jefferson, North Carolina 28640
www.mcfarlandpub.com

Table of Contents

Introduction   1
    Not all the heroes of the Golden Age of Comics wore masks, costumes, and capes. Prepare for the lowdown on their non-super brethren (and sisters).

THE JUNGLE LINE   3
    Take a jungle lord, turn him into a jungle lady, put him in a skimpy leopard-skin suit, and you have Sheena. And Camilla. And Tiger Girl. And Taanda. And Rulah. And … well, go ahead and read about 'em, already.

SCIENCE FICTION THEATER   62
    Think Flash Gordon and Buck Rogers were the only space guys in comics? It's time you met the interplanetary idols of *Planet Comics* and all their rocket-riding cohorts!

THE ADVENTURERS   113
    Possibly the most basic (and no less exciting) heroes of all. Pirates, spies, detectives, soldiers, sailors, and all the other guys and gals who made trouble their business, and business was booming back then.

ONCE UPON A TIME, IN THE WESTERNS   180
    Cowboy heroes were massive in the media of the 1930s to the 1960s, and comics brought them to four-color life. The Vigilante, the Two-Gun Kid, American Eagle, Annie Oakley, and tons of others made their presence known (including a long ton of movie and TV adaptations), and we've rounded up all the ones that started before 1950.

Conclusion   307
Bibliography   309
Index   311

Introduction

If you're a comics fan, and you know about the Golden Age—roughly the late '30s to the early '50s—you might think all the interesting heroes had superpowers and wore colorful long johns to fight crooks, super-villains, and the Nazis.

Believe it or not, you'd be wrong.

Comics racks of the time were loaded down with lots of other kinds of books. Fiction House hardly ever went near superheroes, but still put out a heroic line of titles from 1938 to 1953: *Jumbo, Jungle, Wings, Planet, Sheena, Firehair, Indians*, and the like. Just about every anthology comic boasted science fiction characters such as Spacehawk, the Solar Legion, and Hunt Bowman. Plus, there were just plain adventurers, like the denizens of *Fight Comics* or the long-lived Dick Cole and Cadet. There were Westerns and war stories, horror features, movie adaptations, funny stuff, romances—the Forties comics ran the gamut.

That means the favorites of a lot of readers at that time, and more than a few at *this* time, weren't being covered. As I've found out, if you want something covered, the best tactic is to cover it yourself.

What about Sheena? What about Spacehawk? What about Hunt Bowman and Futura and Fantomah and Camilla and Nyoka and Black Diamond and….

Well, you get the picture.

I wrote *Secondary Superheroes of Golden Age Comics* (2019) to give the heroes who weren't Superman, Batman, Wonder Woman, Captain Marvel, Captain America, Blackhawk, Plastic Man, et al., their memorial. But I always intended to do the same for Sheena, Hunt Bowman, Spacehawk, Tom Mix, and all the rest who deserve a chance at posterity, too. Kids read and loved comics about jungle heroes, spacemen, and adventurers back then, and it's time we found out why.

Since our earlier volume did pretty well, I decided to take a shot at the rest of the heroic lineup. Here it is. You'll probably learn more about heroes you already knew, be introduced to a bunch you didn't, and have some fun jumping into comics' Jurassic era.

Heck, I sure did. So back we go to the days of the late Depression, World War II, and its aftermath. It was a time when we needed heroes, and we got 'em.

And not all of them wore costumes.

Let's get started.

The Jungle Line

There was a very small picture of her on the cover: a blonde in a brown halter and short skirt-garment, spear in one hand, pointing with her other hand toward something unseen. Before her was an African warrior, also carrying a spear, obviously under her command.

She was anything but demure, anything but helpless. But she was almost buried among the cover cartoon and the call-out blurbs for other features in the first issue of *Jumbo Comics*, dated September 1938. The only identification was her name, at the bottom of the picture: SHEENA.

That was the way the first and most famous jungle girl in comics met America.

The initial story, like many from that era, was set up with each page in the form of a Sunday comics page. Since the stories in *Jumbo* were intended for reprint in overseas magazines, some in the form of comics sections, this wasn't surprising. We immediately were thrust into the action. The cover picture was a truncated form of the first panel of the story, and the target toward which the African's spear was pointed was a white adventurer named Bob Reynolds. "In search of the mysterious Sheena, Bob Reynolds and Professor Van Dyke become separated. Alone, Bob is attacked by Sheena's guards," read a caption. Bob, "[t]oo weary to lift his gun," was captured, bound, and marched behind Sheena to a place of confinement.

Sheena herself was one of the sexiest depictions of a woman in the brief history of American comics. In her fur halter and skirt, barefoot and implacable, she conjured up visions of the heroine of H. Rider Haggard's *She* crossed with Tarzan's Jane from the movies. Like Haggard's Ayesha, she ruled a hidden kingdom of Blacks. What else remained of her story had yet to be revealed.

Bob was taken to a hut and placed under guard, to be joined by the missing Van Dyke two days later. Shortly afterward, he overpowered a guard, and he and Van Dyke made off for Sheena's cave. The two of them saw the jungle queen on her throne, guarded by her warriors, and were obviously in danger of being slaughtered. But Van Dyke held up his arms and yelled, "Rumoltai!" This word, meaning "friend" in the natives' language, caused most of the group to pause. Sheena issued an order, and the two white men's lives were spared.

"She's beautiful—beautiful!" remarked the enraptured Bob.

An old witch doctor stepped forward, skull-topped cane in hand, and led them off to a private feast. Over dinner, the mystic spoke of tribal history: "Many centuries ago, the Tartars swept down from the barren plains of the Gobi. When the wild

Jumbo Comics #1: diving into Fiction House's first comic. © 1938 Real Adventures Publishing Co.

conquerors reached Samarkand, they halted and many clans left the main horde to roam and pillage on their own. One party ... rode southwest. Finding the climate warm and pleasing, they pushed forward, and, sweeping all before them, they entered Africa." Unfortunately, the climate was the only thing which was warm and pleasing. Predatory animals, heat, disease, and attacks from natives decimated the warriors, and only a handful of them reached the valley where they made their home.

To that valley, centuries later, came an explorer named Cardwell Rivington, with his young daughter Sheena in tow. Expert in languages, Rivington became friends with Koba, the witch doctor of the tribe. When the time came for the Rivingtons to leave, Koba, not wanting his compatriot to go, prepared a mystic potion that, he hoped, would induce Cardwell Rivington to stay. Unfortunately, it killed him. Koba, struck by remorse, vowed to raise little Sheena Rivington as his own, and so he did.

Sheena, like Tarzan before her, became powerful and skilled at fighting, besting all the males in the tribe. She learned how to hunt and kill the animals of the jungle, but, more importantly, to befriend and master them. Growing in wisdom and beauty, she eventually became the white queen of the lost tribe. She was a cold and brutal ruler when Bob Reynolds met her. But...

...Love conquers all. At least, in comic books.

In short order, Sheena left the hidden valley, Bob in tow, and became a jungle adventuress. Briefly, this is the gist of the story told in *Jumbo Comics* #1–5, reprinted from pages done for the Australian comic *Wags*. The original Sheena appearance in *Wags* was in 1938, some months before Superman's debut in *Action Comics* #1.

Who created her? Both Will Eisner and Jerry Iger laid claim to the jungle queen (who wouldn't?), but the truth may be lost to time. At first, Sheena was mainly a riff on H. Rider Haggard's Ayesha, of *She* fame. But when the artists and writers realized there were more sales to be had in raw sex appeal than in lost world fantasy, they abruptly about-faced and turned her into a female Tarzan. It worked. And how!

After the initial arc

Sheena versus a lion. Really, the lion should have known better. © 1940 Real Adventures Publishing Co.

of tales introducing Sheena, most of her stories were interchangeable. She and her lover Bob would become involved in a situation involving evildoers in the jungle, go through a number of perils, fight with gun (in Bob's case) and knife (in Sheena's), and beat the bad guys in the end. Most comic-book hero stories are formula-fed. Sheena's were no exception. On the other hand, with a figure like hers, nobody expected you to pay much attention to the stories.

In *Jumbo* #10, a fairly insubstantial story depicted Sheena, in a short red dress, going up against Namu, a lion who had killed two villagers. Armed with naught but a knife, she killed the big cat in a four-page battle. Immediately after, Bob shot a leopard that was springing at them. "His skin will make me a new dress!" Sheena declared. A panel later, possibly with the help of a native woman standing behind her, she stood revealed—in more ways than one—in her new outfit.

The leopard skin had been cut into a bathing suit with strips that looped over both breasts (without a connecting bit of material between them), meeting at the belt area, just over a fairly modest suit bottom that covered everything from her waist to her thighs. For the moment, anyway. To say the least, it *wasn't* a dress.

Sheena pirouetted like a model and asked Bob how he liked her outfit. He allowed that even though she was a fierce fighter with the courage of ten men, she was still a woman. Sheena looked a little miffed. But she had gained a trademark wardrobe that would, in its way, become as familiar as Superman's costume. The Queen of the Jungle was finalized!

A few bangles, armbands, and anklets completed Sheena's dress. She was always barefoot, always displayed plenty of leg, and never seemed abashed by it. Or by much of anything else. She killed at least one vicious and powerful beast every story, be it lion, leopard, rhino, python, hyena, or anything else foolhardy enough to chance her wrath. Her pet monkey, Chim, appeared throughout the saga and was often as instrumental in saving her life as he was getting into trouble. Bob Reynolds, with his white-hunter stamina, courage, and bangstick, bagged his quota of beasts and bad guys and was at first presented as Sheena's equal. But, as time went on, it became clear that Sheena was the queen, and he was at most the prince consort. All things considered, it wasn't a bad thing to be.

So, who created Sheena?

The answers to that are as hard to find as the path to her hidden jungle lair. Will Eisner claimed to have conceived of the jungle beauty, as has Jerry Iger. Both seem to have noted that a "female Tarzan" might be as big a draw as Edgar Rice Burroughs's jungle man, but that hypothesis fails to note that, in the beginning, Sheena was based pretty solidly on H. Rider Haggard's *She*. Sheena lost that influence after a few issues, but the template is obvious in the early *Jumbo* issues. (It should also be noted that *She* itself was adapted directly into comics not long afterward, first by DC, then by others.) It was only as the series developed that Sheena turned into the distaff answer to Johnny Weissmuller.

What is known is that she was created in the early days of the Eisner / Iger shop as part of a package for *Wags*, an Australian comic book. Sheena debuted down under in issue #46 (January 14, 1938), with scripting probably by Eisner and art by Mort Meskin. The shop men, including Jack Kirby, Bob Kane, Dick Briefer, Bob

Powell, Alex Blum and his daughter Toni (who produced tons of scripts for the outfit), and George Tuska, pumped out pages for eight months before somebody sold T.T. Scott, publisher of Fiction House's pulp line, on publishing comics. And why not?

So, in 1938, *Jumbo Comics* hit the newsstand. It probably made a loud thud on impact, as the first issue, and seven thereafter, were huge, *Life Magazine*-sized monsters in black and white, with color covers. The first three issues were 68 pages and the next five dropped to 52. Other outfits like DC (with *New Fun*) and Fawcett (with *Master*) had experimented or would experiment with tabloid-sized comics, but all of them would shrink their products down to a manageable, standard size before long. *Jumbo* was no exception, but that's how it got its name.

As noted, on issue #1's cover, Sheena was no big deal. She shared space with *Hawks of the Seas* and *Peter Pupp*, coming up at the bottom on the left-hand side. The main space was reserved for a gag cartoon sequence. That was pretty much the way it was until issue #7, in which three features shared comic-strip billing on the cover. Sheena was the one in the middle. She finally more or less got the cover of #9 (August–September 1939), but the main figure was a troglodytic caveman whom Bob was fighting off with his rifle as a club. If you looked hard enough, you could see Sheena leaping down at some apes in the background.

Cover girl status was hard to achieve, even back then.

Finally, our heroine captured the cover spot in #13, the March 1940 issue, in her barefoot, leg-baring, leopard-suited, knife-brandishing glory. It was pretty tame compared to what would come after, and Bob Reynolds was just about as big on the cover as Sheena. Still, it was a start, and to some kids it must have had the same impact as a *Sports Illustrated* bathing suit cover would some decades down the line. Sheena was hot!

More than that, she was tough.

There would be no Lois Lane–style waiting-to-be-rescued antics for her. Sheena took on the toughest beasts and men the jungle had to offer, armed only with her knife, her wits, and her strong, sexy body, and beat them all. If a great jungle cat was threatening, she leaped atop its back and cut its throat. If power-hungry native chieftains or wandering Nazis got in her path, she outthought and outfought them. Sheena was the queen of her jungle, and she took it seriously.

And yet, she was not a bitch. Sheena was a heroine, a role model of sorts, and it's probable that female readers enjoyed her for a different reason—as a strong and beautiful woman who could fend for herself in a hostile world and who fought for others as well. She wasn't just sex appeal.

Thus, about three years after her creation, Sheena became a breakout character. She alternated on covers with the Lightning, a nondescript superhero, until issue #17, when she grabbed the cover space and held onto it till #160. Both sex object and heroine, Sheena ruled her domain.

For the first couple of years after *Jumbo* shrank to normal dimensions, Bob Powell both wrote and drew Sheena, and the stories had a rough continuity. A few supporting characters, including an evil pasha and two college chums of Bob Reynolds's, carried over into several stories. Even Namu, a lion whom Chim had saved from starvation, teamed up with his monkey pal more than once. Also, Sheena's love for Bob was openly displayed: when an old flame of Bob's stole a kiss, the jungle queen fell into a depression, was captured by slavers, and had to be rescued by her mate and his friends. In the early days, she was a very human heroine.

And in issue #24 (February 1941), Bob proved his humanity, too. Sheena was struck in the eyes by venom from a spitting cobra. Death would come within 72 hours. In response, the native tribes sent in three of their best witch doctors to help. But Bob Reynolds began a 140-mile trek to find the nearest white doctor in Mombasa, pushed himself relentlessly onward without sleep or food and only a bit of water, and made his goal, exhausted, stubble-bearded, and ragged. He explained Sheena's plight to the doctor. The medic said, "Venom of that sort causes death in seventy-two hours … there's absolutely nothing I could do!"

In response, a weary Bob stuck his gun under the doctor's nose. "If you don't come back with me, I'll blow your brains out!" The doctor chose the path of discretion. Both he and Bob ended up fighting their way back to the village where Sheena lay stricken. But they were a little late. The medicine men's efforts had restored Sheena to full health. Astounded, the doctor tried to get his native colleagues to tell him how they did it. They stolidly refused to divulge the trade secret. When he turned to see if Bob could help, the doctor found his friend lip-locking with Sheena. "Well, I can always find out later," he said. "Why break up a happy ending?"

The peerless pair battled their way through issue after issue, tackling a 30-foot super-ape, a mummy raised from the dead, a potentate intent on hunting humans à la "The Most Dangerous Game," and the inevitable evil white hunters. One story touched on racial politics, with a "great black father" stirring up sentiment against local whites, unaware he was only a tool of fascists who wished to use the natives as slaves. The war had come to the jungle, and Sheena and Bob would encounter Nazi troops more than once.

With #27 (May 1941), Powell was gone and Robert Webb, who would handle Sheena for many years, signed on as artist. Ruth Roche and S.M. Iger, among others, became scripters. The quality of drawing remained high, but Sheena's character lost a little in the transition. She'd still be the battle-ready queen of the jungle, but a bit of her humanity had been lost: her love affair with Bob Reynolds was quietly shuffled to the background. Each story became self-contained. It was, sadly, the price of success.

At about that time, in 1942, Sheena graduated to her own title. *Sheena, Queen of the Jungle* #1 (Spring 1942) cover-featured the leopard lady with knife and spear, either fleeing a lion or swiveling to turn it into cat chow. Within, she tackled evil tribal leaders, a vicious huntress, slavers, and the usual quota of wild animals. Bob was on hand, too, getting trapped and rescued at least once, but pulling his weight by slaying a menacing hippo with his knife and saving Sheena from drowning. She finished the issue with a slugfest against a snake priestess, and that was that.

The original Queen of the Jungle helmed *Jumbo Comics* for 167 issues, appeared in 18 issues of her own comic, and made a few reprint appearances in other Fiction House comics. Along the way, she sported some marvelous art by Robert Webb and others. But, after the Forties, it seemed as though the powers that be tried to deemphasize Sheena's sexiness. (As if they could!) Circa 1950, Sheena's bold two-piece suit changed to a one-piece bathing suit, and so it remained for the last three years of her comic existence. For *Jumbo*'s last seven issues, it seemed as though the covers had stepped backward in time: instead of making Sheena the sole cover-feature, she was relegated to a cameo alongside other secondary tales. The anti-comics crusade was heating up, and Fiction House may have gotten gun-shy about selling half-naked jungle queens to prepubescent readers.

Instead, they tried other venues to promote Sheena. A lone 1953 pulp featured Sheena in three stories, and another prose tale or two appeared in Fiction House's *Jungle Stories*. They published the almost obligatory 3-D reprint comic of *Sheena* the same year. But in *Jumbo* #167 (March 1953), Sheena and Bob saved a chieftain's son from a pair of evil white hunters, one of whom was named Nixon, killed the python and leopard from Central Casting, and that was it.

Almost.

A lion horns in on the first cover of Sheena's own comic. © 1942 Real Adventures Publishing Co.

In 1952, film producer Sol Lesser tried his luck at promoting a Sheena movie, not an unlikely move given the popularity of his Tarzan flicks at the time. Auditions were held for a beautiful actress who could pull off athletic feats convincingly, and the search attracted names like Lilly Christine, Debra Paget, and Anita Ekberg. But the emphasis switched to the new medium, television, and the part went to a model and showgirl named Irish McCalla.

Ms. McCalla, whose photo-spreads in men's mags and an album cover or two rarely showed her in more than a bathing suit, was athletic enough (and hot enough) to ace a screen test, which she went to on the advice of a photographer friend, Tom Kelly. The 25-year-old bikini queen said that she had read Sheena comics when she was a kid and liked to pretend she was the jungle queen herself, swinging on ropes with her brothers when they played Tarzan. At least that's what she said, and it may well have been true.

Sheena, Queen of the Jungle debuted either in late 1955 or early '56 as a syndicated black-and-white show and featured Irish in the title role, dressed in a short leopard-skin garment that showed as much leg as just about anyone could have wanted. She spoke pidgin English à la Weissmuller's Tarzan and, with the help of Christian Drake as Bob Rayburn, fought bad guys, did fairly daring stunts, and kept her part of the jungle safe for native tribes and sponsors. The series ran for a respectable 26 episodes, ending probably in early 1957. Irish McCalla, having carried the torch for jungle queens into TV, went back to modeling and then became an artist, but her Sheena stint was never forgotten. She made numerous appearances on the convention circuit, signing pics and selling art to fans who hadn't even been born when the original show ran. McCalla passed away in 2002, and not a few tributes followed.

Sheena just wouldn't die.

Schlockmeister Israel Waldman reprinted an issue of *Sheena*, sans permission (as always), in 1958. Thirteen years later, in company with Sol Brodsky in Skywald Comics, he ran another few reprint tales of Sheena in the back of *Jungle Adventures*, a short-lived title. Jurassic-era comics histories mentioned her in passing, and her iconic, female-Tarzan image was indelible.

Raquel Welch was reportedly to star in a 1966 *Sheena* movie, but it never came to pass. That may or may not have been good fortune, because Tanya Roberts took up the leather bikini to play the title role in the 1984 *Sheena* film, a bomb potent enough to level a city block. (Marvel adapted it into comics in *Marvel Super Special* #34 [1984] and reprinted it in *Sheena* #1 and 2 [December 1984–February 1985]. Neither one was worth writing home about.) In 2000, *Baywatch* alum Gena Lee Nolin donned what there was of the costume to play Sheena in another syndicated show that ran two years. This time, Sheena could mutate into animals. It didn't seem to work.

The comics tried new revivals of Sheena. Blackthorne starred her in a well-intentioned three-issue series written by Bruce Jones (*Jungle Comics* #1–3, May–October 1988), but it didn't take hold. London Night botched an attempt in 1998, taking her out of her leopard-skin outfit and putting her in black leather (*Sheena, Queen of the Jungle* #0–2, February–October 1998). There were also tons of reprints by various outfits.

Finally, in 2007, Devil's Due Publishing did a respectable reboot of the character, retaining her jungle setting and her spotted bathing suit. The first appearance was a one-shot *Sheena Special* #1 (March 2007), by Robert Rodi and Steve Cummings. Sheena was revived as a young jungle heroine in the wilds of a South American country called Val Verde. A five-issue follow-up, *Sheena, Queen of the Jungle*, followed (June 2007–January 2008). She got a new origin but was mostly the same jungle queen in an interesting story. More Sheena comics followed: *Sheena: Trail of the Mapinguari* #1 (April 2008) and *Sheena, Queen of the Jungle: Dark Rising* #1–3 (October–December 2008), plus a couple of reprint volumes. That was the end of her tour of duty with Devil's Due.

Sheena came back in 2014 in a three-issue series from Moonstone, written by

David and Steven de Souza and arted by Jake Minor. *Sheena, Queen of the Jungle* #1–3 continued the Val Verde storyline and pitted the jungle bikini queen against some jaguar men. Then it ended.

But in 2016, Dynamite got her rights, and teamed her up with—of all people—Tarzan! The Lord and Lady of the Jungle co-starred in *Lords of the Jungle* #1–6 (2016) and worked together excellently. A *Sheena, Queen of the Jungle* series ensued (#0–10, August–October 2017). As of this writing, that's her last comic appearance.

She isn't forgotten, and probably never will be. Among all the jungle women, Sheena stands proudly as the true Queen of the Jungle.

But she had many daughters. Some of them came from another Fiction House title that was directly spawned by Sheena's success in *Jumbo*. The new comic debuted in 1940, and the title was a natural: *Jungle Comics*.

The coming of Kaanga! © 1939 Glen-Kel Publishing Co.

Jungle Comics was a direct echo of Fiction House's *Jungle Stories* pulp, and its headline hero was the comic book version of *Stories*' Tarzan knock-off, Ki-Gor. In the comics, he was the longest-lived male jungle hero after Tarzan himself. He was the mighty Kaanga.

The cover of *Jungle* #1 showed a mighty blond jungle-man in leopard-skin briefs, swinging down with a vine in one hand and a knife in the other, ready to save a brunette woman from the attentions of a lion. Within, a story credited to "Alex Boon" (drawn by Alex Blum) got things started quickly. A safari led by one Professor Mason, whose daughter Ann was in tow, was attacked by "murderous slave trader" Bill Blacton. While his hirelings mowed down the native bearers, Blacton declared to the professor, "We've no use for you, old man!" and shot him.

Apparently Blacton had a use of another kind in mind for Ann, who ran as far and hard as she could into the underbrush, pursued by the blackguard every step of the way. She finally fell from exhaustion, and Blacton loomed over her, ready for his own brand of recreation. But then…

…a lithe, blond figure of a man leaped from the trees to land between him and Ann. Blacton had enough time to murmur, "What the?" before the newcomer unleashed a haymaker, then lifted him effortlessly overhead and tossed him into the bushes. After that, Kaanga scooped Ann up deftly and carried her to his "jungle home."

Evidently, Ann knew who to trust. In the next scene, in which a caption informed us that they had been together for "many weeks," she was shown teaching her new captor rudimentary English: "Tree, sky, you Kaanga, I Ann." She knew her Johnny Weissmuller movies from Stateside days. It seemed to work.

Finally, she got down to asking the question, "Tell me, how did you come here?" That opened the gates for an origin flashback.

"Long ago, friends and father killed by natives. I run away, far into jungle, when I hear a sudden sound. It is strange man. He act kind to me. He talk not like me. He take me to village…. Me meet more kind jungle people. Me grow up among them. Learn jungle ways, and soon forget white man's ways and talk."

Well, that just wouldn't do, declared Ann. It was high time he saw the sights of outer civilization, and she was just the woman to show them to him. Kaanga agreed, tentatively, and followed Ann to "an outpost of civilization." Guess who was waiting there?

Bill Blacton and his men chained Kaanga on the spot, noting, "As a slave he will bring a good price!" The jungle lord was thrown in a cell with other captives, and Blacton turned to Ann. "Your hero is kinda on the spot, eh?"

And it appeared the spot Kaanga was on was dismal indeed. He was auctioned, sold, and given to a mine owner, one Slattery, as Ann looked on in horror. But, just after he was marched off between two armed guards…

…Action!

Kaanga kicked one guard in the gut while giving the other a head-butt in the same region. Slattery tried to bring up his rifle. Kaanga snatched it away, bent it "like a twig" with his bare hands, and bounded off into the jungle. Then he headed to a mansion in which Blacton was celebrating his good fortune, swung in on a chandelier, upset all the guests, snatched Ann from the ballroom, and swung off with her into the jungle.

Blacton, of course, couldn't leave well enough alone. He headed up a posse of hoodlums and went after the pair. Kaanga, watching from a tree branch above, bade Ann remain while he made himself visible to the bad guys and led them on a merry chase. And when he had them where he wanted them, the jungle man put his hands to his mouth and gave a "blood-curdling war cry."

That was all it took. In one page-hogging panel, a horde of "ape-men," evidently the same ones who raised our hero, leaped from the trees and made mincemeat of the evildoers. They left Blacton for Kaanga, who snapped, "Kaanga no disappoint you, Blacton. Kaanga very much alive!" before he slugged him with a satisfying SOCK!

After celebrating victory with the ape-men, Kaanga bade them farewell and returned to Ann. He outlined the situation: "Ann, Kaanga must stay here in jungle! White man's way is not Kaanga's way!"

"Well, then I must go back alone," Ann admitted. But Kaanga took her hands and declared she would always have a place with him in the jungle, should she decide to return. He led her to "an outpost where her father's colleagues are at work" and left her. Kaanga secretly kept "a sad vigil" nearby, "for danger still threatens and is imminent."

It sure did, and it was, for a good fourteen years, all told. But there was still some stage-setting to be done. In *Jungle* #2 (February 1940), Kaanga rescued Ann from one Doctor Wratt, a mustached and monocled mad scientist who had a small army of man-apes at his command. Ann wore a leopard-skin outfit on the cover, but sported a shirt and jodhpurs in the story. Fashion-wise, the cover artists were getting ahead of themselves.

The jungle pair were an item, and stayed together for almost every issue thereafter. Issue #3 (March 1940) introduced Sam Broot, a Black American gangster who had made his way to Africa and dominated a tribe by terror. Kaanga gave Broot his comeuppance, but the villain returned for the next issue and several afterward. By issue #5 (May 1940), Ann was down to a sportier, leg-baring red outfit. The art chores had fallen by this time to George Tuska, who did the feature proud.

By *Jungle Comics* #10 (October 1940), a few details of Kaanga's origin were filled in. The jungle king crossed the path of an evildoer who, twenty years ago, had kidnapped him as a child and sold him to slavers. This time, the crook was trying a duplicate scam with the son of a wealthy man, but the blond giant confronted him and identified himself to the wealthy father. "I escaped and grew up with the animals, but I suffered terribly and I don't want that to happen to your son!"

"Then you're..." started the kidnapper.

"My jungle name is Kaanga!" That was as close as we ever got to learning the jungle man's true name. Though the crook took it on the lam, Kaanga finally saved the boy and saw his nemesis perish in a hail of police bullets. Another loose end tied up.

The next issue stirred together Kaanga, Ann, a bunch of dinosaurs, and a pair of Ann's cousins who intended to take her back, dead or alive, to England and claim her inheritance. After the wicked twosome experienced pre–*Jurassic Park* terrors, they agreed to leave Ann and Kaanga be and return to Britain. There, they told an embellished tale of confronting T-Rexes and lost all credibility and standing whatever. That stuff, after all, was straight out of the comic books.

The publisher and editor were gradually learning the draw of cheesecake, and Ann finally sported a leopard-skin two-piece on Nick Cardy's cover for *Jungle* #16 (April 1941) and in the story inside. She was never as strong as Sheena, but before long her presence on the cover came to dwarf Kaanga's. If he objected, we never knew. At least they both kept the cover spot on every issue, until #163 (Summer 1954).

Kaanga finally graduated to his own title in 1949, and swung into action there for 20 issues, finishing the run in 1954. Along the way, he and Ann picked up some excellent rendering, courtesy of Ruben Moreira, Reed Crandall, Rafael Astarita, John Celardo, Maurice Whitman, Dan Zolnerowich, Marcia Snyder, and Art Saaf, among others.

There were a couple of attempts to revive him. The first, and best, was in a three-issue revival of *Jungle Comics*, published in 1988 by Blackthorne Comics. Bruce Jones, late of Marvel's *Ka-Zar*, was the writer, and Hal Jones (credited as Dragan Flaesc) was the artist. Though we didn't get all the details, Kaanga, now spelled Ka'a'nga, was still living in the jungle and had been kept young and vital by a witch doctor's serum. Ann was nowhere in evidence. The witch doctor revitalized an aging Sheena with the same serum, and she and Ka'a'nga spent three issues fighting side-by-side and bickering. Bob didn't seem to be around, either. In the third issue, he was stabbed in the chest by a hypnotized Sheena. We never found out what happened next.

Later, another version of Ka'a'nga was brought out of the Vault, the place where Golden Age characters were kept on ice, in 1990 in AC Comics' *Femforce* #29 and 36 (1990, 1991). He's made a few appearances in other AC comics, as a guest star and in reprints. In 2019, Antarctic Press reintroduced him in a new series of *Jungle Comics*. Though he's hardly known today, Ka'a'nga's long-running stint at the helm of *Jungle* earns him the title of the Golden Age's greatest original male jungle star.

He was, of course, hardly alone.

Camilla was the next important feature to come from *Jungle Comics*. In her earliest version, she was also the most confusing. Pay attention, because this is going to get complicated.

Her original adventure in *Jungle* #1 (January 1940) was drawn by stalwart artist Charles A. Winter, aka CAW, and it cannibalized heavily from Haggard's *She*. There is something to be said for stealing from the best, but the result was more like a new paint job and a phony plate on a stolen car. Here's how it went: the splash panel featured an imposing golden-haired woman in a long red dress, a winged helmet, gold bracelets, and a belt, holding a wooden staff and standing near a city in the jungle. The caption read, "The young scientist, Jon Dale, seeks a lost civilization in Africa, composed of the same Norsemen who went there during the Crusades, and who have found the secret of eternal life. He falls into the power of beautiful Camilla, queen of the Lost Empire." That pretty much sums it up. Details follow.

Young scientist Jon Dale, in pith helmet, shorts, and shirt, got tangled up in

The Mark I Camilla, queen of the Lost Empire and a pretty wicked chick. © 1939 Glen-Kel Publishing Co.

vines attached to a mad elephant and was dragged conveniently to the environs of the Lost Empire. He was welcomed by bare-chested white guards who sported horned helmets, bearskin kilts, boots, and swords. Camilla received him in her throne room and introduced him to another pair of explorers, Dr. Birch and Ruth, his daughter. "You are just in time for the big thunder festival and the human sacrifice!" declared Camilla. "But first, I will show you the city!"

It's nice to have such courtesy shown to newcomers. The Lost Empire's Chamber of Commerce must have made quite a to-do about it.

Camilla gave the trio the grand tour, including the temple of Thor, "where the blood sacrifice is held. We'll see one in a little while!" Also, she showed off a sulphur spring which, though explosive, prolonged life and youth in five-year chunks when mixed with a secret formula. That, she alleged, was why the Lost Empire tribe had managed to survive for over 600 years. Well, some of them survived, anyway.

"Every day during this rainy season comes the thunder and the lightning! It is these gods we worship! And we sacrifice a human being to them *each day!*" Well ... if people are going to live for six centuries, it's obvious corners are going to have to be cut somewhere.

On an altar, a sacrificial victim lay between two electrodes. It was raining. Lightning struck the electrodes. ZAP! No more victim. At all. The unfortunate had simply vanished. Camilla turned to Jon and said, "Why not stay here in the Lost Empire and be my king—we could be so happy!"

"Never!"

In response, Camilla ruled that Ruth would be the next sacrifice. But, of course, Jon Dale was made of stern stuff indeed, and grounded the electrodes. Ruth remained unsacrificed, Jon convinced the Vikings that the gods were angry about the whole setup, and the guys in the helmets thundered, "Down with the queen!" The queen took it on the lam. Jon followed. After shooting a tiger that Camilla sicced on him, he saw the queen aging in seconds. "Eternal life is folly. We should only live our normal span of years. I feel I am going to die now!"

And, as a caption noted, "Queen Camilla dies," and Jon Dale went back to where a mob of Vikings were threatening Ruth and her father. As all red-blooded Americans would, Jon waded in and started dusting jaws right and left. For a finisher, he threw a torch into the sulphur spring and blew it up real good. "The terrific blast completely wrecks the Lost Empire!" After leading his friends to safety, Jon revealed that Camilla had given him the secret of eternal life, but he decided to destroy it. "We should be satisfied with the life God has given us, and not try to improve on His wisdom!" And that, for issue #1 at least, was that.

In the next issue, Camilla got better. She struck a Theda Bara pose on the splash panel, in which we learned that she was "descended from the great conqueror, Genghis Khan." It's kind of strange that Genghis Khan would be a Viking, but you never can tell sometimes. Anyway, Camilla captured a white hunter, one John Stanley, with the aid of a radio-controlled rocket ship. While wining and dining him, she revealed that she was in control of a radium ray by which "[w]e can destroy your Western civilization whenever we wish!" On the spot, she made him a job offer, asking him to stay and be commander of the army. Stanley gracefully declined.

Reasonably enough, Camilla decided to have him thrown in a dungeon. When Stanley fought his way almost free, she decided that he would be put in one of her torpedo-ships and sent into space. It didn't work out that way. The hunter fought free again, got to the radium ray control room, yanked on a switch, and vibrated the entire city to pieces. When Camilla herself fainted, Stanley picked her up and carried her to safety. Her first impulse upon waking up was to chew him out for saving her, and turn back to her flaming city. Evidently, Camilla had major relationship issues.

By the next issue of *Jungle*, Jon Dale and Ruth were back, and Camilla learned from a local prophet with a crystal that if she sacrificed herself in the flames, her city and her people would return. Altruistically, she had the bonfire built, stepped into the middle of it, and raised her hands in the midst of the flames, saying, "O great Bal! Restore my lost empire and my people!" It worked. Not only did the city and the people come back, but Camilla avoided being toasted. And, when Jon and Ruth arrived and Jon still refused to be her king, Camilla threw Ruth into a "blue pool" that turned her into a hag. Jon himself was thrown to a python. Undeterred, he slew the snake with a knife, restored Ruth's youth with a drink from "the spring of eternal youth," and blew up the blue pool while Camilla looked on. "Camilla will soon die of old age, then we will come back and finish our work!"

"Oh, Jon, you're wonderful!" said Ruth.

Camilla was in her familiar mood by the next story, mad over getting older, spurring rebellion in her subjects, and having petty offenders flayed in the torture pit. The people rebelled and Camilla was dethroned and ejected. But, with the help of Jon and Ruth, she plunged into the pool of youth again, emerged hotter than ever, and, with Jon's aid, convinced her subjects she had turned over a new leaf. They welcomed her home, and, this time, she bade a friendly farewell to her two guests, saying, "You will always be welcome guests in the Lost Empire!" That might not have seemed such an attractive proposition, but at least she was trying.

It seemed to work. By issue #5 (May 1940), Camilla was defending her city against Viking raiders, which she did very effectively by placing a knife in the heart of their chieftain. The art improved and Camilla unleashed her short-sword against all invaders and internal threats, often slaying the bad guys personally. In another early issue she descended into a cavern to confront a two-headed monstrosity who claimed to be the Devil himself. She poked him in the eye with her sword, carved a cross out of a rock to repel him, and escaped with a hunchback whom she had befriended. Afterward, an angel appeared to her to grant one wish. The wish was for the hunchback to be transformed into a strong, handsome man, whom she renamed Sir Champion and made her army commander and sidekick. Clearly, Camilla had come up in the world.

Camilla and her consort fought side-by-side for several more issues against foes both material and mystical. In *Jungle* #14 (February 1941), Sir Champion defeated a wizardly foe by turning him into a potato with a magic sword and pinning him to the floor with it. No word was given as to whether or not the wizard was later mashed and eaten with sour cream. Champion seemed to fade from the scene by issue #18 (June 1941). Perhaps Camilla had just gotten tired of him.

The art and scripting seemed taken from *Prince Valiant* by this time, with the winged-helmeted queen fighting off Vikings, pygmies, regular-sized Black warriors, and whoever wandered in from Central Casting. She hooked up with a fellow Northman called Eric and he stayed around for a few issues. Her costume was usually abbreviated down to the helmet, a halter, shorts, and boots. Nobody much complained.

In issue #27 (March 1942), things changed.

The story that unfolded showed Camilla, lost from her Lost Empire for three nights, cold in her bra and shorts (which would be highly ironic in a few issues' time), and slaying a zebra with her knife, making a short dress from its skin to keep her warm. "I'm queen of a jungle empire, now my Vikings would never know me in this skin," she mused. Probably she was wrong about that, but we'd never know. Soon enough, she rescued an aviator from a crashed plane, fought off a tribe of headhunters, and began a new career as a jungle girl. The change seemed to be good for her. She never went back to the Lost Empire, and they never came looking for her.

Even with her long legs and bare feet, Camilla was no threat to Sheena yet, thanks to so-so art and her long mini-skirt outfit. Her new boyfriend, Ben, carried too much of the action, as well. Clearly, the feature hadn't found its way yet, despite the change in format. But Fiction House was willing to give her a chance.

In issue #31 (July 1942), artist Nick Viscardi gave her that chance.

The splash panel told it all: Camilla, swinging in on a vine with a knife in one hand, sported a ragged zebra bikini with lace-up sides at the bottom (a bottom of which male readers were soon more than casually aware). Her face, hair, and figure

The Mark II Camilla, in a jungle bikini and now a heroine. © 1942 Glen-Kel Publishing Co.

had been given a massive makeover, and her curved back, flat stomach, pert breasts, and legs-that-went-from-there-to-here proclaimed her as the latest jungle sex bomb on the block. On top of that, she was swinging unafraid into reach of two poachers on the back of an elephant, and one was shooting at her. Camilla had made a turnaround!

In the story proper, Camilla and Ben were menaced by both a pair of unscrupulous white hunters and the Black Cobras, a snake-worshipping native tribe. Camilla chopped a cobra in half, overpowered a guard, saved Ben from a snake pit, got into a brawl with the tribesmen, and finally wound up leading them against the white bad guys. "Murderers!" she yelled, aiming a spear at them. "This time, you will not escape so easily!" Both villains ended up meeting a bad end, and the Cobra leader offered her a position as his queen. She declined the honor with at least as much grace as Jon Dale when he had a similar proposition, and the chieftain said she would carry the gratitude and loyalty of his people.

Camilla Mark II was a going concern.

She continued on as a beautiful, bikini-clad, barefoot jungle warrioress for year after year, graced by a number of good artists who limned her beauty to the best. Probably the finest of these was Fran Hopper, who, as a woman, was suited to rendering Camilla as an attractive but realistic female. Other fine artists included Marcia Snyder, George Tuska, and Ralph Mayo. Camilla didn't seem as tough as Sheena, but made up for that in grace and beauty. Early on, she lost her sidekick Ben, but she picked up a dog named Fang in issue #63 (March 1945) and he lasted a lot longer.

Finally, another bit of Camilla's history was revealed in *Jungle* #48 (December 1943). In this story, beautifully drawn by George Tuska, we learned that Camilla's last name was Dane and that she was the daughter of Steven and Camilla Dane, two American explorers who were befriended by a trader named J. Davis. Steven was killed by the spear of a witch doctor whom he had angered, though he dispatched the dastard himself with gunshots before he died. The elder Camilla delivered a daughter before passing away herself, leaving care of the infant to the trader. He said that he taught her the "lore of the jungle," but how she got from there to being queen of a lost Viking empire was never explained. The editor might have believed that readers had mostly forgotten about the earlier adventures. It didn't seem to matter.

Camilla's run in *Jungle* continued unbroken till issue #151 (July 1952), after which she made one more appearance in #163 (Summer 1954), the last issue. Then she was gone. AC Comics revived her pretty much in cameo in *Femforce* #29 (1990) along with a bunch of other characters, and she has made a few appearances in their comics since then, but has not been seen recently as of this writing.

Wambi was possibly the third most important feature in *Jungle*, and one of the two to earn its own book. Echoing Sabu of the movies and Mowgli of Kipling's *Jungle Book*, Wambi was a turbaned, loinclothed Indian teenager who could talk to the animals, especially his faithful elephant, Tawn. He showed up in every issue of *Jungle* from #1 to 158 (January 1940—Spring 1953) and headlined his own comic for 18 issues from 1942 to 1952. His appeal wasn't hard to figure out: how many kids dreamed back then of living in the jungle and being able to communicate with the beasts? Wambi held a spot of renown as the first teenage jungle hero in comics. Dynamite brought him back in *Pathfinder: Worldscape* #6 (2017), along with all the other *Jungle Comics* characters that weren't nailed down.

Captain Terry Thunder and the Congo Lancers was another long-lived *Jungle* feature. In the first issue, a six-page story with art credited to Art Peters established that an African fortress had been overtaken by slavers, who had decimated the four patrols that tried to retake it. Enter Captain Thunder, who had re-upped his service on the eve of his enlistment's running out. Assigned to find out what was going on at the fortress, Thunder rounded up some of the toughest guys in his regiment and dubbed them the Congo Lancers. Despite several perils, Thunder and his men captured the slavers and turned them over to the authorities. He was assigned the fortress as his post. One Lancer remarked, "It's dull here, now! No action!" "Mebbe!" said another. "But I've noticed, sooner or later, adventure catches up with Terry Thunder!"

That it did, for many an issue to come, though the early stories were fairly pedestrian. Pretty soon, though, the element of humor found its way into the stories. A stereotypical

Wambi the Jungle Boy's first issue. © 1942 Glen-Kel Publishing Co.

comic Arab named Anderson, accompanied by a stubborn camel named Kismet (whose sarcastic thoughts were amply delineated in balloons) and a vulture named Vincent, arrived and stole the show. With the additional injection of the inevitable Fiction House cheesecake, Terry Thunder was fit to go on adventuring for years to come. He bowed out in issue #151 (July 1952), after a long and honorable tour of duty.

Tabu, Wizard of the Jungle accompanied the other features for many years as well, from issue #1 to 141 (January 1940–September 1951). Henry Fletcher (a pseudonym of Fletcher Hanks) was billed as the artist of the first story, and we got what amounted to an origin story: a powerful blond Tarzan type "once saved an old witchdoctor from a terrible jungle death ... and in return for the favor, the witch-doctor gave Tabu an extra sense, which made him supreme in jungle-land...." It also made him faster than an antelope, a better climber than a monkey, and more stealthy than a jungle cat. In his initial adventure, he tracked down yet another gang of slavers and used his power over nature to make life miserable for them, turning into a gorilla and then a half-octopus-half-tree to confront them, strangling them to death with his tentacles, and then changing back into a man. "It's the justice of the jungle!" Tabu proclaimed. As a reward, the old witch doctor laid hands upon him again and gave him a seventh sense. That seemed to be enough, as Tabu soon was performing magic feats that would have shamed Mandrake. He folded his tent in 1951. Dynamite brought him back in *Pathfinder: Worldscape* #6 (2017); his last appearance to our knowledge.

The White Panther, soon renamed *The Red Panther*, was another early co-star. Dressed in a winged helmet like the Flash, a mask, white long johns, winged shoes, and a cape, he was *Jungle*'s resident mystery man. His father, a "jungle monk," gave him the power to know the future, "[s]o you can destroy all evil, that only the good can survive!" His first task was to play bodyguard to a doctor in search of some magic healing stones. He did so with his super-speed, and saw the bad guy of the story chomped by a crocodile. Fiction House wasn't kind to masked adventurers, and the Panther only lasted 26 issues.

Simba, King of the Beasts fared much better. The title hero was a lion, king of his pride, and such strips have, for some reason, fared well in jungle comics. Simba's first story had him save a rival from hunters and then defeat the other lion in battle, but he led his lioness and cubs away, fearing age had lessened his strength. It must have been a delusion, as Simba stuck around till issue #129 (September 1950).

A couple of generic jungle stories filled out the rest of issue #1 while the staff figured out what to replace them with. By issue #2 (February 1940), they had their answers. Big game hunter *Roy Lance* debuted in the middle of an African tribal uprising during which, surprisingly enough, a Hollywood producer had decided to film an epic. The rebels decided not to let that impede their schedule and snatched Joan Sarrett, the leading lady. Roy single-handedly battled the rebel leader, freed Joan, and, with the help of a movie projector that made it look as though a horde of soldiers was marching on the natives, saved the day. Roy stuck it out through issue #26 (February 1942).

Fantomah (*Jungle* #2, February 1940) was a much more interesting offering. It could hardly be less, having been drawn and probably written by the more-than-offbeat Fletcher Hanks. Hanks, who has come into some renown lately for his stories, which observed fewer imaginative boundaries than the dance of the pink elephants in *Dumbo*, offered up a tale in which an old elephant went to the secret graveyard of his kind to die, with two greedy ivory hunters in pursuit. To the elephant, Fantomah appeared as a beautiful woman in a shimmering dress. To the bad guys, she appeared as a skull with blonde hair. She let one of the villains kill the other and stood by while the other sank in quicksand. It was all relatively subdued for Hanks. By the next issue, Fantomah was flying around and turning two other thieves into lizard-men. In the next, she battled a pair of evil scientists who created a race of talking war-apes, and threw one of them to the horde. (We got to see them throwing his arm and leg in separate directions.) Things only got wilder from there. When the going got rough, she changed into a blue-skinned, skull-faced horror, just to let the bad guys know she meant it.

After issue #15 (March 1941), Hanks left, and things got a little more rational, though that might not have been an improvement. Instead of flying lions and huge, disembodied red claws, Fantomah settled for more conventional jungle sorcery, like

Fantomah, mistress of magic, whose bad side you really don't want to get on. Hint: the bad side has a skull. © 1939 Glen-Kel Publishing Co.

hypnotism and occasionally cutting a path through rock. The new artists improved her appearance quite a bit, putting her first in a blue two-piece and then a regular one-piece swimsuit. But we lost the classic transformation to the blue skull woman, and her shout of "You shall die by your own creation!" Before long, she was hanging out with a black panther named Fury.

Finally, in #27 (March 1942), she underwent a Camilla-like transformation: a "shrouded figure" stepped from the jungle and said, "Legendary daughter of the pharaohs, long and far have I sought thee...." He explained that she came from the lost city of Khefra, where they needed her power. To her, he bequeathed an Egyptian getup. After she put it on, light flashed, smoke billowed, and her hair became red. "The ancient gods approve!" said the mysterious man. "Lo, they bestow mystic hair on you in token, Fantomah!" But, just as he was about to give her walking orders, the cowled man took an arrow in the neck. Fantomah and Fury found Khefra on their own. She rallied her countrymen against a tribe of invaders, turned boulders into clouds and then back into boulders, and saved her people. After that, she was installed as the queen of Khefra.

Billed now as "Fantomah, Daughter of the Pharaohs," she got involved in palace intrigues as Camilla had done in earlier days. Her magic powers seemed to wane considerably, until they were hardly depicted at all. She picked up a rival named Ghazia and took several issues to dispose of her. In the old days, Fantomah would have just turned her into a turnip.

In issue #51 (March 1944), she learned from a foreign prince that her father's name was El Hamid and that he gave the prince a jeweled four-headed serpent bracelet to pass along to her. The serpent, it was said, held the key to four great treasures, and maybe clues about Fantomah's parentage. By story's end, she and her male ally, Horus, had found one of the treasure hoards. A final blurb promised another episode of the quest in the next issue of *Jungle Comics*, but it was not to be. Fantomah ended her trek with that story.

Devil's Due Publishing revived Fantomah as a guest star in *Hack / Slash: Entry Wound* (May 2009), *Hack / Slash: The Series* #29–32 (December 2009–March 2010) and *Hack / Slash* #5 (June 2011), but your mileage may vary on this one. She reappeared in a short story in the back of *Savage Dragon* #209 (December 2015). Dynamite, which will team up any characters they can get their hands on, threw Fantomah into a world with Red Sonja, John Carter, Tarzan, Thun'da, and a number of spear-carriers in *Pathfinder: Worldscape* V. 1 #2, 4, and 6 (2016–2017). Chapterhouse, a Canadian comics outfit, brought her back in the four-issue *Fantomah* (July 2017–November 2017). That's it as of this writing, but Golden Age characters are in a permanent revival tent. She'll be back.

For the most part, *Jungle* kept a remarkably stable lineup for years, consisting of Ka'a'nga, Camilla, Wambi, Terry Thunder, Tabu, and Simba. But shrinking page counts, from 52 to 36 pages in the early Fifties, forced some changes. First Simba was retired, then Tabu, then Terry Thunder. Wambi gave out not long before the end. The space was filled with generic jungle stories and the arrival of *Tiger Girl*, of which more in a moment. Ka'a'nga made it to the end, the Summer 1954 issue, #163. He was accompanied by Camilla and Tiger Girl. Then they were gone.

And as for Tiger Girl...

...she first appeared in *Fight Comics* #32 (June 1944), in an eight-page story that was intended to give the title even more sexual spark than it had with its character Señorita Rio. Tiger Girl was a redhead and wore a tiger-skin two-piece bathing suit. Along with that, she wielded a deadly whip, and was aided by a Sikh named Abdola and two tigers called Togara and Bezali. The first story blurb put it this way: "She was a jungle legend … shadowy, elusive, lovely … and as softly dangerous as the brace of killer Bengal tigers that padded by her side!"

In the first story, she saved the life of Lance Masters, a white hunter, by having her tiger kill a lion that was out to nosh on him. Then she and Abdola brought him into their hidden temple, treated him with native herbs for his injuries, and fought off a horde of invaders who had followed them to their lair. Masters, in turn, saved Tiger Girl from a backstabbing enemy and was sent away, still in a feverish state from a disease. Months later, he returned to Tiger Girl's territory to bring her a jewel necklace from her native land. "How did this strange, beautiful queen come to the jungle? The answer lies in the next Tiger Girl adventure in Fight Comics!"

Tiger Girl prepares to turn a poacher into cat food. © 1947 Fight Stories, Inc.

After the intro story, they got down to an origin with the next issue. Tiger Girl saved the life of a Hindu who identified her as Princess Vishnu by an emerald she wore. According to the Hindu, Mahali, she was the daughter of Rajah Vishnu and an unnamed Irish mother (hence the red hair) who had passed away sometime during her childhood. Saddened by his wife's death, the Rajah came to Africa on a hunting trip with his daughter and two hunting tigers. As it turned out, something in Africa agreed with him, and he turned over the rule of his Indian province to his brother. But, on a lion hunt one day, Rajah Vishnu was turned into cat food. "Before he died, Rajah Vishnu turned your care over to Abdola, your Sikh servant … but now your father's brother is dead … you must come back, princess!"

"No, this is my land!" asserted Tiger Girl. "You will return and see that the right ruler is chosen!"

Meanwhile, both Mahali and Tiger Girl were being stalked by emissaries of a pretender to the throne, and they ended up surrounded, though Tiger Girl held them off as best she could with her mighty lash. However, she'd managed to summon Abdola with a whistle, and the savvy Sikh and his two tiger allies made mincemeat of the baddies. In the last panel, Mahali bowed before Tiger Girl, and she gave him the emerald to give to the ruler he would choose. "Tiger Girl remains, my place is here!"

And so it was. Tiger Girl held forth through issue #81 (July 1952), grabbing the cover spot with issue #49 and hanging on to it till the end of her tenure. Somewhere along the line, her hair became blonde without a hint of Lady Clairol intervention. She switched to *Jungle Comics* with issue #152 (August 1952) and stayed there till the end (#163, Summer 1954). The art, by Matt Baker, Jack Kamen, Robert Webb, and Jack Abel, among others, was frequently excellent and made *Tiger Girl* an enjoyable feature. Like some others, she came back in *Femforce* #29 (1990) and showed up in a few more AC Comics stories.

Of course, there was another jungle character in *Fight* before her, who had appeared in the first issue (January 1940) without much fanfare. *Oran of the Jungle* was a Kaanga clone (who was, in turn, a Tarzan clone) with an origin story fairly well stolen from Kaanga himself. He first appeared as a blond Adonis in leopard-skin trunks on an auction block in Africa. One-time fight promoter Zack Temson saw him there and noted Oran's "fine physique." Later, after the jungle man escaped, Temson shielded him and learned that he had been lost in the jungle since childhood and wanted to go to America to find his father. "Listen, Oran ... you will need money to find your father, and the only way for you to get it, is to fight for it," said Temson.

"I am afraid of no one ... I will fight for you!" Oran testified. Thus it was that the two caught a freighter to the U.S., and quickly turned Oran into a boxing

Oran of the Jungle spars for his next fight. © 1940 Fight Stories, Inc.

sensation. When Oran was told to take a dive in an upcoming bout, he refused, and Temson sacrificed his own life to save the jungle boxer from an assassin. But all was not tragedy: when Oran returned to his locker room, he was greeted by his long-lost dad, who recognized him from a fight poster. After that, father and son caught the next freighter back to Africa, where it can be assumed no one asked Oran to take a dive in a fight with a lion. He did manage to find his way into the boxing ring in most of his adventures, though, and since *Fight* had plenty of pugilists, there wasn't much special about that. Oran hung on until issue #15 (October 1941).

Rangers of Freedom #1 (October 1941) offered Fiction House's only remaining jungle feature: *Rocky Hall, Jungle Stalker*. Actually, Rocky, another Great White Explorer, wasn't the star of his own strip; that honor went to Gay-Ree, a Tarzan clone who saved Rocky from being crushed to death by a python while looking for the temple of Isis. Gay-Ree turned out to be Gary Murray, the son of another explorer who was killed by natives. The strip lasted for twelve issues, which was the longest run of any strip in that first issue except for *Rangers of Freedom*, the title strip.

One quasi-jungle strip appeared in *Rangers Comics* #23-28 (June 1945–April 1946). This was *Kazanda, Queen of the Lost Continent*. The feature was in the tradition of the sarong-clad South Sea girl à la Dorothy Lamour of the movies. She was more than that, though. Kazanda had genuine psychic powers, making her an uncostumed superheroine. She could visualize images from afar and make others see them, communicate telepathically with men and beasts, and start fires with her mind. On top of that, she was a thinly clad brunette beauty on a lost continent. Not a bad start for a story.

Actually, Kazanda had been featured in British and Australian comics circa 1939, and Fiction House merely reprinted her stories, as they had the Sheena stories from *Wags* earlier. Kazanda fit in well with the *Rangers* crew, though, and nobody was the wiser.

Kazanda's tale began when a threesome of explorers, two male and one female, were shipwrecked on the lost continent she inhabited. Naturally, the girl got separated from the other two and fell into the hands of Sylf, a tyrant magician, who enslaved her and turned her into a living statue. Kazanda greeted the two male wayfarers, persuaded her pet tiger not to eat them, and conjured up a vision of the girl's plight. The story continued as a serial through issue #27 (February 1946), with the explorers reunited and the two lovers among them named rulers of the lost continent. Kazanda appeared in one more story and then was gone. The feature, written by Archie Martin and drawn by Edward Brodie-Mack, was nice indeed, but never got a chance to survive.

Later, in *Rangers Comics* #42 (August 1948), *Jan of the Jungle* came forth. Jan was basically a Wambi clone, an Indian boy who hung out with a monkey named Kaang and an elephant called Taj. The strip was nicely drawn but no more remarkable than any other of its kind. Still, Jan lasted through issue #63 (February 1952), missing only one issue along the way.

Many of the prewar and wartime Golden Age anthology comics had their own jungle heroes as backup strips, but few followed the Sheena lead: most were faux Tarzans. One who wasn't was DC's *Congo Bill*, who started out in *Action Comics* #37

(June 1941) and ran continuously, in one form or another, well into the Silver Age. He was an adventurer, a Great White Hunter, and a guide, and his art was well done indeed by Fred Ray. Since his jungle setting made him an easy translation to moviedom, a *Congo Bill* serial was produced in 1948 and he gained his own six-issue title in 1954. The cover of the first issue featured Bill and his jungle kid sidekick, Janu (whom he picked up in *Action* #191 [April 1954]), confronted by a huge golden gorilla. This was prophecy: in *Action* #248 (January 1959), Bill got a magic ring from a dying medicine man that allowed him to exchange minds with that of a great golden ape for one hour. This came in handy when Bill got trapped in a cave and had to switch bodies for the gorilla to dig him out. It also had the unfortunate side effect of putting a raging gorilla's mind into Bill's human body, and he almost always had to be tied up before he made the change. *Congorilla* went on until *Action* #261 and switched to *Adventure Comics* for issues #270–281 and 283, finishing with the April 1961 issue. Every now and then, Bill and Congorilla make an appearance in DC Comics just to let us know they're still there.

The most well-remembered Tarzan clone is Marvel's *Ka-Zar*, who started out as a three-issue pulp hero in publisher Martin Goodman's stable and was reworked as a comics character in *Marvel Comics* #1 (October 1939), renamed *Marvel Mystery Comics* with the next issue. Ben Thompson was the artist, and the splash panel read, "From the famous character created by Bob Byrd" and introduced us to Ka-Zar, his lion, Zar, and his elephant, Trajah. As it transpired, diamond mine owner John Rand was flying in his private aircraft over the Belgian Congo with his wife and three-year-old son, David. The plane developed motor trouble, crashed, and stranded them there. Constance Rand, David's mother, died of a fever, and John never recovered from her loss.

David, though, became best buddies with all the animals of the jungle. After saving a lion, Zar, from quicksand, he gained the beast's everlasting gratitude. Soon enough, though, John Rand (who, like his son, was now wearing a leopard-skin loincloth), encountered the wicked slaver Paul De Kraft, and was killed by him as David looked on. Zar, the lion, killed De Kraft's two henchmen and drove the murderer himself away. David buried his father, swore vengeance on De Kraft, and from that day forward was known as Ka-Zar, or "brother of Zar." Sha, Zar's mate, treated him as an unwanted but tolerated houseguest until the furless one saved her cub.

It took till issue #5 (March 1940) to catch up with De Kraft, who had Ka-Zar tied to a stake and tortured by tribesmen before a monkey friend of the jungle man's found a knife and used it to cut him free. De Kraft shot and missed. He didn't get another chance. "This is the end for Fat Face!" yelled Ka-Zar, and he plunged his knife into the murderer's black heart. After that, "[t]he jungle echoed with the victory roar of a lion ... from Ka-Zar's throat!" Ka-Zar had the opportunity to give his victory cry through issue #27 (January 1942), with a cameo appearance in *Human Torch* #5 (Fall 1941). Then he was gone.

But not forgotten. Marvel Comics revived Ka-Zar as a character in *X-Men* #10 (March 1965), courtesy of Stan Lee, Jack Kirby, and Chic Stone. He looked similar to his forebear, but this time he was paired with a saber-toothed tiger named Zabu and lived in the Savage Land, a dinosaur-filled jungle concealed beneath Antarctica. A new origin was evolved for him, not dependent on the Golden Age version. He has appeared periodically as a headliner or a guest star since then, depending on how the market goes for jungle stars.

Lance Hale originated in *Silver Streak Comics* #2 (January 1940). Lance was a "soldier of fortune" who didn't wear a shirt throughout the whole episode. He was a beefcake specimen on a "dangerous jungle expedition" who opened the story by fighting hand-to-hand with a band of natives. The latter overcame him by force of numbers and brought him to their employer, a white-mustached Caucasian scientist. The old man, whose name was Grantland Grey, needed a strong man to help him crew a rocket ship to the stars. Lance proved his muscle by lifting a 500-pound dumbbell, and the old man put an armband on him that boosted his strength to superhuman status. Before story's end, our hero was throwing a leopard around. Lance and the scientist boarded the spaceship and took off.

That was a weird enough way to begin a jungle strip, and it could have been a science-fiction offering with a few more episodes in that direction. But after the first two stories, drawn excellently by John Hampton, the scene inexplicably shifted. Grantland Grey was forgotten, and Lance was back on Earth. Specifically, he was in Rhodesia, where he encountered the queen of an underground empire. She had him pass through the Flame of Immortality, à la Haggard's *She*, and he fought off a horde of lizard-men before making his way back to the surface world. Eventually Lance settled down to being a regular jungle hero in leopard-skin trunks. He appeared in most *Silver Streak* issues through #13 (August 1941) and teamed up with Daredevil to fight Hitler in *Daredevil Battles Hitler* #1 (July 1941).

Quality Comics' *Samar* moved into *Feature Comics* with issue #32 (May 1940) and stayed till #63 (December 1942). He was blond, wore red trunks, and debuted with excellent art by Reed Crandall. Others who swung into action after Crandall included Rafael Astarita, Ann Brewster, Nick Cardy, Robert Webb, and Charles Sultan. The stories were fairly fun, as most Quality fare was, but Samar was too generic and was dumped in due time. A little while later, *Lion Boy* premiered in *Hit Comics* #6 (November 1941), and his origin was as cut-and-dried as they came: plane crash, father dies, son raised by lioness in the jungle. He teamed up with a lion and had art by George Tuska, and lasted till issue #21 (April 1942).

Champion Comics, from the firm that was eventually bought by Harvey Comics, offered *Jungleman* in its first issue, inexplicably numbered #2 (December 1939). He lived in the Cambodian jungles with an albino tiger and a temple full of jewels and gold. He didn't talk a lot, but at least he got the cover spot on issue #5 (March 1940). Worth Carnahan was listed as scripter and art was by Don Traver and Harry Parkhurst and was usually quite good. We never learned much about him and, truthfully, would have been hard-pressed to care. After issue #17, he was gone.

MLJ Magazines, which later was renamed Archie Comics, threw out *Ty-Gor, Son of the Tiger* in *Blue Ribbon Comics* #4 (June 1940). This one was a bit more interesting, thanks to the energetic art and scripting of the first story. Tyrone Gorman, infant son of an American scientist living in the jungle, was captured by natives and prepared for a sacrifice to atone for the killing of the cub of a tiger, their tribal totem. The kid was rescued in the nick of time by the tigress that lost her cub and was raised as her own. One of the few things he had left from his old life was a laundry mark reading "Ty" and "Gor," which became his cognomen. After his tiger "father" was killed by a tribesman's spear, Ty-Gor took vengeance and became protector of the jungle. Ty-Gor wrapped it up with issue #20. Joe Blair was the writer and George Storm, Mort Meskin, and Bob Montana handled the art.

Fawcett's *Dr. Voodoo* easily trumped them all on art. Not surprising, as the feature was drawn by Mac Raboy, the fine craftsman who would graduate to *Captain Marvel Jr.* and thence to the *Flash Gordon* newspaper strip. As the opening caption in *Whiz Comics* #7 (August 1940) put it, "Deep in the trackless jungles of Brazil, where the fierce struggle for existence makes most men as savage as beasts, life is a constant battle against disaster…. There, because they believe his use of modern medical methods a form of black magic, the Blancas, a head-hunting tribe of white Indians, come to know Hal Carey, young American, as Dr. Voodoo." The narrative commenced with a story from Hal's dying dad, victimized by a vampire bat's bite, recapping their history in the jungle and charging him to remain there to treat the natives. The tribe came to doubt Hal's healing powers since he failed to save his

Dr. Voodoo, medical man and adventurer of the jungle. © 1941 Fawcett Publications, Inc.

father, and decided to kill him. In the meantime, Hal ran across a beautiful white girl in a sarong who could talk to tigers. The two of them attempted to escape on tiger-back but were captured and thrown to a giant carnivorous plant. Hal treated the plant with acid and got them free. After winning a knife fight with a medicine man, Hal was hailed as "Dr. Voodoo" by the tribe and enlisted the girl, Maxinya, as his nurse, with the proviso that she teach him the languages of animals. She agreed, and enrolled him in Dr. Dolittle Tech.

The first story may have been the work of John Hampton, or perhaps Mark Schneider, and was of average quality. By issue #9 (October 1940), though, Raboy arrived and began his revitalization. Panels opened up gradually, Maxinya got prettier, and animals got more menacing. When the villainous Okoro took a punch, his dismayed face resembled that of the later Captain Nazi. By 1941, Raboy was showing the influence of Hal Foster's *Prince Valiant*: Dr. Voodoo saved Maxinya from a colony of knights who had been lost in Africa. With *Whiz* #18 (June 13, 1941), he went all the way and stripped word and thought balloons from the story entirely, confining the narrative to captions à la *Valiant*. It went on that way through issue #34 (September 4, 1942), at which time Dr. Voodoo faded into comic-book memory. Otto Binder wrote at least some of the scripts, and Raboy, who had been auditioning for Foster, instead got to replace Alex Raymond on *Flash Gordon* some years later.

Voodoo, though, was no Tarzan imitator. *Lee Granger, Jungle King*, in Fawcett's *Slam-Bang Comics*, was. He was a white scientist with the build of Johnny Weissmuller, and he got stranded among a tribe of pygmies when a bomb blew up his plane. After helping the pygmies build a fairly modernistic town, Granger gave a lion an electric brain treatment and enabled it to speak English. The lion, named Eric, was the most interesting thing about this feature. Granger lasted all seven issues of *Slam-Bang* (March–September 1940) and four more in *Master* (#7–10, October 1940–January 1941).

Hillman offered the unfortunately named *Blanda, the Jungle Queen* in three issues of *Miracle Comics* in 1940 (February–April). Blanda wore a one-piece leopard-skin bathing suit and had possibly the first female nude scene in comics, bathing sans suit in issue #2. Outside of that, she had little to recommend her, but she was one of the first jungle characters outside of Fiction House to follow Sheena's lead. *Jaxon of the Jungle*, in *Prize Comics*, followed the lead of Congo Bill and did his Great White Hunter thing for the first six issues (March–August 1940).

Beebo, the Jungle Boy, in Street & Smith's *Shadow Comics*, fared somewhat better. He began his run in V.2, #9 (December 1942) with a cover appearance, introduced by the Shadow himself and astride a big black horse. The Shadow: "Hey, pals! Meet Beebo, the bravest boy in the world!" Beebo: "The Shadow knows!" Horse: "Surprised to hear me talk? Just read our adventures starting page 13...." Beebo, whose name echoed that of Bomba, was off and running. Or riding. Whatever.

The story, credited to Otto Binder, August Froehlich, and Ed Gruskin, began with a ship caught in a South Seas hurricane and a couple sending off their only son, a baby, strapped to the back of Fleet, the great black horse. As the boy's mother prayed, "Dear Lord, watch over them, guide them safely to shore!" Fleet leaped into the water and finally, after much hardship, got to land. Behind him, the ship sank in

The Shadow, Beebo, and Botel. A team that couldn't miss. © 1942, 2022 Street and Smith Publications, Inc.

the storm. The next day, a monkey looked in on the scene, and the story got fairly Kiplingish.

Quoth the monkey: "What's this ... a stranger tossed on our shore ... me thinks I will investigate!"

Quoth the horse: "Keep away, breeder-of-fleas, or you will soon be picking them off your ancestors!"

Both monkey (named Cheeto) and horse agreed that the man-child had to be taken care of until he could fend for himself, and they agreed to do so, albeit grumbling at each other all the way. The horse named the kid Beebo, without explanation. The infant grew to boyhood and somehow infuriated a Shere Khan stand-in, a gorilla named Punjab. The big ape vowed to kill the boy for some reason or other (maybe because he materialized a pair of leopard-skin trunks between panels, and the gorilla was jealous of the trick). Eventually, Punjab snatched Beebo away. "Why do you hate me, Punjab?" asked Beebo. "Why do you want to kill me?"

"Your skin is white, without hair … you walk straight without your hands. I would look like you and walk like you—but I can't. So I HATE YOU!" Clearly, Punjab was one bigoted gorilla. Nonetheless, Cheeto and Fleet enlisted the help of an elephant, and Punjab plunged to his apparent death in a lake. Beebo was saved by grabbing onto a simian chain of monkeys, held aloft by the elephant's trunk. "Thank you, my good friends," said Beebo. "Now that Punjab is dead, we will live forever in peace!"

Right.

By *Shadow Comics* V.3 #4 (July 1943), even Lamont Cranston had found his way into the strip. Beebo's uncle wanted his brother's fortune, but Cranston insisted that he explore the islands near which the unfortunate pair, the Botels, had been lost. (Beebo's real name was given as William Botel in this story.) The uncle, James Botel, gathered up a tough crew at a waterfront bar. One of them asked: "What do we do if we find dis brudder of yours?"

"Kill him or his kid … that's why I'm taking a tough, heartless crew like you! Are you game?" They were. Thus began a continued story. Cranston became a "last minute passenger" on Botel's ship, and was himself marked for death by Botel. But the Shadow appeared, and, with Beebo's aid, triumphed over the bad guys and a giant octopus. Afterward, he revealed to Beebo that the lad was the heir to a fortune. Beebo, unable to speak human language, pointed to banana trees and coconut trees, and Cranston interpreted it correctly: the boy had what he needed there, and didn't want to leave. So Cranston himself left on a sailboat. A last caption in this issue's story (V.3 #9, December 1943) advised readers that their letters would determine whether or not Beebo's adventures would continue in *Shadow Comics*. Evidently, vox populi was against him: Beebo was replaced in the next issue by Chick Carter and was never seen again.

But the jungle genre was just waiting for the second wave, as it turned out. The militarism that had ruled most action comics during World War II was fading with war's end, and publishers had to try a different tack to sell comics. On top of that, the G.I.'s, who had been one of their mainstay audiences, were being demobilized, sent home, and faced with reentering civilian life. What to try next?

Simple enough: sex.

Well, that and other things, such as humor, westerns, teen titles, and eventually war comics. But nobody could deny the appeal of a beauty in a bathing suit on a comics cover, and the companies that hadn't tried it yet were getting the hang of things. At Harvey, the Black Cat got her own comic. At Timely, the Sub-Mariner got Namora, the Torch got Sun Girl, and Captain America got Golden Girl. Just to fill things out, Miss America got her own comic and then rapidly left it to superheroine Patsy Walker. Teen humor comics like *Archie* and *Millie the Model* rarely missed a chance to show off feminine pulchritude in swimsuits during the summer months, and whenever else they could manage. Meanwhile, Fiction House chugged along, showing off the same amount of skin they always had on the covers. If it was working for them, why not for others?

Sheena's jungle was about to get a lot more crowded.

It's somehow ironic, though, that the longest-lived and best of the new female jungle stars also kept on the most clothes. Actually, it made sense. If you were a fair-complected Caucasian woman in the heat of the African jungle, with insects about and rough going through fauna and flora unlike that of America, a blouse, shorts, and shoes were a lot more practical outfit than a bikini. The woman in that getup was smart, beautiful, and tough, and is as fondly remembered in her way as Sheena.

She was known as Nyoka the Jungle Girl.

Nyoka's debut in comics was Fawcett's 1942 one-shot, *Jungle Girl*. The comic adapted the then current movie serial, *Perils of Nyoka*, starring Kay Aldridge, a chapter-play remembered well by serial fans to this day. In a 52-page, six-chapter story, we were introduced to Nyoka Gordon, a woman searching for her lost scientist father; to Larry Grayson, a doctor cum adventurer cum love interest; to Nyoka's dad, an amnesiac; and to the wicked but lovely Vultura, who schemed to snatch two golden tablets bearing the secret healing methods of Hippocrates. Nyoka, a brown-haired beauty in a white shirt, green shorts, and sensible shoes, was drawn to reflect the screen image of Ms. Aldridge, who appeared on the cover in a photo inset. She showed up riding a horse, brandishing a pistol, and leading her troops against Vultura's minions. When Vultura threatened her with a spear and said, "You're my prisoner!" she replied, "Oh, no … you are **mine**!" leaping off her horse and bearing her to the ground. The girls started a fight on the spot, but it was interrupted by Vultura's pet gorilla, Satan. The big ape dragged Nyoka off to the villainess's temple hideout.

In the temple, Vultura demanded that Nyoka translate Hippocrates's tablets. "Not I!" said Nyoka, tied to a post. "Those tablets and their secret should benefit humanity … not a pack of inhuman robbers and killers!"

"I'll not argue," said Vultura, briskly. "Torture her."

The two thugs in charge had a tough time transferring the brunette bombshell from post to torture rack. Nyoka fought back and nearly bit the thumb off one of them. But, as it was, the heroine was strapped into a rack, and an attempt was made to increase her height by several feet. Luckily, Larry Grayson arrived, clobbered the bad guys (but not Vultura, who had left), and freed Nyoka. After that, she and Larry got together, starting a relationship that would carry on for 11 years to come.

In the rest of the story, Nyoka was menaced by a lake of flame, found herself under a roof of descending spikes, was caught in an explosion, was threatened by a landslide, was caught under a pendulum blade, and still found time to rescue her father and see his memory restored by an on-the-spot brain operation performed by Larry. At the end, Nyoka closed with Vultura and fought it out. But Satan, seeing an opening, threw a spear. Nyoka ducked it, and Vultura got the point. Seconds later, Larry shot the gorilla dead. Nyoka faced him, hands on his shoulders, smiling. "We've won everything—the tablets—the treasure!" she said.

"Yes, and the battle!" Larry replied. "I'm almost sorry it's all over!"

That statement proved a bit premature. A blurb in the last panel said, "Want to see more adventures of Nyoka, the Jungle Girl?" and gave an address to which to send a postcard to Fawcett. Evidently, enough kids made it down to the post office for her to gain a slot in *Master Comics* #50 (May 1944), two years later. She stayed on through the penultimate issue, #132 (February 1953). By winter of 1945, Nyoka graduated to her own comic, continuing the numbering from the earlier *Jungle Girl* as *Nyoka the Jungle Girl* #2. That ran for 76 issues, through 1953. A year later, Charlton, which had picked up many Fawcett properties, made her the star of *Zoo Funnies* with the eighth issue (October–November 1954). By issue #14 (November 1955), it was retitled *Nyoka* and continued till #22, in November 1957. By emphasizing adventure rather than sexuality, Nyoka outlasted Sheena by four years in comics.

Nyoka, tough, intelligent, and decently clothed jungle girl. © 1945 Fawcett Publications, Inc.

After the initial adventure, Nyoka needed saving a lot, and relied on Larry somewhat, but, as time went on, thought and fought more for herself. She got into peril after peril, but managed to think, muscle, and trick her way out in ways that Batman would have admired. Her initial 17 *Master* stories and most of the tales in her own title were set up as serials, with dangers aplenty, narrow escapes, and action that roared every rip. For the most part, she didn't go in for the wholesale slaughter of animals like her Sheena-style sisters did. But she did throw a heck of a lot of punches at male and female foes, and could run, dive, swing, and swim with the best of them. Menaced by crooks, animals, cannibal tribes, and the occasional rival jungle girl, Nyoka always held her own. And we loved her for it.

Nyoka's dress remained fairly conservative and sensible for a jungle queen, though she switched to a modest halter for a few issues in the early Fifties. On a number of the covers, though, she was portrayed by a fetching model in photographs, sometimes in a bathing suit. Nobody complained. In a genre heavy with bikinis, Nyoka kept her dignity.

All good things must end, though, and Nyoka, like a number of other Fawcett features, finished out her Golden Age career as a Charlton character. She was featured in reprints, a couple of leftover Fawcett stories printed for the first time, and a number of shorts in which she was inexplicably turned into a blonde. Finally, she was gone.

Or was she?

The brunette bombshell hadn't been forgotten by a number of fans, and one of them was Bill Black, editor, writer, and artist for his own company, Americomics. A big fan of the jungle girl genre, he purchased the rights to Nyoka in 1987. By the next year he began a new, short-lived revival with *The Further Adventures of Nyoka*, a black-and-white comic. It only lasted a handful of issues, but the character made appearances in other AC comics and in a couple of Black's fan-style videos with an actress portraying the jungle girl. (Most recently, yours truly scripted a Nyoka story for AC!) Like Sheena, Nyoka somehow refuses to die.

Voodah, the Black king of the jungle. © 1945 Golfing, Inc.

Crown Comics, a 19-issue series published by an outfit known variously as Golfing, Inc., Home Guide, and McCombs, featured an unusual variation on the jungle hero, *Voodah*. It was unusual because, at first, Voodah was, unlike his fellow jungle lords, a Black native African. He was presented heroically, drawn realistically, and, in his initial outing (in issue #3, Fall 1945), saved a beautiful girl of the tribe from the depredations of an evil white interloper. The first story looked to be the work of Matt Baker, or somebody trying awfully hard to look like him. Since Baker was Black, it's nice to think he could have worked on this one. Unfortunately, by issue #6 (Summer 1946), Voodah gained the cover slot, and the Powers That Be changed him into a white man. Thus, what could have been a pioneering feature became just another Tarzan manqué. McCombs apparently forgot and made Voodah a Black man again in issue #13 (May 1948), but he was a Caucasian with the next issue. Nonetheless, the art was good and the scripts were competent enough, and *Voodah* lasted until 1949.

In the real world, times changed, 1947 rolled around, and the world (and America) settled down to civilian life. One result became evident a few years later: returning G.I.'s and their wives got down to business and produced one of the largest generations of kids on record, the Baby Boomers. Morality was gradually loosening up. In 1946, Louis Réard debuted his design for a new swimsuit, named for an island recently subjected to an atomic test—the bikini. Fiction House had been doing well all the time with their good-girl covers and art. Comics took the hint and ran with it.

Nedor (also known as Better, or Standard, or Pines) tested the waters with a relatively modest entry, *Kara, Jungle Princess. Kara* premiered in issue #39 of *Exciting Comics* (June 1945) and starred Jane Howell, Army nurse, who got stranded with her male lead, Maj. Kit Kendall, among the hidden Arohitan tribe in New Guinea. She was adopted as their ruler, given a tiara, halter, and slit skirt, as well as a "magic powder" to protect her from physical harm, and was made their ruler, since they mistook her for the absent princess, Kara. This did not play well with the evil Targala, an archpriest who schemed to rule all of Arohita himself. Most of the action was handled by Kit, who was vulnerable to harm, but Kara did a bit of spear-slinging herself. Her reign lasted till issue #49 (July 1946), with a last appearance in *Fighting Yank* #21 (August 1947). Then she retired. She has been revived since, in Antarctic's *Jungle Comics* #2 (2020).

But Nedor wasn't about to quit. The first of a triple-threat punch landed in *Thrilling Comics* #56, in October 1946. Her name was Princess Pantha.

The double-page splash of her first story depicted a gorgeous brunette in a two-piece leopard-skin bathing suit, backed against a tree, holding a knife, and kicking an ape in the face with her bare foot. Other apes were advancing on her, but a cavalry of elephants were coming to her rescue … we think. The opening caption read thusly: "The world knew her as Princess Pantha … ace animal trainer of the National Circus! Little did they dream what would happen when this lovely lass traded the tanbark for the drama and deadly danger of the deep jungle! Here's a strange and stirring story of a grim mystery of the wilds … of how Princess Pantha pitted the powers of a mere girl against the fierce challenge of the dark continent!"

The first panel of the story proper cut to a meeting between blond good-guy Dane Hunter and Pantha's employer, Gilt-Edge Gates. There had been a rumor of a monster gorilla in a sector of French West Africa, and Gates had sent Pantha to trap the beast. Pantha hadn't been heard from for a month, and now the circus owner was hiring Hunter, an explorer and adventurer, to find her. Or to find out what happened to her. As it was, the Princess and her party encountered a tribe of huge, hostile natives, the Kodus, and the rest of her band were wiped out. A Kodu had his hands around her throat when Pantha flipped a switch and played the recording of a giant gorilla's growl. The tribesmen, fearing the wrath of the legendary giant gorilla M'gana, fled for their lives. Pantha, dressed in shirt and jodhpurs, mused, "Now what do I do? I'm alone in the jungle, equipment destroyed, only a little food left! Miss animal tamer, you're in quite a spot!"

But she made do with what she had, and did that well. When Dane Hunter and his bearers came in search of her and got captured by the Kodus, Pantha, now dressed in a leopard-skin bikini and carrying bow and arrows and a knife, incited a herd of elephants to tear up the Kodu village and herself put a knife blade through the shoulder of a witch doctor intent on sacrificing Dane. As she untied him, a bare-chested Dane quipped, "Dr. Livingstone, I presume?" The twosome fought their way to safety, with Dane snatching a part of the witch doctor's necklace as they fled. Later, while Dane scoffed at the tale of a monster gorilla, he opened his hand and saw the image of just such a beast on the bauble he had taken. "Perhaps my search isn't so nonsensical, after all!" remarked Pantha. "This seems to indicate that such a gorilla really exists!" Dane scoffed again. Above them, in the trees, a huge, hairy shadow-thing looked on.

Princess Pantha pounces! © 1946 Standard Magazines, Inc.

It took several more issues, but Pantha and Dane (now clad in a Tarzan-like leopard-skin loincloth) finally found and captured M'gana. By that time, the Princess had commandeered the cover from Doc

Strange and was rendered finely by Alex Schomburg on each one. She usually took advantage of a two-page splash, like other Nedor headliners. The Princess and Dane made it back to America, but they found their way back to the jungle every issue for more adventures. The art, by Ralph Mayo, Gene Fawcette, Art Saaf, Rafael Astarita, and Marcia Snyder, was usually excellent. Pantha battled her way through issue #74 (October 1949) of *Thrilling*, and then disappeared.

That is, until 1990, when AC Comics (again!) revived her as part of their "Vault Heroes" package, along with a ton and a half of other unclaimed Golden Agers. The Princess, freed from suspended animation, appeared in living black and white in a handful of stories, starting with *Femforce* #30 (1990). But, since Nedor heroes were in the public domain by then, Pantha didn't have to be satisfied with just one revival. In Alan Moore's *Tom Strong* #10–11 (2001), another version of her, this time called Princess Panther, was rescued, along with duplicates of her Nedor mates, from a time-warp bubble. This Princess became the lover of Tom Strange, the analogue of Doc Strange, and went on to co-star in two mini-series entitled *Terra Obscura*. Recently, Princess Pantha has returned, her hair miscolored red, in *Jungle Comics* #2 (2020) from Antarctic.

Judy of the Jungle jumps the shark. © 1947 Standard Magazines, Inc.

The cover of *Exciting Comics* #55 (May 1947), besides featuring a large illustration of the Black Terror bouncing a bullet off his chest, offered a small inset illo at bottom right, showing a brown-haired beauty in a one-piece bathing suit, holding a knife. A blurb read: "Introducing … *Judy of the Jungle!*" Inside, she was redheaded, but that mattered little. Nedor's second jungle girl was off and swinging.

The story commenced in a jungle cabin, where Judy was hearing a speech from her naturalist father. "You're no longer a child, Judy! Your whole future lies ahead! I'm sure your dear mother would have given you the same choice! Because I never trusted my fellow man, I brought you up to despise people! Alas—how wrong I was! Now you are completely at home in the jungle!" Judy's father said that she needed to learn about the outside world, but, hugging him closely, Judy said, "Oh, father, how could I ever leave you?"

In comic books, that kind of question is just begging for an answer. Within a page, Judy's father met up by accident with one Kurt Von Saber and his band of cutthroat exiles, and was shot dead on the spot. Judy, shocked, came upon her dad instants before he died. His last words to her were, "Live for revenge, Judy … and trust no man!" In tears, Judy said, "I shall never rest until I have found his killers! I swear it!"

Before long, Judy found Von Saber's camp, and was captured. But she was freed by one Pistol Roberts, a government agent out to capture the German, and repaid the favor by killing a leopard that had its claws out for Roberts. He said, "Wow! You are an amazing girl! You saved my life!"

"I hate all men, but you had just saved mine!" she responded.

"In that case, let's each thank the other—like this!" Pistol grabbed her quickly and smooched her. Judy didn't seem to mind. But, offstage, Von Saber vowed, "If it is the last thing I do—I will kill those two with my own bare hands!"

By the next issue, Judy had those Schomburg covers all to herself. In *Exciting* #57 (September 1947), she met with Von Saber in battle again and knocked him off a rope bridge into the mouths of some crocodiles below. "At last I have avenged my poor father!" she said. Afterward, when Pistol asked if she would be leaving the jungle, Judy admitted, "There's something that holds me—here! I just wouldn't be happy in the outer world! Especially without you, Pistol—" On cue, she embraced him and kissed him. She was making great strides at not hating men.

Judy held on until issue #69 (September 1949) and then, save for a few reprint stories, was gone. Fawcette, Mayo, Saaf, and Sheldon Moldoff handled most of the art, but one story, in #59 (January 1948), was the work of Frank Frazetta.

Tygra, the third of Nedor's jungle trio, debuted in *Startling Comics* #45 (May 1947). She was billed as Tygra of the Flame People and was a pretty blonde in a tiger-skin bathing suit. But at the story's beginning, she was modestly clad in a red dress and, as Lynn Thomas, was helping her dad, a doctor, at an African medical mission. Dr. Thomas sent her to London to get a vitamin named Autorene, which could cure a disease a nearby tribe was suffering, from its inventor, one Terry Wilton. "Whoa!" said Terry on seeing her. "You can't be Lynn Thomas! No pigtails? No freckles?" And Lynn, for her part, noted, "You used to be so—stodgy!" By the end of the page, they were kissing. But Lynn had to fly a private prop plane back to Africa, and that was going to prove problematic.

A thunderbolt from a storm sheared off her wing, and Lynn went down but survived the crash. Exhausted, she drank the Autorene, thinking it was beef extract. (Evidently she had a real thing for beef extract.) At once, Lynn developed Captain America–style strength, and soon wrestled and beat a lion that was attacking some tribesmen. "The Autorene! That was what I swallowed—the whole bottle!" When the warriors attacked her in fear, she clobbered them. One of the band bade his brothers hold: "She is the tawny one!" he said, and the men dropped to their knees and called her "Master!" Which, probably, was better than calling her "mistress."

Before long, she was decked out in a tiger-skin outfit and gold bracelets and made queen of the tribe. "No one shall fear me!" she proclaimed. "If I am to rule … it will be as one of you!" The tribe said that legends declared she would lead them back to their homeland, wherever that was. "And Terry, please," she begged in private, "do what is in your power—and come to me!" Meanwhile, we suppose, the tribe and her dad waited for the medicine.

Tygra did soon meet up with her father and Terry Wilton, saving them from a pack of Amazons. She said that she was staying in the jungle, and Dr. Thomas gave her into the care of Wilton, or perhaps it was the other way around. She was tough, but she didn't last long, hanging on only until *Startling* #53 (September 1948). Most of the art was by Shelly Moldoff, but Art Saaf showed up toward the end. Unlike Pantha and Judy, Tygra never got a cover to herself. She did, however, show up in a few mid–Nineties stories from Americomics. Most recently, she returned in a team with Princess Pantha and Kara in *Jungle Comics* #2 (2020) from Antarctic.

But the real mother lode of postwar jungle characters came from one of the Golden Age's most renowned exploitationist publishers. Fox Comics unleashed a phalanx of half-naked male and female jungle monarchs on their audience, practically overpopulating Africa with them. And the most famous of the lot was Rulah.

Rulah, briefly (about as brief as her outfit), was the jungle girl stripped down to her essence, with about as much subtlety as a Mack truck. In a world 15 years away from Ursula Andress's debut in a white bikini in *Dr. No*, Rulah wore several strips of giraffe hide strung together with leather thongs, and that was it. As silly and violent as most jungle queen stories could be, Rulah's were even more silly and more violent. She

Comicdom's runner-up queen of the jungle, Rulah! © 1947 Fox Feature Syndicate.

was cheap thrills packaged for sale at 10 cents a pop, and, as such, she made a name for herself and for Fox Comics as well. What kind of name she made will be left to the reader's discretion!

The first story, in *Zoot Comics* #7 (June 1947), told her tale, opening with a splash panel of a leopard trying to claw Rulah while she, in turn, plunged a knife into its shoulder with a big (big!) blood splash. "Jane was a bored American girl.... Was it chance that brought her winging over the vast jungle terrain? ... Chance? Or fate? For that brief flight soared her into the most incredible adventure you have ever read about!" A panel later, we faded back into the recent past, in which aviatrix Jane Dodge, a gorgeous brunette, piloted her plane over the African wilds while asking herself, "Who are you trying to kid? Flying around like a lone eagle ... no home ... no family ... just money and a yen for adventure." A minute later, she checked her instrument panel and thought, "Just a minute! While I daydream, something's happening ... something that's not so good!"

An understatement. Thanks to her not paying enough attention, her fuel line snapped, setting the plane afire. Jane, tastefully attired in flight cap, blouse, jodhpurs, and boots, parachuted out of her craft, which darn near landed on top of her when it crashed. She picked herself out of the wreckage and, taking stock of her shredded outfit and a giraffe that had been killed by the plane crash, stitched herself a bikini from its hide and the strings from her chute ... essentially, the world's first "string" bikini. Jane Dodge displayed her bared-down body in a fairly large panel, and then got down to the business of survival.

After she walked away, the plane's wreckage was found by a band of natives led, incongruously, by a spear-wielding white woman in a skimpy outfit straight out of a burlesque show. The woman advised her group to spread the word that "Nurla, the moon-goddess, comes!" Meanwhile, Jane was learning the pleasure of tree-swinging, and came upon a local village in time to steal some food and see Nurla go into her goddess act. "Hey! Something phony here! She's wearing bits of silk from *my* parachute!" Jane remarked. Within seconds, Jane alit before the locals and, hands raised, proclaimed, "I come to warn you, Nurla lies!"

"You must prove such words, else we kill you, strange one!" answered one of the crew. Quickly, Jane led the group to her fallen plane, which still had her name painted on the tail. "You see, she claims she came from the moon in this flying bird. It is mine. The name on my bracelet proves it...." Evidently the tribe there was good enough at recognizing English letters to note she had enough proof of identity. "We shall follow you, white one," said a tribesman, who a few panels earlier had probably been ready to follow another white one.

Instants later, Jane got her baptism of fire, or whatever, when a cobra attacked her. She wasted no time dispatching it with her knife. Nurla, for her part, was looting a chief's burial chamber of its pearl treasures. Conflict having been set up, it wasn't long in commencing. Jane jumped out of a tree at her adversaries, holding her knife in her mouth. To get the tribe's attention, she set off a gasoline explosion near her plane with a cigarette lighter. After explaining that Nurla was a baddie and they should return the pearls to the tomb, Jane won their loyalty ... almost.

The tribe insisted she had to be proven a goddess by a test of strength. For the task, two men hauled in a furious leopard and told her to kill it or be killed. Not having much to say in the decision, Jane grappled with the cat and stabbed it, gaining several bloody claw wounds herself in the process. A final stab to the heart killed the leopard. Exhausted, Jane sank to her knees while the tribe proclaimed, "You are a goddess! You have proved your wisdom and your strength! We name you, Rulah!"

"Rulah ... a jungle goddess!" mused Jane.

"But I hadn't planned on being here forever," she said. "Still I guess a girl can change her mind ... a goddess, eh? ... I'm sure they don't really mean that ... but confidentially, shame on me, I like it!" And thus was Rulah born.

The first cover was the work of Jack Kamen. The script was probably by Manning Stokes, and the art was most likely not by Matt Baker, but somebody working in his style. Rulah headlined *Zoot* from that issue onward, getting two stories a book with #9 (October 1947) and three with #10 (November 1947). By issue #17 (August 1948), Fox retitled the comic *Rulah, Jungle Goddess*, and that was it.

Rulah dwelt in a world in which all native women were white, beautiful, and bikini-clad; all native males were Black and primitive but usually willing to take her advice; and the usual outlanders were after gold, jewels, or women, not always in that order. She adopted a kid sidekick, Tombo (or Nimbo), who was sometimes white, sometimes Black, not that anyone seemed to notice. Integration was a fact of life in her jungle long before it hit the United States. There was no explanation as to why so many good and evil white women were there. Possibly a plane carrying a chorus line crashed, but we never knew. In issue #15 (June 1948), Rulah acquired a black panther named Saber. The big cat stayed with her to the end of the series, and made himself quite useful indeed.

The stories were extremely simple and were loaded with cheesecake, bondage, and the not infrequent catfight. Rulah got trapped a lot, escaped a lot, and triumphed a lot. Also, the stories never shied away from gore. In one episode, a maiden was crucified with knives through her wrists, and we got to see it in detail. It didn't make it into Fredric Wertham's book *Seduction of the Innocent* about the harmful influence of comics, but it probably should have.

In issue #20 (November 1948), in a story titled "The Twisted Fates," we found out that Rulah had an American boyfriend in her previous life. The man, Tim Pointer, had lost his memory while soldiering in World War II and regained it afterward in a hospital. Mrs. Dodge, Rulah's mom, informed Tim that Jane Dodge (herein called "Joan Grayson" for some reason) had been lost two years ago on that fateful African flight. Tim went to Africa in search of the girl, and both he and she wound up being captured by Sivo, a jungle dictatress. In chains, Rulah looked upon her new cellmate and thought, "A white man! Looks familiar! No—No! It couldn't be! But it is! Timothy Pointer!"

When Tim learned of Rulah's identity, he remarked, "Blast these chains.... I've got to kiss you ... just once before..." And he did. But while she was smooching, Rulah thought, "Dear Tim! Came all this way! But I'm not the same! The girl he knew is dead!" The two of them did make an escape, with Rulah killing two panthers with chains, beating Sivo in a knife fight, then almost strangling her to death. A wide-eyed Tim protested, and Rulah granted the villainess her life, though she sent Sivo into exile. "I'm going home tomorrow, Rulah ... alone," said Tim. "I understand a great deal now."

"Thank you, Tim," said Rulah. "You loved a different girl.... I belong here now...."
She saw him off the next day with a wave of her hand, and never saw him again.

Rulah's reign ended with issue #27 of her comic in June 1949, by which time she'd also managed appearances in *All-Top Comics* #9–18 (January 1948–July 1949). She ruled as Fox's premier jungle queen and, in appearance, was the anti-Sheena, which may have been the main reason why she stood out so well (that and the kinkiness of her stories). Other companies grabbed the rights, and she was reprinted quickly, sometimes with her name changed to "Pulah," sometimes with a fuller bathing suit inked onto her body. The Code came, shut all of that down, and relegated her to comic book limbo for a few years.

Then IW-Super's *Jungle Adventures* reprinted a few issues of *Rulah* and *Zoot* in the early Sixties, usually with Rulah depicted on the cover as a redhead in a one-piece bathing suit. Circa 1971, Skywald featured her in further reprints in a new, short-lived *Jungle Adventures*, and kept the character somewhat alive. Inevitably, AC Comics brought her back in reprints and in a few new stories in *Jungle Girls*. More recently, Antarctic Comics has featured new Rulah stories in a revived *Jungle Comics* in 2020. If Sheena was the Beatles, Rulah was the Rolling Stones.

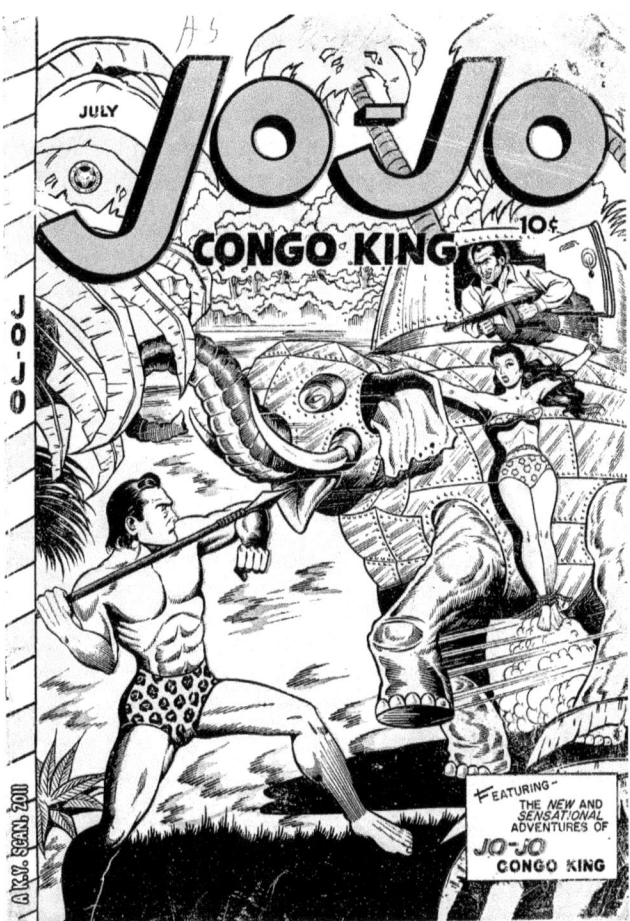

Jo-Jo the Congo King goes against an armored elephant and a thug with a machine gun. We're still betting on Jo-Jo. © 1947 Fox Features Syndicate.

Jo-Jo was Fox's answer to Tarzan, or perhaps to Ka'a'nga. His comic, also named *Jo-Jo*, had been a funny-animal book up till issue #7 (1947). With that number, we got a cover depicting a loinclothed, black-haired white man wielding a spear against an armored elephant with a machine-gun-toting hood on its back and a swimsuited girl tied to its side. The blurb read, "Featuring—the *new* and *sensational* adventures of Jo-Jo, Congo King!" That was where it started.

We never got an origin story for Jo-Jo, and somehow it didn't seem to matter. The first tale concerned the cover situation of an American gangster who outfitted elephants with armor plates and led them against the domain of Gwenna, the white queen of a Black tribe (yeah, *that* trope again), to seize her copious gold supply. The bad guys initially took their objective and Gwenna, but Jo-Jo trapped the tusked tank with an interlocking trap of fallen trees, smoked out the gangster by shoving a torch inside his turret, and, in the end, saw the baddie trampled to death by his own elephant. Later, holding Gwenna's arm, Jo-Jo proclaimed, "You will be a better queen for this, Gwenna, and remember what a jungle sage has spoken … 'True gold is only found in an honest heart.'"

"You are wise, Jo-Jo," said Gwenna. "I will heed you in the future, I promise!"

She didn't have much time to do that. In the next story, Jo-Jo went to the aid of one Geesa, and saved her from the experiments of the evil Dr. Gotha. In the next issue, he saved Princess Yolda, the white daughter of a Black chieftain. (The story blatantly ripped off the Frank Stockton story "The Lady or the Tiger?".) After that, he saved his "beloved," Safra, from a tribe of blonde, six-foot Amazons. If left to himself, he might have racked up a long enough list of conquests to make James Bond look like a piker.

Soon enough, though, he settled down on a brunette looker named Tanee, who wore a leopard-skin two-piece, went barefoot, and followed closely on all his adventures. She was also handy when a villain needed somebody to torture. The art, by the likes of Jack Kamen and John Forte, was pretty good and gave Jo-Jo what he needed to survive. The stories, probably by Manning Lee Stokes, were fairly standard Tarzanesque fare, stealing from *Tarzan and the Ant Men* in one story (and changing the tiny warriors of Burroughs's tale to tiny women … but of course!) and putting a modern metropolis, complete with automobiles, in the midst of the jungle in another. It went on through issue #29 (1949), with a regular slot in *All-Top* as well. Like Rulah's, Jo-Jo's stories were reprinted by Star, IW-Super, Skywald, and AC Comics. Of late, like a lot of others, he's shown up in Antarctic's *Jungle Comics*.

Of course, Victor Fox couldn't be content to leave it there. Fox liked sex, liked garish covers, and liked the fact that jungle comics gave him a big avenue for exploitation. So, like it or not, there were more Tarzan-style titles. None of them lasted very long, but it probably didn't bother him all that much.

Jungle Lil was the proverbial only survivor of a plane crash that claimed her parents' lives when she was just a baby. A witch doctor wanted to sacrifice her. The chief of the tribe didn't, and got his way. She grew up to be a redheaded, bikini-wearing jungle queen with lousy art. It lasted one issue (April 1950).

By #2 (June 1950), the title was transformed into *Dorothy Lamour, Jungle Princess*. Miss Lamour, a real-life movie queen famed for wearing sarongs, was transmuted into a sarong-wearing jungle queen. In the comic, she was the daughter of a pair of scientists who took her with them to Africa (unwise move!) while looking for moss as an ingredient for a wonder drug. The inevitable happened: the parents were killed, and the young kid was raised to be a jungle empress by a native tribe. The art on both issues, and a third which came out under the covers of Rural Home's *Red Circle Comics* #4, was mostly the work of a very young, very crude Wally Wood.

Dorothy Lamour, star of stage, screen, radio, and jungle. © 1950 Hero Books, Inc.

Zago, who showed up in 1949, was a blond clone of Jo-Jo and may have well been reworked from Jo-Jo stories; the first *Zago* issue lineup, with Blue Beetle and Toni Luck, looked suspiciously like the just-cancelled *All-Top*. The comic lasted four issues (September 1948–March 1949). *Tegra* (August 1948) was really a renamed Rulah, and fought Amazons from Saturn in her first story. She bleached her hair blonde, changed her name to *Zegra*, and lasted four more issues (#2–5, October 1948–April 1949), often wearing slip-on shoes to protect her feet. There was also *Jungle Jo*, in 1950, who was blond, had mediocre art and stories, and did a four-issue stint (#0–3, March–September 1950), with an unpubbed fifth issue ending up in Star's *Terrors of the Jungle* #21 (February 1953).

Sabu, Elephant Boy (June–August 1950) adapted the then-current jungle movie star to the comics pages and lasted two issues. The art, again by Wood, was more developed this time and showed more promise. He also rendered the short-lived *Frank Buck* series in 1950 (#70, 71, and 3, May–September 1950), featuring the real-life big game hunter. By this time, Woody was showing traces of what would soon flower into brilliance at EC and other houses.

Dagar, Desert Hawk, not quite but almost a jungle book, was a bit better conceived and executed. Drawn by Edmond Good, the strip featured an American adventurer who wound up ruler of an Arab land and lover of the beautiful Ayesha. Dagar wore Arab clothes, wielded a scimitar, and went after dastards of the desert in about two years' worth of rip-roaring stories. He began his term in *All-Great Comics* #13 (December 1947) which was renamed *Dagar, Desert Hawk* with the next issue (February 1948). The series ran till issue #23 (April 1949), with an encore appearance in *All-Top Comics* #18 (July 1949). In the back of his comics lurked a legitimate jungle girl, *Tangi*, who was blonde and wore a flowered bikini and shoes.

By 1951, Fox threw in the towel for their comics operation. The rights to their characters were sold to several companies and mostly used for reprints, although their main star, the Blue Beetle, got a few new stories from Charlton. The days of Rulah, Jo-Jo, and Dagar were gone.

Tarzan movies were still fairly big, though, and the comics weren't quite ready to give up on jungle characters. Avon, which got into the comics game fairly late, offered up five issues of *White Princess of the Jungle* (July 1951–November 1952). She was Taanda, a redhead in a leopard-skin bikini. Her parents had been white explorers who were killed by an enemy tribe, and she herself was raised dutifully to be a jungle girl by a chieftain. Louis Ravelli did the first few stories. Then Everett Raymond Kinstler

The White Princess of the Jungle, with a title that would never make the grade today and a bikini that would. © 1951 Avon Periodicals, Inc.

stepped in and rendered Taanda in some of the most exquisitely drawn jungle stories of all in issue #2. Gene Fawcette took up the pencil after that, but Taanda (renamed Taarna in the last issue) vanished shortly afterward, along with Avon's comics line. She got her share of reprints from IW-Super, Skywald, AC Comics, and IDW, but has never been revived.

A one-shot jungle queen, *Saari*, popped up from an obscure company named P. L. Publishing in November 1951. She was a redhead, her bathing suit was a leopard-skin one-piece, she was shown on the cover fighting off an ape with a knife, and she never turned up again after her two stories in the issue. Saari was backed up in her only issue by Congo Jim, a white hunter, and Tambor, a blond jungle king. She's mentioned here for the sake of completeness.

Alani, Matt Baker's pulchritudinous South Sea Girl. © 1946 Universal Phoenix Features Syndicate.

Alani, aka the South Sea Girl, was another almost-jungle heroine who can be made to fit in here. She appeared in all six issues of *Seven Seas Comics* (April 1946–July 1947) and sported a sarong that ofttimes covered about as much as a bikini. The splash page of her first story showed her lounging pin-up style against a tree on a tropical island, looking enticingly at the reader. A caption read: "Above a volcano floor, shrouded by whispering mists, and hemmed in with deep waters treacherously studded by reefs, lies the **Vanishing Isles ...** where the pounding surf sweeps adventure against lush shores, demanding a challenge from the young beautiful ruler and protector, **Alani ...** known simply as the **South Sea Girl!**"

As the story opened, two bad guys were boarding a boat captained by one Ted Trimble and crewed by an islander named Tanaka. They had heard of oil deposits on the Vanishing Isles and wanted to stake a claim. Though Captain Ted protested that typhoons would make the journey dangerous, Tanaka pointed out that they needed the money, so they reluctantly agreed. But before they took off, a veiled woman in a red dress was rowed up to the craft and asked to be taken aboard and go to the Isles herself. "That woman, Marty, we saw her in Saigon!"

"Yeah, Bill, I think she's following us!"

And so she was. But, despite the villains' protests, Captain Ted let her aboard. Later, one of the baddies noted, "There is a legend about a queen who lives in the mists." Later than that, they ran into one of the aforementioned typhoons. Ted and Tanaka wanted to turn back, but the dastards pulled guns, winged them, and threw Ted into the woman's cabin. To his astonishment, he found the brunette beauty clad in a sarong that bared her stomach and legs, with a garland of yellow flowers in her hair.

"I am Alani, ruler of the Vanishing Isles," she explains. "Those men plan to seize my lands as a hideout for international intrigue. But no more talk.... I have a plan for escape!"

As it was, Alani jumped out of a porthole in the cabin's side, struggled to swim against the currents of the typhoon, and clambered back aboard the ship by climbing up the rudder chain. From there, she managed to free Captain Ted, and the two of them reclaimed control of the ship. Alani herself took the wheel and steered them toward the Vanishing Isles. "We near the isle of Patna, where I was born ... fear not, Ted!"

Once past a ring of mists thrown up by undersea volcanoes, the ship and Alani were greeted by canoes full of Patnan islanders. The crooks, meanwhile, liberated machine guns they had stored in crates in the ship's hold, and took to murdering the natives. Alani, saying, "I will avenge the slaying of my people!" swam underwater, killed a shark with her knife, and then overturned the bad guys' boat. With the two villains in the drink, she directed her people to throw chunks of the chopped-up shark into the water. The blood drew the attention of very-much-alive sharks, and the predators settled in for a two-and-a-half-course meal. "Ug ... those screams," remarked Ted.

"Yes," noted Alani, climbing from the sea into a canoe, "but the penalty for murder must be harsh!" Later, after the mists lifted, Ted and Alani said their goodbyes and he sailed off. "What a gal..." he thought. "If only..." Matt Baker, who signed the first story, drew all Alani's exploits and made her a desirable lass indeed. Scripts were most likely the work of Manning Lee Stokes.

The South Sea Girl defended her tribe for five more issues, even once against a gang of crooks that had atom bombs in their possession. Then she was gone, although Ajax-Farrell changed her name to Vooda (not to be confused with Voodah) and put her in three issues of a reprint comic with that name. Interestingly enough, Alani also appeared in a short-lived comic strip written by "Thorne Stevenson" (Manning Lee Stokes) and drawn by John Forte.

Magazine Enterprises, a relative newcomer to the comics game, got into the jungle a little late in 1952 but made up for it with one of the most quality offerings ever. The title character's adventures were written by Gardner Fox and drawn by Frank Frazetta. His name was Thun'da, King of the Congo.

The cover of issue #1 (1952) showed a man in a fur loincloth, with muscles Johnny Weissmuller could only dream of having, fighting off three grotesquely rendered, spear-wielding tribesmen at the same time. In the foreground, a beautiful brunette in a skimpy fur outfit gaped in fear as another tribesman reached out for her with a clawed hand. His hand was at the level of her breasts, and his expression was plain enough to read. The cover's animalistic depiction of Africans reflects the racism of its era.

Frank Frazetta's fighting fury, Thun'da! © 1952 Magazine Enterprises.

But inside, we got down to business. On the splash panel of the first story, Thun'da showed off his musculature as only a Frazetta hero could, holding a bow in one hand. Then we faded back to the time of World War II, when pilot Roger Drum was ferrying a plane of supplies to Allied troops in Africa. He hit a mountain peak with one wing and, like Rulah some years before, came in for a crash landing. But this part of Africa wasn't shown on the maps. Indeed, it was covered in mists and populated by dinosaurs ... and cavemen. One such dinosaur gaped wide its jaws, bit into the plane's fuselage, and "As a dog would shake a rat, he shakes the big plane ... and a limp figure drops earthward...."

No sooner had Drum dropped earthward than a big raptor grabbed him and dragged him skyward ("Holy cow!"). He dropped the winged saurian with two shots from his sidearm, but, when he was on terra firma again, admitted, "I—I can't seem to think ... to remember who or where I am ... as if I was just born ... almost like a baby ... and yet ... I know this uniform ... and I have a gun...."

Abruptly, he was accosted by two cavemen, and, in gentlemanly fashion, decided not to use the gun on them when they attacked. Instead, he waded into them with both fists, as any good Frazetta hero minus a sword would do. But numbers prevailed, and Roger Drum went down. The cavemen carried him back to their lair, a cliff dwelling. Using a bit of deductive reasoning, he took away the ladders that enabled them to climb to their cliff cave homes, and escaped. The residents took umbrage at this abuse of their hospitality, and went after him as soon as they could. Three of them came upon him. He shot two and killed the third with the man's own club. "When they find you three ... if they ever do ... maybe they'll think twice about coming after me...."

Roger Drum trekked on, and we cut to a shot of another kind of people, a more civilized bunch (barely), fronted by the girl from the cover. She said to the leopard-skin-togaed man beside her, "The cave people are as numerous as gnats on the hide of a sabretoothed [sic] tiger. If there were only some way we could make them fear us...."

"We are an old, dying race, Pha," replied her companion. "They are younger. Soon they will kill all us valley people...."

As fate would have it, Pha caught sight of Roger Drum, though he did not notice her on a rise above him. She noted that he was no caveman, but was unsure whether he was on her side or not. Thus, Pha and her tribe faded into the jungle, leaving Drum to himself. He had things to do.

Said things included fashioning a bow and arrows for himself, becoming expert at their use, and building his already considerable musculature into Charles Atlas territory and beyond. He also learned how to swing on vines, as all jungle heroes and heroines must do, and, when the time came, saved Pha and her tribe from a raiding party of cavemen with his deadly shafts. After he used up all his arrows, Drum took on the last surviving caveman ... bare-handed.

"Reeling and panting, his fists like steel hammers pounding into the caveman's ribs, the lost aviator knows the taste of victory!" He also told the loser to run back and tell his tribe he'd be waiting for them, with "sharp sticks."

Not long after, Drum caught sight of a caveman army marching toward Pha's village. Unable to make the villagers understand his talk, he lassoed Pha, carried her off with him, and showed her the threatening party. Then he and Pha took to the hills, leading them away from her tribe. A panel or two later, they had led the cavemen to a hill with a big hole in its side and a big gong in front of it, complete with a hammer. Drum took the logical course and banged the gong.

A page later, the biggest snake ever on record crawled out of the hole. So much for logic.

The raging reptile responded to the gong as if it were a dinner bell. Drum shot several arrows at it, to no avail. Then, finally, he grabbed his gun and pumped his remaining lead into it. That worked. As he stood beside the slain snake, Drum accepted the accolades of the cavemen: "Thun'da—lord of the magic drum! Thun'da—who killed the snake that surrounds the world! Thun'da—king of the lost lands!" Pha, for her part, kept Thun'da between her and the snake.

A caption explained, "And so, Roger Drum, who is henceforth to be known as Thun'da, comes at last to peace and friendship with the queen of the valley people ... and with the people of the caves!" In the rest of the issue, Thun'da and Pha fought monkeymen, made a pet of a saber-toothed tiger they logically called Sabre (Rulah, for some reason, didn't sue), and fought off Commies who wanted to loot some local uranium deposits. It was an impressive debut, and the last panel of the issue promised there would be more.

There was, but in a different tone.

Two things happened in short succession. First, editor Ray Krank asked Fox and Frazetta to cut out the dinosaurs and cavemen, making Thun'da just another Tarzan clone. This, reportedly, did not set well with Frazetta. Second, Columbia Pictures was on the prowl for another comic book subject for a movie serial. They saw *Thun'da*, liked it, and optioned it. Frazetta was notified that he wouldn't be getting any bucks from the movie. He quit.

Thun'da itself carried on for five more issues (#2–6, 1952–1953), which weren't shabby at all, being written by Fox and drawn by Magazine Enterprises' excellent mainstay, Bob Powell. The books, indeed, were good. But they weren't Frazetta, and the serial, *King of the Congo* (starring Buster Crabbe), couldn't save the comic. With the sixth issue, Thun'da was gone.

Cave Girl was a spinoff

The curvaceous Cave Girl, taking on seven Amazons at a time. © 1954 Magazine Enterprises.

from *Thun'da*, and a good one indeed. She debuted in a rare crossover story in *Thun'da* #2 (1952), written by Fox and drawn by Powell, the team that would handle all of her stories. Under her own logo in the splash panel, the blonde jungle girl in a leopard-skin one-piece fought side-by-side with Thun'da against a tribe of pygmies and a huge ape-god. In the story proper, Thun'da and Pha came upon Cave Girl, who was crawling away from something and surrounded by a bunch of birds. She mistook them for enemies, backed against a tree, grabbed her knife, and spat, "Come then! I will die fighting you!"

"I do not seek to harm you, only to help!" said Thun'da. He disarmed Cave Girl, who, exhausted from a prior battle, collapsed. But she sent up a trilling call to the birds, informing them that Thun'da was an ally, and they dispersed. It seemed to work for an introduction.

At that point, a tribe of ape-men from the land of Kor (possibly borrowed from Haggard's *She*) fell upon them, overwhelmed them, and took all captive, lock, stock, and saber-toothed tiger. Thun'da survived combat with a big cat (not Sabre) in an arena, but for assaulting the tribal leader, Boorg, he was sentenced to death. But Cave Girl, sharing a cell with Pha, received a knife borne by a bird ally, and used it to pick the lock.

The next day, with Thun'da chained and facing three tigers, Cave Girl jumped in front of her newfound friend and told the big cats in their own language to lay off. She freed Thun'da from his bonds. He responded by taking a spear and running Boorg through with it. Then the three of them, four counting Sabre, headed for home.

Cave Girl appeared in two more solo backup stories in *Thun'da* before getting her own comic (#11, 1953). On the cover, she sported a zebra-skin swimsuit and fiercely charged two enemies, bearing a long knife and backed up by a black panther. If anyone had tried groping *her* chest, he would have soon become handless.

The first story of the issue, "The Pool of Life," finally gave us her origin. Her real name was Carol Mantomer, and she was an English baroness, of all things. She had been taken as a child with her explorer parents into the jungle and, when attacking tribesmen killed her mother and father, was abducted by an eagle. The eagle was killed by a wolf. Little Carol called the wolf a "nice doggy" and decided to join his family. Within the space of a few panels, she grew to maturity and full sex appeal, wore a zebra-skin swimsuit stitched together at the sides with leather thongs, used a bow and arrow, threw a mean knife, and fought like a wildcat. Cave Girl was born.

For the rest of the issue, Cave Girl had to save the hides of two white men who wanted to bring her back to civilization, restore her to her proper position, and marry her. She wasn't having any of it, and they finally conceded, after facing hostile tribes, gangsters, ape-like "snowmen" and the occasional jungle beast, that she probably had the right idea. But that didn't mean they were giving up on the marriage idea.

Cave Girl, often accompanied by her would-be beau, Luke Hardin, fought on for three more issues of her own book (#12–14, 1953–1954) and more backup stories in *Thun'da*. In her second issue, she encountered a tribe of enemy Amazons, who became recurrent nemeses of sorts. She got into almost as many catfights as Rulah as a result. She also found time to battle Mau Maus, a mad scientist, and occasional evil tribesmen. Obligingly, she gave Thun'da a backup slot in her own comic after his mag folded. Both she and Thun'da made their last appearances in a one-shot comic, *Africa*, in 1955.

Well, almost their last, anyway. AC Comics did their inevitable reprinting and reviving, the former in 1989 and the latter in 1990 for Cave Girl. After a bunch of reprints in various books, she returned to original stories in AC's *Femforce* #29–31 and 35–36 (1990–1991). Cave Girl also made further appearances in *Femforce*, *Jungle Girls*, and *Fighting Yank*. *Thun'da* was reprinted first in 1987 by Fantagraphics, then in 1989 by AC, then in 2010 by Dark Horse. Thun'da also made new appearances in AC's *Fighting Yank* #2–3 (2002) alongside Cave Girl. In 2012, Dynamite Entertainment did a five-issue *Thun'da* mini-series (August–December 2012), with new stories supplemented by reprints. Finally, both Thun'da and Cave Girl appeared in the *Pathfinder: Worldscape* series (2016–2017). At this writing, that's where their appearances stand.

Timely Comics had started out with Ka-Zar and a couple of other one-off jungle strips for its early '40s anthologies, then abandoned them. In the early '50s, with their superheroes similarly abandoned and their comics diversified into a jillion other genres, the company—now called Atlas—made another stab at the jungle line. Their heroines didn't show quite as much skin as those of Fiction House, but they made do quite well in their own way, and remain memorable to this day ... a nice trick, since they haven't been revived, for the most part.

Lorna the Jungle Queen (changed after five issues to *Lorna the Jungle Girl*) came first, in 1953. With that timing, it's hard to believe that Atlas's Stan Lee wasn't keeping tabs on Fiction House and waiting till Sheena was canceled to make his move. Whatever the case, Atlas came up with a winner in its first jungle girl. Lovely, blonde Lorna wore a red-and-black-striped top that stretched from her neck to her waist, while still suggesting a chest to compete with Sheena's, along with a leopard-skin miniskirt that soon was converted into shorts and sandals, which were often left off in favor of bare feet on the cover. She was strong but good-natured and could swing from vines and slay beasties with the best of them.

The origin story, in issue #1 (July 1953), introed us to Lorna and her father, who had been living in Africa for many years. By the second panel of the story, Lorna's dad got attacked by a lion and his leg was so badly mauled that M'Tuba, their native friend and guide, had to amputate it with a hot spear-blade, much to Lorna's anguish. (Lorna's dad undoubtedly had a good share of anguish, too.) Later, while Lorna was hunting, she was charged by a rhino and almost gored when her gun jammed. She dropped under the beast as it charged, then sprang up afterward and scampered into the trees for safety. M'Tuba arrived and dispatched the animal. From then on, Lorna was leery of guns. They seemed too undependable.

Her friend had worse news than that, though: her father had just died. After Lorna buried him, she declared, "My father always wanted a son who could be a great hunter as he was! I am not a man ... but I will be what father wanted ... with your help, M'Tuba!"

"Mikki and I will teach the little mistress all I know," agreed M'Tuba, and Mikki, his pet monkey, agreed: "Eep!" So it began.

Lorna, Marvel's sexiest jungle queen, fights off baddies with the help of Greg Knight and a pair of pachyderms. © 1954 Official Magazine Corp. and © 2022 Marvel Publications. Used with permission.

Thus, Lorna learned to throw a spear and use a knife even better than her teacher, and learned other feats of junglecraft, such as the time-honored art of tree-swinging. Shortly after M'Tuba admitted there was nothing more to teach her, both of them were captured by a band of headhunters. With the help of Mikki, they escaped being sacrificed, and Lorna won a death-duel with the local witch doctor. That got her appointed to the post, which she generously handed over to M'Tuba. In return, M'Tuba gave her Mikki. "I shall travel deeper into the jungle," she announced, "as my father would have wanted me to … to seek out others who may need help!" And M'Tuba waved goodbye to Lorna as she left on a 26-issue, four-year journey.

By issue #2 (August 1953), Lorna encountered Greg Knight, hunter and guide extraordinaire, and had a decided reaction: "So handsome ... so young ... so strong! I didn't know there were such creatures in the world! I—I want to know him ... to be near him ... always! What's happening to me? Why do I feel this way?" Mikki offered "Cheee!" but said nothing further. Greg had earlier admitted to the client he was guiding that he had been in love once, it had ended badly, and he didn't want another woman. In short order, Lorna appeared, saved him from a lion, and then saved both him and his client from a rogue elephant. Greg was grateful, but griped, "Well, anyway ... the jungle is no place for a woman!" And that was about the way it stayed for the length of the series, with Greg reluctantly falling in love, insisting that Lorna was unqualified for jungle work, and having his bacon saved by her time and again. He also earned a solo story in that second issue and for the rest of the run.

Refreshingly, Lorna wasn't out to depopulate the jungle. "White hunters kill for the sport ... not for food or protection! ... They kill and leave the young to starve by themselves! It's wrong, Mikki, **wrong!**" So, although she had to deal with animal threats in every issue, her attitude was that of a conservationist, not a conqueress.

Lorna's leggy sex appeal put her somewhere between Sheena and Nyoka, and that was just fine. She handled various threats with Greg and Mikki by her side till issue #26 (August 1957), with cover art by the likes of Bill Everett and Russ Heath helping out. Jay Scott Pike replaced Werner Roth on the interior art and did a creditable job. In her last story, Lorna and Greg were transplanted to the United States, where she trapped a manticore-like "Night Beast." When a cop remarked that the beast belonged back in the jungle, she said, "And so do we! Don't you agree, Greg?"

"Hate to admit it, but you're right, Lorna!" said Greg. "Back we go!"

And that was the last we saw of Lorna. Which, in a way, was a shame. She did field a few reprints in the early issues of Marvel's *Jungle Action* in 1973. Later, in 2010–2012, all her stories were reprinted in Marvel Masterworks editions. But, to our knowledge, she was never revived.

Having seen Atlas test the waters with Lorna, publisher Martin Goodman, who never missed a chance to flood the stands with copycat books, struck again. *Jungle Tales* came out in September 1954 and *Jungle Action* followed a month later. Under a Joe Maneely cover, *Jungle Tales* #1 produced the first rival to Lorna at Atlas: *Jann of the Jungle*.

In contrast with Lorna, Jann was a brunette in a dark one-piece bathing suit affair with a knife buckled to her belt. Her real name was Jane Hastings, and she was a stunt girl on the set of a jungle movie being filmed in Africa. When she told the local natives who she was, they proclaimed, "No! You are Jann!" "Jann? Hmmm! That's a nice professional name! I'll adopt it as my own!" In a couple more pages she proved her stuff by heading off an animal stampede and slaying a huge snake.

Afterward, the local chieftain said that a white woman had come to them many years ago, served the tribe well, then fell in love with a white hunter and left them. "That Jann they're talking about was my grandmother!" said the current Jann. "I'm staying here! This is where I belong ... to carry on the work of the first Jann ... and help the people of the jungle!"

Marvel's runner-up jungle girl: Jann. © 1956 Classic Syndicate Inc. and © 2022 Marvel Publications. Used with permission.

"And I'm staying too!" said Pat Mahoney, film producer-cum-African exile. "Somebody's got to watch over the new Jann!" Thus was the stage set for the series.

Don Rico and Jay Scott Pike were the creators of the first Jann story and all the rest of her *Jungle Tales* run. With issue #8, the book was converted into *Jann of the Jungle* and ran till #17 (June 1957). Rico and Pike handled all of Jann's stories through #15, but by the penultimate issue, the jungle queen found a new artist: Al Williamson. As could be expected, Al did an excellent job, limning the long black tresses of Jann and adding authenticity to the jungle setting. But after only two issues of his work, the book was canceled.

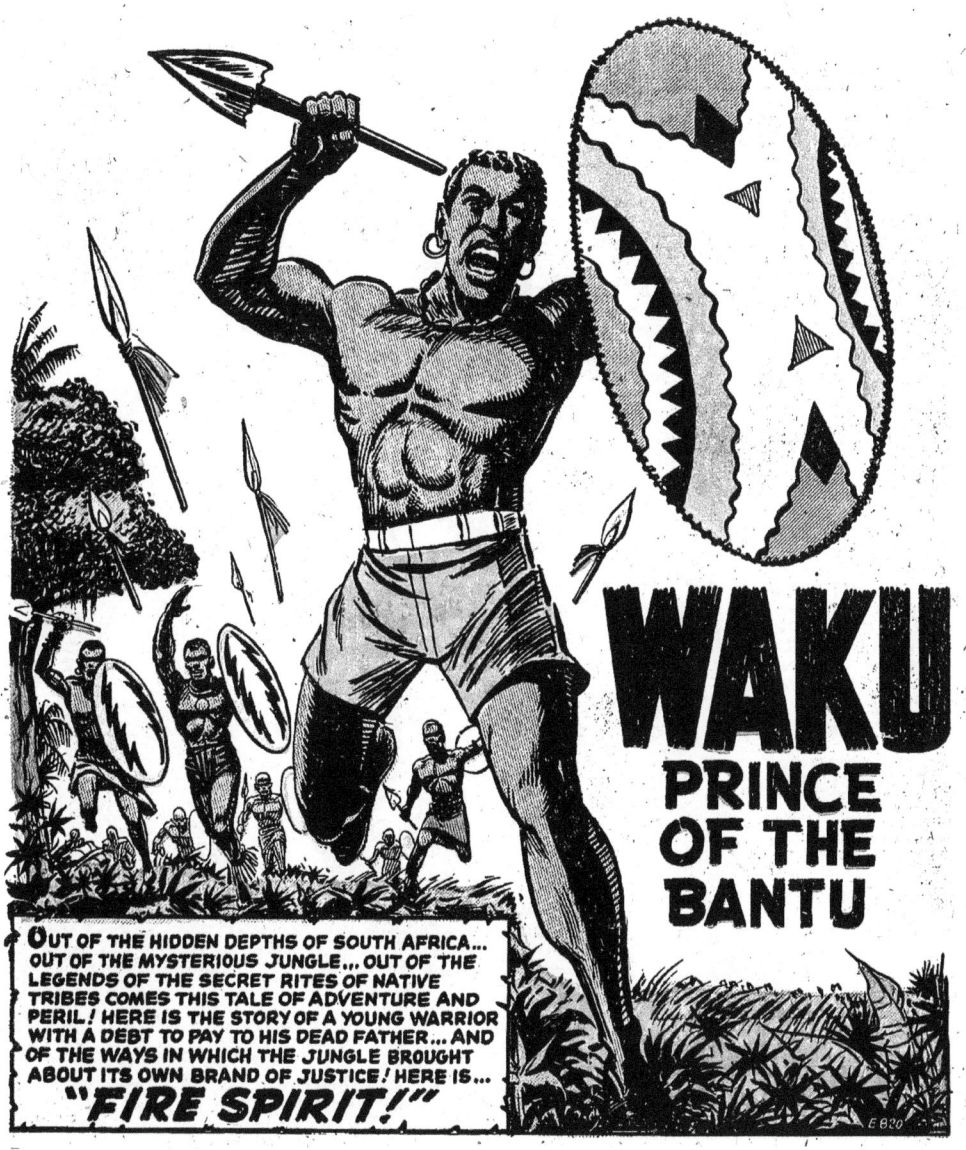

Waku, Marvel's first solo-featured Black hero. © 1954 Classic Syndicate Inc. and © 2022 Marvel Publications. Used with permission.

The rest of *Jungle Tales* was filled by three strips: *Waku, Prince of the Bantu*, about a heroic Black tribal leader; *The Unknown Jungle*, featuring a different animal "star" each month; and *Cliff Mason*, about a white hunter. All were written by Rico and the artists included Ogden Whitney, Syd Shores, Sid Greene, John Romita, George Tuska, Joe Maneely, and Don Heck, among others. *Cliff* and *Unknown Jungle* carried over into Jann's own comic.

Jungle Action didn't fare as well. The first cover, by Joe Maneely, was good enough: in four vignettes, Lo-Zar, Leopard Girl, Jungle Boy, and Man-Oo the Mighty were introduced. They were, respectively, a Ka-Zar knockoff, a girl in a full-body leopard suit, a stand-in for Bomba, and a gorilla. Leopard Girl, who was the only jungle heroine to have a secret identity, might have had the most promise, but the art wasn't that great and jungle girls who don't even show off their legs have a short shelf life. After six issues, the book folded its tent.

Lo-Zar, Marvel's king of the jungle. His brother Hi-Zar did not appear. © 1954 Interstate Publishing Corp. and © 2022 Marvel Publications. Used with permission.

Marvel paid heed to its jungle heroes and heroines of times past in 1973, when they reprinted Lorna, Lo-Zar (now called Tharn), and Jann in the first four issues of a new *Jungle Action*, just before it became home to a new Black Panther series. Jann made a cameo in *What If?* #9 in 1978, in a story laden with Atlas-era characters. None of the Atlas jungle characters have been seen since.

This leaves only one major American jungle comics character to cover. As might be expected, we've saved possibly the best for last. The remaining swinging superstar is ... *Tarzan of the Apes!*

Tarzan, the progenitor of the entire jungle hero genre, had, of course, been created by Edgar Rice Burroughs in his 1912 novel *Tarzan of the Apes* and maintained by him through 23 sequels. The jungle man got into the movies within a few years and into the comic strips shortly after that, with the art of Hal Foster creating an indelible image in the public mind and setting a marker to inspire generations of artists to come. The first collection of Foster's Tarzan strips was probably *The Illustrated Tarzan Book* from Grosset & Dunlap in 1929. It was a hardbound reprint of the adaptation of Burroughs's first novel. Of course, things didn't stop there.

In 1936, with comic books taking off for the first time, Tarzan strips were reprinted first in *Tip Top Comics* #1 from United Feature Syndicate. The cover showed Tarzan and Li'l Abner boxing in a ring with characters from the other strips in the book watching. The reprinted newspaper offerings continued in *Tip Top* through the mid–Fifties. At the same time, other Tarzan strips were recycled in *Comics on Parade* and Dell's *Sparkler*. The first regular-sized solo comic of Tarzan in America was United's *Single Series* #10, an entire book of Foster reprints. Outside of some anonymously written Tarzan text stories in *Popular Comics*, there were no original Ape Man comic stories until 1947. Perhaps Burroughs didn't think there needed to be any.

But by the late Thirties / early Forties, the original-story comic had supplanted its strip reprint forebears. Burroughs, who was proficient at marketing his famous creation, gave the go-ahead to Dell Comics, the master makers of licensed comics, to try an adaptation of Tarzan in an original story. The result was *Tarzan and the Devil Ogre*, a book-lengther that appeared in *Four Color Comics* #134 (February 1947). The front cover showed a grinning Tarzan, waving at the reader from elephant-back. The writer of the story is lost to history, but the artist of the cover and the book was Jesse Marsh.

The story was a fairly exciting tale of Tarzan helping a woman find her lost father, who was being held by an isolated, tyrannic tribe. The Devil Ogre of the title was a gigantic white ape which, of course, Tarzan had to fight and defeat. Marsh's art was never spectacular, but was serviceable. He continued as the artist of Dell's *Tarzan* through 1965, by which time the title had been acquired by Gold Key. The next Tarzan tale was *The Fires of Tohr* (*Four Color* #161, August 1947) and again proved a winner. By this time, Tarzan had acquired a full-time writer: Gaylord DuBois, who would stay with the series till the end of Gold Key's holdings, in 1972. Dell's next offering was *Tarzan* #1 (January–February 1948), and it ran for 206 issues. To say the least, it was an impressive run.

DuBois and Marsh salted the stories with fragments of Burroughs's novels, all tied up in a "jungle world" of their creation. Jane soon appeared, as did Tarzan's son, who was called "Boy" in deference to the movies. In the Sixties, the youth would adopt the name Burroughs gave him and spin off into his own series, *Korak, Son of Tarzan*. It was excellently drawn by Russ Manning, who had been working on Tarzan's backup strip, *Brothers of the Spear*, for years, and on *Magnus, Robot Fighter* since 1963. That had to give the Powers That Be ideas for Marsh's replacement, and it did. In 1965, Manning took over the art chores on *Tarzan* and quickly commenced a nonpareil series of adaptations of the Burroughs novels, which efforts have been reprinted again and again unto the present day. Manning left to help the *Tarzan* newspaper strip and was spelled by Doug Wildey, Mike Royer, and others.

The Burroughs adaptations were cued by a bootleg effort from Charlton Comics entitled *Jungle Tales of Tarzan*, which came out in late 1964. This four-issue series was made possible by a copyright hassle which temporarily seemed to throw Burroughs's creations into the public domain, and Charlton, which felt (as did many fans) that the Dell / Gold Key versions were too tepid, turned Joe Gill and Sam Glanzman loose on adaptations of the short stories in Burroughs's *Jungle Tales of Tarzan*, which were tales of the jungle man's early life. Soon enough, the courts ruled in favor of Burroughs, and Charlton had to pulp the entire fifth issue before it hit the stands.

Marsh's art was never that exciting, and his women, no matter what their state of dress or undress, would never be mistaken for a Fiction House offering. But the low-key action fit the young kids who were Dell's target audience, and, best of all, the lack of graphic violence and sex appeal let *Tarzan* (and Dell itself) weather the comics crackdown of the mid–Fifties without a scratch. If Tarzan is still around in comics today, in large part it's because Marsh and DuBois set the foundation.

Tarzan's franchise was given over to DC, then Marvel, then Malibu, then Dark Horse, then Dynamite unto the present day, with a few years in between. Those later publications are beyond the scope of a Golden Age history, but can be covered if later projects come to fruition. Tarzan is the ur-jungle man, and it's only fitting that he still survives, even though his reign is oft interrupted.

But after 1955, he was pretty much alone. Fredric Wertham's anti-comics crusade of the time specifically targeted jungle comics, among others, for their blatant sex appeal (hey, why else were they there?), for violence (which was never nearly as bad as in the gangster and horror comics), and for racism (which may have been an undertone, but which mostly was in the eye of the beholder). Parents in the conservative Fifties suddenly became aware that their kids were hooked on comics featuring a bunch of hotties in bathing suits on the covers and in the interiors. In an era in which *I Love Lucy* couldn't even use the word "pregnant" when Lucy was about to give birth, something had to give. What gave, sadly, were the jungle comics.

Fragments of the era still survive. Sheena continues as an icon of sorts, with scattered reprints and revivals. After the sexual liberation of the Sixties, bikini-clad heroines weren't frowned upon as much, and a couple of token attempts, such as Marvel's Shanna and DC's Rima, were made, though they didn't last long. Tarzan's movies faded out in the mid–Sixties. Jungle adventure, as a genre, isn't that popular anymore. And, without a basis in current pop culture, the genre can't survive in comics. But the continuation of Tarzan and Sheena and a few newbies like *Jungle Girl* give us hope.

Sheena, Rulah, Lorna, Ka'a'nga, and all the rest still have their place in the saga of comics. They can never be forgotten. The lords and ladies of the jungle still live!

Science Fiction Theater

Long before we ever got to the moon, we were among the stars.

Writers like H. G. Wells, Jules Verne, and Edgar Rice Burroughs showed us the way. Others, like Isaac Asimov, Robert Heinlein, and Ray Bradbury took up the cause. From the classic science fiction of the nineteenth century to the pulps that started with Hugo Gernsback's *Amazing Stories* in 1926, we were there, in space suits, rocketing into the void. Every kid with a dime and an imagination knew all about it.

Magazines like *Thrilling Wonder Stories, Fantastic Adventures, Captain Future, Super-Science Fiction, Planet Stories, Astounding Stories,* and *Amazing Stories* served up pulpwood space voyages every month from the Depression years through World War II and beyond. In time to come, even mainstream mags like *The Saturday Evening Post* would publish the occasional SF tale. But it all started on the cheap, in SF pulps with garish but imaginative painted covers and text and illustrations within, fueling the desire of kids for adventure. Not just down mean streets, in the Wild West, on the battlefield, or in the jungle, but beyond. Places where humanity had not yet set foot, if they even existed.

The comics were there too.

Flash Gordon and Buck Rogers, the comic strip forerunners, set the pace. Comic books, most of them created by teens or young adolescents who had read the funny papers, tried to come up with new spacefaring tales to rival their antecedents. A few succeeded, a few failed, and most were in between. But they were all part of the graphic entertainment of their time, and most of the early comic anthologies sported a science fiction feature or two. Yet, there was one comic full of blasters, babes, and BEMs (bug-eyed monsters), as the cliché goes, and it's our first focus. Fiction House had a pulp named *Planet Stories*. It wasn't such a jump for them to make to create, in 1940, *Planet Comics*!

Planet wasn't the biggest seller for Fiction House, or its longest-running publication. But it did survive on the stands for over 13 years. Also, it was the first successful science-fiction comic in America. Admittedly, the SF in *Planet* wasn't anything to give readers of *Astounding* or *Amazing* pause. It was more the sort of beauties and monsters, rocket ships and Ming the Merciless type of title. Lots of sexy, bikini-clad heroines and villainesses populated the pages. But such themes have never lost circulation for comics, or much of any other magazine.

Even some of the female comics fans of the time have commented favorably

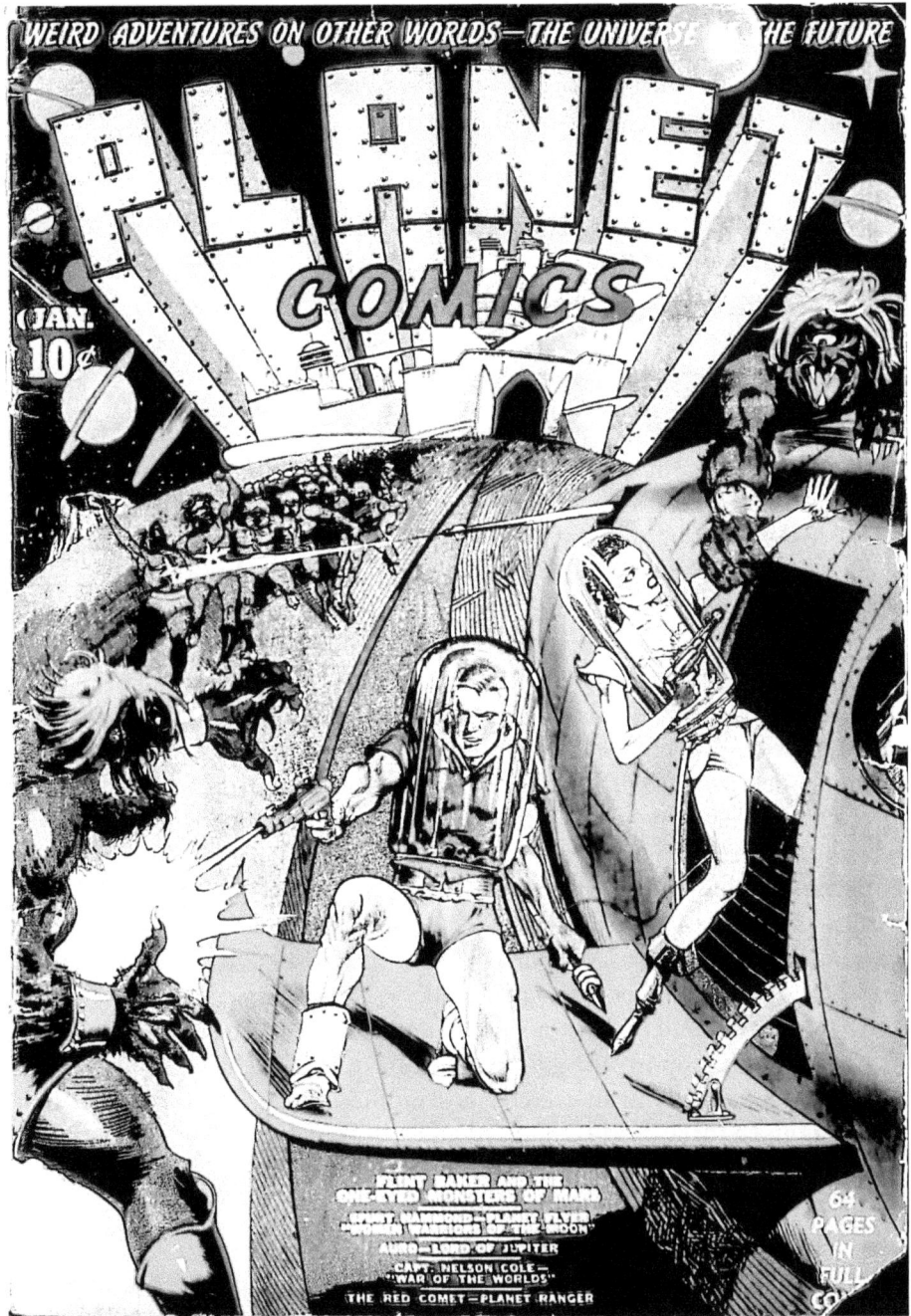

Planet Comics premiers! © 1939 Love Romances Publishing Co., Inc.

about Fiction House's portrayal of women. The ladies of *Planet Comics* didn't stand around shivering in their swimsuits to be rescued by the nearest clone of Flash Gordon. They piloted the spaceships, zapped the ray guns, and were as good at bringing in the baddies—or wasting them—as the men. And since *Planet*'s male heroes weren't bad in the beefcake department, the women probably didn't object to them either.

So *Planet Comics* was neither *Weird Science* nor *Strange Adventures*. But if you were a kid looking for some rip-roaring interstellar adventure, *Planet* was a good place to land. For a while, it featured straight science-fiction scenarios on its covers. Then, with issue #13, the Powers That Be threw up their hands and required that every cover from then on had to have a beautiful woman in an action scene ... and every one of them did!

The cover of *Planet Comics* #1 (January 1940) was drawn by Will Eisner and Lou Fine. Eisner didn't appear to be at home doing SF art, and it showed. But he gave it a darn good try. The logo "PLANET COMICS" arose against a black background, with the arcing "PLANET" riddled with metal rivets, possibly to suggest the metal plating of a spaceship. A shoutline above the logo promised *"Weird adventures on other worlds—the universe of the future."*

In the cover scene, a steely-jawed space hero knelt on the wing of his red metal spacecraft and dealt out deadly ray-gun blasts to an army of one-eyed, fanged, clawed, green monstrosities who were streaming in a conga line from an alien city below the logo. A girl in space helmet and boots was almost inside the ship, but her arm was grabbed tightly by one of the green ghoulies, and the three fangs in his mouth (two on top, one on the bottom) suggested that he wanted her as an hors d'oeuvre. A cutline below the spaceship wing identified this as a scene from "Flint Baker and the One-Eyed Monsters of Mars." It wasn't Alex Raymond or Dick Calkins stuff, but publisher Thurman Scott, editor Malcolm Reiss, and feature editor S. M. Iger did the best with what they had. And for 1940, it wasn't too bad.

"The Planetary Adventures of Flint Baker and the One-Eyed Monster Men of Mars" commenced on page one, written and drawn by Dick Briefer of *Frankenstein* fame. No human being was on the splash page, just a big cannon, the huge, gear-driven mechanism around it, and, apparently, an unseen spaceship to be shot from its mouth. A caption read, "When Fletcher Baker's scientist father died, Fletcher was left with the task of completing his rocket ship, to be sent to Mars. Now it is finished, and is ready for its magic flight!"

The story commenced with a shot of a red-and-yellow roadster as long as a stretch limo, pulling up to "the grim gray walls of a state prison." Our hero, Flint Baker, a black-haired guy in an overcoat and muffler, consulted with the prison warden and was given three death-sentenced guys pardoned by the governor. They were released in his care to work as his rocket crew. "I'm not offering you too much freedom. Perhaps you will soon long for a comfortable prison!"

Perhaps they would. Later, Baker explained to his men, Grant, Godwin, and Parks: "Your lives aren't worth much more now, for I don't believe you'll ever see this Earth again. Nobody will sign up as my crew on a trip to Mars, so I chose you three ex-mechanics for my crew." A caption admitted the men were skeptical at first, but after two weeks, they were "raring to go." Cut to a big shot of a huge red-and-yellow rocket ship (maybe they were Baker's school colors) heading into space. When Mars came in sight, they broke for lunch.

Once in the provision room, they found a girl, sitting on a table and smiling. "Hello boys! Mind if I have a little sandwich? I'm Mimi Wilson, of the N.Y. *Globe*, here to write up this flight!"

Baker, not pleased at all, snapped, "You little fool! You'll never get back to Earth! I ought to turn around and dump you out." At that, the ship swerved to avoid a meteorite, and Mimi fell into Flint's arms. "Well ... er ... ah.... I guess you can stay—heh heh!" It was a good thing Tom Godwin's story "The Cold Equations" wouldn't be written for 14 years yet. Given that her weight would throw off the trajectory of the rocket, Mimi's stowing away should have been disastrous. Under those circumstances, she probably *would* have been thrown out.

"After weeks of monotonous traveling, they reach Mars!" another caption told us. (Given that there was a crew of four men and one girl, perhaps it wasn't *too* monotonous.) The big old red-and-yellow spacecraft touched down, and Flint and Mimi emerged in space suits and clear space helmets. Just after Flint remarked that they were the "first Earth people to land on Mars!" Mimi pointed out the ruins of a rocket ship nearby. That had to have been a bummer.

Inside the ship, they found the remains of a space traveler with a metal canister on his chest. The canister held a letter which noted that he wrote it on August 21, 1933, a month after his own Mars landing, and warned any future readers to "*KEEP AWAY FROM THE* DARK SIDE *OF MARS!*"

Mars rotates.

"Looks like we'd have some fun on the dark side!" remarked one of the men.

Anyway, Flint and his crew wheeled out a "motor car" from the ship, which was orange, not red-and-yellow, and headed out on one of the great highways spanning Mars, which were mistaken from Earth for canals. After being bypassed by several vehicles, they ended up at a great city, and were greeted by a half-lizard watchdog creature on a chain and its mistress, a black-haired beauty in a red dress and helmet. She was Princess Viga, she knew both Martian and English, and she brought them all to see her dad, the ruler of the city of Ru.

The mayor of Ru revealed that Mars was at peace until July 1933, when a group of evil Earthmen landed. "Cruel and scheming, they were banished by us from the light side."

(Mars rotates.)

"They set up a dictatorship on the dark side of Mars, using the monsters there to war upon us...."

"You may enlist us in your army to rid Mars of these fiends!" ventured Flint, and Parks chimed in with, "Hot-dog!"

Cut to a shot of Sarko, the imposing, uniformed, evil-eyed "last of the wicked Earthmen," and another of a one-eyed monster in his thrall. The monster, unlike those on the cover, consisted of a one-eyed head stuck between two legs, with a tail protruding from the back of the head. Presumably, these things were pretty nasty biters and kickers. Sarko "plans to rule over the warm, light side of Mars!"

(Mars *rotates*.)

Sarko bellowed, "ATTACK!" and we got down to the action. A whole big flotilla of flying ships departed from the dark side (Mars ROTATES!) to the light side, and Flint and Mimi, finding they could breathe Martian air, took off their space suits and witnessed the city of Ru being covered by a clear protective dome. The dome withstood the enemy attack, and the attacking ships went home.

This, of course, led to Plan B. Sarko waited till the dome was lowered, then sent his monsters to leap over the walls of Ru, grab Mimi and Viga with their tails (despite Flint busting them in the chops, which in this case were between their thighs), and bound off. Flint and his boys loaded up with Martian ray guns, went back to their ship, and blasted off for Sarko's fortress, "into the darkness of the other side of Mars."

(MARS ROTATES!!)

Once there, Flint directed his crew to "[p]ut on these black robes, we'll be invisible here on the dark side!"

(*MARS ROTATES!!*)

Our band of brothers scaled a wall, peeked inside a window, and saw a scene that gave Grant, especially, pause: Sarko had Mimi and Viga hooked up to a machine which, he said, would take the life from Viga and give it to Mimi, giving her "immortality, to be with me forever!"

Grant crashed through the skylight, grabbed Sarko, and said, "Back on Earth you were called 'Sappo' before you broke jail to come here on that rocket! And you're the guy who hypnotized me into committing murder and left me to take the rap!" Vengeance should've been his. But Sarko drew a ray gun and blasted Grant in the chest, killing him. Flint Baker dived down upon the fiend, but Sarko got the upper hand and was about to make him eat a ray blast. In timely fashion, Parks shot Sarko in the back. "You can keep your ol' ray guns! I'll put my opponents out of commission with my .38!"

Flint, Mimi, Viga, Parks, and Godwin clambered aboard their rocket and took off. A passing flying saucer let them know that the last of the one-eyed monsters had been conquered. "What a story that would make in our newspapers!" said Mimi. "Perhaps I can show you some more material for 'good stories,'" replied Viga, and the story ended.

No, it wasn't Asimov or Heinlein. It wasn't even very good E. E. "Doc" Smith. But it was a beginning, and Flint Baker and *Planet Comics* were on their way!

Bob Powell may have been the artist on the next Flint Baker story, credited to "Starr Gayza." Flint and company wanted to return to Earth, but Princess Viga begged them to stay and defeat the "dreaded monster" who menaced them. Flint said, heroically, "The trip to our Earth will be postponed—I will stay and fight this thing!" Said thing looked like a King Kong-sized, four-armed ape. Our heroes got into their rocket, flew it into the creature's open mouth, and smashed out the back of its head. Then they jumped up a mountain on super–pogo sticks, met with a mad, megacephalic, green-skinned Martian mad scientist, and blew the bad guy up with one of his own machines. Flint then freed hundreds of Martian slaves, got their thanks, packed up Mimi, and headed back for home. Parks and Godwin must have stayed on Mars. They were never heard from again.

Dick Briefer was back with the next issue. It turned out Mimi liked adventuring too much to return to Earth and newspaper assignments. She changed the course of Flint's rocket and they headed for Pluto. After a battle against evil Plutonians (were there any other kind?) and replenishment of their fuel tanks, the two of them headed back for Earth. This time, Flint didn't let her set the course.

Art Peddy did the art chores for the next issue, which saw Flint and Mimi's trip interrupted by space octopi and the usual evil ruler of another planet. It was an improvement, visually, over the last three issues. After a between-issues stop on Earth, Flint and Mimi rocketed beyond the solar system in *Planet* #5 (May 1940) on a mission of interstellar exploration. Adventures continued in this fashion for a couple of dozen issues. In one story, Mimi's editor became skeptical of all the crazy Buck Rogers stuff she was reporting and fired her. But when a cadre of aliens invaded Earth and Flint and Mimi helped defeat them, he rehired her and gave her a raise.

By issue #9 (November 1940), Flint and Mimi had decided, like John Carter before them, to stay on Mars, which gave them a more interesting base for action. Peddy continued as artist till issue #11 (March 1941), giving way to Nick Cardy, Leo Morey, Frank Schwarz, Art Saaf, and others. Both Flint and Mimi often made it onto the covers, facing monsters and machines galore. The storyline, originally set in the present, shifted to an undefined future. Nobody seemed to object. Flint, Mimi, and their ship, the *Rogue Star*, continued adventuring through issue #25 (July 1943). Then there was a change. Describing it will mean dropping back to cover another *Planet* feature, so here we go.

Flint Baker zaps the Brute of Mars. Probably will take more than one zap. © 1941 Love Romances Publishing Corp.

Reef Ryan made a landing in *Planet Comics* #13 (July 1941). He was another generic space explorer and his initial six-page story may have been drawn by Al Gabriele. In his first story, he went far below the surface of Neptune, learned it was inhabited by long-lost Earth people, and saved a girl named Vara from an evil tyrant, all while wearing a yellow shirt and jodhpurs. Reef hung around sub-Neptune for several issues, fighting the same tyrant and saving the same girl, usually from underwater perils. The art improved in issue #16 with swashbuckling action and a full-page panel. Reef and Vara shared a few covers as well, before getting down to waterlogged action in their own strip.

Finally, at the end of his story in issue #25 (July 1943), Reef explained to his girl: "Have you heard the news, Vara? We're leaving Xalan!"

"But why ... when ... where are we going, Reef?"

"Search me! All I know is that a gent named Baker.... Flint Baker ... is picking us up by order of the interplanetary council!"

"Flint Baker? Oh, Reef, I'm dying to meet him!"

At the end of Flint's story that issue, when Mimi was faced with yet another potential rival for her lover's hand, a closing caption advised, "Psst! Hey, Mimi! Relax! Maybe Flint'll have the worry next time ... for you're going to meet Reef Ryan!" Thus, it began.

The change was probably necessitated by *Planet* dropping from 68 to 60 pages with that issue. And Mimi should have been worried, because with issue #26, she was dropped.

At any rate, Reef Ryan met with Flint ... actually, it was a mightily smitten Vara who met with Flint, with Reef around for window dressing, which didn't please him too much—and a rivalry developed, but both of them united to battle a space pirate called Braxo. After the villain was defeated, Vara and Reef were back in love, and the two men were partners. *The Space Rangers* made it through almost every issue of *Planet* up through #64 (Spring 1950). They endured a couple of reprints in issues #68 and 70, had a new four-page adventure in #71 (Summer 1953), and that was it.

Fiction House's main gimmick in its early titles was to see how many different riffs they could play on a given genre. *Auro, Lord of Jupiter* was such a riff: Tarzan of the Planets.

Appropriately, Auro was shown in red trunks and boots, displaying Weissmuller-ish muscles as he hefted two alien, claw-fingered bad guys overhead, one in each hand. Then we dropped back for an origin story. "Early in the twenty-first century, a cruise ship streaked through the heavens, somewhere between Uranus and Jupiter!" The spaceship looked as much like a pickup truck as a spacecraft can look. Aboard it was a family: Prof. John Hardwich and his wife and child. They were headed back to Earth from a pleasure cruise but—surprise!—a meteoroid hit their ship and forced them down on Jupiter. Both adults died on impact, but the boy, Auro, was thrown to safety. Well, about as safe as you could get on a jungle in Jupiter.

This version of Jupiter didn't have the gravity that would turn the boy into currant jelly, or the noxious atmosphere that would have poisoned him like cyanide. On the other hand, this was 1940. About all we knew about Jupiter then was that it was out there, it was big, and we'd given it a name. This Jupiter was like a jungle veldt, and the boy was found by a Jovian saber-toothed tiger and brought up like Mowgli or Tarzan. Jupiter's great gravity in turn gave him great strength. In the first story, he helped a girl liberate her friends who had been taken slaves by the king of Neptune. *Auro* eventually developed into a pretty decent strip, and its first run ended with issue #29 (March 1944). It came back in issue #41 (March 1946) and stayed through issue #61 (July 1949).

Planet Comics #1 continued with another riff: a superhero in space. *The Red Comet.*

The truncated splash panel showed us a red, comet-like spaceship, "[h]urtling

The origin of Auro—and what an intro! © 1940 Love Romances Publishing Corp.

through space with the speed of light (186,000 miles a second)" and assured us that "[t]he Red Comet, mystery man of the universe, is out scouting for some new adventure...." A rocket full of Earthmen had landed on a "strange planet" in the "Valley of the Spiderpeople" and got caught in a steel web. The spiderpeople, who had two human limbs and six spidery ones, looked like the eight-limbed Peter Parker from

The Amazing Spider-Man #100–102 (September–November 1971). They clambered out of their caves and abducted the Earthlings.

"Meanwhile, having traveled over 22,000,000 miles in two minutes [the writer seemed to have a thing about light speed, but unless he traveled faster than that, the Red Comet would be at a virtual standstill in deep space], the Comet arrives on the scene!" The hero, clad in a sort of blue athletic suit and hood with a red cape, used his Intra-Atomic Space Adjuster to turn himself into a giant. Then he ripped up the spider-people's steel nets and grabbed up his own rocket and the explorers' craft. Finally, he returned to normal size, had a fight with a spider-sentry at the cave's entrance, and tied all the guy's limbs up.

The Red Comet, battling astral evil in his BVDs. © 1940 Love Romances Publishing Corp.

The Red Comet turned himself tiny, found out where the spider clan held three humans caged for sacrifice, became a giant again, and crushed hundreds of spider-men and spider-women to grease spots under his feet. He managed to lead the explorers to safety. When they asked his name, he replied, "I am the Red Comet, Robin Hood of the universe. As to where I come from—that is my secret—" And so it stayed, as he bid them farewell, got back in his spaceship, and blasted off.

We didn't learn a lot about the mystery man of space in early issues, but maybe that just made him more mysterious. In one story, he met a giant from Jupiter who was stomping on and scooping up people, so he turned to giant-size himself, took on the big baddie in a tremendous battle, chased him off the Earth and into space, and kayoed him with a titanic haymaker. The space forces of Earth towed the giant back to Jupiter, gratefully.

Finally, in *Planet* #9 (November 1940), the Red Comet got down to the details of his origin story. "Years ago I shot out into outer space; something went wrong with my ship. As I climbed out to investigate, a jolting shock, some outer space force, passed through my body, and I found I had suddenly outgrown my ship...." The spacefarer learned he could alter his height to giant-size and tiny-size at will, and opted to become a superhero of the spaceways. It was about as good as 50 percent of the other character origins of the Golden Age.

The Red Comet's costume varied, but mostly he settled for a red hood, cape, tunic, trunks, and boots. In issue #17 he picked up a girlfriend called Dolores Taylor and a sidekick named Rusty, but it was pretty late in the run. He missed issue #2, came back in #3 (March 1940), and held on till #20 (September 1942). In that issue he lost his hood and his powers, got a new artist, and was retooled more as a space hero than a superhero. (Dolores and Rusty called him "Red" a lot.) That was his last story. The Comet got reprint appearances in issues #37 and 69 (July 1945, Winter 1953), and that was it.

Next up was *Captain Nelson Cole of the Solar Force*, by Alex Blum (billed as "Alex Boon"). Blum, a classically inclined illustrator and mainstay of the Eisner shop, had a way to go in his comics development at the time he turned out this one, but it was okay. In the story, Captain Cole, a "young and fearless officer of the Solar Force," was summoned to command an armada of ships against an unknown enemy who was stealing starcraft. They met with dictator Zan and his "army of living dead" on the volcanic planet Volcus, freed the slaves, blew up a giant magnetic device, and saved the day. Cole did much the same thing in each issue up through #14 (September 1941).

After that came a quite decently drawn strip, by Henry Kiefer: *Spurt Hammond, Planet Flyer*. There are only so many decent variations on the name "Flash Gordon." This was not one of them. We can only hope he didn't get his nickname from his girlfriend.

Spurt Hammond looked like a forerunner of the *Planet Comics* to be. It had bitchy villainesses, Amazon armies, enslaved males, and green demonic monsters called "mooniacs." The opening caption told us, "There is a war on the Moon, which is overrun by war lords, much the same as in present day China. The polar region of the Moon is inhabited by Lunerzons, fierce women warriors, who want to rule it.... The Lunerzons plan to rob the planetary transports...."

We got a shot of two Lunerzons, dressed like Asian temple dancers, plotting to bring down Spurt's ship, which they did. He was captured when he trailed them to the Moon, but blew up their munitions plant, forced his way to their radio room, and called Earth to negotiate a peace treaty. Seeing how brave he was, both head Lunerzons decided they'd marry him, and promptly got into a catfight. Spurt said, "Now, girls, don't fight over me!" gallantly before escaping to Earth in his ship. Spurt made his presence known for the first 12 issues of *Planet*.

Buzz Crandall of the Space Patrol was another inductee in *Planet* #1, but was only allotted four pages. Buzz was a troubleshooting Earthman wearing a space helmet and swimming trunks. He ran for an incredible 14 issues. His page count increased to nine at one point, and he was drawn by the likes of Gene Fawcette, Charlie Sultan, and Henry Fletcher. In his first story, Buzz fought a horde of "shark-men" who looked like big, upright grasshoppers.

Following Buzz Crandall came a strip about a villain: *Quorak, Space-Pirate*.

This one ran for 12 pages in its one and only installment. Quorak was a bald mad scientist on the planetoid Spectremus who was out to conquer Pluto, "greatest of known planets." A hero named Lt. Blake and a heroine named Miss Perry, both of Earth, saved the Plutonians from freezing to death. (If Quorak could freeze Plutonians to death, he had to be *some* kind of scientist!) In the end, Spectremus and, presumably, Quorak were blown to bits and Pluto returned to its normal orbit.

So went *Planet Comics* #1's lineup.

It's easy to fault Golden Age comics in the light of later developments. But, really, that's like criticizing the Stanley Steamer for not being a Maserati. *Planet Comics* was the first original science fiction anthology comic in America. It was a shop product, done by writers and artists who, in 1939, were still trying to discover what made an adventure comic really work. It was primitive. But without the cave paintings of Torremolinos, we couldn't have progressed to the masterpieces in the Louvre.

Even though *Planet Comics* never progressed to the level of *Weird Science* or *Strange Adventures*, it did get better. And, when many rival SF comics of the Forties might get canceled within a year or so, *Planet* hung on for an amazing 13 years.

A guy named Planet Payson turned up in the lead spot in *Planet* #2 (February 1940) with good art by George Tuska. He reappeared in issues #6–8 (June–September 1940) and was gone. There were several one-shot strips in the early issues: *Amazona, Mighty Woman; Tiger Hart; Kenny Carr; Jim Giant; Space Admiral Curry.* Mostly, what they signified was that *Planet Comics* was still in search of a working lineup.

Then came *Gale Allen of the Women's Space Battalion* in issue #4 (April 1940). She was more in line with what *Planet* would come to stand for: great-looking women in space.

For her earliest adventure, Gale was clad modestly in a red jacket, red flight helmet, and yellow jodhpurs. On the splash panel, she was piloting a twin-prop airplane. In fact, throughout the story, the entire Space Battalion was piloting such planes, making one think the story could have wandered in from *Wings Comics*. But it was in *Planet*, and that made it science fiction.

The story opened with Captain Jack North of the Universal Space Patrol picking up an SOS from a scouting party on a satellite of Saturn. They were being captured by the pirates of Pluto. Captain Jack radioed for a battalion to back up his brigade. The next caption read, "When they arrive, he is shocked to find the ships unloading nothing but *women!*" Gale, a pretty brunette in this story, handed him an order from the commandant. "I asked for men to help fight pirates!" groused North. "I didn't send out bids to a knitting circle!"

But Gale and company piloted their prop-planes to Pluto (a trick not even Blackhawk could have matched), on which Jack North's plane cracked up, leaving him to be led away by Plutonian giants. "Letting them take him without even putting up a fight! That's real he-man stuff, eh?" remarked Gale.

Within two more pages, the Women's Space Battalion had bombed the pirates' city, freed the men, and won high praise. Gale herself broke off to ray down North's captors personally and rescue him. When the two soared back over the pirate city, they found it deserted and destroyed. "Guess your girl friends have been defeated!" said Jack, misinterpreting the situation.

"Defeated!" snapped Gale. "You'll find your fine, male squad safe, on Saturn—*now*, who's a sissy?"

The art and scripting improved by the second story, set in the far-flung future of 1990 AD. The strip was now titled *Gale Allen of the Girls' Patrol*, which made her sound like a crossing guard. On page 1, we were introduced to a recurring villain: Prince Blaga Daru, "notorious interplanetary buccaneer" and aspiring conqueror of Earth. He sent his warships toward Earth, interrupting a date Gale and Jack North had at a soda fountain. This time Gale got captured, and Jack had to rescue her. In the interim, Blaga tried to get better acquainted with Ms. Allen.

Gale: "Still the same old Blaga—Oh-h, keep away from me!"

Blaga: "You know how I feel about you since we met. Marry me, Gale, and I'll make you the wealthiest girl in the universe!"

But Gale wasn't that kind of girl. Jack burst into Blaga's apartment and walloped him. Gale grabbed the baddie's gun arm when he went for his blaster. In the last panel, after Gale expressed her gratitude, Jack snarled, "Your entire squadron is captured! Bah! Women should stay at home where they belong!"

Gale apparently didn't forget that remark. After issue #19, Captain Jack North was not heard from again. Blaga Daru appeared three more times and then bit the dust in issue #11 (March 1941). Bob Powell drew the first ten stories. He was succeeded by Al Bryant, Art Saaf, Lee Elias, and others. Gale got prettier post–Powell and the romance between her and North actually deepened until he fell out of sight.

Her costumes got sexier.

By issue #12 (May 1941) she had traded her jodhpurs for an open wrap-around

Gale Allen saves a green woman from a dinosaur. (And no, we don't think that's the Yvonne Craig dancer from *Star Trek*.) © 1943 Love Romances Publishing Corp.

skirt, underneath which she wore tights. (This story also contained one of the more memorable lines from her series. When observing a toad-man held captive by amphibians, Gale commented, "Looks like these fish people have grafted gills on the horny guys!") By the next issue she was wearing shorts, a blouse, boots, and a blaster. In the next, she wore a modified red bathing suit with a neckline cut down to her belt. Her artists changed a lot before issue #28, and each gave her a different outfit. Sometimes she wore a more conservative midi, other times a short Supergirl-like outfit with a cape. Finally, in issue #18 (May 1942), Gale and her Girl Squadron got their standard uniform: a bikini, boots, and a ray gun.

Apparently, fighting off menaces in outer space was hot work.

By 1942, Gale was a gutsy, pulchritudinous battler, leading her crew of curvy combatants through alien adventures galore. Jack North was forgotten. But by issue #23 (March 1943), she met a handsome space pirate named Captain Saracen, who bore more than a casual resemblance to Clark Gable. She captured him, he broke free, and she and her girls were taken prisoner. Finally, Gale challenged Saracen to a sword duel for their freedom. In a steel-clasher straight out of *Captain Blood*, Gale faced her foe, but was "no match for the super-skill of Saracen! …But wait! Did his foot slip on the stair? Suddenly he is staggering back, and Gale's red thrust bites into him!" The smiling Captain Saracen admitted defeat, and let Gale and her charges go free. Luckily enough, that wasn't his last appearance. He came back as a roguish ally to Ms. Allen in issues #24 and 26 (May and September 1943) and then, sadly, was never seen again.

Gale carried on through *Planet* #42 (May 1946). By that time she had lost the Girl Squadron and had become a space pilot and female troubleshooter. She was dumped after that in favor of the *Futura* strip, but she still had a legion of supporters who wrote in to the "Viziograph" (*Planet*'s letters column) and asked where she had gone. The editors replied that she was on a seven-year space voyage. Gale reappeared in reprints in *Planet* #65–70 (1951–53), but not in an original story.

Ages later, in 1982, AC Comics revived her as part of a spacefaring ensemble in *Star Fems* #2, and reprinted some of her earlier stories in later comics. Maybe someday, we'll find out what happened on the seven-year journey.

Several other short-lived strips popped up in *Planet*'s early issues. Briefly noted: *Fero, Interplanetary Detective* (#5–8, May–September 1940) was a "ghost detective" strip which, with a little finagling, was converted into an SF offering. The finagling, in issue #5, amounted to saying the vampires and werewolves in the story came from Pluto.

Crash Parker and his Zoom Sled (#6–16, June 1940–January 1942) was begun by Charles M. Quinlan of *Cat-Man* fame. It was about a rocket inventor, his pal "Wheel" Barrow, and their adventures in space with the Zoom Sled, kind of a rocket on runners.

Don Granval (#6–11, June 1940–March 1941) featured a young, mustached scientist who had adventures in a sub-atomic world with his girlfriend, Claire.

Cosmo Corrigan, aka *Cosmic Corrigan* (#9–11, November 1940–March 1941) was a nicely written and drawn (by George Tuska) strip about a hell-raising, clueless pilot who got stationed on Pluto for pulling one stunt too many, and had fairly funny adventures.

Through all of this, *Planet* was improving. Its bad artists were gradually supplanted by decent ones and, by the mid-war years, *Planet* was a competent-looking book. Pencilers and inkers like George Tuska, Lee Elias, Murphy Anderson, Joe Doolin, Lily Renée, Leonard Starr, and Fran Hopper passed through its pages, with Dan Zolnerowich handling covers from #10 to 25 (January 1941–July 1943) and Joe Doolin doing a masterful job on most from #26 on. Lily Renée spelled him on issues #33, 35, and 39, and #66–73 were by Maurice Whitman. Most of it was Good Girl Art, with pin-up beauties in skimpy suits fighting off various evildoers, but Fiction House made a great job of it.

Finally, by issue #12 (May 1941), *Planet* started assembling the lineup that would carry it up to its last days. The moribund features were out and *The Star Pirate* was in.

Standing tall … the Star Pirate! © 1941 Love Romances Publishing Corp.

Star Pirate was the next character in *Planet*'s winners circle, and he was quite fun. We never learned his real name, but his friends all called him "Star." He roamed the spaceways in search of a little ill-gotten gain, as long as it didn't hurt anybody much (except his competitors). Star had to keep clear of both the law and other outlaws, but managed to do enough unofficial jobs for the Space Patrol that they looked the other way once he wound up a case. Like most good pirates, he knew his way around with a sword, and was usually rescuing or being threatened by a beautiful girl in each story. Sometimes, the heroine and villainess doubled up.

The first story, credited to "Leonardo Vinci," showed a splash of a smiling Star Pirate, dressed in transparent space helmet, red shirt and trunks, diaphanous leggings, and green gloves and buccaneer boots, with a ray gun belted to his waist. He was symbolically towering over a craterous moonscape while spaceships zipped by behind him.

The story commenced a panel later. Star and his partner, Trody, of whom more later, in their hideout somewhere in Saturn's rings, saw a pirate freighter approaching. "The interplanetary smugglers! And in our own back yard!..." noted Star. "Let 'em have it!"

The pirates' ship, the *Revenge*, engaged in battle with the enemy craft and brought it down with a ray blast. They pulled a single, metal-helmeted survivor from the wreckage and found it to be, incredibly enough, a girl. Since Star was really a gallant sort, he took her back to his secret base after blowing up the other ship. He gave her a tour of the hideout, showing her a bunch of spaceships he had captured. "A pirate! Why?" she asked.

"Driven by the ruthless interplanetary smugglers.... I was forced to turn outlaw," said Star, and that was about as much as we learned of his origin. As it happened, the girl was a traitor, hoping to capture Star and Trody for the star-spanning pirates, but she died from a ray burst and our heroes went on to win a brief space battle with the competition. That was it for the first story, all five pages of it.

Usually, Star Pirate worked with a partner, but he traded up once he got tired of them. His first aide-de-camp was Trodelyte, Trody for short, who was the size and shape of a human in his first appearance. Well, except for the fact that he had only one eye, and it was in the center of his forehead. By issue #32 (September 1944), he was hanging out with a Martian named Gura who looked and talked like a Native American. Then, in #36 (May 1945), he encountered a fat, black-bearded, hero-worshipping pirate named Blackbeard, originally in the pay of a rival. When there was a conflict with management, Blackbeard switched sides and became his idol Star's sidekick. He remained that way for the rest of the series.

The first Star Pirate artist was Al Gabriele, then Rey Isip. They were followed by George Appel, who did issues #14–31, being spelled at times by Isip and George Tuska. The next artist was a very young Murphy Anderson.

Murphy, who would make a name for himself at DC doing *Hawkman*, *Strange Adventures*, *The Spectre*, and many others (plus lending excellent inks to Adam Strange, Superman, and other characters), as well as drawing the *Buck Rogers* strip for a number of years, was learning his craft at the time. About the only way one can recognize the work as his on the early *Star Pirate* stories is by the signature.

Nonetheless, it is looser than his later hyper-realistic work, and has a spirit of fun about it. Also, Murph was no slouch at drawing gorgeous women, and that skill served him well at Fiction House. He did almost all the *Star Pirate* stories in *Planet* #33–51 (November 1944–November 1947). After that, John Celardo, Maurice Whitman, Leonard Starr, John Rosenberger, and others kept the Jolly Roger in space-flight through issue #65 (1951).

Anderson's best art jobs came on the two-page features titled *Life on Other Worlds*. These featurettes speculated on what the inhabitants of other planets would look like, and it was a given that every planet and moon of the solar system was inhabited. Murphy did a convincing job on Martians, Saturnians, Jupiterians (they didn't know the term "Jovian" back then, I guess), and all the rest, with decorative borders and delineation that made unreality look believable.

Star Pirate and Blackbeard had a nifty habit of running into half-clad female pirates and getting the best of them. The ladies kept showing up and neither Star nor Blacky complained. It was a relief from having to dodge the Space Patrol, anyhow. The two of them shared their last caper at a Universal Fair in *Planet* #64 (Spring 1950), saving a couple of girl robots from crooks. After that, Star appeared in reprints in issues #65, 67, 68, and 70, in *Jumbo Comics* #165 (December 1952), and in the one-shot *Man O' Mars* comic (1953). He was reprinted at various times by IW-Super and AC Comics, but never made another original story appearance.

But, as good as he was, Star Pirate wasn't headline material, just a good backup strip. *Planet* was in need of a good lead feature, and Fiction House knew it. So the experimentation went on.

One of those experiments was humorous. *Norge Benson* snuck in during issue #12. In his splash panel, he and his pet bear, Frosting, were revealed to us, thawing out of ice bubbles in a polar-like region complete with penguins. Norge was a brown-haired youth in a red parka. Frosting was a white polar bear. The caption told it like this: "Norge Benson, a 'Wrong-Way Corrigan' of the space-ways, finds himself on Pluto. His new home is a fantasy of ice and snow, with icicles and ice cubes in profusion.... The hauty penguine [sic] population, arrayed in formal attire, waddle their way through our adventures with Norgie and Frosting, his pet polar bear, in 'Snowland.'..."

The first story commenced with Norge in his spaceship, buzzing the Plutonian mountains and neglecting his piloting to play with Frosting. Abruptly, his craft ran into a peak, touched off a dry-ice volcano, froze their rocket, and sent them into a crash in an arctic sea. The Plutonian penguins, capable of thought and speech, right out of a Disney cartoon, thawed out Norge's rocket and gave him a vial of something to drink. The drink made him, and anyone who tasted it, fly through the air in great somersaults. This led him and his bear to a confrontation of sorts with the predatory, walrus-like Sebars. In the end, he poured some of the stuff on his rocket, and he and Frosting took off. The series continued in much the same way through the final story, in #32 (September 1944). Along the way he picked up a bikini-clad, frost-resistant girlfriend named Jolie and met characters like Mr. and Mrs. Weatherman and the Snomads.

Al Walker did the art through issue #22 (January 1943), doing a job similar to what he was doing for Greasemonkey Griffin in *Wings Comics*. The remainder were done by Fran Hopper, Jim Mooney, and Lily Renée. Norge was fun, but he wasn't going to drag many readers to the book by himself.

By issue #15 (November 1941), *Planet* had its first great strip. With excellent art, a good concept, and passable writing, *Mars, God of War* debuted, and held on till issue #35 (March 1945). Joe Doolin did all the art. And, as usual, he did it well.

Mars, god of war, the Darkseid of *Planet Comics*. © 1941 Love Romances Publishing Corp.

The splash of the first story showed Mars, clad in Roman soldier's gear and brandishing a spiked mace, towering over a battlefield on Earth. Planes were strafing combatants, tanks were overturned, and soldiers were getting bayoneted and machine-gunned by other soldiers. On the horizon, a town was in flame. A caption read: "Down through the ages, a foul spirit has infected the universe, a god of hate, creating strife through the injection of his personality into the bodies of the evil, and now, leaving his planet in chaos, this invisible horror invades Earth.... Mars, god of war!"

Actually, he'd been here in spirit for a good long while, certainly since 1939. A similar Mars had been making trouble for Wonder Woman since 1940. But the Mars of the *Planet Comics* universe was a more hands-on kind of guy. His modus operandi was to take over the body of a person who had opened himself to invasion by evildoing, and then raise as much hell as he could get away with. It usually involved warmongering on a planetary scale.

In *Planet* #15, Mars (who was usually rendered in blue tones, like the Shadow when he was invisible) saw a hit-and-run in which a driver killed a little girl without stopping. He took over the scumbag's body. "The flyer convulses violently as Mars's spirit enters his body. Soon he is at the wheel of a great passenger rocket, hurtling through space.... Leaping up, he seizes a wrench and smashes the instrument panel.... The craft plummets down...."

The passengers of the rocket ship are killed in the crash. The only survivors are the two pilots, and the Mars-possessed one tries to kill the other. They fight, and the non-possessed pilot, John Freeman, kayos his former partner. Mars tries to possess John, but the pilot's "strong will" prevents his entrance. John is convinced that some weird power underlies the accident, and takes his de-possessed partner in for a mental exam.

Mars goes shopping for another body, takes one belonging to a stickup artist, has him shoot an ambassador and his wife (apparently for fun ... there isn't much method to Mars's madness in this story), and sees his host body arrested, tried, and sentenced to death. In the prison, Mars goes lurking again, sees a guard beating a prisoner, enters his form, and has the guard shoot the convict down in cold blood. Mars then takes it on the lam, muttering, "I'll teach those fools to respect the war god!"

John Freeman, in the meantime, confers with law officers, who are already convinced "something supernatural" is going on. For his part, John opines that they're in for "a reign of terror ... the like of which America has never known!"

The next caption confirms: "Freeman's prediction proves true...." Mars jumps into the body of a corrupt skyport official and blows up a rocket coming in from another nation. Said nation is called Axia, and as you might expect, the Axians speak with a German accent and call their leader "der Fuehrer." Actually, "der Fuehrer" looks more like Stalin than Hitler. Even more surprisingly, the Axians aren't portrayed as the monsters and dummkopfs that passed for Germans in most comics of the time. But, just to keep the ball rolling, Mars leaps into the Axian Fuehrer's body and declares war on America.

"The fiery-eyed dictator addresses his people, filling them with hate and lust for blood...." Luckily, John Freeman joins the American espionage service, is sent to Axia, and guesses the truth when he hears of the Fuehrer's "fiery eyes"—a sign of Mars-possession. He sneaks into the dictator's palace, is confronted by the big cheese himself, and knocks him out with a solid right cross. Mars abandons the Fuehrer's body, assumes solid form, picks up a sword, and prepares for battle. Freeman belts him again, saying, "So you're the cause of the world's troubles! Take this! This too!" Knocked off his pins, Mars goes ghostly again and retreats.

The Fuehrer wakes with a "Vere am I?" Shortly afterward, he signs an armistice, saying, "America iss our best friend!" To top that off, the last panel proclaimed, "Once more the rising sun finds a planet at peace..." and the rays of the sun, though colored yellow, look suspiciously like those of the Japanese flag.

To be this "reasonable" about the Axis powers, only a few months before we entered World War II, makes one consider just what was going through the writer's mind back then. But that was in another comic, and besides, the book is dead. The last caption promised, "Mars, god of War, returns to sate his blood-lust in the next *Planet Comics!*"

Mars was even more impressive in the next issue, tearing apart a spaceship with his bare hands on the splash and standing side-by-side with Death himself. Meanwhile, rocket ships hurtled down toward an Earth that was already aflame with war. This time, Mars managed to foment war between Earth and Jupiter, taking solid form to kill the maker of an anti-war device in order to make things work more smoothly, or maybe because he just had a jones for it. Jupiter invaded big-time, devastating America's factories, its navy, and its cities, led invisibly by the war god himself.

All was terrible, but Bill Dixon, the son of the murdered scientist, teamed with Mary Dale, daughter of another scientist who had invented a paralyzing ray. While they were heading toward Professor Dale's laboratory, Mars got there first, assumed material form, bellowed "Nothing must stop WAR!," and smashed the scientist's lab. Mary and Bill entered, and Bill, recognizing Mars as his dad's murderer, punched him in the stomach. "I will avenge this insult on the entire Earth!" hollered Mars, tying Bill up and kidnapping Mary.

Earth got conquered, but Mary, thinking quickly, challenged Mars to fight Bill in a duel. Mars agreed, flooring Bill with an iron-fisted punch. But Bill recovered, smashing Mars with a "pile-driver right," and forced the war god to assume spirit form and slink away. Mary fell into Bill's arms. Probably the invasion was withdrawn, but that was the end of the story, so we didn't find out.

Mars raised hell on Earth and other worlds for his 21-issue stay, challenging the heroes and heroines of each story to thwart his warlike ways. A woman soldier named Telma, her Amazonian corps, and her boyfriend, Bruce, battled Mars in *Planet* #17–19 (March–July 1942). They gave way to different casts of characters on different worlds. But, always, Mars was seeking the key to plunge the universe into war, and only seemed a step or two away from finding it. Like Jack Kirby's later Darkseid, Mars demonstrated the appeal of a powerful villain.

Unfortunately, *Planet* didn't seem to pick up on it much in its other strips. The nemeses of the other players were usually one-shot nonentities, memorable only if they were lady pirates in bikinis. If Fiction House had put out a one-shot like Lev Gleason Publications' *Daredevil Battles Hitler*, in which all the *Planet* good guys and gals teamed against Mars, it would have been a classic beyond compare. But Charles Biro wasn't writing Fiction House comics.

The editors finally decided there was only so much mileage one could get out of a villain strip. In *Planet Comics* #35 (March 1945), the first page of his story depicted Mars standing behind a confident blonde heroine who was clad only in red halter, shorts, gloves, and sandals. (For *Planet*, she was almost overdressed.) The caption read: "A world went mad at his maniacal whim; a universe of slaves bowed to his evil will—and Mars was master of men! But then a girl defied him. Her name was Mysta—and the moon her home!"

The war god encounters his shapely nemesis: Mysta of the Moon! © 1945 Love Romances Publishing Corp.

In a horrifically prophetic sequence that seemed to foresee the 1960s college riots, we saw a mob of students waving torches, yelling, "Down with the autocratic intellectuals!" They smashed up a university, looting libraries, labs, and the campus chapel. "And books—the printed greatness of mortal men, records of the past and dreams of the future, flame in bonfires to please the wanton mob!" A professor, in mortarboard and gown, held up his hands before the rioters, trying to reason with them. A student pulled out a ray gun, snarled, "Class dismissed, professor—for good!" and murdered him on the spot.

Seconds later, Mars left the body of the killer, noting that this was Earth's last university. "Without knowledge, the fools are no better than pigs! ...But, no—I remember a laboratory on the Moon.... Mars, you grow careless—"

The god of war betook himself to the moon. The author explained: "Long years ago, a scientist foresaw the coming madness ... and so he mysteriously disappeared—The same day, two infants were stolen from their Plexiglas cribs. Exiling himself to the moon, Dr. Kort built a laboratory to house all culture of the decaying universe.... There also, he reared the two children, instilling in their eager minds the knowledge their fathers scorned! And now comes MARS...."

On the Moon's surface, within a domed environment, the bearded Dr. Kort was electronically infusing knowledge into the brains of a young man and woman who reclined on tables. He noted: "They will plant anew the seeds of learning in the universe ... the god of War is licked!"

Invisibly, Mars entered, and thought: "Hmm ... *is* he?"

Dr. Kort revived the girl, Mysta, and her brother, Norg, charging them to fight human warlust. But Mars inhabited the body of a robot Kort had intended to give the pair, and used it to almost kill the threesome. Mysta tripped up the robot and caused it to fall into a disintegration pit. All were relieved, but Norg was a bit put out: "Why did it have to be *my* robot?"

Sensing Norg was the weakest of the three, Mars possessed him. Kort announced that they would soon begin a tour throughout the universe, spreading knowledge like Johnny Appleseed planting tree seeds. But after they boarded Kort's spaceship, Mars used Norg's body to bludgeon the old man to death. Then he laughingly smashed Kort's laboratory to bits and set it afire. He almost bluffed his way past Mysta. But, somehow, the girl managed to see the blue-overlay form of Mars over her brother, and grabbed for Norg's gun. As they struggled for the weapon, Mysta twisted it until the muzzle pointed under Norg's chin and pulled the trigger.

"My almost-brother!" mourned Mysta. "I did not want to kill you, but Mars stole your soul. I will avenge you, Norg—the god of War is my sworn enemy!" Mars ghosted away, thinking, "She is as strong as I—strong with knowledge of culture. But I will not be gone for long! Twenty years, perhaps! And then—the god of War returns!"

In the last panel, Mysta stood defiant before her robot, which towered a good two heads over her. The final caption said, "She, a living temple of Man's essential goodness, is his last hope! Can Mars still win?"

Probably not. Mars made a final cameo in the next issue, beneath the first *Mysta of the Moon* logo. Except for a couple of reprints, he never made it back again.

Meanwhile, Mysta hung out her shingle in that issue (#36, May 1945) and made it all the way to issue #62 (September 1949), clad in her red interplanetary bikini and backed by her mighty robot. Her first mission was to save a space station whose crew had been turned into mesmerized zombies by Superbrain, a big-headed villain with mental powers. His main helper was Bela, a good-looking brunette in a one-piece bathing suit. Her purpose, mostly, was to wrestle with Mysta for a gun, and she lost. The heroine released the crew, who were either bald men in trunks or women in bikinis. Mysta later felled Superbrain with a fungus of his own design and had the crew paint the villain's ship with two coats of fungus. Then they stood back and watched it rot.

The next issue, Mysta battled a mad scientist and his army of plant-men. She watered them until they burst over him and dissolved him with their acid, and that's all that needs to be said about that one.

Mysta soon developed the ability to infuse her spirit into another person's body, like Mars (or Deadman). This and her telepathically controlled robot helped keep the stories interesting. In later issues, she gained a human assistant: Bron, a reformed bad guy. By *Planet* #55 (July 1948), she assumed a secret identity as Ana Thane, Technician 3A, aide to one Dirk Garno, and thus passed her last seven issues.

The art on Mysta was usually quite good, with Fran Hopper's efforts from issues #37 to 49 (July 1945–July 1947) probably the best. Other "Mystafiers" included Joe Doolin, Ruben Moreira, Charles Sultan, Maurice Whitman, Matt Baker, Harry Sahle, and Chuck Winter, her final artist. In *Planet* #62 (September 1949), she helped a race of merman farmers defeat a bad guy named Kark. Mysta made one reprint appearance in issue #68 (1952) and called it quits. AC Comics picked her up for a brief one-shot teaming with Futura and Gale Allen in *Star Fems* #2 (1982) and reprinted a batch of her older stories, but did nothing more with her. Outside of a cameo in a text story by Alan Moore (in a 2003 volume of *The League of Extraordinary Gentlemen*), Mysta has not been seen since.

With all of that as prelude, we come to the most well-known *Planet* strip of all. In issue #21 (November 1942), *Planet* finally found the strong headline strip it had been hunting. Quite appropriately, the hero's name was Hunt Bowman. And the feature was *The Lost World*.

The splash panel of the first *Lost World* story was devoted to a Chinese-style dragon breathing smoke and threatening an unconscious blonde woman and her protector. Said protector, Hunt Bowman, was a guy in a green Robin Hood outfit with a red cape. He already had an arrow nocked to his bow and was ready to let fly. A caption clued us in: "Only one man could win the fight for survival of Earth in the 23rd Century … this superb specimen is Hunt Bowman, a lonely archer knowing nothing of his forebearers' [sic] sciences…. But Hunt's tireless search for a human mate reaches a fantastic climax when a wild voyage through space ends on a world the universe forgot!"

In the ruins of Chicago, Hunt stood, muttering, "Three seasons have passed since my brother died. My search for another human is hopeless." His reverie was interrupted by a spaceship that lands nearby. The occupants emerged and were revealed as sallow-skinned pygmies known as Voltamen, plus one human woman.

Iqor, leader of the Voltas, said that they will capture Hunt and put him on exhibition back in Volta. Well, that after starving him half to death to give the Voltas the impression that humans are an inferior race.

Hunt, rightly thinking the Voltamen are the murderers of his brother, let fly an arrow, but Iqor destroyed it with a disintegrator gun. After a brief fight, the Voltas stunned Hunt with a globe of noxious "comet vapor" and loaded him aboard their ship.

Later, with the vessel already in space, Hunt awakened in the presence of the woman, who asked him his name. "I was called Hunt Bowman by the last on Earth to die! But who—where are you from?"

"I am Lyssa, queen of the Lost World! My people are descendants of early space voyagers from Earth! But these brutes from Volta killed or captured all the women before they caught me. If you can break your bonds, we can escape together!"

Hunt, who had been bound head and foot, made a Steve Reeves effort and broke his bonds one by one. Iqor and his henchmen made an inspection entrance, and the two underling Voltas were killed when Hunt smashed their electro-blasters with his chain. Iqor fled in a space-lifeboat, warning Hunt, "You'll crash the next planet!" "They must be afraid of me to do this," mused Hunt as the Voltan escaped.

Hunt admitted, "I cannot read, and I know nothing about machines." He turned to Lyssa, who had evidently earned her space driver's license. She piloted the Volta ship to a rough but safe landing on her Lost World, which turned out to be populated by cavemen. Hunt was encouraged to see his own kind again, after a fashion. But the Lost World Welcome Wagon decided that Hunt was after Lyssa's throne, and only her appearance a few moments later stopped them from killing him.

One guy, a leopard-suited character named Basil, was still unimpressed and arranged for Hunt and Lyssa to encounter the Spirax, which is the dragon from the first page. Even the Voltas were afraid of the beast, but Hunt was made of the stuff of *Planet Comics* heroes, and destroyed it with an arrow. Afterward, Lyssa offered Hunt the chance to rule the Lost World with her as her king. Basil took it on the lam, and Hunt, remembering a vow he made not to kill humans, let him go.

And that was the first *Lost World* story.

As such, it wasn't too impressive. But the strip was still in its formative stages, and improvements were coming. Plus, the concept of humanity finding its way back from the ruins of war, whether the opponents were Voltans or Nazis, carried a lot of weight in those times. Post-holocaust settings were newer in 1942 than they are now, and soon, *The Lost World* would be a strip to remember. The kids who read it back then certainly did.

Originally, the title *The Lost World* referred to Lyssa's world, and the initial adventures took place there. But by the third story, Hunt and Lyssa were faced by a revolt fomented by Basil. They boarded the captured Volta spaceship, took along a scientist who was one of Lyssa's people, and headed back to Earth. By this time, the Volta-ravaged Terra was indeed a "Lost World," and there was no need to change the title.

The Voltas changed appearances in the early episodes, becoming gray brutes of normal size in #22, then human-looking, pale-skinned beings by #23. But the conquerors of Earth needed a more impressive look than that. So, in a two-page short in issue #25 (July 1943) that was really, believe it or not, a war bond promo, Hunt and Lyssa faced the new model Voltans. These boys sported coal-scuttle helmets that identified them with America's current enemy, the Nazis. They were of normal size, but their skin was grey and wrinkled. (They were probably intended to look like animated corpses.) Often as not, they also had protruding upper and lower fangs.

But the real identifying mark of the Voltans didn't appear for eleven more issues. In *Planet Comics* #36 (May 1945), the Voltamen began to speak in Latin syntax. Like the Blackhawks' accents, it was a brilliant identifying move. At first, the new Voltaspeech was used sparingly, as the writer(s) got used to it: "Drowned are they?" "The Earthling it is!" But before long, phrases like "I plan have for destroying Hunt Bowman!" were gliding off their tongues as if the Voltans were Anglicized Romans. It was such a neat bit that comics historian Dick Lupoff titled his own *Planet Comics* history "Me to Your Leader Take"! It also, in modern times, seemed strangely similar to the patois of Yoda in the *Star Wars* films….

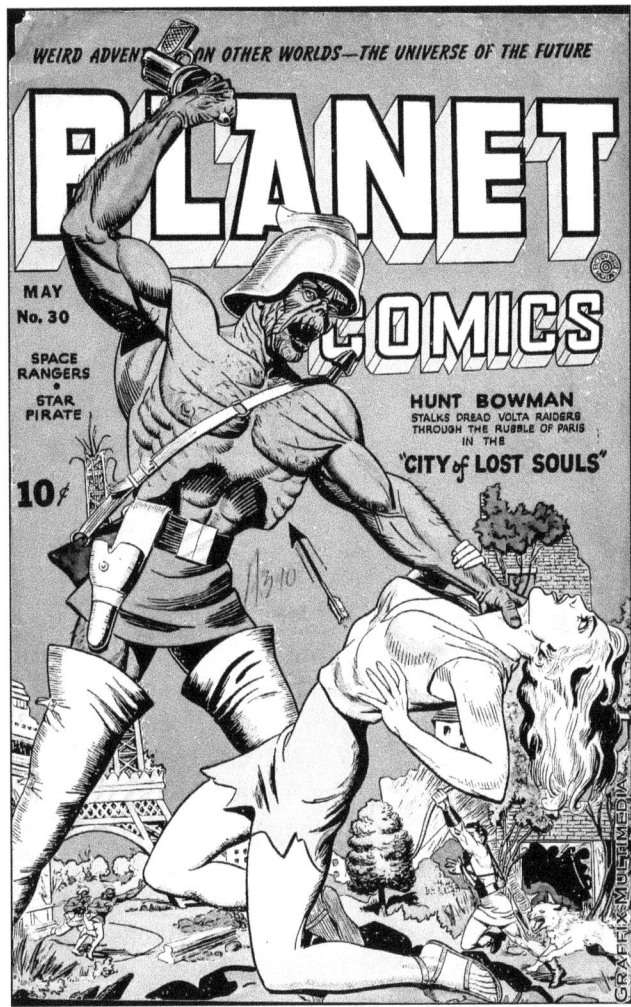

A Voltan threatens to kill Lyssa, but Hunt Bowman's arrow should take him out first. © 1944 Love Romances Publishing Corp.

Hunt and Lyssa's crusades against the Voltamen lent themselves to continued stories. One of the best began in issue #36, when Hunt and Lyssa fled to the Cornell Medical Center in New York City. There they discovered three teenaged humans in suspended animation within glass capsules. A Volta patrolman passed by, idly threw a switch, and restored them all to life. The kids, Bonnie, Bruce, and Robin by name, had a joyous reunion. It was cut short by the Voltamen, and by the sight of their father's skeleton nearby. "Interesting very!" snapped one Voltaman. "You live … you die … you live … now we see if you die again!"

Before the baddies could make a move, Hunt Bowman sent shafts into their vitals and helped the threesome escape. Bonnie explained, "Our father was a great scientist, back in 2110. He made us the subjects of an experiment in suspended animation. I can't imagine why he died without waking us up again!"

Robin, a dark-haired boy, replied, "I guess it was these creatures who interrupted his work, Bonnie! Looks like they interrupted just about everything."

After Lyssa explained about the Voltamen, whom she described as "hard to kill," one Volta left for dead suddenly reared up, leveled his weapon, and blasted Bruce in the back. Hunt killed the enemy on the spot, but Bruce was dying.

At that point, Robin exclaimed, "Wait! What did Dad train me to be a surgeon for?" In a short time, he performed a brain transplant and brought Bruce back to life … in the body of the Voltan soldier! He came back to consciousness just in time to see Hunt, Lyssa, and his two siblings in front of a Voltan firing squad. Bruce, in his new body, bluffed his way into letting him execute them himself. He turned his weapon on the Voltans and mowed them down like ducks in a shooting gallery.

Afterward, Bruce reluctantly turned to Bonnie and said, "Can you … can you stand the sight of me?" She said, "You'll always be brother Bruce to me … and you know it!" The three kids walked away, arms around each other's shoulders. Hunt, looking on, praised the bravery of his newfound friends.

As it was, Bruce hadn't been put into the body of just any old Voltaman. After Hunt and Lyssa stopped the Voltans from destroying the Declaration of Independence in Washington, D.C. (#37, July 1945), the three teenagers joined them in blitzing a Voltan patrol. They commandeered a Voltan ship and took off, only to be halted for inspection by another enemy craft. The human-looking humans hid in lockers. Bruce, in his Voltan body, met with the boarding party. To his dismay, they knelt and salaamed him. "Hail to our lost leader, Prince Guth!" "You must return to Volta! Our father, the king, dies of grief!" Playing along, Bruce brought his ship into line with the others. For the first time, Bowman's band went to the planet of the enemy.

On Volta, Bruce was embraced by his body's father, Klarg, king of Volta. The humans were discovered and captured. "What means this, my son…. Earth creatures on your ship?" asked Klarg. "I did not tell you—they my prisoners are!" improvised Bruce.

"Then they are a gift to me, son? You recalled my experiments on humans!" Wide-eyed, Bruce agreed.

The Earthmen were strapped to tables in an operating room and Klarg made ready to dissect them. Bruce decided it was time to pull a Gary Cooper and shot his semi-father dead. At gunpoint, he forced away the other Voltans and freed his friends. Bruce personally piloted their escape craft back to Earth.

As might be expected, the killing of the king did little to improve Earth-Volta relations.

Bruce and company appeared in a spate of other stories. But by this time, Hunt Bowman's concern had shifted from just destroying the Voltan invaders to uniting the surviving Earthmen and rebuilding their government. Despite the Voltans and their planetary allies (which included the Venusians), despite the dissenters and the traitors who made life interesting for an issue or two, progress was being made.

Earth was fighting back.

The problem was that Hunt Bowman couldn't really defeat the Voltans, unless he wanted to lose his reason for existence. So, no matter how badly they got beaten, the corpse-skinned crudités were still hanging on through *Planet Comics* #64 (Spring 1950), in the last original *Lost World* story. By this time, Hunt had acquired some polish, was the de facto mayor of a city, the leader of a human resistance group, and could probably see the light at the end of the tunnel.

Did he make it? Were the Voltamen finally sent packing from Earth, cursing their foes in Latin syntax all the way across the galaxy?

No one knows. But the real question for comics historians is, "Why did *The Lost World* work better than the rest of the *Planet* offerings?"

Most of it comes down to the concept. In Bowman's world, humans were neither space conquerors nor members of a galactic federation à la *Star Trek*. They were persecuted underdogs, fighting valiantly to survive and to win their homeworld back from their oppressor. Hunt Bowman represented our Last Great Hope, and we cheered him for it.

But there was another factor. The razed cities, the occupying armies, the horrible engines of war, and the underground resistance movement signified one thing: *The Lost World* was a war story. Most *Planet* strips, being set in the future, had few ties to the readers' own era. But a kid reading *The Lost World* could easily compare it to his own time, with Hunt Bowman's Earth a stand-in for wartime Europe. The Voltans looked like corpses, wore coal-scuttle helmets, and were fiendishly brilliant in devising weapons of war. The Nazis were their soul brothers.

Even today, the finely drawn scenes of a bombed-out New York, Washington, or Paris can send a chill up one's spine when beholding them. *The Atomic Knights* covered much the same ground twenty years later in *Strange Adventures*, and it's interesting to note that the Knights' artist, Murphy Anderson, was a *Planet Comics* alumnus.

On top of that, *The Lost World* featured a lot of great action and adventure in an interesting setting. It had good art and better writing than most of *Planet*'s other strips. So it was that Hunt Bowman and *The Lost World* became the most-remembered feature in *Planet Comics* ... deservedly.

Roy Thomas admitted being influenced by Hunt Bowman when he created Killraven, a similar character, for the *War of the Worlds* feature in Marvel's *Amazing Adventures* in the early Seventies. Killraven was an updated Bowman (his first suit even looks like one of Hunt's old outfits), and H. G. Wells's Martians took the place of the Voltamen. But even against Killraven, a well-written-and-drawn strip for a good part of its existence, *The Lost World* looks mighty impressive.

Any feature we can remember over 70 years later has to be.

The writers of *The Lost World* are lost to the ages, but it's a safe bet that Ruth Roche, one of Fiction House's most prolific scripters, contributed to the strip. Jay Bixby, a noted SF writer of the time, may have been another hiding behind the "Thornecliffe Herrick" house name. Rudy Palais drew the first episode. After one-shot offerings by Rey Isip and Nick Cardy, Graham Ingels (some years before his "Ghastly" tenure at EC) was the first regular artist, on *Planet* #24–31 (May 1943–July

1944). Probably the best work was done by Lily Renée, whose stint lasted from issues #32 to 49 (September 1944–July 1947). Then George Evans took over and rode out the strip till issue #64 (Spring 1950). After that, Hunt Bowman appeared in reprints in issues #65–68 and 70 (1951–1953), and then faded away, just three issues from *Planet*'s demise.

They tried to revive him. Blackthorne Publications, in 1988, published a three-issue series of *Planet Comics*. The writer and artist were Bruce Jones and Ken Hooper, respectively. This time, Hunt was an astronaut sent into space in suspended animation, just minutes ahead of an atomic war that ravaged the Earth. He woke up in 3189 AD. There were cavemen, sky-sled-riding Amazons, and even a doppelganger of Hunt, but no Voltans, and nothing much more to recommend the strip. It was an okay strip but not a good enough successor.

Hunt Bowman, Lyssa, and all the rest belong in their time, on their Lost World, and so we leave them. Reluctantly.

The well-drawn adventures of Futura begin. © 1946 Love Romances Publishing Corp.

One last *Planet* strip deserves mention, and it's one of my favorites. When Gale Allen was sent packing, she was replaced in issue #43 (July 1946) by Futura. And even though Futura wasn't a female Hunt Bowman, she managed to get her gutsy, beautiful self into a horde of Flash Gordonish perils. She moxied her way through every one of them. Not a bad showing for a gal who started out, more or less, as a secretary.

The *Futura* strip was rendered in the "illustrated text" style used by *Flash Gordon*, *Tarzan*, and *Prince Valiant*, without word balloons. Any dialogue was set between quotes in a caption. Rafael Astarita was probably the artist for her first five escapades, with John Cavallo taking over for issues #49–64 (July 1947—Spring 1950). Both were capable artists and made Futura a pleasure to look at.

And there was no question that Futura was made to be looked at! The lovely black-haired girl was clad only in a skimpy halter, an abbreviated skirt, and high heels in the first panel of the story. She was trotting down a deserted street in a skyscraper-filled city of the future, motivated by an unnamed fear. Behind her was a white silhouette with pointed ears and long clawed fingers. The caption read: "Terror, blind, reasonless terror. Marcia Reynolds felt it that evening as she came home from work ... one minute she was just an average girl, walking down a familiar street in Titan City ... and then she was swept into a wierd [sic] fantasy of horror...."

Being swept into a *Weird Science* of horror would seem more appropriate, but that title wouldn't be published for a few years yet. Marcia checked into a police department and had the cops scan the streets for pursuers. They found none, and told her to go home. "Imagining things?" thought Marcia. "Maybe he's right ... why should anyone waylay a second-grade technical secretary? No money, no family ... only a norm-plus rating in intelligence quota.... Who'd be after me? Haunts and hobgoblins ... nonsense! This is Titan City, most civilized city of Earth.... This is the 21st Century, not the Dark Ages."

Well, maybe.

Marcia probably underrated her mating potential, but it soon became academic. The white silhouette chose that moment to bust through her window, grab her arms, and be beamed up with her to an orbiting spaceship. Her captor, who looked like a cross between a hobgoblin and a well-veined bodybuilder, chained her to a wall. His master, Mentor, was a huge-headed, shrunken-bodied Martian munchkin who designated her as "Specimen Nine from Terra-Belt Green for Project Survival! ...If you find our methods ruthless, Specimen Nine, it is because our needs are desperate.... The life of our Cymrad race is at stake.... Strong new flesh and blood is needed to feed and house our treasures of the mind...." What it meant was that the Cymradians were looking for suitable bodies into which they would transplant their brains.

With that, the spaceship arrived on Cymradia. A battery of tests were performed on Marcia off-panel. One of the big-heads admitted, "Your Specimen Nine has possibilities!"

"Yes," agreed Mentor. "Give her a base-tab of 113 and mark her lab name as 'Futura.' Take her away, K-4!"

The newly named Futura was endungeoned with a group of humans from various worlds and began plotting escape with them, exactly as Mentor anticipated. "She has leadership potential as well!" Mentor noted. "Why delay her final test?" When she and her fellow prisoners were marched outside to board a transport rocket, she saw her chance, elbowed free, and took over the ship herself. After the ship took off, Mentor chortled, "No Earthling yet has survived this test, but perhaps—hee-hee—she'll surprise me!"

But Mentor got more than he bargained for. Futura soon hooked up with a tribe of cavemen called the Aborotes, fought against them and then alongside them, and flung a challenge back at Mentor by telescreen: "Futura by your naming, Mentor ... and by that name I'll conquer you. Take warning, big-head ... this tower is ours, and not until I lead my Aborotes to Cymradia will I return to Earth as Marcia Reynolds."

Now there was a woman worthy of Magnus, Robot Fighter!

Futura won past the dangers Mentor placed before her, including beating a Cymrad-brained, human-bodied woman specially bred to destroy her. Shortly afterward she allied herself with a race of butterfly people, captured Mentor, forced him to release his human prisoners, gained a magic sword, and engaged in final, terrible battle with the Cymradians. Project Survival was destroyed, but so, alas, were Futura's allies. The latter perished in a geyser of molten lava, thanks to Mentor's machinations.

Mentor finally met his end in the crash of a spaceship (*Planet* #53, March 1948). Futura, bikini-clad and spacebound in an escape capsule, was catapulted into further adventures on other worlds. She was captured by space pirates, smashed a slave market, and ended up as a lady pirate herself by story's end, in issue #64. One of her crewmen was the son of the buccaneer she had deposed, and he plotted revenge. If the previous 22 issues were any indication, he probably failed but catapulted the plucky Earthgirl into another set of adventures.

Too bad we'll never see them.

By this time it was 1950, and the axe was starting to fall. *Planet Comics* had been a monthly only during its first half-year. After that, it went to bimonthly status. With issue #63, it became a quarterly. After #64, it became a reprint comic.

One issue was published with a 1950 date. Another single issue was published in 1951. The next year, 1952, saw three undated issues come out. After #70, in 1953, even the reprints were cut.

Fiction House decided to try a new tack with *Planet*. EC was making a go of it with *Weird Science* and *Weird Fantasy* at the time. DC's *Strange Adventures* and *Mystery in Space* were thriving. All of those were anthology books. Thus, *Planet Comics* was converted into an anthology science-fiction title.

Only one of the old series, *The Space Rangers*, crept in for a last appearance in issue #71 (1953). The rest of the books were made up of unrelated SF stories. The art, by the likes of Bill Benulis and John Belcastro, was quite good. The stories weren't bad, either. But comics were in the midst of the Wertham Era, and sales were dropping across the board.

Fiction House decided to call it a day. *Planet* #73 (1953) wound up a 13-year run with five well-done stories. The last, appropriately enough, was called "Among the Missing."

Planet left behind a legacy as the first successful science fiction–based multi-character comic. It left us with memories of Hunt Bowman, Mars, Futura, Gale Allen, Flint Baker, Star Pirate, and all the rest.

Planet may not have racked up the triple-digit numbers of *Jumbo*, *Jungle*, or *Wings*, but it wound up being one of the most-remembered Fiction House titles of all. And beyond that, of course, learn did we Voltaspeak from it.

But there were other spacefaring heroes in other comics. Many of the anthology books carried at least one science fiction strip to rope in the Flash Gordon / Buck Rogers crowd. Since there were a bunch of them, we'll try to cover some of the more interesting rocket-jockeys.

Centaur Comics carried its share of space heroes, and one of the earliest ones was Dan Hastings. He debuted in *Star Comics* #1 (February 1937) and was restricted, like most of Centaur's features back then, to two pages an issue for the first couple of stories. Then they expanded the stories from four to eight pages an episode, and Dan had space, pun intended, to breathe. Hastings started out as a poor man's Flash Gordon, dressed up in military finery in a future Earth at war. A "loose planet" named Mexady was approaching (just like Mongo) and Dan, aided by the scientist Dr. Carter (standing in for Dr. Zarkov) and his offspring Gloria (a substitute for Dale Arden) and Bob, had to help fight off Mexady's cruel ruler Eutopas (a faux Ming the Merciless).

The penultimate issue of *Planet*. No series, but a great Maurice Whitman cover. © 1953 Love Romances Publishing Corp.

Dauntless Dan's early strips were drawn quite nicely, first by Clem Gretter, then by Fred Guardineer, the latter doing a spectacular job on the feature. The hero appeared in ten of the first eleven issues of *Star*, with a stop-off in the one-shot *Cocomalt Big Book of Comics*. After a couple of appearances in *Amazing Mystery Funnies* (V. 2 #4–5, April–May 1939) and one in *Keen Comics* #1 (May 1939), Dan jumped ship and landed in MLJ Comics' spaceport. This was not an unusual thing in the early days, as many comics were the products of shops and they often took their characters with them when they changed publishers.

At any rate, Dan's crusade against the Mexadians continued in *Blue Ribbon Comics* #1 and 2 (November–December 1939), lay fallow for a couple of years, and returned with a brand new publisher, Harry "A" Chesler, who had supplied the feature to both Centaur and MLJ. Dan held down the space-fort in *Scoop Comics* #1–3 (November 1941–March 1942), sometimes drawn by a young George Tuska. Later, he made his home in *Dynamic Comics*, starting with issue #8 (1944?) and ending with #21 (July 1947). It was as good a run as most early spacemen got, outside of the Fiction House camp.

Amazing Mystery Funnies carried the exploits of *Skyrocket Steele*, an early rocket-ranger strip by Bill Everett. His real name was Steele Dodge, about as heroic a moniker as you could ask for back then. Skyrocket lived in the year X, according to his first strip, and usually was a troubleshooter for one King Kurt on the planet Mannin. Steele appeared first on the cover of *Amazing Mystery Funnies* #1 (August 1938) but had to wait for the next issue before he showed up in a story. He lasted through V. 2 #6 (June 1939).

Everett also tried out another SF hero with *Dirk, the Demon* (*AMF* V. 1 #3 and V. 2 #3, November 1938 and March 1939). The "Demon" was a 24th-century boy who was a baron's son and an archeologist of sorts, getting into trouble with his friends when he stole a hydroplane and broke into a 400-year-old chamber, reviving a 400-year-old hermit. In his second adventure he saved a princess from crooks. Both stories were all of three pages long.

In *AMF* V. 2 #3–9 (March–September 1939), Carl Burgos's *Air-Sub DX* appeared. The titular Air-Sub could function either in the air or underwater, and was the creation of Professor Grey, with heroic duties by his crew, Tim and Rita. The strip was set in an undefined future and the villain had the awe-inspiring name of Curley.

But *Space Patrol*, in issues numbered V. 2 #12, 18, and 21–24 (December 1939–September 1940), outpointed both of them with art and writing by Basil Wolverton. Nobody had drawn like Wolverton before, and nobody would equal his grotesque and baroque imagination or sense of humor in times to come. His elaborate cross-hatching, his sense of lighting, the weight of the objects he drew, the Freudian symbolism of his aliens and rockets, and his offbeat scripting set Wolverton aside as a true original. He couldn't have imitated Raymond or Calkins if he tried.

Space Patrol's first story was all of seven pages long. The first page, lacking a splash panel, was divided into a standard grid of six panels. The second panel showed a cylindrical spacecraft moving past the face of Venus. A caption explained, "Patrol pilot Nick Nelson and his Martian partner, Kodi, receive a call from the Venusian space station." A panel later, we saw both of them at the controls of their ship. Nick was a resolute, humorless black-haired man in a blue-and-orange uniform. Kodi was bald, high-browed, squinty, and had the longest eyebrows this side of the Sub-Mariner.

Both of them got the message to be on the lookout for Owen Kosterman, "notorious space-bandit," who had killed four men in a robbery attempt at a Venusian radium mine. "Train the electroscope on Venus, Kodi!" ordered Nick. "His ship will show up sharp against that white cloud blanket." Sure enough, it did, and the heroes gave chase.

After forcing Kosterman down with a blast of blue flame from their craft's "powerful shock gun," Nick and Kodi followed him down to an impressive landscape below Venus's cloud cover, full of volcanoes and jungles. Even though the enemy ship crashed, Nick doubted their foe was dead. He and Kodi suited up, landed in the jungle, and went on the search for him amid the weirdest-looking flora and fauna presented in comic books.

Kosterman couldn't be obliging enough to die in the crash, and he got the drop on Nick and demanded "the keys to your ship!" (One wonders why he didn't demand the fuzzy dice on its rear-view mirror as well.) "If you want anything from me, you'll have to get it for yourself!" snapped Nick.

At that point, a newcomer crept up behind them: a "spider-man," with four tentacular arms, a speckled, round body, and a human face ... well, more or less human, anyway. The spider-man snuck in behind Kosterman, who couldn't believe Nick's warnings to him weren't a trick. As a result, the villain was grabbed about the neck, and both he and Nick were captured.

Things looked dire, with another spider-man about to bop Nick over the head with a tomahawk and eat him. But Kodi arrived to zap the monster dead with a ray gun, and killed the monster menacing Kosterman. Did the baddie show any gratitude? Hardly. He grabbed for Kodi's weapon, but Nick knocked him off a cliff. And "in the murky waters below, ravenous river denizens swarm upon him...." Said denizens were three in number, looked like refugees from a particularly effective nightmare, and gave us to believe there would be no last-minute escape for the terrified Kosterman.

"Well, Nick, this is one time we didn't get our man!" said Kodi, watching from cliffside.

"Perhaps it's just as well, Kodi," said Nick. "I don't think he would have been very good company on the way back to headquarters!"

The plotting and dialogue may have been cut and dried, but Wolverton's art more than offset that. *Space Patrol* came back three issues later, and then settled in for a four-issue run beginning with *AMF* #21 (June 1940). Nick and Kodi fought off the strange balloon men of Jupiter, a Plutonian gambler, the Sand Rats of Mars, and a great green cannibal monster from a pygmy planet. One could get hooked on *Space Patrol* just to see what alien forms Wolverton came up with next. After issue #24, though, it was over.

Wolverton wasn't. His career in comics was pretty much defined, from then on, by space opera, screwball humor, and horror ... sometimes all three. He had already reached for the stars a second time, and this time a little more successfully. The June 1940 issue of Novelty's *Target Comics* (V. 1 #5) featured the first adventure of his signature character: *Spacehawk*.

The spaceman in question appeared in the last story of the comic. The first panel showed him in a green suit with red gloves and an all-covering head mask. He was carrying a hand-weapon and stood against a Martian landscape. The first caption read: "With the coming of interplanetary travel, the legions of the law find it impossible to cope with the pirates, killers, and other criminals lurking in space.... Then, apparently out of nowhere comes the superhuman enemy of crime, the mysterious SPACEHAWK! Thereafter, bandits of the void begin to disappear, for they soon learn to fear the amazing powers of the Spacehawk, who strikes without warning. For example, here is the case of Gorvak, notorious Martian space pirate who boasts he is too clever to be caught by the Spacehawk...."

Bad guys in comic books usually end up eating words like that. Gorvak and his aide-de-camp, both of whom looked like bug-eyed lizards wearing football helmets, were rocketing to the Grax Mountains of Neptune. Hearing their destination, the underling said, "Then you mean you're going to capture more of the—the Creeping Death? Master Gorvak, we shouldn't go there again! It's unsafe! It's—"

"Silence, you white-livered dolt! I'm paying you well to pilot my ship—not to advise me!"

Gorvak and his crew, in an orange, cylindrical rocket, landed on a moon of Neptune just outside a cave. Upon touching down, the bandits got a trap ready and pulled out the bait—by the hair: a beautiful human brunette in a red mini-dress. They clapped her into a metal tube with an opening for her face, put it in front of the cave opening on a long waldo, and waited for the Creeping Death.

A few minutes later, it crept up: a white, amoebic, amorphous mass which extended several handlike protrusions, all of them probing toward the face of the woman in the metal tube. The white "hands" approached her from all sides of the opening. She waited, silent and wide-eyed. Then...

...a rayblast from above struck the Creeping Death, repulsing it, forcing it back into its cave. Gorvak, looking on, was not amused. He howled, "Open the door! I'm going out and kill whoever fired that bolt of flame!" A couple of steps later, he stopped dead, dropping his ray gun.

"The Spacehawk!" he gasped.

The paladin of the planets stood on the ridge above the parked spaceship, inscrutable in his mask. "All right, Gorvak! Come and get me—if you have the nerve!"

Gorvak knew how to get out while the getting is good. He clambered back into his rocket, cut loose the trap, and blasted off. However, when his first mate commented that they'd never escape the Spacehawk, Gorvak corrected him roughly: "I, Gorvak, never flee from my enemies! I outwit them—and that's what I'm doing now!"

Meanwhile, Spacehawk freed the brunette from the tube, and noted, "If that protoplasmic creature from the cave had reached you, it would have devoured you! This old-fashioned flame gun is the only kind of weapon that monstrosity respects! Now let's get away from here!"

A shot followed of Spacehawk holding the woman in one arm and rising "by the controllable anti-gravity element in his attire," taking her to his windowed spaceship, which appeared to be parked amidst a crop of fire hydrants. "Don't worry about falling captive again to Gorvak! He has captured his last ship!"

"But how can you say that?" asked the girl. "Gorvak is still at large!"

The Spacehawk made no answer. But in short order, we learned that he had mind-reading powers and could "feel" that Gorvak was still on-planet, but not near at hand. He took his spacecraft to the mouth of a tunnel "bored by huge extinct ants," met with a green-faced "bat-man" who was glad the hero had come to deal with Gorvak, who had killed many of his people, and journeyed on. Finally, he found the ship, and the mental impulses of the pirates within clued him in to danger.

Within, Gorvak outlined his plan to his crew: he'd take their supply of liquid Creeping Death, pour it into receptacles that could be opened by remote control, and stash them on spaceships they wanted to burgle. Then, after opening the receptacles, letting the Creeping Death eat the crew and later die of starvation itself, they could burgle the ships to their hearts' content. Gorvak truly seemed to have the mind of a good executive.

But, while they were bottling up the supply of Creeping Death, Spacehawk burned his way through the ship's hull and confronted the master pirate. After a brief exchange, Gorvak blustered, "Well—what are you going to do?"

"Don't worry about what I'm going to do! Start worrying about what you're going to do!"

Both foes drew and fired at the same time, and the blasts from their respective ray guns canceled each other out. Gorvak hollered for help. When the crew heard who he was up against, they headed for the hills.

"I can read your foul thoughts like a book!" snapped Spacehawk. "I know now where you've hidden all your loot, and I'll see that it all gets back into the proper hands!" But, since Gorvak asked for a chance, the hero obligingly broke both his own gun and the pirate's weapon, and told him to get ready for a fight.

Both grappled powerfully, but Gorvak won out by strangling Spacehawk into unconsciousness with his tentacle-like arm. After that, he opened up a can of Creeping Death and sent it flowing toward the trussed-up hero. Things looked grim.

But, as usual, all was not what it seemed. The Spacehawk arose in time, burst his rope-bonds, and declared, "Now you are going to die by your own infernal device!" Gorvak tried to lam out of there. Spacehawk caught him by the collar, pulled him back, got out of the room, and jammed the door shut.

"Let me out! Let me out! It's going to get me!" yelled Gorvak. A panel later he stumbled right into the mess, and the Creeping Death devoured him like an hors d'oeuvre. Spacehawk made it back to his ship, magnetically towed Gorvak's craft with him, and finally sent it whirling into the sun. He stood looking at the fading ship through a viewport, as enigmatic at the end of the story as at the start of it.

The next story (in V. 1 #6, July 1940) concerned a lost tribe of Mercurians who were living as mermen under the seas of Venus. They had a horde of treasure with which they'd fled the planet Mercury in ages past, and some present-day, air-breathing Mercurians (though the kind of air was debatable) with larceny on their minds rocketed to Venus, found the mermen and their treasure, and killed their chief to get it.

But Spacehawk was known to the mermen as a friend, and their new leader, Borlo, clamped himself into a thought projector (which looked for all the world like an electric chair) and contacted the masked hero. Quickly bringing his rocket below Venus's sea surface, he came to the aid of the aquatic Mercurian men, who were known as Draxions. In the meantime, Greebo and Rogg, the two diving-suited thieves, fell out and had a showdown. Greebo won.

Then a newcomer spoke from behind him: "Murdering your friend was stupid, Greebo! It won't help you get any more of this platinum—because you won't get *any!*"

Greebo shouted the Spacehawk's name and dropped his weapon in terror. But, seconds later, he used his armored diving suit to come to grips with Spacehawk, and ended up beaten. "Don't turn me over to the Draxions!" Greebo begged. "Let me go, and I'll never come back!"

"I'll let you go—and I'll also be certain you'll never come back!" Spacehawk jammed the anti-gravity control on Greebo's suit in the "up" position. Greebo flew up, through the waves, through the air, and into the void of space. There, the pressure within his suit caused it—and himself—to go pop. Exit one more space bad guy.

In the rest of the story, Spacehawk transformed the Draxions into air-breathers with a ray machine and helped them build a new city on land. Then he left, saying, "Borlo was getting the idea that I'm not quite human—and that's an uncomfortably close guess!"

Through all of this, the Spacehawk never removed his mask. Was he human or ... something else? (Considering what Wolverton was capable of drawing, we might have not *wanted* to see what was beneath his mask.) How long would readers be kept wondering?

One more month, actually. *Target Comics* #7 (August 1940) presented Wolverton's first Spacehawk cover, and he was shown maskless, a black-haired, dashing human male, facing off with a clawed lizard-being on a distant planet. The blurb on the cover informed us: "With one lightning blow Spacehawk crushed the planetoid monster." It was nice to know he wasn't a planetoid monster himself.

Spacehawk takes the cover for the first time and prepares to wallop an alien. © 1940 Novelty Press, Inc.

The first panel of the story had a brunette beauty hugging Spacehawk, and the caption related: "It takes a beautiful girl to finally unmask him." Beneath that was another half-page panel showing our villains of the piece, Jark and Zorg. They were grinning, they were pockmarked and hairy, and—let's get this out of the way right here—they looked like a pair of male generative organs. This might have been the first time that Wolverton played this kind of gag, but it wouldn't be the last. Not by a long shot.

Jark and Zorg had a portable planet, moved around by huge jets, and they used it to maneuver into the path of space freighters, causing them to wreck and yield the villains a hoard of plunder. After causing their first rocket wreck, the planetoid pair unleashed the "bloodthirsty Snurls" on the survivors. The Snurls looked like beetles, or perhaps snapping turtles, and they made short work of the passengers who were left.

The only one left was the aforementioned brunette, and Zorg snagged her, declaring she was "Just the person to keep me from becoming too lonely on this barren little planet!" The girl's expression was just about what you'd expect when a giant phallic head loomed in your direction. Jark got into a hassle with Zorg over her, but Zorg prevailed. After that, he cooed to the woman, "Come now! I will put you under the surgical ray! It will alter your appearance completely, and you will be truly beautiful by *my* standards!" Considering what Zorg was modeled after, one shudders to think what she would have been turned into. But one doesn't have to speculate too far, really.

Spacehawk was on the job. Having seen the traveling planetoid, he landed on it, debarked from his ship, polished off a couple of Snurls with his knucks, and leaped toward Zorg's fortress. Jark cocksurely aimed his atom rifle at Spacehawk's chest, pulled the trigger, and blasted him. The hero fell like a sack of potatoes. Jark traipsed outside in ecstasy, examining the fallen spaceman, and declaring, "I'll give him a fitting funeral by letting out two more Snurls to pick his bones!"

At that, Spacehawk grabbed the dastard by the leg. "Speaking of bone-picking, I have one I'm going to pick with you, my friend!" Within a couple of panels, he lifted Jark up, whirled him around his head, and sent the enemy flying through the air, long-stemmed neck and limbs flying, as Jark's scrotal body was "crushed to a pulp against the steel wall of an oxygenerator." Meanwhile, Zorg had the girl strapped into his surgical machine and was about to proceed, but he was distracted by "Jark's last blood-curding screams." Given the Freudian symbolism, Jark's screams were understandable.

Spacehawk burst into Zorg's lab and was greeted by the sinister genitoid, who brandished a ray gun and snarled, "Looking for trouble, eh? Here's where you find it!" An instant later, Spacehawk took another burst in the chest, and crashed to the floor. This time, for keeps. Zorg unmasked his foe….

…and found that Spacehawk was a robot.

He couldn't wait to spill the news to his female captive. But, even clamped to a laboratory slab, she answered, "Then you did not meet the Spacehawk! I have seen him and I'm sure he is human!"

A panel later, the real Spacehawk appeared, stage right: "The Earth girl was right! You only shot at one of my robots! Now you have me to contend with!"

Sometimes an alien is … just an alien. © 1940 Novelty Press, Inc.

"Robot or flesh and blood, I'll tear you to pieces!" said Zorg, extending his head erectly toward Spacehawk as he charged into battle. The alien grabbed the hero with his tentacles and pulled him close in to his globular, hairy body. But Spacehawk got the enemy by the neck, "and with one swift, powerful motion, breaks Zorg's spinal column. Zorg shivers convulsively, and slumps to the floor—dead." By that time, probably more than a few male readers were shivering convulsively themselves.

Spacehawk proceeded to release the girl from Zorg's contraption. She pointed out that he had rescued her a few weeks ago from a Martian, and that she wanted to see his real face. "Since I arrived in this solar system I have allowed no one to unmask me or my robots—until today!" said Spacehawk, starting to peel off his mask. A second later, he revealed his true face, the one we'd already seen on the cover. "But now I am going to claim that kiss I didn't take when I saved you from the Martian pirates!"

And he did.

Later, Spacehawk demonstrated that his robot double could still get up and walk, and towed the porta-planet out of the space lanes. He then gave the girl a lift to her original destination, Pluto. After he said goodbye, the girl thought, "Hmm! I guess it's up to me to see that it isn't too long until we meet again!"

She never appeared again, though. In the next saga, Spacehawk dealt with a couple of vulture-men named Glak and Orad who were based on Earth's moon, and who sent a giant gas-bearing missile at New York. The missile exploded, spewing forth acidic vapors that ate the flesh off people's bones. The panels of Earthmen running away in terror from the gas, and then skeletons littering the streets, were a grim precursor of the even more horrific illustrations Wolverton would do later for the Book of Revelation on behalf of Ambassador College Press. In this one, they were horrible enough. After setting things to rights, Spacehawk gave Glak and Orad a dose of their own gas, and swooped down in his spaceship to catch a last glimpse of their fleshless skeletons.

Spacehawk continued with more starfaring sagas, with grotesque aliens, even more grotesque alien creatures, and spaceships and gadgets that probably owed more to Dick Calkins than Alex Raymond. But his visuals were so distinctive, and so oddly appealing, that the Spacehawk stories (and others he drew) continue to be reprinted unto the present day. You might not recognize the art of a number of *Planet Comics* workers, but nobody ever mistook Basil Wolverton's work for somebody else's.

Then something happened to change the strip's focus: World War II. *Target Comics* V. 2 #1 (March 1941) appeared and, even though Pearl Harbor was many months away—possibly a year, since comics were cover-dated months in advance—Uncle Sam himself commanded the cover, and the *Target* characters were lined up below, uniformly saluting the U.S. flag. Spacehawk was third from the left. Within, Sam himself rallied the heroes and heroines and told them they must work for national defense. "It will be your duty, Spacehawk, to patrol the stratosphere and prevent invasion from other planets!" he said. Spacehawk said nothing.

But in his own story, a tale in which Spacehawk rescued the beautiful queen of Noom from a pickle-headed villain named Droon, some dialogue had been added at the last moment. After revealing Droon's evil plan, Spacehawk's speech balloon was obviously edited and expanded to include the words, "You intend to use them in your plan to conquer the Earth now that they are embroiled in a war and are at your mercy. But as long as I live to defend the great nation of America, no one is going to do that!"

As Wolverton later put it, the editor thought that it was unpatriotic for Spacehawk to be uninvolved with World War II. But this abruptly changed his milieu from the far-flung future to the present day, and Spacehawk's adventures became increasingly Earthbound ... a deadly blow for a feature that had thrived on weird landscapes, weird critters, and even weirder villains.

By the next story, Spacehawk was saving modern-day Americans from asteroids being guided at them by two evil Asian scientists in a spacecraft. Wolverton got in some great shots of Spacehawk's rocket zipping over the craggy surface of the asteroids, but things were subtly changing. With *Target Comics* V. 2 #3 (May 1941),

Spacehawk's logo was colored red, white, and blue, with the cutline "Defender of America" underneath. He fought an undersea tank manned by Nazis. No spaceward voyages were made.

With every issue, Spacehawk became more and more involved in the war effort. The stories were still somewhat fun, but the great sense of wonder that had propelled the earlier strips was gone. In *Target* V. 2 #7 (September 1941), he picked up his first recurring villain, a psycho scientist named Dr. Gore, who made three more appearances. It helped a bit, but not enough.

Finally, with *Target* V. 3 #10 (December 1942), with a not particularly memorable story about spies in Mexico, Spacehawk called it quits. Wolverton went on to other things, including the more successful *Powerhouse Pepper* feature in Timely's *Joker* and other comics. In the Fifties, he returned to science fiction, doing a number of memorable tales for Marvel and other companies, plus a wealth of magazine illoes and a couple of jobs for *Mad*. (His drawing of Lena the Hyena, a particularly grotesque character, was picked as the winner in a contest held by Al Capp for his *Li'l Abner* strip.) Later, he became a minister in the Worldwide Church of God and, for some years, did "The Story of Man," a retelling of the Bible in prose and illustrations for the church's *Plain Truth* magazine. In the Seventies, Wolverton returned tangentially to comics with covers for DC's humor mag *Plop!* By then he had been rediscovered by comics readers, mainly due to reprints of his Forties and Fifties comics fare. And a lot of those reprints were of Spacehawk stories.

One of these reprint books, Dark Horse's *Spacehawk* (1989), featured the first new Spacehawk story in 47 years. It appeared in the first two issues, was written by Jerry Prosser and drawn by Gary Davis, and pit Spacehawk against the Brain-Bats of Venus, another Wolverton creation. Rich Heddon and Tom McWeeney did another Spacehawk tale for the third and last issue. Though no new Spacehawk stories have appeared since then, Wolverton's stories refuse to die. They are periodically reprinted, and because of that, the Superhuman Enemy of Crime will continue to guard the spaceways.

Of course, there were others.

In *Mystery Men Comics* #1 (1939), Rex Dexter of Mars made his first appearance. He was the creation of Dick Briefer, and the first panel of the story informed us that a rocket ship had been sent to Mars from the 1939 World's Fair. That was one event that was not recorded by contemporary accounts, but there's always something new to learn. The ship was crewed by Montague Dexter and his wife, and, after a few hours, they were not heard from again.

Switch to the year 2000. Montague and his son Rex, in a Martian valley, are repairing their rocket. The elder Dexter, 85 years of age by now, observed to the Martian-born Rex: "There she is, son—completely fixed, after 61 years. Our rocket is ready to fly again—but this time, you will pilot it!"

Rex, a blond, long-haired young man, was bade farewell by both his father and native Martians. He took off in the repaired ship for Earth, but didn't get far: he crashed into the side of a much bigger spacecraft (which had wings and tail fins like an airplane) and made his way inside safely. The ship was crewed by Earthmen, who had heard of Montague Dexter's efforts: "He created that 'flivver' ship back in 1939!"

"I don't know what I am going to find in your world, but the prospects are bright!" said Rex, ready for adventure.

Our hero was given a great parade, fitting for a hero from a lost era. But we were about to get down to business: Europe, which had been reduced to "ruin and decay" from a war that had happened in the 1950s (missing things by about 10 years), was home to one Boris Thorax, an evil, one-eyed guy who was allied with people from the Moon, who were apparently as evil as himself. They wanted slaves, and he promised to get them American ones. How did he propose to do it? By having them send a small planet, Tarsis, plummeting toward America, forcing the population to move to Europe, where they could be snatched. Simplicity itself.

"To be dictator of the world was once a mad dream," said Thorax, relaxing with a cigarette. "What will people say, when Boris Thorax rules over the universe!"

And the dire destiny might have come to pass, had not Vesoff, a disgruntled former employee of Thorax, burst into an audience Rex was having with President Grover of the United States. Tarsis was sighted, and Vesoff revealed Thorax's plans. "A plane can get to Thorax's laboratory, in Europe, in 8 hours. Only one plane! If Dexter will volunteer, we can stop this catastrophe. My reward will be in breaking Boris Thorax's neck!"

Rex and Vesoff took off, with Cynde, a woman Dexter had met aboard the spaceship, looking on. "There he goes, into my life one hour, out the next. Moral: don't fall in love with a Mars man." But it was too late. She was already signed on as a supporting character.

Vesoff and Rex invaded Thorax's castle, and Vesoff was promptly shot. He fell across a lever that changed Tarsis's course. For his part, Rex said, "Vesoff only wanted one thing—to break your neck! Although he can't do it now—I can!" Rex laid him out with a haymaker. Tarsis plunged into the ocean (which was probably as devastating as anything out of a Philip Wylie novel) and Vesoff, who rose from the floor, admitted he had been prepared for the gun Thorax used on him. After all, he invented it. The story ended with Rex looking toward Mars, but seeing only Cynde.

Rex Dexter took over the next cover of *Mystery Men* with Cynde, both of them fighting enemy robots with ray guns. The art, by Lou Fine, was the best that Dexter ever had. In the story, Cynde revealed that she was a licensed space pilot, and helped Rex bring a radium-bearing planet close to Earth so that its radiation could cure a worldwide plague. There were battles with grotty aliens, too, just to keep things interesting.

But in the next issue (#3, October 1939), Rex and two others explored a cone-shaped planet, brought back a hairy, 150-foot-tall monster as an exhibit, and were somewhat surprised when the beastie rose up, broke his bonds, and went on a city-destroying rampage. The citizens were none too grateful toward Dexter for that, even after he leaped onto the monster's shoulder, plunged a knife through its eye and into its brain, and killed it. The populace responded, "Down with Dexter! Kill him for bringing that monster here!"

Faced with such political turmoil, the president told Rex he'd better leave, and he got in his rocket and headed for space. Cynde went along with him, vowing her love. The last panel showed Rex's rocket heading for the stars. Evidently, the space-hero gig wasn't all gravy.

Heading for Mars in the next episode, Rex and Cynde were diverted onto a planet named Ursis, controlled by a villain yclept Lord Marvel. He wanted to destroy the Earth because he intended to rearrange the solar system, apparently because the old model was too boring. Things looked grim, until Rex discovered that a robot menacing him was built by his father. Speaking Martian to it, Rex took control of the robot, stopped Lord Marvel from crashing the Moon into the Earth, and had the robot destroy the laboratory around him and Lord Marvel with it. "On to Mars, Cynde, where I shall reprimand Father for selling robots so carelessly!" Rex said.

The dauntless Dexter got back to Earth in issue #6, helping the people of Terra kill off some invading "protoplasmen," flat amoeboid creatures of sorts. They forgave him the incident of the 150-foot monster and welcomed him and Cynde back to their planet. They didn't stay there long, and the swashbuckling continued.

Along the way, a one-shot issue of *Rex Dexter of Mars* (1940) was published, and the usual expanded origin story was told, courtesy again of Dick Briefer. Actually, it was a major revision of the earlier stories. This time, Rex's exploits were moved up to 2040, and we got more in-depth coverage of Montague Dexter's World's Fair flight. Montague told a reporter, "My wife and I, and two other couples, are leaving the Earth—for Mars! There is nothing but war and strife and misery on this planet. We have nothing to lose by our experiment." So saying, he donned his helmet and blasted off.

We got our first glimpse of Montague Dexter's wife, Norma, as he told his rocketmates, "In this tube is a set of instructions. One century from now my descendant will open it! And he will return to Earth, to give to our people the results of our experiment!"

Finally, our intrepid crew made Marsfall, and Montague planted a flag on

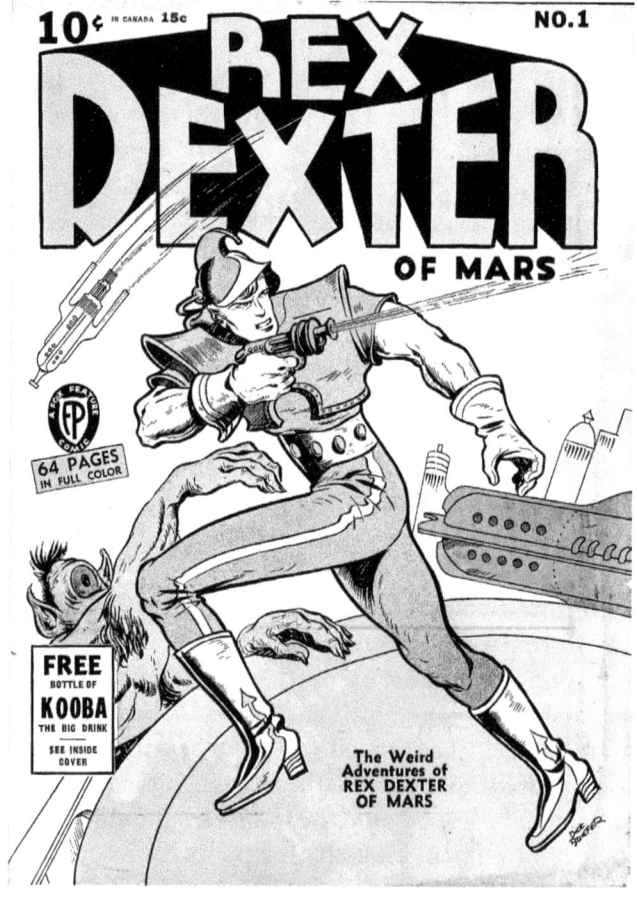

"The Weird Adventures of Rex Dexter of Mars." And who are we to disagree with that? © 1940 Fox Publications, Inc.

it, saying, "In the name of God and the planet Earth, I set foot on Mars!" Meanwhile, Earth blew itself up really well in a war, and in 2015, the "great-great grandson to Montague Dexter" was born. Evidently Briefer had done some calculating since the original story.

Baby Rex became awesomely strong on Martian cow milk, had a rattle full of meteorite fragments, and became an artist and scientist. And who should show up but Cynde, not an Earthwoman here but a daughter of one of the families who had come with Montague Dexter to Mars! She dared Dexter to come into the cave of the dangerous Hoogi beast with her, and, naturally, he ended up slaying the beast and saving her life. Just as naturally, she covered him with kisses.

When 2040 rolled around, Rex opened his ancestor's cylinder, took out a sheet of paper, and learned from Montague's handwriting that he was to return to Earth, see how well they'd done in the interim, and give them a report of how things were on Mars. Cynde insisted on coming along. They revved up the old rocket, made it to Earth, and got a parade, as before.

However, Earth nations were at peace, and they didn't think much of space travel. "Here is your apartment where you're going to stay!" said a modern Earthman. "Look—there is the old Empire State Building! That used to be the tallest structure in the world! Tomorrow we're going to tear it down. Out of date, don't you know!" Rex reflected on how happy Montague would be to learn that Earth had abandoned war, and we segued into some reprints. The adventures of Rex and Cynde continued, ending with *Mystery Men* #24 (July 1941).

Fox's *Fantastic Comics* #1 (December 1939) offered the first adventure of Space Smith, as basic a name for a rocket-wrangler as one could hope for. Luckily, it was written and drawn by Fletcher Hanks, which meant that it would definitely be skewed toward the odd end of the spectrum. In the first panel of the first story, a claw-handed, orange-skinned midget whose head was pretty much the shape of an egg lying on its side declared, "The Brain wants all Earth people destroyed!" Space and his girl, Dianna, were galivanting about amid the planets when their red rocket was attacked by thousands of "Martian imp men," who looked like lizards and shot sound rays (a real achievement, in space), radium rays, and anything else the author felt like. The culprits put belts on the unconscious Space and Dianna, "transmitted" them to the planet of Skomah, the egg-headed villain, and tried to enlist them in his upcoming war against the Earth. Dianna, burying her head against Space's chest, declared, "I'll die first!"

At that point, Skomah loosed the Martian imps on them, and they started attacking Space like a horde of piranhas. The Earth pair jumped through a window to safety (every villain's plan has to have a loophole), fought off a gigantic red man-eating Martian mosquito, got to a "transmitting station," and teleported themselves back to Earth. "We'll have to return to Mars!" said Space. "We must destroy that monster before he ruins the universe!"

That was the end of the first story. The next few issues continued Space Smith's valiant fight against Martian invaders, with the wildest space battles Hanks could come up with (and that was pretty wild). Space and Dianna fought off the ogres of Mars, the leopard women of Venus (who rode flying lizards through space and shot rays from their foreheads), headless soldiers with eyes on their chests, grasshopper men from an island in space, and just a whole big bunch of others. Hanks left the strip in the middle of its run, and it became a conventional space opera. Such is comics.

Space Smith was accompanied in *Fantastic* by *Flick Falcon in the Fourth Dimension*, whose name was changed to Flip Falcon by issue #4 when Fox realized how his first name would read if the second and third letters ran together. The first stories were drawn and probably written by Don Rico (as "Orville Wells"). The debut story began with a ball returning to Flick and his girlfriend, Adele, after being thrown into his Fourth Dimension machine. It had been turned inside out. "Does that mean your invention is a success?" Adele queried.

"I don't know—but there is one way to find out! Goodbye, Adele!" Flick threw himself into the machine. He was thrown through space in a fetal position, woke up on Mars (not unlike John Carter), and declared, "I have never felt *so queer!*" After determining that his body had pretty much been reversed (heart on the right side, and so on), Flick was picked up by a giant hand, thrown head-over-heels into the lair of a green, three-armed man who stood on what looked like a giant jukebox, and told he was his first Earth victim. "But that's not fair!" protested Flick. "I came to Mars of my own free will!"

"Ha, ha!" laughed his host, as other green Martians surrounded him. "There is no justice here—only activity!" They got right down to being active. Flick punched his way through the Martians, met with the giant again, threw himself back into the Fourth Dimensional portal, and reemerged in his Terran lab again. He stopped the machine just as the giant was reaching through it.

"The Martians have started their invasion!" he said, taking Adele by the shoulders. "I must go back, to find some way to stop them!"

"I'm going with you!" said Adele, dooming herself to a life of writing with the wrong hand. Flick, later Flip, and Adele adventured on through issue #21 (August 1941).

Science Comics was home to *Cosmic Carson* and *Perisphere Payne, Interplanetary Explorer*. Both of them appeared in all eight issues of the book (February–September 1940). *Cosmic* was drawn by George Tuska and *Perisphere* wasn't. They were run-of-the-mill spacers, and their mill ran out quickly. *Cosmic* made an appearance in *Big Three* #1 (Fall 1940) and *Perisphere* made one in *Samson* #3 (February–March 1941), and that was it.

Depending on when you read it, Fox's *Rocket Kelly* was either a mediocre space strip or a mediocre war strip. Our titular hero wore the conventional flight cap, jacket, and jodhpurs of a World War II–era pilot. In his first couple of adventures (*Everybody's Comics* and *Bouncer* #10 [both 1944]), he and his wingmate Punchy wound up somehow on an alien planet called Selura. After a couple of adventures, he got home and became a wartime pilot against the Japanese, and nothing was said about his science-fiction exploits. Then the war ended, Rocket got his own title and a real rocket, and he tooled around saving Earth from alien threats. His career stretched through a number of Fox Comics, ending up with a one-shot story in *Tegra* #1 (August 1948), and we've spent as much time on it as we really need to and more, really, than we want to.

Rick Evans was a bit more interesting, mainly because the writing was a bit better, probably the work of a young Bob Kanigher. Rick was a spacefaring crusader who lived in a future city (named, appropriately enough, Future City) with a sidekick named Stringbean and a girlfriend named Astra. He dressed in a yellow helmet and red-and-blue costume and periodically rocketed from Earth in a spaceship of his own design to right wrongs in the universe. His adventures started in 1944 in the Fox one-shots *All-Good Comics* and *Everybody's Comics*. They proceeded fairly irregularly through other books and ended with *Zoot Comics* #8 (August 1947).

Dell Comics, that giant of licensed features, stepped into the science-fiction ring with an impressive offering: *John Carter of Mars*. Starting in *The Funnies* #30 (April 1939) and continuing till issue #56 (June 1941), the stories were adapted from Edgar Rice Burroughs's *A Princess of Mars* and introduced us to the comic-book versions of Captain John Carter, Tars Tarkas, Dejah Thoris, and all their Martian cronies. Carter would return to the comics again and again over the decades, but he acquitted himself well in this nicely done strip, written and drawn by John Coleman Burroughs, ERB's son.

Rocket Kelly steps out. Um … where's the rocket? © 1944 All Comics Library.

Over at Quality Comics, *The Ace of Space* lifted off in *Feature Comics* #38 (November 1940) for a four-issue run. The strip was credited to Harry Francis Campbell and H. Weston Taylor. In the first episode, "young millionaire sportsman" Ace Egan, out in his plane for a jaunt, was dismayed by the landing of a large yellow spacecraft on his estate. A three-eyed, yellow-skinned giant emerged and telepathically granted Ace some info about alien invaders coming to Earth to conquer it. It also granted him a belt that could expand him to giant-size, give him great strength, and make him invisible. The alien benefactor died, unable to breathe Earth's atmosphere. Ace commandeered the giant's spacecraft and, when a horde of one-eyed, green-skinned invaders approached in an armada, defeated them single-handedly. His run wasn't long, but it was fun.

Crack Comics offered *The Space Legion* in its first 20 issues (May 1940–January 1942). The strip was the work of Vernon Henkel and introduced the very heroic-looking Rock Braddon in the first panel. The first story, drawn and written well for the time, pitted Rock and his planet-hopping police force against Harg, a bearded space pirate. The good guys forced Harg's vessel down on the Moon, blasted it in half, and engaged the villains in spacesuited battle in caves below the surface. Rock finished the story by ray-gunning down Harg personally. Most of the time, the strip wouldn't have been out of place in early *Planet Comics*. Henkel was just that good.

Blaze Barton and the World of Tomorrow helped fill the back of *Hit Comics* from issues #1 to 13 (July 1940–July 1941). This strip, also of decent quality, was by Henry Kiefer. The inspiration seemed to be the story of Noah: in the year 50,017 AD, Professor Solis, a scientist, determined that the Earth would pass so near the Sun that human life, and most other kinds, would perish. The strong-jawed Blaze believed him, and so did his daughter Betty, but the government did not. So the three of them built a domed, heat-proof city and survived when the heat cataclysm arrived. The temperatures split the Earth open, unleashing a race of subterranean mutant-men, and Blaze and the professor had to save Betty when she was nabbed by them and offered to their king. The trio foiled their pursuers by luring them into a subway, raying out the ceiling supports, and letting a river thunder in on them. The science fiction and swashbuckling were both of a decent caliber, and Blaze was a Quality feature indeed.

Rocket Riley takes on four bad guys. He's got them outnumbered. © 1939 Hillman-Curl, Inc.

Rocket Comics #1 was dated March 1940 and, on its cover, promised "*Action! Thrills! Adventure!*" Hillman was the publisher and, though they tried to deliver on all three, things never really clicked until Airboy came along a little later in *Air Fighters Comics*. The lead character of *Rocket* #1 was *Rocket Riley*, a he-man type in flight jacket, jodhpurs, and goggled helmet.

He was shown fighting bare-handed against four ray gun–wielding attackers on the cover, even though he had a holstered gun himself. For three issues he and two friends, Professor Sterling and his daughter Griselda, and a foe, enemy agent Von Stengle, blasted off and got into dangerous adventures on other planets. No data exists on who wrote or drew the strip, and it's just as well.

Speed Comics featured five stories of *Mars Mason of the Interplanetary Mail Service* (#7–11, April–August 1940). Munson Paddock drew the adventures of the planetary postman, who delivered his loads via spaceship (take that, FedEx!) and ran into all sorts of alien grotties who were determined that the mail would not go through. He fought off menaces like Killraye and seemed a throwback to the Pony Express drivers in his valor. When Harvey took over the title, they sent him packing.

Along with early *Dan Hastings* stories, MLJ featured *Scott Rand in the Worlds of Time* (*Top-Notch Comics* #1–3, December 1939–February 1940). This strip, written by Otto Binder and drawn by his brother Jack, sent the Flash Gordonish Rand and Dr. Joel Meade through different centuries in a "time car." In the first adventure they picked up a Viking warrior named Thor and an Egyptian princess called Elda. They saved the latter from a troop of ancient Egyptians by mowing them down with a submachine gun. Then they left to fight Martians in 2000 AD in the next episode.

Nedor Publications got into the SF act with *The Space Rovers* (*Exciting Comics* #2–9, May 1940–May 1941). The Rovers were 20-year-old Ted Hunt and his "pal," 15-year-old Jane Martin. Both were stocking up supplies on a spaceship created by Jane's dad, Dr. Matthew Martin, when spies attacked, intent on stealing the ship for nefarious purposes. Jane pulled a lever, blasted off, and got the ship, herself, and Ted out of the hands of the spies. They made it to Mercury, where they saved a bikini-clad cavegirl from a primitive tribe that wanted to sacrifice her. Evil aliens and other elements found their way into the story before they could get back to the rocket and blast off again. Max Plaisted took over the art in the next issue, and the Space Rovers wound up on four covers in a row. In the last episode, Dr. Martin and his assistant picked Jane and Ted up in another spaceship and returned them safely to Earth.

Lance Lewis, Space Detective debuted in *Mystery Comics* #3 and 4 (1944). Lance was a Buck Rogers–style hero, troubleshooter for Earth at the command of Montague of the space patrol. He did little detecting, but he did a whole bunch of swashbuckling. In his second adventure, he rescued Marna, a beautiful astronomer captured by Saturnians, and she promptly became his girlfriend and sidekick.

For three years after that, Lance dropped out of sight. Then he took over as lead feature of *Startling Comics* with issue #44 (March 1947) in a series of adventures drawn, early on, by Graham Ingels. Lance and Marna tangled in a two-part story with Mercurians who were out to pull Venus and Earth into the Sun with a force beam. The Mercurians were four-armed beings with potato-like bodies, and their faces were plastered on their torsos. At the end of the two episodes, Lance and Marna destroyed the device and Lance blasted down the Mercurian Sun King, who had a protruding mustache in about the area of a human's belly button. Lance and Marna continued their troubleshooting through the solar system up to issue #53 (September 1948), and did it quite well, under covers provided by Alex Schomburg.

Unlike most Golden Age space heroes, Lance actually got a revival, appearing with other Nedor heroes in *Tom Strong* #11–12 (January–June 2001). Unfortunately, he got killed by a villain in *Terra Obscura* #2 (September 2003). So it goes.

Black Terror #23 (March 1948) featured the one and only appearance of *The Space Speedsters,* who were reporter Jinx Johnson and astrophysicist Randy Colman. In this story, drawn by Stan Asch, the pair boarded Randy's rocket and saved the Earth from invasion or possible destruction by the planet Hecate, which was being piloted near the Earth by the evil Princess Venia. Despite a promising debut, Jinx and Randy never showed up again.

Tara premiered in *Wonder Comics* #15 (December 1947). Introduced by an Alex Schomburg cover, she

Lance Lewis exterminates a big bug. © 1947 Better Publications, Inc.

was a futuristic, beautiful, blonde pirate-wench in a two-piece, short-skirted outfit with buccaneer boots. Tara was one of a trio of space pirates, the other two being her mates Robin and Malo, who were, as the saying goes, "Honest men, driven into piracy by tyranny!" Their art, by Gene Fawcette, and their adventures were quality indeed, and it was a shame she only made it to issue #20 (October 1948), when the book was cancelled. A last *Tara* story ran in *Thrilling Comics* #71 (April 1949). In recent times, Will Meugniot has added her to his cast of revived Nedor characters at AC Comics.

Lev Gleason and Charles Biro offered up a few science fiction strips. The first of these was Joe Simon's *Solar Patrol,* which lifted off in *Silver Streak Comics* #2 (January 1940). The first story featured space-cop Ken Kurage, who patroled the solar system tracking down spies from other planets. He wore a modified policeman's uniform and his partner wore an aviator's cap from World War I. In their first exploit, they met the Tree Men of Uranus. Kurage was thrown in prison with a sexy Martian Amazon, and between the two of them they escaped and cut the Trees down to size.

By the next issue, the feature was renamed *Planet Patrol* and remained so till its last appearance (#6, September 1940). Years later, *Rocky X of the Rocketeers* began in *Boy Comics* #80 (August 1952), but that's one for the Fifties. Gleason also published *The Amazing Adventures of Buster Crabbe* (#1–4, December 1953–June 1954), featuring the serial star in various comic adventures, some set in space.

Fawcett's *Slam-Bang Comics* featured *Mark Swift and the Time Retarder* (#1–7, March–September 1940). Mark was an orphan living with schoolteacher Rodney Kent, who had discovered the secret of time travel in his spare time and built a spaceship-like "time retarder" in even more of his spare time. Mark and Rodney went back to the time of the Vikings (an ever-popular choice) in their first adventure, and continued that way pretty much through the series. They had one last appearance in *Master Comics* #7 (October 1940) and called it quits.

Tara outrays an enemy and looks fashionable doing it. © 1947 Better Publications, Inc.

Captain Venture and the Planet Princess debuted in *Nickel Comics* #4–8 (June–August 1940), then shifted to *Master* (#8, November 1940) after *Nickel* bit the dust. Venture was introduced as the "king of space-flyers" and, in his initial adventure, landed on Saturn. There he revived Princess Zyra from suspended animation (her people, emigrants from Earth, had died of a plague long ago) and helped her fight off the green-skinned Kashas. After that, they boarded Venture's ship and took off. "We have left Saturn behind, Captain Venture," she said. "Yes, and we have the whole universe before us," he said. The series ended with *Master Comics* #22 (January 1942).

Street & Smith's *Shadow Comics* provided *Iron Munro, the Astounding Man* (V. 1 #1 [1940]). Theodore Sturgeon, soon to be a noted SF writer, was the first scripter, and art was provided first by E. C. Stoner. Like most of S&S's early heroes, *Iron* was adapted from its pulps: in this case, John Campbell's *Aarn Munro* tales from *Astounding*. Our hero was a blue-suited space-type whose parents had been marooned on Jupiter and who, as a result of growing up under 2.5 times the gravity pull of Earth, had developed great strength. Iron was sent to Earth in the Jupiter colony's lone spaceship to try to bring back supplies. On his way to see the Earth president, he had to punch out a gaggle of guards, leap over tall buildings, and do all that sort of lower-gravity stuff. President Carlisle decided to go back to Jupiter with him, and the two set out in a brand-new ship of Iron's design.

But they hit an asteroid, were shifted into a "new universe," and were intercepted by alien invaders in flying saucers. Battle ensued. Iron assured Carlisle in the next episode that Earth would help out Jupiter in a spaceship of his own design. Our heroes fell in with a beautiful space princess, Anto Rayl, and helped her fight off a race of planetary satyrs. Munro continued his crusade through V. 2 #1 (November 1941), taking time out for a one-shot in *Army and Navy Comics* V. 1 #2 (August 1941).

Whiz Wilson and his Futurescope was the first SF offering from Ace Comics. The strip began in *Sure-Fire Comics* #1–3 (June–October 1940) and, when the title changed to *Lightning Comics*, continued there from V. 1 #4 (December 1940) to V. 2 #4 (December 1941). Whiz was a scientist who had perfected a "futuroscope," a box-like contraption he strapped onto his chest, which he used to project himself into Los Angeles in 1960. At that time, apparently, we were still fighting the Nazis, who had taken over Europe. Whiz used his device to save an Allied fleet of ships from destruction, then returned to 1940 to tell his girlfriend all about it. In the next episode, he traveled to 2040 and found out there had been four world wars already. The art was a little better than the prophecy.

Sun Publications, in their lone issue of *Colossus Comics* (March 1940), tried out *Colossus A.D. 2640,* credited to (Mark) Reinsberg and (Bernie) Wiest. Therein, Earth of 700 years in the future was threatened by Plantaliens, who looked pretty much like potatoes with faces. Dr. Blitzmann injected his human guinea pig Richard Zenith with a hormone extract that turned him into Colossus, a giant of over 2,000 feet in height (or at least that's what the captions said ... he didn't look over 60 feet tall). It also drove him insane and made him declare himself ruler of the Earth, though he had a little conquering to do first. Still, he didn't much like the Plantaliens, so he smashed them first. At story's end, Colossus had leaped into the ocean and was swimming toward Europe, and the heroes of the piece vowed to intercept him. We suppose they did, but frankly, we don't care all that much.

Hugo Gernsback's Komos Publications published *Superworld Comics.* In its three issues (April–August 1940), it presented *Mitey Powers*, scientist and space adventurer, and *Marvo 1-2 Go+*, a boy of the future with a super I.Q. Having noted both, we shall move on. The book was no *Amazing Stories.*

Bruce Barlow, Conqueror of the Planets held forth in Nita's *Whirlwind Comics* #1–3 (June–September 1940). He was a troubleshooter for Earth in the far-flung future of 1980 AD. Barlow was as notable as Nita's other characters, which is why the series lasted only three issues.

Hawley Publications' one-shot *Hi-Spot Comics* #2 (November 1940) had a promising cover and lead feature: *Dave Innes of Pellucidar.* This was an authorized adaptation of Edgar Rice Burroughs's Pellucidar series, featuring David Innes, a hero who journeyed to the center of the Earth in a mole-machine, encountering a lost race of humans and the sentient, evil, telepathic Mahars. After the first 12-page story was published, *Hi-Spot* went back to being *Red Ryder Comics*. Another episode had been prepared, though it had to wait decades before being printed in an issue of the *ERB-dom* fanzine. David Innes made a cameo in a late-Sixties issue of *Tarzan of the Apes* and, some years later, helmed his own stories in DC's *Tarzan* and other comics.

In Progressive Publishers' *Bang-Up Comics*, Cosmo Mann held forth, a super-scientist who had perfected a "sun-ray gun" that could melt tanks. Quite naturally, he fought Axis agents who sought to steal the weapon. The art was credited to "Sam Hill," who was pretty good, whoever he was. Cosmo appeared in all three issues of *Bang-Up* (#1–3, December 1941–June 1942).

Of course, Flash Gordon and Buck Rogers themselves got reprinted again and again. But in Flash's case, Dell Comics offered him a home away from home. He appeared in *Four Color Comics* #10 and 84 (1940 and 1943), in Alex Raymond strip reprints. However, in #173 (1947), the cover proclaimed, "Introducing for the first time.... *Flash Gordon comics* especially written and drawn for this book!" The guy who drew them was Paul Norris of *Brick Bradford* fame, and he did a great job with Flash's rip-roaring, book-length adventures on Mongo. The series continued with five more *Four Color* issues, ending with #512 (1953), and a solo *Flash Gordon* comic, numbered #2 (1953). After that, Flash would appear in comic book reprints, but not until King Comics took him over in 1966 would he again get original coverage in comic books.

Buck Rogers, for the most part, settled for reprints. But some of those reprints, in *Famous Funnies*, featured cover art by Frank Frazetta, who outdid himself on portrayals of the spaceman hero. They still stand as some of Frazetta's best comic work ever—and that's saying a mountain.

In Magazine Enterprises' *Manhunt*, Space Ace plied his trade.

The Space Ace, one Jet

Space Ace prepares to give a monster an oral cleansing. © 1952 Magazine Enterprises.

Black by name, was a member of the Space Patrol in the future. He was written possibly by Gardner Fox and illustrated by somebody or somebodies really good, maybe Frazetta himself. He was as generic a space hero as space heroes can get. Briefly: in his first adventure, the Space Ace was assigned the task of nabbing the Prism Pirate, a villain who used a cosmic ray–powered prism to bring down cargo spaceships and steal their uranium. A kid named Jak Tal had stowed away on one of them. Jet Black rescued him and the two quickly brought down the Prism Pirate. The stories improved in future issues, written by Gardner Fox and drawn by Fred Guardineer. Space Ace and Jak Tal lasted in *Manhunt* from issues #1 to 7 (October 1947–April 1948). Another Space Ace showed up in *Jet Powers* #1–4 (January 1951–[month unknown] 1951), having no relation to the earlier feature. Neither did *Major Inapak, the Space Ace*, who had a one-shot giveaway comic in 1951. The original Ace got his own comic full of reprints (*Space Ace* #5, 1952) and was reprinted time and again, most recently by Boardman Books in *Jet Black and Jak Tal: The Complete Space Ace* (2014) and *A-1 Comics: A Retrospective* #142–143 (2015).

The Forties drew to a close, and with them, most of the superheroes. But other genres of comics were taking their place, and one of those was science fiction. The early Fifties would see the birth of EC's classic *Weird Science* and *Weird Fantasy*, and DC's excellent *Mystery in Space* and *Strange Adventures*. Other publishers would unleash a horde of SF anthology comics and tomes of steel-jawed space opera stars like Rocky Jones and Tom Corbett, Space Cadet. The Forties space comics had been fueled by the visions of the Thirties' SF pulps, but the Fifties would be propelled by something new: the rocketry experiments of Wernher von Braun, the rivalry between America and Russia which culminated in the space race, and the launch, later in the decade, of the USSR's Sputnik satellite.

The old cliché: science fiction becomes science fact.

The comics had already been there.

The Adventurers

Not every hero in comic books wore a costume or a jungle outfit. Some of them wore business suits without masks. Or soldiers' uniforms. Or ... well ... whatever the situation dictated.

Superheroes, jungle characters, and sci-fi guys and gals only made up a part of the adventure comics roster. Another set of them might easily be labeled as Adventurers.

The Adventurers, who went about their heroic duties usually without benefit of superpowers or costume, were the staple of Fiction House comics. Hardly any of them walked around in a colorful union suit, although the women walked around in as little as they could get away with. If you subtracted their jungle heroines and heroes, their *Planet Comics* rocketeers, and their aviators, you still had a sizable amount of characters. They were the mainstays of *Rangers Comics*, *Fight Comics*, and most of *Jumbo*. Adventurers also rode shotgun to the superheroes in most of the anthology comics, and sometimes starred in their own titles.

They were soldiers, they were sailors, they were spies, they were private detectives, they were cops, they were ghostbusters, they were prizefighters, they were pirates, they were explorers, they were just about every stripe of non-costumed hero imaginable. And they were all in comic books.

Jumbo was the first of these, a mixed bag of adventure, humor, period pieces, and true-life features. It started out as a huge, tabloid-sized comic, without color; hence the name, *Jumbo*. *Peter Pupp*, by Bob Kane, qualified as both adventure and funny-animal humor. In *Jumbo* #1 (September 1938), the titular Pupp and his sidekick, Tinymite, were kidnapped by a mad scientist and sent to the Moon in a rocket ship to find out if the Earth's satellite was made of cream cheese. (If it was, Pupp was to bring back a sandwich of it.) Kane did a fun job on this one, and the feature continued through *Jumbo* #24 (February 1941), though the latter issues were reprints.

Hawks of the Seas, later retitled *The Hawk*, was a more long-lasting effort. Obviously influenced by movies such as *Captain Blood*, Will Eisner wrote and drew the initial episodes of the strip for Australia's *Wags*. The Hawk was possibly Eisner's first adventure hero, and certainly one of the best of his pre–*Spirit* efforts. And he lasted for over a hundred issues. He started out in America in Quality's *Feature Funnies* #3 (December 1937), stayed there through issue #12 (September 1938), and then jumped ship for *Jumbo Comics*.

The Hawk swords things out in a magnificent Eisner cover. © 1939 Real Adventures Publishing Co.

The Hawk was a nameless Englishman turned pirate. As he put it, "We don't fight for money, we fight for the freedom of weak slaves and for adventure." His first adventure in *Jumbo* (#1, September 1938) involved him braving the wrath of English slaver Merrystone in order to free a group of slaves and get them back to their homeland. It took several issues, but the Hawk, his first mate, Fluth, and his Indian ally,

Sagua, finally freed the slaves and brought their enemy to justice. It didn't hurt that a colonial governor was on the Hawk's side.

In *Jumbo* #4 (December 1938), the Hawk revealed his origin story. "My boyhood was spent in luxury. When I left my tutors, I was sent to an exclusive college. Like other rich men's sons, I was content with idle pleasures. One day I was asked to write a theme on some worthy topic. I chose the barbarism of slavery." He was ridiculed for his paper. His fiancée, daughter of a wealthy slave-owner, bade him give up his beliefs or give up her. He chose the latter, or so he thought.

The sight of a slave being beaten by his fiancée's brother caused the future Hawk to knock the slave-beater down. The villain challenged him to a duel and lost, being wounded in the process. Later, the slave recovered, killed the man who beat him, and fled. The Hawk-to-be was blamed for the crime, tried, convicted, and put on a prison ship for life.

He managed an escape, got to his ex-fiancée, tried to explain, and failed. He was sentenced to another ship, but, at sea, a huge wave swept the helmsman overboard. Since our hero was the only one who knew how to navigate, he took the wheel, lashed it, dropped into hiding, and began to wage a guerrilla war against the crew. "They attributed the disappearances to a hawk!" He liberated the prisoners, overcame the crew, and put the survivors into a boat. The remaining prisoners were of two minds. One faction wanted to turn pirate. The Hawk wanted only to prey on slave ships. He faced down the enemy faction's leader in a knife fight, and won.

"From then on, we were the Hawks of the Seas, preying on slave ships only." The governor offered to help him clear his name. The Hawk refused. "I'd have to tolerate slavery, and that can never be! As long as there are slaves, I remain the Hawk!"

In the next issue, the Hawk picked up a kid sidekick, Jeremy Clogg, the son of a fellow pirate who had died. The boy was menaced by Dr. Synde, a fiend who wanted the treasure map that was tattooed on the boy's chest. Synde was just as likely as the Joker to kill for insubordination, and he demonstrated it more than once. His crew did battle with the Hawk and his cohorts, and came perilously close to victory. But, in the end, the heroes triumphed and Dr. Synde worked out a deal to save his life, though he was put out to sea in a boat. By that time, the Hawk stories were formatted as regular comic stories rather than Sunday comic page broadsides. The feature was retitled *The Hawk* by *Jumbo* #9 (August–September 1939).

With *Jumbo Comics* #9 (August–September 1939), the book shrank and went to color, and the Hawk ended his black-and-white phase. The pirate hero fought a multi-issue battle against another band of slavers, picking up a love interest, Maria Mantilla, along the way. He encountered Dr. Synde again in issue #13 (March 1940). This time the villain fell to his death.

The *Wags* reprints were evidently used up by *Jumbo Comics* #14 (April 1940). Will Eisner continued to write and draw the feature for a while. It wasn't unlike the pre-war *Spirit* in visuals and tone. But, by issue #16 (June 1940), with the impending birth of *The Spirit Section*, a comic book inserted into Sunday newspapers, Eisner had left the *Hawk* feature and it went back to strip reprints for a single episode. With the next issue, #17 (July 1940), Eisner shop artists, possibly Dan Zolnerowich and Chuck Mazoujian, took over the feature. The Hawk continued his adventuring.

John Celardo, later to draw the *Tarzan* comic strip, came on board as artist with issue #19 (September 1940). Two issues later, a new artist, Art Saaf, signed on with new instructions. He was to take old Eisner panels, modify them a bit, and turn them into new stories. This, alas, probably shows what the editors thought of their young readers' intelligence. Anyway, it was take it or leave it.

The recycling of old *Hawk* strips continued all the way until issue #44 (October 1942), where Robert Webb took over the art. Maria was gone, but Jeremy remained, and Dr. Synde was recycled as a new villain named Dr. Crawshaw, who died at the end of the story. Well, they had to recycle something.

The Hawk's adventures, though exciting, became formulaic. He fought a lot of adversaries, went through a lot of back-whipping, and met a lot of women. As Fiction House was going whole-hog on sex appeal, the last wasn't surprising. Finally, though, in *Jumbo Comics* #65 (July 1944), they settled on a continuing leading lady. She appeared on the splash panel in what amounted to a tattered bikini, barefoot, with a gun in one hand and a sword in the other. A caption introduced her: "Adventuress, hellcat, vixen, this lass known as 'Velvet' ... backed by a swarthy crew, she charged the seas, leading the kill ... that is ... until she unwittingly attacked the Hawk and became his prisoner! Yet she's running true to form, this fiery, captivating captive.... Will the Hawk manage to tame her?"

Whether he could or not, it'd be fun watching. We were thrust into the story *in medias res*, with Velvet, a true sister of Anne Bonny and Mary Read, and her crew in the brig of the Hawk's ship, the *Lady Scarlett*. She pulled a quasi-epileptic act and was taken to a separate cabin, from which she easily escaped and then freed her crew. Velvet captured Jeremy and battle ensued, but, as her men began dropping like flies and not from wounds, she realized that they had been infected with a plague. The she-pirate abruptly called off the melee, ordered her plague-ridden men into her former ship, and stayed aboard the Hawk's own craft herself.

Velvet's last order to her men was to land their ship on a place called Rock Beach. When the Hawk asked her why she was giving doomed men landing orders, she tearfully explained: "The breakers will smash them to bits! My order was for mercy's sake. They're men of the sea, let them die of it, not of the plague!"

True enough, the longboat holding the men broke up on the rocks and the crew drowned. The Hawk approved. Well, they would have taken longer to die of the plague, but still.... The Hawk proposed Velvet as a new member of the crew, and Fluth wondered if she could cook as well as she could fight. "Cook, hmmm!" said Velvet. "With what, a harpoon?" "Aw.... I s'pose she'll be with us for keeps now!" groused Jeremy. And she was. Velvet stayed on for the rest of the strip.

The Hawk, still under the byline "Willis Rensie" though Eisner had left long ago, sailed on through *Jumbo Comics* #162 (August 1952), missing only issue #78 (August 1945), when the book shifted from 52 to 36 pages. Jeremy, Fluth, and Velvet were there till the end. The Hawk fittingly lifted a glass in a toast in the last panel of the final story. What became of him, no one will know.

Jack Kirby and Dick Briefer weighed in with an adaptation of *The Count of Monte Cristo*, which ran for *Jumbo*'s first 17 issues (September 1938–July 1940). *Spencer Steele*, a gentleman detective strip possibly written by Eisner and drawn by Edwin

Laughlin and George Tuska, appeared in issues #1–14 (September 1938–April 1940). It then jumped to *Fight Comics* and went from issues #7 to 14 (July 1940–August 1941). Briefer also tackled a retelling of *The Hunchback of Notre Dame* (*Jumbo* #1–10, September 1938–October–November 1939), foreshadowing his later *Frankenstein* strip for *Prize Comics*.

As "Curt Davis," Kirby was also responsible for *Wilton of the West*, possibly his first Western strip, in *Jumbo Comics* #1–24 (September 1938–February 1941). This was an action-packed but fairly conventional oater in which most of the first four-page episode was devoted to a fistfight between Wiley Wilton and bad guy Bart Luger. Around that, Kirby fitted in some gunplay. Wilton finally rode off into the sunset sans Kirby, who had migrated to Timely, Novelty, and other publishers. The stories beyond him were handled by Lou Fine, Charles Sultan, and George Tuska.

The Diary of Dr. Hayward, also by Kirby (as Curt Davis) at first, fared better both in conception and longevity. It probably started out in *Wags*, because the first *Jumbo* episode began *in medias res*, with an evil scientist named Kromo menacing a blond Flash Gordon type named Stuart Taylor, "a young scientist." Kromo sought vengeance on Dr. Hayward, Stuart's mentor, and on Hayward's daughter Lora. He actuated it by putting his mind in Stuart's body and posing as him, menacing the Haywards secretly.

Kromo kidnapped Lora and made her witness what was to be the doom of Stuart's mind within Kromo's body in an acid bath. However, Dr. Hayward, speeding toward Kromo's lab in an automobile, picked up a strange hitchhiker who called himself Mr. Eternity, and who knew all about the Kromo affair. "I am a being whose size extends beyond the limits of space and time," he said. "When visiting Earth I use countless shapes and forms." Mr. Eternity debarked from the car just before Hayward arrived at his destination, saying, "I will return—for I play a principal part near the ending." And apparently he did, because Stuart was back in his old body before long and things were set to rights.

After the first story arc, Kirby was gone and his place was taken by Lou Fine. Lora was renamed Laura and the foe was one Ali Pasha, a mystic. In the course of the new story, Stuart Taylor was transformed into energy, transmitted to a far-off Mongol land, and reassembled into his human self. But after that issue (#8), *Jumbo* was resized to more normal comic book dimensions and the storyline was slightly made over. *The Diary of Dr. Hayward* became *Weird Stories of the Supernatural*. Instead of transmitting Stuart Taylor halfway across the world (which storyline was forgotten), Ali Pasha sent him back in time and across space to the Asian city of Manchung. He became involved in a war between two city-states, helped Manchung to victory, and returned to his own time by story's end. The format was set.

By issue #10 (October–November 1939), the series was billed as *Stuart Taylor in Weird Stories of the Supernatural*, and the stories almost always followed the pattern of sending Stuart, Dr. Hayward, and Laura back for an adventure in other-time and restoring them to their normal era at the final panel. They seemed to be able to time-travel at will, which made things easier for the writers. Stuart continued his trans-temporal swashbuckling, fighting the Devil himself in a Faustian early episode. Then he went into the future, to battle giant insects. The backdrop changed with every issue.

Stuart Taylor continued through *Jumbo Comics* #140 (October 1950), dropping back to the seventeenth century in his last adventure to help convince the Indians to sell Manhattan to Peter Minuit. After that, he faded into the limbo reserved for Fiction House characters that never got a revival. All in all, he had a great run.

ZX-5, Spies in Action started in *Jumbo Comics* #1 (September 1938) and was possibly the first of Will Eisner's several espionage strips. The title character, ZX-5 (a name possibly cued by Secret Agent X-9 from the newspaper comic strips), was an undercover man who was thrust in the first adventure into a war between Transovania and Chesterland, two European nations. He proceeded to bust spies across the world, through World War II and beyond, and finished things up in issue #140 (October 1950), pacing Stuart Taylor.

Inspector Dayton, another cop strip, began in *Jumbo*'s first issue and was an Eisnerian police detective in a trench coat. The inspector fought a bunch of dope smugglers called the Ace of Spades Gang in his first story arc and continued fighting the Good Fight through issue #67 (September 1944). Along the way he picked up a sidekick called the Creep, who took over top billing in the last four stories.

In January 1940, Fiction House brought forth two new comics: *Jungle Comics*, which we've already covered, and *Fight Comics*. Both were named for their pulp parents, *Jungle Stories* and *Fight Stories*. *Fight* covered two-fisted adventurers of varying stripes, with a first cover by Will Eisner. It depicted a torn-shirted he-man beating up two tough guys and about to lay them out with two others he'd already knocked out, lying right beside an opened-up treasure chest and a skull. Three others

Nobody jumps the Shark! –Brodie, that is. © 1939 Fight Stories, Inc.

and a horde of natives led by an Amazon were making for him, but that was all right. Shark Brodie could take them all.

Shark, drawn quite well in his first outing by George Tuska (as "George Aksut"), was billed as "[t]he toughest, two-fisted adventurer in the South Seas." We never learned all that much about him, but maybe there wasn't that much to learn. He stood on the splash, smiling, legs spread, hands behind hips, and a big gun belted at his waist. That was all we needed to know.

In the story, Shark Brodie rescued a beautiful island girl at sea and learned her tribe had been overtaken by the stereotypical Evil White Men who forced them to dive for pearls and abused them, including her chieftain father, whenever they felt like it. Shark hit on the idea of hollowing out coconut shells and filling them with gunpowder. Our hero got caught by the villains and thrown in a brig with the heroine's father (who looked like a mustached white man with a towel around his waist), but Shark signaled the natives with a flare gun to attack the baddies' ship.

A great half-page battle scene followed. Shark rammed the brig door open with just his own strong shoulder and got in on the action, losing his shirt in the process. At the end, he shot down two bad guy guards to get to Nemo, the chief brigand, and the chief's daughter knocked the villain into the ocean with an oar. A school of real sharks beat Shark to the punch and had Nemo for a buffet. The chief asked Shark to stay, but he said that he had to "keep roving about!" The girl kissed him and then watched as he sailed away.

Shark Brodie carried on as a seagoing Conan through issue #43 (April 1946), missing only #40 (October 1945). Later issues were done by somebody doing a fair imitation of Matt Baker, if not Baker himself, and featured appropriately sexy South Sea girls. One such girl, Lily, stayed on for many issues as Shark's sarong-clad partner. It was a good enough run for any mariner at the time.

Next up was *Kayo Kirby*, whose art looked suspiciously Eisnerian in the first story. Kayo's intro wasn't unlike many of the boxing movies that proliferated in that day. An old boxer past his prime, one Chris Hardin, needed to keep fighting to put his son through college. He took one last beating in the ring and a thug promoter had his goons administer another one in an alley. By chance, a youth named Red Kirby happened by, clobbered the goons by himself, and impressed Hardin mightily. It turned out he'd come to the city to learn boxing to fund his way through law school. To Hardin, it was kismet, and he offered to train Kirby. In the kid's first fight, he won by a knockout. Similar results followed, and his nickname Kayo Kirby resulted.

Kayo went against a seasoned veteran of the ring in mid-story and took the guy apart. He also met Hardin's pretty daughter and, predictably, took a shine to her. Kirby's next opponent was juiced with adrenalin to amp his ferocity, but Kayo managed to defeat him as well. The loser's boss tried to have his men destroy Kirby afterward, but the premier pugilist laid them out on the sidewalk.

For the last fight, all the clichés were pulled out. Kirby was matched against the champion, but Mary, Hardin's daughter, was kidnapped. Deprived of her support, Kayo barely hung on. When Hardin found out that Mary had been snatched and passed the word to Kayo, the contender found new strength and knocked the champ cold in the ninth. Then he rushed out with Hardin, rescued Mary from the thugs, and came back to tell his mentor, who'd been wounded in the struggle and was in a hospital bed, that he was going home and quitting the fight game. Hardin pointed out Mary, who wanted to pay her respects. The last panel featured a silhouette of Kayo and Mary kissing, and Hardin asked the nurse to pull a screen in front of them.

Kayo Kirby kept fighting all the way through *Fight Comics* #81 (July 1952), at which point it shifted format and became a war comic. Later issues featured the work of a young Jack Kamen, on his way to becoming an EC star. After 12 years, Kayo was entitled to hang up his gloves.

Kinks Mason was the next offering, about a deep-sea diver who was swept by a storm into "the graveyard of lost ships!" He fought a pile of living seaweed and aided a tribe of good guys in an assault against the caveman-like Goors in his first adventure. After his triumph, he said goodbye to the girl he'd met and returned to the surface world, promising to come back someday. Steve Broder drew the story and all that followed. Most of Kinks's adventures involved him finding undersea civilizations and battling green mermen. He lasted through issue #15 (October 1941).

Big Red McLane was a feature done by the inimitable Fletcher Hanks, as "Chris Fletcher." Big Red was a huge lumberjack, and he and the villain of the first story had chins you could stand on. At the first lumber crew which he wanted to work with, Big Red found a "lumber racketeer" trying to force workers to sign up with his outfit. "Not so fast there, smart guy!" said Red. "I don't like the way you do business, and I don't like your face!! I can't change your business, but—I can change your face!" And he did. Red, whose neck was appreciably wider than his head, vowed to send the first lumberjack who pulled a fast one home with a lily in his hand. After a barroom brawl and several other altercations, Big Red routed the racketeers. Things continued pretty much in that

Kinks Mason shrugs off the danger of a cut air-line and an approaching shark. The treasure's the important thing. © 1940 Fight Stories, Inc.

vein through issue #9 (October 1940). He met a girl in that issue, became a boxer, and never came back.

Terry O'Brien, Gang Smasher, was the work of Maurice Gutwirth. He was apparently a private detective hired by a group of six masked city fathers as the best candidate to break up a city-wide insurance protection racket. He waded into the thieves with his bare knucks and cleaned up the bunch in five pages. He made it to issue #2 (February 1940) and was gone.

Strut Warren represented the Marines, and was written and drawn by Klaus Nordling. He was stationed in China and helped keep a bunch of Japanese invaders from endangering a group of American female settlers. Thankfully, the women weren't drawn as typical Fiction House pin-ups, being rather on the plain side (though played for laughs). Strut got mad at the Japanese, beat the heck out of them, and then asked his griping sergeant if he was off duty. When told he was, Strut knocked the man down. Strut remained at his post through issue #18 (April 1942).

Chip Collins, Sky Fighter rounded out the first issue. He was, in his first story, kind of a proto-Blackhawk. Standing in his Navy whites aboard a ship, smoking a pipe, Captain Chip Collins mused, "It won't be long now! The Skull Squadron will soon be a reality!" A superior called him in and said, "Remember, Chip, your squadron is on its own—don't expect any official aid from the government!"

The Skull Squadron proved to be a team of Navy fliers stationed aboard an aircraft carrier who did troubleshooting in red planes with a skull painted on the fuselage. Their first job was to save an American refugee in China from Japanese invaders. (Now, where have we seen that plotline before?) The refugee had a beautiful daughter named Wendy, and the Skull Squadron saved them both. George Tuska did his

Chip Collins shoots up an enemy plane on the way down. If he'd had time, he'd have bagged two. © Fight Stories, Inc.

usual great job on the art. Chip lasted through issue #30 (February 1944), missing only issue #27.

In *Fight* #10 (December 1940), Frosty North came in from the cold, more or less. North was "a fighting man of the vast and dangerous polar regions … a new courageous adventurer and secret agent." He was sent to Alaska to stop foreign smugglers from taking liquid explosives out of the country. In the process, he met a beautiful fellow agent, got blown up with a train and survived unhurt, and repaid the favor by blowing up the Nazi agents, who got hurt quite a bit. Frosty took the cover for that issue and trudged on through issue #16 (December 1941).

By issue #19 (June 1942), the editors of *Fight Comics* decided it was time for a housecleaning. Kayo, Shark, and Chip got to stay. They were joined by three new characters. Their names were Rip Carson, Señorita Rio, and Dusty Rhodes. One issue later (#20, August 1942) they were joined by Hooks Devlin. Along with Tiger Girl, who arrived in #32 (June 1944), they formed the vanguard of the comic for most of its run, except for Dusty, who didn't last that long. *Fight Comics* had finally found some contenders.

Frosty North teaches some wolves to heel. © 1940 Fight Stories, Inc.

Dusty Rhodes, which came first, was an engaging strip about a kid who stumbled frequently into adventure. And we do mean stumbled: in his first adventure, he was carrying lunch to his Marine brother on board a torpedo boat when an alarm was sounded for an engagement with the enemy. Dusty got knocked belowdecks by accident, pushed the wrong button, and ended up confronting an entire Japanese battalion. This being an American comic book, he defeated them all. His adventures went pretty much like this through issue #31 (April 1944).

The next newcomer did a lot better for herself. In the splash, we saw a beautiful black-haired woman in a low-cut dress with a slit that exposed a lovely leg all the way to the thigh. She was pressed against a brick wall, hiding from a Luger-toting Nazi agent. The caption read: "Into gay and song-loving Rio where Axis agents ply their sly and murderous wiles, bursts a new sensation—SEÑORITA RIO! Who is this shapely mysterious woman in red? Where is she from? Why did she come to Rio? The answer is written in blood in a tawdry music hall, in a moonlit palace garden, and in a warship at the bottom of Pearl Harbor."

Clearly, Señorita Rio was a woman with a mission. The story that followed was good, hard-hitting espionage stuff, mixed with as much sex appeal as artist Nick Cardy and the unknown scripter could handle. In the opener, the beauty from the splash page leapt at night from a ship leaving Rio and, clad in a two-piece black bathing suit, swam through shark-infested waters to a small boat. From thence she was taken to a wharf, where she boarded a cab in which another black-haired beauty, tied, gagged, and in a red dress, sat on the back floorboards. The driver told her, "You must get the forged papers or else relations between the U.S. and Brazil will be shattered!"

"I'll remember," said Señorita Rio. "Now, Countess, I'll borrow your dress!"

After trading dresses with the trussed-up villainess, the Señorita was taken to a club where she would pose as the enemy agent, a singer. Problem was, a few miles down the road, the cab driver stopped the cab in a deserted place, kindly eased the Countess's bonds—and got a knife in the chest.

A panel later, a newspaper story clued us in that Rita Farrar, an American actress, had apparently leapt to her death from the ship that was leaving Rio on page 1. The reporters chalked up her suicide attempt to depression over losing her fiancé at Pearl Harbor. Little did they know....

Rita, aka Rio, sang her heart out at the bistro. A Nazi agent sitting at

Neither leopards nor hook-handed goons shall stay the course of Senorita Rio! © 1946 Fight Stories, Inc.

ringside, one Von Stutz, summoned her over with a note. After giving Von Stutz the countersign, she was accepted as the Countess. It took a little more doing to get the forged papers that would stir up trouble between the U.S. and Brazil. But Rio showed fine temperament, almost threw a fit, and bluffed her way through it. She also fended off Von Stutz when he tried to steal a kiss.

She was not so lucky when she entered her dressing room. The club owner was lying face down, stabbed in the back. The Countess, saying, "The newspapers were wrong about your death—but only by a few hours!," grabbed the papers from Rita/Rio at gunpoint, gagged her, tied her to a chair, and left, promising to return and take her to "her last big performance!"

Luckily, the she-spy banged hard enough with her high heels against the wall, alerting some lingerie-clad dancing girls to come in and free her. Rio left just as Von Stutz and the Countess returned, and hitched a ride on the back of their car when they left. The good guys, or good girl, hadn't lost yet.

After sneaking up on the Countess, stunning her with a punch, and switching clothes with her again, Rio yelled for Von Stutz to stop the American girl from leaving with the documents. Duped, Von Stutz shot the Countess to death. "Dummkopf, you have killed me!" were her last words. The Nazi tried to flee but was caught by guards. Rio watched him being carried away. In the last panel, she burned the forged papers and dropped them into the bay, saying, "For Bill ... and Pearl Harbor!" The Allied Mata Hari had closed her first case.

Señorita Rio continued to show us the South American way of spying. Nicholas Viscardi, as Nick Cardy, drew her initial assignments, combining espionage, romance, action, and sex appeal in equal portions. In her second exploit, a Nazi spy killed her second suitor with a knife in the back. At the funeral, she dropped flowers in the grave and swore a double vengeance on the Axis for him and her dead fiancé.

In issue after issue, the sensational she-spy took on fascist enemies all over South America. She could fight, she could shoot, she could use a knife, and frequently she had cause to use all three skills. Posing as any number of other females, but somehow never having much use for a disguise, Señorita Rio struck deadly blows against Axis operatives and kept up our end of the Good Neighbor Policy in a most effective way.

Through it all, Rio never stopped fighting, never stopped spying, and never stopped showing off her legs. In one adventure, she saved herself and a fellow agent from a jaguar by leaping atop its back and cutting its throat with a knife. Sheena and Tiger Girl could have done no better.

Lily Renée replaced Viscardi after a while, and sustained the feature in fine fashion. In fact, Renée's talent for drawing fashionable, as well as capable, women gave the strip a little extra oomph. And if the guys read for the sex appeal and the girls read to fantasize themselves as a glamorous, swashbuckling lady spy, who could quibble?

But the war couldn't last forever. In *Fight Comics* #37 (April 1945), with the "Nazi menace in its death-agonies," Señorita Rio went back to Hollywood. Clark Gable, Jimmy Durante, Lana Turner, Abbott and Costello, and all the rest welcomed her back, probably all on leave from the *Black Cat* strip. Then she was whisked away by plane to Mexico to deal with an ex-Nazi agent suspected of fooling around with atomic energy. The war might be over. Spying was not.

By the next issue, Rio picked up a sidekick of sorts in a girl called Suzy. She caught the little one playing dress-up with her wardrobe. "Golly gee, Miss Rio, Ah sure hope yo' wont mind too much," said Suzy. "Y'see, back in Texas, well … you were kinda my idol. So—Ah decided Ah'd be a movie star, too!" Rio had her put on a new suit of clothes, more suitable for action, and went to save the girl when she later got captured. Luckily, Suzy was capable of a mean kick or two herself, and ended the story by hog-tying the main villain quite smartly. Unfortunately, that was Suzy's only appearance.

Renée gave way to other artists, including possibly Jack Kamen. But by *Fight Comics* #65 (December 1949), a spectacular but brief creator change was made. Fiction House was publishing *The Spirit* as a comic book. For all of two issues, the crew of *The Spirit*—possibly including Eisner himself—produced the Señorita Rio stories in *Fight*. They were well-nigh as excellent as a *Spirit Section* themselves.

The first such story, "The Affair of the Liquid Gold," started with an achingly beautiful headshot of Rio beside what appeared to be a calendar, dripping leaves with an amended origin story on them. In this version, Señorita Rio was said to be Consuela Maria Ascencion De Las Vegas, whose husband, Luis De Las Vegas, was killed by fascist agents in 1940. We can put this down to mere revisionism and continue with the story.

Señorita Rio, accompanied by a reporter named Jack Stat, who was to be a short-lived supporting character, survived numerous attempts on her life with the unique perspective and balloon lettering of the Eisner crew. After these brushes with death, she bewigged herself in one of her rare disguises and offered herself to gangsters as the woman who could find Señorita Rio and deliver her. An expertly thrown knife convinced them.

The case proceeded with an oil well fire, an attempted swindling, and another attempt on Rio's life. She saved herself by turning a stream of gushing oil on a car full of hoodlums, and survived for her next case, offering Jack Stat a date. All in all, it was easily the best-drawn Rio story to date.

Fight Comics #66 (January 1950) continued in the same vein, with the *Spirit* crew pitting Rio and Jack against a German baron who planned on carving out a South American empire. The fact that Jack didn't know Rio in this story indicates that it might have been prepared before the story in the previous issue. At any rate, what mattered was the art and writing, and there was quality aplenty in that.

With issue #67 (March 1950), Rio was back to the regular bunch of Fiction House artists and writers. She continued on, missing only #69 (July 1950) along the way, before ending her run in *Fight Comics* #71 (November 1950) with a story of phony flying saucers.

Was that the end of the fair Señorita? Of course not. Bill Black at AC Comics made sure to reprint a batch of her original stories and had her as part of the original, World War II–era Femforce in *Femforce Special* #1 (1984). Later, in *Femforce: The Untold Origin* #1 (1989), Señorita Rio—often referred to as Rio Rita—was revealed

Will Eisner's studio steps in for a two-story run on Señorita Rio. © 1949 Fight Stories, Inc.

to have stayed in undercover work for the government up to that day. By that time, she had a granddaughter, a new Rita Farrar, who was a spy herself. The new Rio Rita undertook more than a few missions with the modern Femforce, and did her grandma proud.

Rip Carson lasted even longer. He also premiered in *Fight Comics* #19 (June

1942) and went all the way to #85 (Spring 1953), the penultimate issue. He was billed as Rip Carson, Chute Trooper throughout the war years, which was appropriate: Rip was an Army guy who parachuted into danger, of which there was a lot. Other than that, and being the toughest guy in the stories, he was a cipher.

The first story, credited to "Rollin Bell" but drawn by Jack Kamen, introduced us to Rip. He was shown parachuting on the first page and in a silent inset profile panel. No captions, no dialogue. The story itself began in the first panel proper, dated January 20, 1942, only a few weeks after Pearl Harbor. Rip was shown pounding the heck out of Japanese soldiers ("Come on, you #$%?!! Rats!"). He suffered an unknown injury, apparently to his arm.

Rip Carson rips into a scene to save a bunch of good guys from Japanese torture. © 1942 Fight Stories, Inc.

The story segued from the battle to a hospital bed, with Rip in pajamas and his right arm in a sling. A comely nurse, Peg, was feeding him medicine. ("If you don't take it, I'll pour it down your throat, you lug!") He went out on the drill field, still arm-slung, to watch his buddies drill. The sergeant (referred to as "Sarg," and named Mulligan a few issues later) told him to get on the field or go back to the hospital. A few seconds later, Sarg wanted "the toughest, meanest guy in this outfit to step up!"

Who could it be other than Rip?

He might be "half-dead," he might have his arm in a sling, but this was America we were talking about. "The trouble with these gents is that they want to live too long…. I'm your man, Sarg!" The Sarg gave him the assignment and made a point of escorting Peg off the field. Even with his injuries, Rip Carson parachuted into enemy territory, knocked out a troop of Japanese, blew up a building, and might have won the war right there if a sneaky guy hadn't bonked him on the head with a rifle butt from behind.

Following this, Rip got tortured with bamboo shoots under his fingernails, fainted, came to, was betrayed by a Nazi girl-spy and shot in the shoulder, knocked her out, blew up another building, captured a machine gun, and was pot-shotting the enemy by the time American paratroopers showed up. Sarg was on hand: "Say, don't look now, but you're bleeding to death!" In the next scene, Rip was back in a hospital bed. He didn't want to be, but this time Peg was firm: he was going to stay there, and she'd go to a dance with Sarg just to show him. Oh, well, you can't always get the girl.

Rip was hardly out of place in a comic world of Axis-smashers, but he did well enough to hold his place in the comic for all but one of the rest of the run, and on 23 covers to boot. By issue #34 (October 1944), he'd made sergeant. Sgt. Mulligan and Peg had faded away months ago. There were also the usual surfeit of pin-up girls, a requirement of almost every Fiction House strip, but few complained.

When the war ended, as it did for many a comic hero a year beyond the real thing, Rip wound up with a new gig. *Fight Comics* #45 (August 1946) had him and three new pals, Tex, Brooklyn, and Chet, waiting for a flight home. Instead, they got captured by a gang of hoods who had commandeered a plane and were trying to use it to hijack a shipment of gold. Our heroes took command, blew up a shipload of pirates, and "persuaded" the crooks to sell them the plane. They painted a name on the plane's exterior: RISKS, UNLIMITED. And for all but the last couple of stories, the strip was billed as "Risks, Unlimited Starring Rip Carson."

Rip and company did their share of global troubleshooting, but by the time of the Korean War they were back in government service. By the last few issues, Rip appeared to have rejoined the service, and in the last two stories the title reverted to just *Rip Carson*. *Fight* managed only a couple of issues in 1953. By 1954, it was converted to a war comic with no continuing characters. That was its last gasp.

Hooks Devlin, Special Agent, started his assignments in *Fight Comics* #20 (August 1942), an issue later than Rio and Rip. He was introed on the first page of his debut story as private eye Armitage X. Devlin, locking up his private eye office and dressed in a Navy outfit, having just been drafted into the Marines. His nickname was Hooks, evidently in reference to the punches he threw. On page 2, a damsel in distress he rescued handed him a naval order countermanding his orders to report for duty. She was an admiral's daughter, her daddy had been kidnapped, and they needed Hooks to find him. So, with the help of the girl (one Peaches Tootly), he did, rescuing the admiral from a nest of Nazi spies. All he wanted, he said, was to see some action with the Marines.

Hooks eventually got with the Gyrenes, but Peaches kept hanging around and, for his early issues, Naval Intelligence kept giving him detective work. He did it so well, who could blame them? Before long, Hooks was assigned to something called the "X-Bureau" and was put to work detecting and fighting homeland spies, with Peaches hanging on in every episode. He was out of uniform before the war's end and went back to his civilian life in 1945 as a detective. The strip finally ended its run with *Fight Comics* #69 (July 1950).

In issue #44 (June 1946), *Shark Brodie* went overboard and the crew piped on *Captain Fight*. He had nothing to do with the superhero of the same name who was in issues #16–19. The new Captain Fight was an old English buccaneer, roughly a clone of the Hawk. The first caption had this for an intro: "Who is he? A murderer? An honest sea captain had been killed! A looter? The dead man's ship had vast wealth aboard! This swashbuckling adventurer's crew would follow him to the ends of the earth. Yet others would follow as far to see Fight hang!"

That being said, and with a pic of Captain Fight kicking an armed enemy in the gut without rising from his chair, we got down to the story. Fight (who apparently had no other name) came into port with his mate Hawkins, carrying in the brig of his ship a villain named Trent, who had murdered said "honest sea captain," Sutton by name. To make things complicated, the rumor in town was that Fight had actually killed Sutton, and Sutton's young son Rusty was out to get revenge. The boy threw a mean knife, but missed. Trent's sister Jane Clark (hey, we didn't say the names had to match) inveigled the boy into helping her sneak aboard Fight's ship and freeing the pirate. The dastard took Fight captive and threatened to blow up his enemy's ship. But Rusty overheard Trent admit his guilt, put out the fuse, and banged into Trent's craft with Fight's ship. With a sword at his chest, Fight kicked Trent in the labonza, drew sword, dueled with him, and ran him through. Afterward, Fight asked, "Well, Rusty, think you could learn to be a cabin boy?" "Gee, sure!" responded the kid.

Captain Fight was penciled ably by Alex Blum, and possibly written by his daughter Toni. The captain's swashes were neatly buckled through *Fight Comics* #69 (July 1950).

The only other character of note in the book was Madame Zero, who had three 4-page adventures in issues #82–84 (September 1952–Winter 1952–53). She was a mysterious blonde Commie-fighting spy, not exactly Señorita Rio but in the same business. Madame Zero wasn't bad but didn't last. She probably wasn't meant to.

Fight continued through issue #86 (January 1954), with none of its usual heroes lasting to the final issue. Fiction House was folding its tent.

There was one other notable title (besides *Wings Comics*, which has been covered in other histories): *Rangers Comics*.

Originally, *Rangers* was titled *Rangers of Freedom*, with its first issue dated October 1941. It was named after the costumed kid gang, the Rangers of Freedom, that appeared on the cover and in the first story. Dan Zolnerowich did the cover shot, depicting the three red-white-and-blue-costumed kids and a bunch of factory workers (and the inevitable pin-up girl) fighting the megacephalic Super-Brain and his Fascist followers.

The splash of the first page was thematically the same, except the Super-Brain wasn't among the madmen the three Rangers were fighting. We got their names in a caption—Biff Barkley, Tex Russell, and Percy Cabot—and saw some newspaper headlines indicating sabotage was running riot in America. (It seemed to do that just for superheroes to have something to do.) This time all the lunatic asylums were opened, decades before that happened in real life, and all the inmates were turned loose to riot on America. Also, political radicals "seize[d] the chance to attack Democracy," and things were in pretty bad shape, obviously.

All but three boys, the aforementioned Biff, Tex, and Percy, who were posing onstage in swim trunks as the winners of a bodybuilding contest. They got their prizes from a bathing-suited Miss America and were whisked off by the FBI

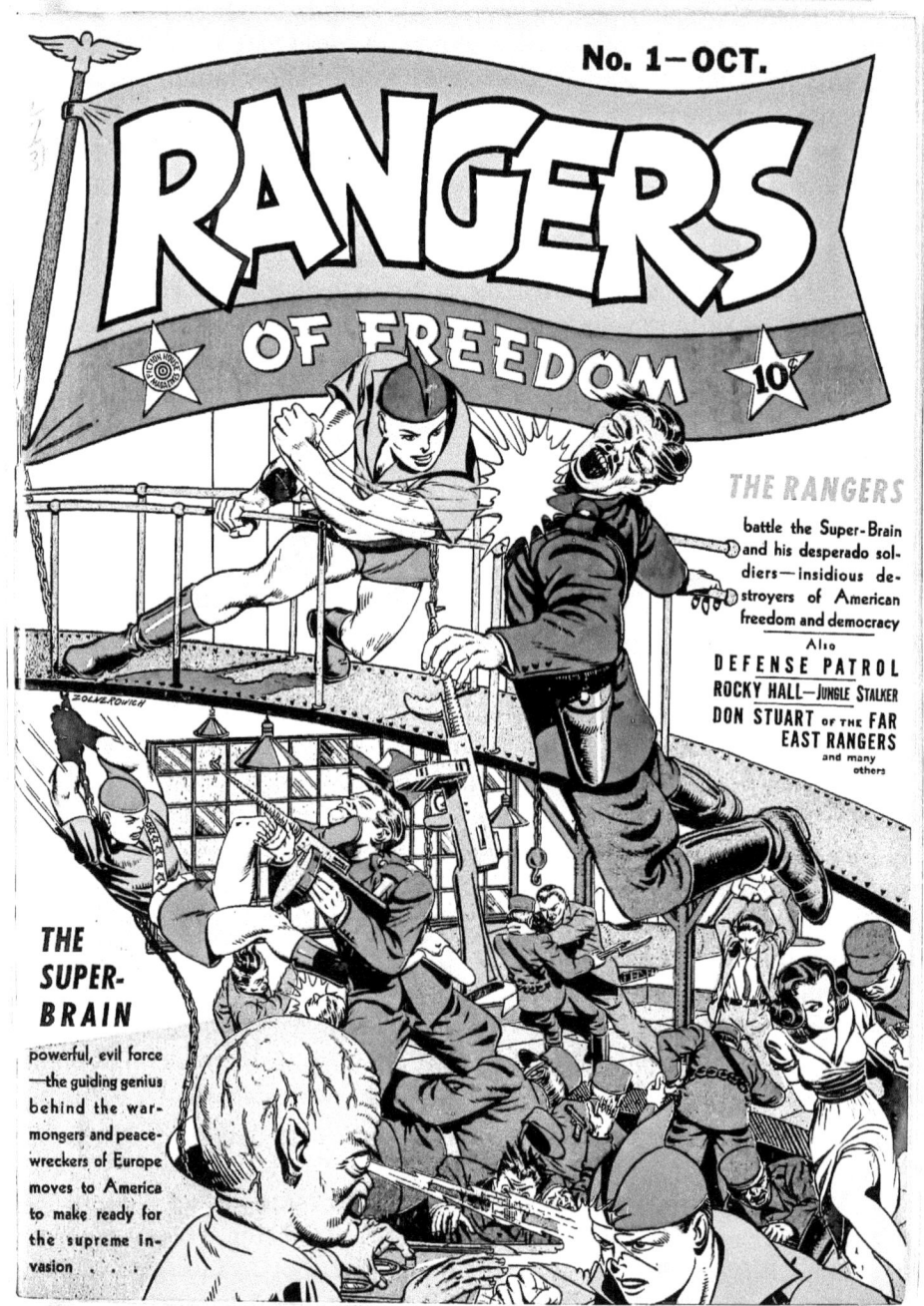

The Rangers of Freedom battle the Super-Brain! © 1941 Flying Stories Inc.

afterward. All three of them went to a behind-closed-doors meeting in Washington, D.C. There they were told that "a mysterious mental force" which only "young minds" could resist was threatening the country, and "America calls on you to risk your lives as the Rangers of Freedom!"

"You bet!" said one of the three. "When do we start?"

The three Rangers donned "impenetrable uniforms" of red and blue, which somehow didn't cover their very penetrable arms, legs, or faces, and beat the heck out of a loony mob which was out to destroy a factory. With his dying breath, a wounded saboteur mentioned the "Super-Brain." More mayhem followed until the young heroes were subdued and brought to meet the Super-Brain himself.

The Brain, definitely the most impressive part of the story, was a villain with a small body but a truly swelled head, at least three times normal size, his regular-sized face grinning ruthlessly at the bottom of it with fangs. He got around in a wheelchair, which made him almost a forerunner of Green Lantern's 1960s foe, Hector Hammond. The Super-Brain appeared without benefit of origin or explanation. He simply was, he hated America, and he had a mind-control gimmick that could bend people to his will. It even looked, for a time (Gasp!), that he had the Rangers in his power. He also had Miss America in tow and threatened to marry her. But somehow (I really don't want to rehash the whole story), the doughty Rangers of Freedom saved Miss America, saved the president, resisted the mind-machine, and sent the Super-Brain packing. "We just made it!" said one Ranger. "America is free again!" said another. (It was awfully hard to tell which Ranger was which.) That was it.

The art was decent and the story no more boneheaded than dozens of others out there (not really a recommendation). With the next issue, it was revealed that the saga was really taking place in 1948, that Hitler was alive in that year, and that he was Super-Brain's stooge. The Brain forced Der Fuehrer to take over South America so he could use it as a strike-point against America. New York was taken (Boo! Hiss!). The Nazis were apparently unharmable. Even Washington, D.C., fell. It began to look as though the writer was cribbing from the Purple Invasion saga in *Operator No. 5*, a pulp of the time.

The brass found out that the Nazis were inoculated with a death-proofing serum. The Rangers, accompanied by Miss America, whose name was given as Gloria Travis, finally succeeded in de-immortalizing the Nazis. The U.S. armed forces beat the Nazis back, the Rangers drove away the Super-Brain, and Miss America showed herself an excellent fighter pilot while she wasn't busy showing off her legs.

By the next issue, Miss America was dubbed "Ranger Girl" and was wearing the same outfit as the boys. There was a little artistic effort expended to distinguish Tex from Percy from Biff. But Super-Brain was still around, and still making trouble. They also encountered a Chicago gangster named Scarface and a midget detective called Phineas B. Tutts. The plot involved a plan of the Brain's to sabotage a combat exercise between two Army groups. The story, thankfully, seemed to be set back in 1942. Altogether, the scripting was vastly improved and the feature lurched toward the readable.

Super-Brain was still around for *Rangers of Freedom* #4 (April 1942). But that story, a rip-roaring episode set in Hawaii, was the last for him. Things had gotten serious in the meantime with Pearl Harbor, and the young Rangers of Freedom were about to start playing with the Big Boys.

Though the kid Rangers showed up in costume on the cover of issue #5 (June 1942), on the inside the story featured American soldiers trapped during the Japanese offensive of December 7, 1941. The opening scene showed a blond American soldier hefting a Japanese adversary on the end of his rifle's bayonet, a boy blasting bloodily away at other enemies with a machine gun, and the other Japanese from Central Casting getting what-for. The soldier was one Captain Morgan, the kid was Peter Rogers, son of a missionary who had been killed by the invaders, and a third member of the group was Native American John Red Hawk, another soldier. They vowed to fight a guerrilla war against the Japanese until aid could be gotten from the U.S., and to find Peter's missing mother.

In the meantime, Ranger Girl had opted to join the Red Cross as a nurse, and Tex, Biff, and Percy, in Army uniforms, got a radio message from Captain Morgan and came to his aid. The story that followed pitted Morgan, the Rangers, Peter, and a girl spy against the Black Dragon Society and a Nazi agent called the Tigress. After running a gauntlet of deadly perils and deceits, the heroes won the day and stayed under the supervision of Morgan. A new, more realistic incarnation of the Rangers of Freedom had taken shape. Captain Morgan, John Red Hawk, and Peter now constituted the group. Tex, Biff, and Percy were gone by the next issue.

With issue #8 (December 1942), the book was renamed *Rangers Comics* and Captain Morgan's feature was redubbed *U.S. Rangers*. They waged guerrilla warfare against the Japanese on the Malay peninsula for another issue, and then somehow hooked up with the U.S. Command, were liberated, and went on to fight on other fronts. The art, by the likes of Rudy Palais, George Tuska, and Bob Lubbers, was usually good and sometimes excellent.

Red Hawk got lost somewhere along the way, leaving Captain Morgan and Peter to fight the Japanese some months beyond V-J Day in the real world. There was almost always a good-looking girl, sometimes two, sometimes on our side, sometimes not. The two heroes subsisted on occupation tales and now-it-can-be-told stories until issue #29 (June 1946),

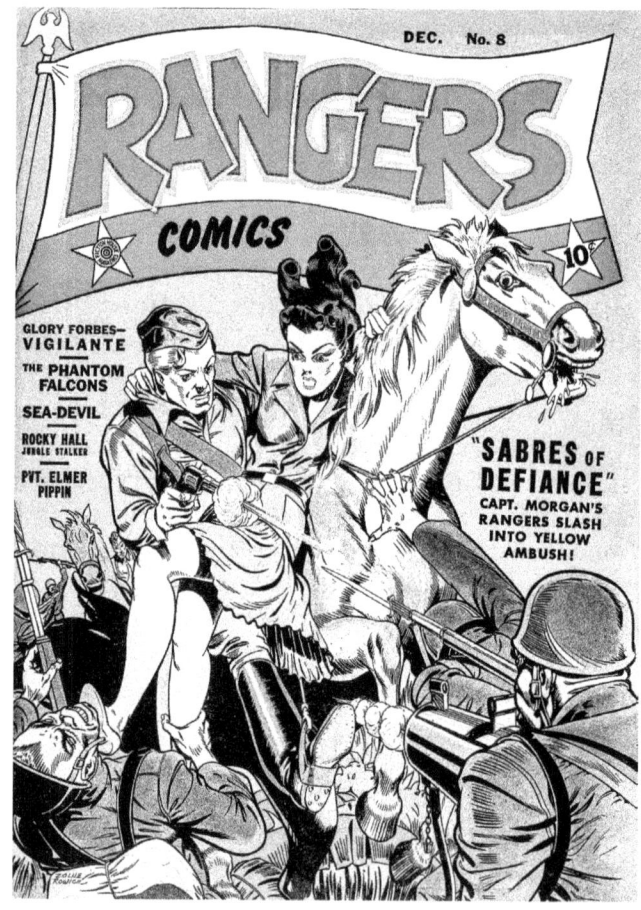

Captain Morgan thoughtfully lets a woman ride sidesaddle as he blasts the Japanese. © 1942 Flying Stories, Inc.

when a final caption promised "[a] startling new role for Captain Morgan in the next Rangers Comics!"

The "new role" was signaled by the renaming of the feature to *Sky Rangers* with the next issue (#30, August 1946). On the opening page, we learned that Morgan and Peter were out of the service, that Morgan had bought a plane with his savings, and that the two of them were employed as troubleshooters by an oil tycoon named Graham, aka the "Tall Texan." They saved Graham's hash from evildoers in the first of the new-format stories and continued in the same way through *Rangers Comics* #55 (October 1950). By that time, the feature was being drawn by Jack Kamen quite competently. But it was put quietly away, never to be revived.

Outside of *Rangers of Freedom*, only the *Rocky Hall* strip from *Rangers Comics* #1 lasted very long (12 issues), and we've covered that in chapter 1. The other features in the first issue didn't last beyond issue #4. Just about all of them were about kid gangs. *The Royal Watch* was a group of British youth in the Night Watch, looking for spies and often finding them. *The Defense Kids* were eight boys from Steel City who caught and beat up a saboteur and became special agents for the FBI. *Jeep Milarkey* was a military policeman in a semiserious vehicle played for laughs as much as action. *The Anzac Hawks* were three Australian kids, two boys and a girl, who patroled the coast in an autogiro. *The Sea Squad*, one of the few strips about adults, featured five seagoing friends in search of treasure, their only resource an old salt who knew about pirate booty but couldn't remember where it was stashed. *Don Stuart of the Far East Rangers* was an American youth in China who partnered with his pals Sing Hi and Sing Lo to fight the Japanese. All of these features perished with issue #4 (April 1942), apparently the first post–Pearl Harbor issue, except for *The Sea Squad* and *The Anzac Hawks*, which died after their debuts.

Two new offerings came up with issue #2: *Pvt. Elmer Pippin and the Colonel's Daughter* and *The Double-Slango Kids*. *Elmer* was a typical Army-laughs strip, with the title hero a Wrong-Way Corrigan kind of guy and the colonel's daughter a beauty he longed for. It had some staying power, surviving till *Rangers Comics* #18 (August 1944). The Double-Slangoes were a waste of time, being a couple of kids who sent verbally coded messages to each other in a variant on pig Latin. They managed a whole two appearances.

A little more interesting was the short-lived *Tex Rainger* strip, which debuted in *Rangers of Freedom* #4 (April 1942). Tex was a kid cowboy, son of Ace Rainger, a sheriff who was killed in the first story by outlaws he'd sent to jail previously. With his dying breaths, Ace made Tex swear not to kill, not to be "judge and jury," but left him his guns and saddle. Tex grimly buried his dad, swore "to help bring law and order to Texas," and then rode off with his horse Calico and brought the dastards in.

The odd riff in Tex's strip was his sidekick, Jackie Taylor. He met up with her in issue #5 (June 1942) and she was a rough-ridin', sure-shootin' daughter of a gun. But from the way she was dressed, in shirt, 10-gallon hat and jeans, Tex thought for sure she was a guy. Since Jackie took a shine to Tex, and was afraid he'd desert her if he knew she was a girl, she took up cross-dressing with a vengeance. This led to some interesting shenanigans in the strip, especially, for example, when a swimming hole presented itself. Tex's strip ended with issue #8 (December 1942). If he ever learned Jackie's secret, it was after that.

Of course, by *Rangers of Freedom* #5 (June 1942), America was at war and the editors took things in hand, clearing out deadwood and building a lineup of strips that could and would endure. The kid strips were mostly booted out and grown-up Adventurers came aboard. Thankfully, they were more interesting and they endured.

The Phantom Falcons had a dynamite premise: a bunch of "misfits" who couldn't join the Army Air Force but weren't about to miss out on the action. The first story commenced with Japanese planes firing on a small life raft off the jungle coast of Australia. Said raft bore two occupants, an adult male and a kid, who managed to escape being perforated. But just as the man shook his fist and vowed vengeance, three Airacobras with a silver bird insignia dropped in from nowhere and shot down three Japanese bombers, forcing the rest to flee. The man, one John Lovelace, and his cabin boy pard, Bud, trailed the Airacobras to a secret cave hangar nearby. There they were taken captive by the Phantom Falcons, who couldn't afford to let their secrets get out.

The Falcons were led by Jock Sturtevant, a "rich New York sportsman"; Ace Ely, "holder of many air records," who had lost his legs and had to be helped into his cockpit; and Peg Darnell, a beauty who was darned well determined to show them she could fly and fight as well as any man. And she could. Jock said, "You're the worst of all—a woman who wants a man's glory!" The look she gave him would have detonated a ton of TNT.

Several other mechanics and aides made up the Phantom Falcons. John Lovelace wangled his way aboard Peg's plane when she needed a tail gunner. When enemy planes made a pass-by, the Falcons went up after them. Peg was wounded in battle, forcing Lovelace to take over. He shot down every Japanese plane in his way, and even though his tailfin was damaged, brought Peg and himself back safely. "Why didn't you tell me you could fly?" asked Peg. "You didn't ask me," he said. Lovelace and Bud were welcomed into the Falcons, and the story ended. Art Saaf was the artist on it. Their missions continued through the war, all the way to *Rangers Comics* #21 (February 1945).

Glory Forbes, Vigilante came next. For an intro, the splash panel showed a monstrous fanged Japanese about to stab an American to death in a rat-filled cellar. But up from a trap door appeared Glory Forbes, a brunette beauty in a red dress, toting a gun and ready to use it.

"The vigilante spirit of the roaring Old West comes to life as alert America battles Axis lawlessness in defense of our lives, our fortunes, our sacred honor.... Glory Forbes proves that wits and courage can defeat the most ruthless enemy...."

Well, that, a killer body, and an ever-ready gun. She was, as it happened, the daughter of one Ludwig Forbes, a designer of bombers for Uncle Sam. Glory got kidnapped in San Francisco, and was doped by an Asian bad guy called Yaki Su who worked for a spy ring called the Scarlet Crab. Yaki assigned Glory to kill her own father while in a hypnotized state. Her swain, FBI agent Randy Duncan, and her pal, a paperboy named Billy, got on her trail and prevented her from sinking a knife into

Glamorous Glory Forbes, Vigilante. © 1942 Flying Stories, Inc.

her dad's back. She came to her senses and led the crew on a counterattack against the Japanese agent. The Scarlet Crab apparently committed hari-kari, and Glory had her first recorded adventure.

Rey Isip was the first *Glory* artist and continued on the feature for the next few issues. In the next story, Randy was posted to Naval Intelligence and Glory found her way into more trouble. Yaki Su was still alive and fomenting trouble at a Tijuana racetrack. Glory got drugged again the same way and this time, under her enemy's spell, shot a guard for him. But the shock of the incident brought her back to sanity, and she and Randy once again foiled the Japanese spy's plans.

The next story went pretty much the same way with the same cast. Yaki Su remained the villain through issue #10 (April 1943), after which both he and Randy Duncan did a vanishing act. Glory got into a number of catfights with female enemy agents and won every one of them. On the logo, the "V" of "Glory Forbes, Vigilante" was enlarged in a big V-for-Victory motif. Glory was on her own, and she was ready for it.

Glory functioned as an amateur spybuster for a few more issues and then switched to solving regular crimes. Every now and then daddy Ludwig showed up, but Randy and Yaki Su were gone for good. The strip got more cheesecakey with our heroine decked out in bathing suits as often as possible. Nobody much complained. George Tuska assumed the art chores with *Rangers Comics* #17 (June 1944) and rendered the brunette bombshell quite effectively. Glory was definitely a Fiction House femme fatale.

The "Vigilante" label was finally dropped from the strip and she was revealed (appropriately, while bikini-clad) as an FBI agent. Her enlistment happened offstage, but a lot of things in early comics were like that. Humor became as much of an ingredient in the Glory stories as mystery and good-girl art.

George Tuska departed circa issue #35 (June 1947). In the following issue, either Matt Baker or somebody trying awfully hard to look like him took over the feature. Glory, formerly a black-haired bombshell, now had a light brown hair color. With it came a ditzier personality and a status as a private investigator. By issue #43 (October 1948), Glory had become a blonde. It seemed appropriate. Glory Forbes finally wound up her tour of duty in *Rangers Comics* #48 (August 1949), and has not been heard from since.

The Sea Devil was the next strip to see the light of day, in *Rangers of Freedom* #5 (June 1942). The *Sea Devil* was a two-man sub, designed by inventor Alexander Dewey, captained by his son, Ensign Heck Dewey, and crewed by a guy named Swenson. They sunk a Nazi U-boat in the first adventure. Heck got captured by Germans, then freed by a beauty in a bathing suit, and clambered aboard the sub again to sink the enemy craft. The girl, one Cora Wood, was revealed in the next issue to be a double agent working against the Krauts. It was an unremarkable strip, but it existed till *Rangers Comics* #22 (April 1945).

Rangers still had a few more changes to undergo. The next one was the addition of *The Werewolf Hunter* in issue #8 (December 1942). This was *Rangers*' first outright plunge into the supernatural, as a bona fide werewolf menaced a girl in the splash panel, with the hero, Danny O'Shea, entering from stage left. The opening caption read, in part: "Werewolfery (see lycanthropy, Encyclopedia Britanica) plays a prominent part in the legends of almost every land. …[I]t has never been accepted by science or modern research, yet is not wholly unsubstantiated. …It is hardly strange, therefore, that in this year of 1942, when war rages all over the earth, when nations are locked in a death-struggle and men are being slaughtered by tens of

PAGE 19

Who's afraid of the big bad werewolf? Not the Werewolf Hunter! © 1942 Flying Stories, Inc.

thousands, there should be an awakening of this usually dormant wolf-like lust to kill."

Indeed. The story was set in New Orleans, the home of Professor Broussard, who had made "a life-long hobby of studying werewolfery and the black arts...." In short order, a girl named Marie was set upon by a werewolf. She managed to contact

Broussard by telephone. He came running with Marie's grandfather Michele, who came too late to stop the attack but in time to save her life. Broussard's assistant, Danny O'Shea, burst in a few seconds later. They tracked the culprit to an artist's garret at the wharves, fought the werewolf, and dosed him with chloroform. Luckily or unluckily, the dosage was too much, and the werewolf, an artist while in human form, died. That finished up the first story.

George Tuska became the artist on the next episode, and Broussard and Danny kept the fur flying in their vendetta against the lycanthropic menace. Broussard's daughter Lily joined the group in *Rangers Comics* #10 (April 1943) and helped them track down yet another werewolf, who turned out to be a female this time. If Lily had been the lead, the strip could have been a precursor to *Buffy the Vampire Slayer*, only with Lon Chaney types instead of Bela Lugosis.

Since werewolves weren't specifically tied to the war (and the strip wasn't, either), *The Werewolf Hunter* continued all the way to *Rangers Comics* #41 (June 1948). By that time, the three heroes had dropped out of the strip and it became a collection of weird tales from Professor Broussard's casebook, sometimes not even involving wolf-men. The feature faded away.

In *Rangers Comics* #9 (February 1943), the *Commando Rangers* made their brief stand. The first splash showed an effective scene of a squad of American soldiers in battle with a horde of Nazis. On the next page, we were introed to the Rangers themselves, a four-man unit led by Sgt. Dan Austin of Waco, Texas. They were sent into occupied France just for reconnaissance, but quickly found themselves bound to save an underground newspaper publisher, a British girl-spy, and a guerrilla chief from execution. The boys took on the extra work and, with the help of local patriots, saved the day. For the Rangers, it was another day's labor. They held forth till issue #12 (August 1943).

Commando Ranger, a masked hero treated elsewhere, replaced them in the next issue. The lineup held more or less stable until 1945. With issue #21 (February 1945), Fiction House began looking toward the post-war future. Though the cover didn't show it, *Rangers* produced its first new star: the furious *Firehair*!

The opening caption read: "It happened yesterday ... yesterday, when America was wild and raw and young.... Beginning an epic saga of the West that will never die, and of a girl that fate named 'Firehair!'"

The story was written by John Marshall as "John Starr" and drawn by Lee Elias. The opening page depicted two Bostonians, J. B. Smith and his daughter Princess (revealed some issues later as a nickname, but it was the only name she had in this story), who came West to a frontier town in a stagecoach. "From now on we're Westerners, Princess.... Boston, the past, we'll forget it all, eh?"

"If you say so, Dad!" said the lovely redhead. She got fixed up with more frontier-friendly clothes and accompanied her dad aboard a wagon train. But folks of a more unsavory sort had taken notice, and among them was a mustachioed gent named Fingers. Said gent dressed himself and his gang up as Indians and led a raiding party on the train to grab the guns and wealth it was transporting.

J. B. Smith died of an arrow to the chest. Princess tried to hold the reins of the horses pulling the wagon, but couldn't control them. Within minutes, the members of the wagon train were massacred, and a locked satchel belonging to Smith was taken away. Princess was left for dead, and certainly looked the part.

However, a true Indian, one named Little Ax, had been watching the scene from afar. When the raiders left, he approached, found the girl still barely alive, and took her to his tribe's village. Specifically, he took her to a shaman named Two Horns, who managed to bring her back to life. But Princess's mind had been harmed by the tragedy. She could barely remember anything of her former life. Many of the tribe, fearing her presence would cause white men to blame them for the massacre, were in favor of cutting her loose.

But Little Ax was the son of Chief Tehama, and was allowed to decide her fate. "The black of death still shades her mind—she cannot speak her name—but until she can—I claim her my captive by the ancient laws—and my knife defends the claim!" So saying, he threw his knife into the ground near Princess. "She is mine, Great Spirit—my sister ... and I will make her well and take care of her!"

The furious Firehair saves an Indian kid from an eagle. No talk of symbolism, now. © 1948 Flying Stories, Inc.

"And the days passed and the seasons changed, and tomorrow she would win the name that the Western winds had carried far—FIREHAIR!" That finished the first episode. Though she wasn't on the cover, Firehair was destined to be the star of *Rangers Comics*.

The next issue continued the story. Fingers and his gang, on the next spring after the massacre, tried raiding Firehair's village when the men were out at the horse races. But he hadn't reckoned on the redhead's recovery, her strength, or her skill with the bow or her horse. She took down one thief with a tomahawk to the skull. Then she grabbed her victim's gun, shot down two other crooks, and drove away Fingers, who was now wounded, and the rest of his gang. Later, nursing his wound, Fingers revealed that he still couldn't force open the chest that had belonged to Firehair's father. He further opined that the girl could tie them to Smith's murder, and that she'd have to be sent to the happy hunting grounds.

In the next issue (*Rangers Comics* #23, June 1945), Firehair, who now wore a blue halter and fringed skirt, was targeted for death by Fingers, who had finally smashed open the chest and found money, jewelry, and deeds to valuable property within. Firehair was grazed by a gunshot, but it brought back her memory. She tracked down her father's murderer and his minions and gave battle. The tribe followed her, played backup, and captured Fingers and his men. By story's end, Firehair had to decide what to do with the wealth from her father's chest.

The decision seemed to be made by the next issue: Firehair said her tearful farewells to the tribe. Her given name was revealed as Lynn Cabot, and her father was inexplicably renamed John Cabot. But it wasn't as though anyone was keeping a tally of names. At any rate, Firehair boarded a packet boat to return to Boston and claim her estate. As one might expect, it wasn't that easy. Villains aboard the ship threw her overboard and a girl crook donned a red wig to impersonate her and claim her wealth. The whole thing was a plot of lawyer John Prescott, who'd schemed to take the Cabot estate for himself. But Firehair fought, shot, and stormed her way back to bring the gang to justice, and claimed her wealth herself. She was no wilting lily.

The Firehair stories surged on, with a heroine midway between the white and Indian worlds, rich enough and tough enough to protect herself and those of her clan. Fiction House didn't put her on the cover for some time after issue #22, but she was the lead feature from her debut. Finally, in 1948, they came to their senses, plastered Firehair on the cover spot again with issue #40 (April 1948), and kept her there through her last appearance (*Rangers Comics* #65, June 1952).

Lee Elias drew the redheaded rider through issue #29 (June 1946), after which he was spelled by August Froehlich and Bob Lubbers in #30 (August 1946). Then Lubbers, some years away from his syndicated *Robin Malone* strip, soloed on the feature. Like Elias, Lubbers was great at drawing attractive women, and *Firehair* didn't falter in his hands. As "John Starr," John Marshall probably wrote all the stories.

Such was the heroine's popularity that she won her own comic. *Firehair* #1 was dated Winter 1948 and featured four stories of the Western wildcat. By issue #3 (Spring 1950) it was renamed *Pioneer West Romances*, but carried a big FIREHAIR on the logo. With #8 (Summer 1951), it went back to being just plain *Firehair*, and so it continued to its last issue (#11, Spring 1952).

Firehair was a great character in a memorable strip. Unfortunately, Fiction House was closing up shop, and the Wertham-era criticism of sexy comic book females took its toll. Four issues before the end, with a redrawn story from an earlier script, Firehair faded from *Rangers Comics*. It didn't last long without her.

Six years later, IW-Super exhumed a copy of *Rangers Comics* #57 (February 1951) and reprinted it with a different cover as *Firehair* #8 (1958). AC Comics had her do an unheralded cameo in *Bizarre Thrills* #1 (1977) and reprinted some of her stories from 1991 to 2011. But, since 1952, she has not reappeared in a substantial new story.

Rangers expanded from 36 pages to 52 in the postwar era and used the allotment to premier its next new feature. Though the cover space of issue #28 (April 1946) was given to the U.S. Rangers, the cover blurb read: "The strange tale of a man's death—and from that death rises an unknown figure—a living ghost that strikes terror to the underworld. *Tiger Man!*"

The strip, with art by Rodlow Willard, opened with a splash panel of one Lt. Robert Benton, bare-chested and next door to dead, bleeding (yellowly) on the slab where he was placed while a Burmese witch doctor performed surgery on him with a bone knife. Surprisingly, there was a female nurse of sorts in a sarong, with a tray of surgical instruments that looked more modern; maybe the doctor just liked the old style. Chained to a board, standing upright, was a tiger. The spirit of Benton was rising from a pool of water in a basin. Altogether, it needed a bit of explanation.

We faded in on a U.S. bomber doing a run over Burma, apparently just after the dropping of the first atomic bomb. The bomber, crewed by Benton and his planemate Doc, promptly got hit by lightning and crashed. Neither one was particularly adept at jungle survival, Doc was wounded, and Benton went bonkers, seeing Japanese that weren't there. One of those things he superimposed a Japanese fighter over was a tiger. The tiger was menacing some natives, but Benton didn't give that much of a damn. He just took a stick and attacked the big cat.

This didn't turn out too nicely, and the Burmese intervened to finally kill the tiger after it had done a number on Benton. Doc, dying from exposure, poured sulfa powder on Benton's bleeding chest. A witch doctor put Benton on a table, chained the tiger next to him, and performed a spell that infused the spirit of the tiger into Benton. He stirred from the table, alive, alive-o. But, still delirious, he saw an image of a tiger menacing his long-time fiancée Jan, took an axe, and smashed the idol behind his hallucination. Benton, recovering (though Doc was a goner), was given a secret ring and custody of Pali, the native whose life he had saved from the tiger.

Then he was picked up by the Americans, who found him sporting thirty more pounds of muscle and two inches more of height. He returned to the States as a civilian, Pali in tow, and found that the ring glowed whenever danger was near. There was danger aplenty, and when it struck, Benton found he could summon the tiger's spirit as a totem (shown as a ghostly figure) and strike with a tiger's force. Hence the name Tiger Man.

For all that, Tiger Man prowled through issue #46 (April 1949). He was featured on the cover of *Fight Comics* #86 (January 1954) and in two reprints inside, but that was it.

In *Rangers Comics* #30 (August 1946), another fun series kicked off, even getting the cover spot with the next issue. *Crusoe Island* lasted just eleven installments, and each one was a gem.

Opening with a cameo of Daniel Defoe's Robinson Crusoe, the story splash featured two women and one man asea on a raft, with the man chunking a can of something at a shark who was out for a triple-course lunch. Other cameos introduced us to the dramatis personae: Connie Courtney, a brunette, bespectacled reporter en route to China for an assignment; Paul Harris, Jr., son of an American general; and Princess Loo Fey, out to rejoin her parents in their homeland. With that covered, things commenced to happen.

All three were aboard a China-bound plane which crashed in the sea, apparently killing the two pilots. Connie, Paul, and Loo Fey donned life jackets and survived the crash, within sight of an island, but also within sight of a shark. Paul borrowed Loo Fey's ceremonial knife and fought off the piscatorial predator. Then all three hustled their way across water to the island, where they prepared to learn to survive.

Loo Fey soon had to rescue Connie from a Komodo dragon by jamming a stick in its jaws ("My warrior ancestors would be pleased could they behold their daughter!"). Paul gathered wood and, with the others, began constructing a house. He also found evidence of a trap, which was an indication of another island inhabitant. Said inhabitant was Old Ned, a crazy, white-bearded, peg-legged guy who didn't like company and wasn't about to put up with it. He pushed a boulder onto their log cabin and demolished it, though the threesome escaped. Now our heroes knew that survival on the island would be more than a matter of just finding food and shelter. The story, like those to come, was drawn by H. L. Larsen.

Loo Fey takes aim at her fellow castmates on *Crusoe Island*. © 1947 Flying Stories, Inc.

On the next cover (#31, October 1946), Connie was tied to a dead tree while a horde of half-dressed natives menaced her with a mechanical fire-breathing dragon. Way in the back, Paul charged in, brandishing a gun. For all that, the cover blurb didn't mention Crusoe Island, but you can't have everything.

The next splash did feature Loo Fey and Connie in their bras, which made up for it. In the story, though, both women were fully clothed, which was a lot more logical. Anyway, the threesome found an abandoned ship (which wasn't quite abandoned—Old Ned was secretly aboard), fought off a giant turtle and an octopus to get there, and clambered aboard to find provisions. The women were more intent on trying on the clothes they got there, miraculously in their size.

Old Ned snuck up behind Paul, conked him on the noggin, and threw him to the fish. Then he trapped both Loo Fey and Connie and prepared to do much the same with them. Luckily, Paul revived in time to save the girls from being pitched overboard, and tossed off Old Ned in their place. He was tough enough to survive, though he ended up getting trapped in a net that Loo Fey had rigged on the island. So ended the second story.

By the third, Loo Fey had developed a yen for Paul and was jealous of Connie. That didn't stop Old Ned from escaping his cage, but when a fall from a cliff restored him to sanity, he was there to help the three castaways fight off a bunch of native islanders who didn't like strangers any more than Ned had. The old man died in the conflict, and Connie shed tears for him behind her schoolmarm glasses. So did the other two, even Paul, who turned his back to the others.

The Crusoeites were menaced by a newcomer named Singapore Sid in the next issue, but sent him to a watery grave. Loo Fey proved to be able indeed both at survival and getting rid of bad guys. The story continued onward with her, Paul, and Connie facing various dangers until issue #40 (April 1948), when a rescue ship finally got them off the island. In the last panel, the ghost of Old Ned waved them goodbye.

In the very next issue (#41, June 1948), *I Confess* took their place. This was more or less an anthology series, framed by a radio show hosted by one Myra Maxwell, who also had the byline for the stories. Myra, broadcasting from station WSSI, billed herself as the "radio voice of conscience." She brought on guests who told stories of murders or other crimes they had been involved in or perpetrated. The series was decently drawn and written, and it lasted through issue #53 (June 1950).

The Secret Files of Dr. Drew was the last truly impressive strip to debut in *Rangers Comics*, which it did in issue #47 (June 1949). The feature was initially produced by the Eisner shop, and if the Spirit had chased ghosts instead of crooks, his strip would have looked like this. It was that good.

The same innovative visuals that went into *The Spirit*—oddball angles, deep shadows, panels that leaped off file folders, and the like—were part and parcel of *Dr. Drew*. He appeared in an opera cloak on the splash panel of the first story, lighting a Sherlock Holmes pipe, and saying, impassively, "Good evening. Interested in the supernatural, eh?" If you weren't, you would be by the end of the story.

The opening caption told us that Dr. Drew lived in an old house at the top of Bone Hill in an unnamed city. When you reached it, if he liked you, he would regale you with one of his cases set "in the eerie world that lies somewhere between reality and infinity. If you are made of stern stuff, you will retain your sanity … some of his guests have, you know."

Outside of the fact that he was a consulting detective of the supernatural, we never learned much about Drew. His first name, we learned in issue #49, was Desmond. A later tale revealed that his ancestor, Hamilton Drew, had been a witch-burner. But that was about all we got, and all we needed.

His first story, "The Case of the Absent Floor," dealt with a skyscraper built, like many others, without a 13th floor. An elevator operator from the building came to consult with Dr. Drew. Two passengers, a man and a woman, had entered and demanded to be let off at the 13th floor. There should only have been a blank wall there. Instead, when the operator opened the door, he found another floor, a darkened one, onto which the two passengers stepped. When the operator went back—you guessed it. A blank wall.

Dr. Drew, smoking his meerschaum, went back with the operator to the building at midnight. There, the two of them did manage to emerge onto the spectral 13th floor. They saw a psychodrama of double murder, involving both the passengers who had been taken up earlier—now dead. Seeing Drew and the other man, an angry ghost said, "I created this world for your eyes—and I can destroy it!" He snapped support beams, bringing the spectral world to an end. Drew and the operator raced to the elevator, instants away from disaster, and got away.

Well, for a while, at least. When the operator learned that there was $50,000 in cash from the murder still waiting to be found, he went back in and tried to ascend to the 13th floor. An unexpected but now-familiar guest materialized in the cab, and an explosion occurred between the 12th and 14th floors. The operator's body was found later in the elevator shaft, clutching $50,000 in bills. An inspector, Mr. Beedle, consulted with Drew later and asked how he was going to explain that to his insurance company. "There are things, Mr. Beedle, that simply cannot be explained to insurance companies," said Drew, and filed the case away in a filing cabinet topped with a human skull.

Dr. Drew was written by Marilyn Mercer and drawn up by Jerry Grandenetti and the Eisner shop, all of whom did an exceptional job on the early stories. In the second tale, Drew met the legendary Count St. Germain and discovered the fabled Philosopher's Stone. In the third, he tackled a voodoo doll menace. And on it went from there, every *Spirit*-inspired moment of it.

Vampires, Atlantis, pirate ghosts, they all had their chance, and Dr. Drew vanquished them all. By issue #57 (February 1951), though, Grandenetti's art changed. Whether some Eisnerian help departed or his style was deliberately altered, the artist's work became a bit simpler, less *Spirit*-like. The strip only lasted from then till issue #60 (August 1951). Fiction House reprinted three Drew stories in *Monster* #1 (1953) and *Ghost Comics* #10–11 (1954) and then let him go. Later on, IW-Super reprinted two of his tales in *Eerie* #8 (1958) and *Firehair* #8 (1958).

Comics fans in later days discovered Dr. Drew and reprinted him repeatedly. *Eclipse Comics*, thanks to Michael T. Gilbert, reran three of his stories in *Doc Stearn, Mr. Monster* #4 and 6 (December 1985–October 1989) and *Mr. Monster's Super-Duper Special* #2 (August 1986). AC recycled another Drew drama in *Femforce: Night of the Demon* (1990), and *The Mammoth Book of Best Horror Comics* did another in 2008. But, to our knowledge, Dr. Drew never reappeared in an original comic story.

King of the Congo took up space in *Rangers Comics* #50–53 (December 1949–June 1950). He was a jungle pilot who, refreshingly, had an unglamorous female sidekick named Bertha, and he had the usual kind of adventures for his four appearances. Two of his stories were reprinted in the last couple of issues of *Sheena*. They took up space there, too.

With issue #61 (October 1951), *Rangers Comics* entered into a period of some flux. Dr. Drew was gone, and Firehair and Jan of the Jungle held on for only a few more issues. *Suicide Smith*, an aerial strip from *Wings Comics*, was grafted into issue

#61 as a reprint, took two issues off, appeared in another reprint in #64 (April 1952), and began a new stint with an original story in #65 (June 1952). *Rangers Comics* became *Rangers*, pretty much a war book, with #66 (August 1952), and Suicide rode it out to the end (#69, Winter 1953).

Cowboy Bob, a kid Western strip, was offered in issues #62–66 (December 1951–August 1952). *The Space Rangers*, a well-drawn but very short-in-length science fiction feature, appeared in #63, 64, and 67–69 (February 1952–Winter 1953). *The Eye*, featuring an anti-communist trench-coated spy, was in #65–66 (June–August 1952), and a couple more war strips, *Commando Rangers* (#66–69, August 1952–Winter 1953) and *G.I. Jane* (#67–69, October 1952–Winter 1953), finished things out. Then *Rangers* was gone.

Outside of their Indian books (*Indians, Long Bow*), war comics (*War Birds, Wings Comics*), *The Spirit, Ghost Comics, Toyland*, and miscellaneous one-shots, that was pretty much it for Fiction House. The anti-comics backlash of the mid–Fifties was in full swing, and FH's sexy covers and female leads made them an easy target no matter how much they reined in the glamour in the last two years. Sales were probably down, too. Like many, possibly most, of their peers, Fiction House called it quits in 1954.

There were other adventure strips. Two of the most important came from Novelty, and the most famous of the two was *Dick Cole*.

Dick Cole was one of the noble line of collegiate athletes that seemed to come to a comic in the early days, but he had more going for him than most: a better concept, better scripting, and art which was always distinctive if not excellent. He entered in *Blue Bolt* V. 1 #1 (June 1940), and, before he exited, made over 100 appearances, got his own series, and fielded his own radio show as well. Not that bad for a kid from military school. Of course, Dick Cole was not your average kid.

Billed as "Dick Cole, Wonder Boy" in his first appearance, with art by Bob Davis, our hero sprinted onto the splash panel in an athletic uniform that might as well have been a superhero costume. As the opening caption read: "Introducing that wonder boy of American youth—Dick Cole—the newest, most startling character in action picture magazines. The story of this super boy opens at Farr Military Academy where…"

…Dick Cole, in his green cadet's uniform, observed a pole vaulter at practice and asked the coach if he could try it. He admitted he'd never done it before, and Coach Bradly was loath to let him try. The vaulter presented his pole to Dick and said, "Here you go, plebe. Break your neck!"

Dick took off his coat, grabbed the pole, gave himself a running start, and cleared the bar by several feet. "Look at that!" "It's a new record!" "Holy jumping cats!" The coach allowed in amazement that Dick had broken every existing world record for the pole vault. "Who are you, son? What are you?"

"Well, it's quite a story, sir," said Dick, and proceeded to give the coach his origin. As a baby, he was abandoned in a basket on the doorstep of one Professor Blair. A note was included with him, penned by his mother. It stated that the baby's name was Richard Cole, that his father was dead, and that she had no way of caring for him. But Mother Cole had heard that Blair had developed a method to raise a child to be a superman. (Probably he'd been a consultant on the upbringing of Doc Savage.) "I beg you to keep him—and make him the finest man in the world!" finished the note.

"By thunder, I'll do it!" said Blair, hoisting the baby Dick Cole on his shoulder. "No one would believe me—no one would give me the chance to prove my theories. But now we'll show 'em, Dick! I'll make you the finest specimen of humanity in the world!"

That he pretty much did. Professor Blair, seeming more of a mad scientist than a dad, shot his kid full of vitamins just about from Day One (we'd probably call them "steroids" today), exposed him to various kinds of radiation, had him talking with a three-year-old vocabulary in his first year, and turned him pretty much into a juvenile Captain America.

By age five, Dick was in school and at the head of his class. By age 10, he graduated as valedictorian of his junior high. By age 12, he was a graduate of high school and probably missed out on all the good parts. After that, Professor Blair took him on a five-year tour of Africa, had him study fencing in France, had him learn to ski in Switzerland, and showed him how lousy things were in Germany. At age 17 (which means that five-year tour was either shorter than five years, or the European adventures were in a time warp), the Prof and Dick came home, and Blair revealed that Dick's mental and physical powers would only grow stronger with time. "I want you to promise me that you'll never use those powers to bad advantage."

"I promise, Dad," said Dick Cole, and that was that. Shortly thereafter, he was enrolled in Farr Military Academy. He would spend the next 10 years there as a student, which means we are talking time-warps here. But such things are the rule in comics, except for *Gasoline Alley*, so let's go on.

The coach remarked that Dick must have been the Dick Cole who was recently awarded the Carnegie Medal. When the coach asked him what that was all about, Dick replied, "Oh, it wasn't much." All it amounted to was that Dick was walking downtown one day and chanced upon a scene in which a madman holding a crying baby was standing on the ledge of a skyscraper's upper story and threatening to jump. Really, not much of anything at all.

Anyway, Dick "shot into the building," grabbed a rope, ran up to the roof, tied one end of it to a fixture, and then swung down like an urban Tarzan to grab the madman (who had just jumped) and his baby burden. Dick hung onto the rope with one hand, snagged them both with his free arm, and swung into an open window and into the hands of the police. "But I didn't want a lot of fuss, so I went downstairs, and slipped away unnoticed." Those pesky Carnegie people found out who he was from the cops, and insisted on giving him a medal. You know how that goes.

At that point in Dick's tale, the coach's daughter Laura came running up, in tears. Farr BMOC Jack Payton, the Conceited Snob of the piece, had decided to ride a horse yclept Wild Black. Said horse was not tame, had not been ridden before, and was dangerous. Also, it was running like a locomotive off its tracks, a cowering Payton holding onto its back for dear life. When the horse came by, gallant Dick leaped over a tall wire fence, caught Wild Black's bridle in his hands, and bulldogged the stallion to a standstill.

Jack Payton's reaction? "What are you, a wise guy?" Things only went downhill from there, and the rivalry and love interest of the strip had been set up. That was the end of the story, but the last blurb promised more in the next issue.

In that next issue, Dick was present when Payton, taking Laura Bradly for a reckless ride in his boat, hit another boat on the lake, wrecked it, and saw an unconscious Laura thrown to her apparent drowning death. Dick saved Laura, fought off a menacing snapping turtle, and gained the redoubled hate of Payton. Shortly after that, Dick was framed for the theft of a chapel bell, endured repeated taunting from Payton and his droogs, and beat up two truck driver thugs who were in league with Payton. Though the bell was down in the bottom of a well, Dick drew it back up, clobbered the drivers into taking him and it back to campus, and lifted it back into its proper place by brute force. He refused to implicate Payton, though. That would get rid of a good villain.

Cole's action-packed stories didn't have him in the headline spot yet, but he was giving the other characters in *Blue Bolt* competition. In issue #3, he met Professor Blair again and, with sufficient fistic action (including bursting through a ship's door, which may have been metal), stopped two spies from stealing the super-formula which turned Dick Cole into a super-cadet. In issue #4 (September 1940), Dick had the chance to tangle with an escaped gorilla. The ape slammed him up against a wall. "Now I'm getting mad!" said Dick. "You hairy—*PALOOKA!*" The 17-year-old superboy waded in, walloped the heck out of the hairy ape, and chained him up. Even gorillas dared not mess with Dick Cole.

Dick finally made the cover with issue #6 (November 1940), riding the wing of a plane with a gangster inside pulling a gun on him. He had a multi-issue adventure in Hollywood over the summer, in which he got mixed up with crooks, cleaned their clocks, and did feats of derring-do that would have tuckered out Douglas Fairbanks. When he came back to Farr, he found out that inmates at a nearby prison had broken out, attacked the campus, holed up in the armory, and taken Laura captive. Naturally, Dick did a daring one-man rescue, tear-gassed the cons, saved Laura, and cracked a few jaws in the process. If you weren't jealous of him, Dick Cole was decent hero food.

Finally, by issue #11 (April 1941), Dick again got the cover spot, rendered by Bill Everett, and took over the lead position in the comic. (The fact that Joe Simon and Jack Kirby had just left the *Blue Bolt* feature might have had something to do with it.) In the story, he stopped Nazi spies from stealing an Army robot by crawling in the thing himself, taking control, and tearing the heck out of the bad guys' airplane. He could get kayoed, he could have trouble, but it took an awful lot to give Dick Cole competition.

And by *Blue Bolt* V. 2 #1 (June 1941), he got it. Another Everett cover, under the cutline "Dick Cole battles his double!" we saw Cole grappling and fighting a powerful, menacing cadet in uniform who could match him blow for blow. No Jack Payton here: the enemy this time was Simba Karno, and he was Dick Cole's mirror image of evil.

One Dr. Karno was the villainous counterpart of Professor Blair in his own right. He used the methods that made a superboy out of Dick Cole to make a super-bully of his son, Simba. Upon finding out about Cole, Simba jealously—and angrily—enlisted at Farr Military Academy to confront his rival. He confronted him all over the place, and one issue wasn't enough for the battle. It spilled over into the next, and the next, and the next after that. Daredevil had the Claw, Crimebuster had Iron Jaw, and Dick Cole had Simba Karno.

In V. 2 #2 (July 1941), Dr. Karno drafted his son into breaking a gang boss out of prison single-handedly with a bomb. Laura inevitably got kidnapped. Dick stepped in, fought Simba, and brought the gangster to bay, but the Karnos escaped. With no evidence to link Simba to the crime, he survived to menace Cole in the next issue.

Dick Cole first encounters his evil double, Simba Karno.
© 1941 Novelty Press, Inc.

After that, Simba hooked up with Payton (now called Rayton, but we'll keep calling him Payton here for simplicity) and went after Dick and his pal Eddie, who, over summer vacation, were searching for a sunken treasure in the Mississippi River. All arrived at an ancient riverboat along the way, and Dick and Simba got into a no-holds-barred battle. The two smashed each other about the boat until one of Dick's punches hurled Simba into a kerosene lantern, setting the boat afire. The good guys and the bad guys escaped to fight in the next installment.

As fate would have it, Simba and Payton learned that Dick carried the treasure map on his person, ambushed him, had a terrific fight with him, and finally kayoed him with a blow from behind. Simba donned diving gear, went inside the sunken riverboat, and brought up the treasure chest himself. Cole arrived on the scene shortly after, but Simba stalled him with a boulder to the labonza. That only slowed Cole down. He leaped aboard the jalopy Simba and Payton were driving, walloped them both, and threw them out. Then he got the treasure back to its rightful owners. Another episode gone by.

The cover of the next *Blue Bolt* (V. 2 #5, October 1941) bore a Bob Davis cover showing Dick Cole and his car blown sky-high by a dynamite bomb set off by a grinning Simba. As it turned out, Dick happened onto a movie being shot on location by his old Hollywood pals. They invited him to do stunt work. Simba, happening by with Payton, rigged a bomb of his own in a shoot where Cole drove over planted explosives. When the unexpected blast went off, Simba swung down on a rope, saved Cole's life (and got Cole's gratitude), and proposed himself as a stuntman, too. The crew accepted.

However, this time, there was a plot swerve. Simba, hanging onto an airplane wheel while it was in flight, found that the landing gear was stuck. Dick got airborne, risked his life in the usual manner, and saved both his and Simba's lives by unsticking the gear and parachuting them both to safety. After that, both Simba and Dick teamed up to fight off crooks who were trying to hijack the movie studio's payroll truck. Cole and Simba shook hands afterward, with Simba opining, "Between us we could lick anybody!" Even Payton seemed to have turned over a new leaf.

The good feeling continued into the next issue, in which Simba saved Dick from taking a deadly fall and teamed with him in a tough football game against a rival academy. In mid-story, though, a figure from the past entered: Dr. Karno, who insisted his son go after some military plans in the desk of Major Farr so he could sell them to the enemy. On bended knees, tears in his eyes, Simba pleaded with his father not to make him do the deed. But Dr. Karno insisted, and still had enough hooks in the boy to force him to thieve the plans and turn them over to him.

It didn't sit well with Simba, though, and he made a confession to Dick. The two of them took after Dr. Karno, sliding bare-handed down an electric cable and smashing through a window to battle the villain and a spy ring. Simba himself throttled Karno, yelling, "Darn right I'm mad! And I'm through with you!" Cole clobbered the spies, recovered the plans, and saved the day. Later, back at Farr, Simba admitted his part in the plot, with Dick testifying in his behalf. Major Farr allowed that Simba might be facing jail time, but that he'd do his best to get him on probation. The story ended there, with readers sympathetic, probably, for the ex-villain.

Things might not have been all that rosy, though, if the next cover (on *Blue Bolt* V. 2 #7, December 1941) was any indication: Simba had his hands around Cole's throat, and both of them were falling off a bridge. In the first pages of the story, Simba got his probation, and both he and Cole did acrobatic stunts of joy at the news. But—and there's always a "but"—Dr. Karno was still about, having been released for lack of evidence. He and a brutish accomplice broke into Farr, subdued Simba with force and a hypo full of sleeping stuff, and kidnapped him.

Once in their Hideout of Evil, Karno and his accomplice, Krog, performed a brain operation on Simba to turn him into a creature of evil again. It worked. Simba, his head in bandages, was loyal to Dr. Karno again, and only too glad to take up fists against Dick Cole again.

Dick picked up on a clue, forced the truth out of Krog with strangling fingers on his throat, and confronted Simba on a train in the midst of a radium robbery. The two of them fought, fell out of the train car over a river, and ended the fight when Dick's strong right hand crashed into Simba's jaw. Shortly after, Dick's fist did similar duty on Dr. Karno's chin, and he forced the dastard to reverse his brain operation. While Dick tended to a recovering Simba, Dr. Karno and Krog escaped.

The two villains weren't around for the next issue, but Jack Payton was. Driven insane by his hatred for Cole and Simba, Payton stole bullets and grenades from the armory and planned to murder both of them during Farr's war games with another academy. Simba was wounded, but Cole braved live fire to bring Payton in. At the end of the episode, Payton was sent to an asylum. The two wonder boys each got a medal.

In between that and the next arc of stories came *4Most Comics* V. 1 #1 (Winter 1942). Dick Cole joined in on the cover with his co-stars the Target, the Cadet, and Edison Bell in whupping up on Nazis. He also had the lead story, a 30-pager, his longest ever. Therein, a freighter which must have come back from *King Kong*'s Skull Island docked with a dinosaur, about the size and shape of a brontosaurus, in its hold. It was brought out in chains, but the saurian broke the restraints and menaced a crowd on the docks. Into the breach leapt Dick and Simba, who had a hard time with the dinosaur but finally managed to leg-scissor its throat and choke it into unconsciousness. Even a *dinosaur* had to watch its step around Dick Cole!

The real meat of the story came with the appearance of Reggie Mocton, a very short, very bespectacled, very nerdy-looking guy, who approached Dick and Simba afterward. He appeared to hero-worship them, told them he was going to enroll at Farr himself, and offered them a lift back to campus—in his family limo. The two boys accepted.

Actually, Reggie had an ulterior motive, as all curious characters in such stories did. "Bah! Strong boys! Athletes! Muscle lads! They make me sick!" It transpired that Reggie was born short, puny, and intellectual, and his brother, Steve, was everything he wasn't: handsome, athletic, and probably C+ on his report cards. Reggie assuaged himself by studying ancient tomes of sorcery, swinging cats around by their tails, and, finally, taking things into his own hands. He pushed his brother off the top of a skyscraper and watched him go splat.

That was the beginning. Reggie developed a potion from the magic books which gave him mental power over anyone who drank it. After the effects of the potion wore off, the victim would remember nothing he had done in the interval. Reggie dosed one dupe with it and had him murder a cop. The dupe brought the cop's hat and billy club back to Reggie, who gleefully assured him he'd forget it all in the morning. As the narrative assured us, Reggie used his potion on a batch of athletes.

It took a while, but Reggie administered the stuff to Dick Cole. The wonder boy was induced to steal secret airplane plans from a factory, got caught in the act, and was thrown in jail. Even though he remembered nothing of the act, Dick Cole was sentenced to death by firing squad.

Simba Karno helped break his pal out by aiding him in pulling the window bars out of his cell. The usual—or unusual—rip-roaring adventure followed, with Dick and Simba stowing away on a freighter, saving it when it got torpedoed, Dick regaining his memory of his actions and Reggie victimizing him, and a showdown with the shrimp mastermind when the latter climbed aboard the dinosaur's back and used it to menace the students at Farr. The wonder boys managed to drown the beast in a lake, Reggie was nabbed, and Dick was cleared. To say the least, it was epic.

With Simba in the good guys' column and Dr. Karno and Reggie making no return appearances, a new villain had to be found. He turned up in *Blue Bolt* V. 2 #9 (February 1942) in the person of Ted Dare, Major Farr's nephew, who introduced himself by skywriting his name over Farr Academy with a plane. Ted made trouble for a few more issues and was dutifully packed off. Other menaces took his place.

Dick Cole was one of the elite comic book heroes to star in his own radio show, introed by the rousing school song, "We'll always be near to Farr." This tune made it into the comic books as well, whenever the cadets felt like singing it. The radio show debuted in 1942 with Leon Janney playing Dick, and it probably owed a lot to *Jack Armstrong*. Nonetheless, it was a pretty good show and lasted a number of episodes.

In the comics, Dick Cole lasted in *Blue Bolt* through V. 10 #2 (September–October 1949), in *4Most Comics* through V. 7 #6 (November–December 1948), and in *Dick Cole*, his own comic, from issues #1 to 10 (December 1948–June–July 1950). Star Publications took over from Novelty with Dick's sixth issue (October–November 1949), which contained Cole's last original stories. He held on in reprints for several more issues. Then the book was converted into *Sport Thrills* with issue #11 (November 1950) and he ran on for a few reprints there. Accepted Publications reprinted the first three issues of *Sport Thrills* in 1958 and that was the last anyone ever saw of Dick Cole. Did he ever graduate? Did he become part of the Farr faculty? We'll probably never know.

There was, however, a spinoff of the strip. It was called *Young King Cole* and the title character was Kingston Cole, Jr., Dick Cole's cousin. Dick himself appeared in the first issue (*Young King Cole* V. 1 #1, Fall 1945) to give Kingston his imprimatur. The youthful Cole had just graduated college and got busy

Dick's buttoned-down detective cousin, Young King Cole. © 1945 Novelty Press Division of the Premium Service Co., Inc.

setting up a detective agency. He ran through V. 3 #12 (July 1948) of his own title before it was retitled *Criminals on the Run* with V. 4 #1 (August 1948). That lasted to issue #10 (December 1949–January 1950), when it was picked up by Star Publications. The book was retitled *Crime-Fighting Detective* with #11 (April–May 1950) and Young King Cole appeared in a few more issues, all reprints of earlier stories. His last Golden Age hurrah was in issue #17 (December 1951). Later, IW-Super reprinted a few of his stories in *Top Detective Comics* #9 (1958) and *Master Detective* #17 (1964), and that was it.

A more obvious Dick Cole clone, but a successful one, was *The Cadet*.

The Cadet, aka Kit Carter, had a two-page text story origin in *Target Comics* V. 2 #4 (June 1941), written by Ray Gill. The slam-bang affair detailed how Kit was born to a World War I hero and his wife, the latter of whom died in childbirth (common in comics). Kit's father died about a paragraph later, trying to foil a bank holdup. That left 15-year-old Kit in the care of his uncle, whom he left after he found the uncle was a crook. Carter hitched a ride in a truck that was abruptly hijacked by criminals, but found a way to foil the ne'er-do-wells by filling the truck's tank with hi-test gasoline and making its engine blow up. All that took place in a two-page text.

The comic story that followed didn't coordinate precisely with what Gill had written, though. Kit Carter hitched another ride (the text ended with a cop giving him a lift), *that* truck got hijacked, too, and Kit got wounded in the shoulder fighting off the crooks who did it. The trucker drove Kit to the nearest medical facility, the infirmary of the Daunton Military School. The young hero was patched up and put in a hospital bed, and fate continued taking its course.

Headmaster Judd, the director of the school, recognized Kit Carter, Jr., as the image of his war hero father, Kit, Sr. Kit allowed he'd love to be part of the school, and Judd informed him he'd do just that, once he was out of the hospital. "Oh gosh!" said Kit, eloquently. So it began.

Actually, it began with Kit in uniform and getting an insult from a wealthy cadet named Van Kleek. The matter was settled, for the moment, when Kit delivered an uppercut to him. But that didn't set well with the rich kid and his cronies, and they pilfered a secret "anti-gas formula" from a school professor, intending to frame Kit for the theft. It didn't quite work that way, with enemy spies kidnapping Van Kleek and swiping the formula from him. Nonetheless, Kit captured the spies, recovered the formula, and got a letter of commendation from the president himself. The Cadet's career was underway.

Art Gates was the Cadet's initial artist, and carried him through the next story, in which Kit's villainous half-uncle returned. The miscreant inveigled Kit into helping with a prison break, but our hero left a clue with a cop that enabled him to foil the escapade. Carter's half-uncle escaped to bleaken another day. That day never came.

In *Target Comics* V. 2 #8 (October 1941), Judd was replaced as head of Daunton by one Colonel Tilghman, and *The Cadet*'s art and storyline changed for the better. Art Gates and Jim Jordan were the creative team, with Gates disappearing partway through the run. Jordan took the strip by himself for a while and then was partnered with George Kapitan. Kit's fun-type sidekick Dan Merry, a bespectacled short guy, turned up in *Target* V. 3 #3 (May 1942) and stayed through the end of the run. Though

The Cadet was never quite as inspired as *Dick Cole*, it still managed a lengthy run. Kit made it through *Target* V. 10 #3 (August–September 1949) and appeared in *4Most Comics* #1–40 (Winter 1942–April–May 1950). He was never heard from again.

Bill Barnes, America's Air Ace blew in from the Street & Smith pulps, where Bill had been winging it since March 1935. When the company went into comics, he debuted in the back of *Shadow Comics* V. 1 #1 (1940). It was duly noted that the story was "illustrated by a prominent aviator and all of the incidents are accurate." In that tale, Bill, an airborne seeker of justice, was spurred into action by the death of a friend and soon began tangling with the Yellowjackets, a secret fascist underground group not unlike the later Hydra. It took him two issues to beat them, but they later returned, and there were always other threats. In *Shadow Comics*, he ran through V. 1 #6 (August 1940).

The Cadet leads his pals to Victory in a big V. © 1942 Novelty Press, Inc.

Within the year, Street & Smith started up *Bill Barnes Comics* (later *Bill Barnes, America's Air Ace*) with V. 1 #1 (1940). The Yellowjackets returned for the inaugural. After that, Bill appeared in a 27-page illustrated text story that could have come straight out of the pulps, and may have. He bowed back in for a tale of the Bill Barnes Aviation Cadet Corps, and that finished the issue.

A truly disturbing story, from a modern viewpoint, was in *Bill Barnes* V. 1 #7 (July 1942). The cover showed a bare-chested Bill whupping up on four Japanese soldiers at the same time, while a cutline below proclaimed, "How to wipe the Japs ACTUALLY off the map based on cold scientific fact." Brother, it was cold indeed.

In the tale, written by Walter Gibson and drawn by Jack Binder, Barnes (now a commander in the Army Air Force) was summoned in for a special consult with representatives of the United Nations. Briefly, his next mission was to cause earthquakes in Japan big enough to wipe out their industrial complex and thus cripple their war effort. And how would they do it?

Bill Barnes, America's Air Ace, proves himself a hands-on kinda guy. © 1941, 2022 Street and Smith Publications.

"With U-235!" a scientist explained.

Bill was to dump a crude atomic bomb, laden with 10 pounds of separated U-235, into the volcanic Mount Fuji and cause a quake that would fill the bill. The scientific explanation went on for pages. After sufficient aerial battle, Bill and his aide, Sandy, landed on Mt. Fuji, threw in the bomb, and got out. And, some hundreds of miles later, their plane was jostled by a terrific shock wave.

A huge atomic explosion was visible, even at their distance, and great tidal waves started devastating Japan. The wave was described as "4500 feet high—approaching at 400 to 500 miles an hour!" Tremors were felt all across the Earth. And finally…

…in a horrific double-page splash of a huge mushroom cloud and great walls of water like the fingers of a god, engulfing the island nation most graphically…

…Japan was no more.

The entire island nation was destroyed.

The booms of the quake were heard for weeks. Volcanic dust hung in the air for

Possibly the most horrifying sequence in Golden Age comics: the total destruction of Japan. © 1942, 2022 Street and Smith Publications.

about as long. One official said, "No need for armies now!" Another noted, "The sea has done its work!"

Everyone in Japan had been wiped off the face of the Earth.

And all of that, all of that, about three years before the real bomb was actually dropped.

It had to be about the most horrifying war propaganda in comics.

Bill Barnes continued through V. 1 #12 (October 1943), after which it was transformed into *Air Ace* with V. 2 #1 (January 1944). Bill only appeared in that issue, V. 2 #5, and V. 3 #7 and 8 (September 1944–February–March 1947). The book was a half-comic, half-text hybrid geared to nonfiction articles and features about planes, and Bill was quietly pensioned off.

There were many more Adventurers, most of them backups, easily forgotten. Two that we won't forget are *Gregory Gayle, Gunmaster*, and his daughter, *Toni Gayle*, a model detective. Both of them worked for Novelty Press, and Toni started out first, in *Young King Cole* V. 1 #1– V. 3 #12 (Fall 1945–July 1948).

Toni, a ravishing brunette, was in the middle of a bathing suit shoot when she got word that her father, Gregory, a police detective, was a victim of the brutal mugger, the Ape. In his hospital bed, the elder Gayle revealed his attacker's name to Toni just before passing out. The tearful model-girl vowed, "Pop, I'll get the Ape for you…. I'll carry on for you!" Biff Muggson, a reformed crook, was framed for the murder, but Toni went undercover, got caught by the Ape, saved herself by strangling the mugger with her necklace, and brought him in herself. A grateful Biff said,

"You'll need a strong-arm guy—and I know just the one!" "My woman's intuition says you'll see plenty of action!" said Toni. That was the beginning.

Toni Gayle continued catching crooks and showing off her legs throughout the entire series, with her early adventures drawn by Wayne Boring of *Superman* fame. After *Young King Cole*, she moved to *Guns Against Gangsters* (V. 1 #1–V. 2 #1, September–October 1948–September–October 1949) and *4Most Comics* (V. 8 #1–5, January–February 1949–September–October 1949).

Then, curiously, Toni's format changed. Apparently the Powers That Be saw more bucks in a teen strip than a feature about a gorgeous detective, so Toni was turned into a teenager and set in high school

Toni Gayle, model and detective, surfs into danger. © 1948 The Premium Group of Comics.

adventures in Star Comics' *School Day Romances* #1–4 (November–December 1949–May–June 1950). After two issues, she was rechristened Toni Gay. (The word "gay" didn't have the popular connotation it does now.) The title changed to *Popular Teen-Agers* for issues #5–8 (September 1950–July 1951).

After that, Toni's string ran out. She was reprinted sporadically, first in Star's *Thrilling Crime Cases* #45 (July 1951), then in Merit's *Secret Mysteries* #18 (May 1955), and then in three IW-Super comics, *Teen-Age Talk* #9 (1958), *Teen Romances* #10 (1963), and *Danger* #18 (1964). Finally, Eclipse reprinted one story in *Mr. Monster's Super Duper Special* #7 (May 1987), mainly because it had characters named Toni Gay and Butch Dykeman. Toni hasn't been heard from since, but she was nice while she lasted.

Gregory Gayle, Gunmaster was all business. He appeared in *Guns Against Gangsters* V. 1 #1–V. 2 #1 (September–October 1948–September–October 1949) and got his star turn, looking a lot tougher than when he'd been mugged by the Ape. The first cover, by L.B. Cole, showed a gangster being pinned against a wall by the interlacing shots of four cops. Nobody much talked about gun control in those days. At least, not in this comic.

Cole was apparently the artist for Greg's stories. In his first episode, the gun-toting detective, helped by a cameo from Toni, set out to discover why men in green suits were being murdered all over the city. Wearing a green suit, Greg Gayle baited the crooks (who used garbage trucks as cover), got captured by them, broke free, and took them in using one of their own trucks. The series was off and running. It only ran the length of the title, but Gayle got reprints in Star's *Thrilling Crime Cases* #42–45 (April–July 1951) and in IW-Super's *Danger* #18 (1964).

Bert and Sue were a husband-wife detective team, probably conceived as knockoffs of Hammett's Nick and Nora Charles. They headlined *Super-Mystery Comics* from V. 6 #1 to V. 8 #6 (August 1946–July 1949). Bert and Sue Smith were a couple of upper-crust newlyweds who stumbled into mysteries issue after issue and promptly solved them with much derring-do and wisecracking. Ken Battefield and Bill Walton were among their artists. After their run, they got a couple of reprints in *Penalty* #47 and 48 (October 1955 and January 1956).

Gregory Gayle, Gunmaster, defies crime (and perspective). © 1948 The Premium Group of Comics.

Note should be taken of *The Saint*, Leslie Charteris's famed detective, who first showed up in an adaptation of the movie *The Saint Strikes Back* in DC's *Movie Comics* #2 (1939). Three years later, Lev Gleason struck a deal with Charteris and featured the Saint as the cover star and prime feature of *Silver Streak Comics* #19–21 (March–May 1942). Charteris was credited with the scripting and Edd Ashe did the art, pitting the Saint against Nazis undercover. After three issues, Simon Templar had to wait till August 1947, when his option was picked up by Avon. Jack Kamen did the art quite well, pushing the Saint through regular detective capers. *The Saint* ran from issues #1 to 12 (August 1947–March 1952). He also managed to star in an illustrated text story in Avon's *Captain Steve Savage* #2 (December 1951). After that, the Saint's comic career was up, except for a reprint of his syndicated strip in Malibu's *Private Eyes* #4 (May 1989). He was only featured in

The Saint crashes in to save a beautiful blonde from something or other. © 1947, 2022 Estate of Leslie Charteris.

books, magazines, movies, and TV shows in between and afterward, which kept him busy.

Radio's *Jack Armstrong*, the All-American Boy, had his chance in the comics, but it didn't last nearly as long as his airwave career. He was, as the inside front cover described it, "A clean-cut American boy who exemplifies the motto, 'A sound

Jack Armstrong, the All-American Boy! © 2022 General Mills, Inc.

mind in a sound body.'" Really, he exemplified a teenaged Doc Savage. Jack was a football hero and an adventurer who always accompanied his best pal, "blundering" Billy Fairfield; Billy's sister Betty, an "outdoors girl" who served as love interest; Uncle Jim Fairfield, an ex-Army colonel, aviator, and owner of an airplane manufacturing plant; and Vic Hardy, a science-based crime detector, in various hair-raising adventures. Their main go-to villain in the comic was the evil Professor Proteus, who was "The Man of a Million Faces!" and did dirty deeds for pay, though presumably not dirt cheap, for the highest bidder. Jack was so wholesome that Parents' Institute, Inc., which published the most antiseptic comics in print, produced his books. That didn't keep his tales from offering action, well-drawn by Edd Ashe. Billy Fairfield got his own funny strip, Betty got adventures in which she often saved people, and Vic Hardy helmed his own Sherlockian detective stories. It started with issue #1 (November 1947) and ended with issue #13 (September 1949). Jack is lost to the ages now, very often satirized as the too-perfect American boy, but he was fun while he lasted.

Don Winslow of the Navy was much more successful in comics. And why not? He'd been appearing in a popular syndicated comic strip since 1934, he'd been on the radio and in a movie serial, and there was already a young adult novel based on him. It took a little while, but the comic books got hold of him soon enough.

Briefly: in the early Thirties, the U.S. Navy was becoming concerned that not too many Midwesterners were enlisting in the corps, as opposed to residents of the East and West Coasts. To stimulate interest, they commissioned one Frank V. Martinek to create a comic strip about a heroic naval man. He did, producing naval spy-chaser Don Winslow, a stand-up, white-uniformed hero who went against the likes of the Scorpion, Doctor Thor, the Duchess, and Owl-Eyes. He was aided by a fat but strong comic relief character named Red Pennington and answered to one Admiral Colby, and apparently enlistments went up from mesmerized kids in the Heartland.

The syndicated strip, drawn by Leon A. Beroth, crept into comic books with *Popular Comics* #1 (February 1936) as two-page reprints. It stayed in *Popular* till issue #27 (April 1938) and then switched to *Crackajack Funnies* for issues #1–43 (June 1938–January 1942). Don then made a brief stop in *The Funnies* #64 (May 1942) before shipping back to *Popular*, where he remained in port for issues #75–84 (May 1942–February 1943). Along the way his reprints appeared in two issues of DM Publishing's *Don Winslow of the Navy* (1937–May 1937), Western's *Mammoth Comics* #1 (1938) and Dell's *Four Color Comics* #2 (November 1939) and 22 (1941).

All of those were strip reprints. Fawcett Comics, home of Captain Marvel, had something more original in mind.

Don Winslow of the Navy #1 (February 17, 1943) hit the stands with Captain Marvel himself introducing him to the readers on the cover, as was his wont in those days. Don gave us all a brisk salute on deck while battleships and planes busied themselves in the background. These stories would be new ones for the comics, not a reprint among them.

"The Coast Guard Menace" was the first such story, and it started with a Nazi sub torpedoing a little fishing smack. Winslow and his pal Red Pennington wondered why the Krauts would have bothered with such a trivial target. As it turned out, the Germans were using it as a ruse to draw the Navy's attention while they landed spies elsewhere. Said trio of spies made it into the home of Admiral Colby, took him and his pretty daughter Mercedes prisoner, and demanded the plans for a secret submersible aircraft carrier from him. (It must have been some secret. The Navy never deployed such a thing in the entire war or afterward.)

Before the spies could torture the admiral, Don and Red turned up at the front door, as Winslow had a heavy date with Mercedes. She managed to give them a clue that all was not well, and after detecting another few clues, the naval nabobs broke in and treated the Nazis to some knuckle-dusting. One bad guy pulled a gun, gaining the upper hand, and tricked the admiral into giving away the plans' hiding place. Then they tied up Don, Red, Colby, and Mercedes, and put them in a garage with a car running, belching out carbon monoxide. The spies left, and things looked appropriately grim.

But Don Winslow was never without resource. He found a gasoline spill on the floor, managed to ignite it with a match, and set a fire that burned off his bonds. Luckily, it also burned through the garage wall, preventing them from using up what was left of the oxygen in the place. After getting themselves, Mercedes, and the admiral to safety, Winslow and Pennington tracked down the spies again, clobbered them in a battle aboard an inflatable boat, and were again endangered by the Nazi sub before a Coast Guard bomber laid an egg on it and sent it to the bottom.

Captain Marvel pipes Don Winslow aboard the Fawcett fleet. © 1940 Fawcett Publications, Inc.

In the last panel, Don delivered the recovered plans to a grateful Admiral Colby. "You—er—may take my daughter out tonight!" responded the admiral, and that finished the story.

Don and Red sailed through three more adventures in that issue, using more space than the syndicated strip had to offer. Since World War II was underway, the Hydra–like menaces of the Thirties were absent; Winslow was too busy fighting the Germans and Japanese. The adventures continued, four to a comic, as long as the 68-page size lasted. Each story had enough action, both on land and sea, to satisfy the connoisseur. Edd Ashe did a number of the early stories and Rod Reed, Otto Binder, Kermit Jaediker, and Eric Messman were among the writers. Later on, John Jordan, L.B. Cole, Dick Krause, Shelly Moldoff, and Carl Pfeufer drew him.

Don Winslow of the Navy shrank to 60 pages with issue #9, to 52 with #11, and to 36 with #19. It stayed at that thickness till #33 (April 1946), when wartime paper restrictions apparently let up. The 52-page count resumed with #33, continued through #49 (September 1947), and finally deflated to 36 again for issues #50–69.

All this time, Commander Winslow and his pal Red Pennington alternated straight wartime adventures with the Navy, the Coast Guard, and the Marines with more exotic spy missions, keeping up their troubleshooter status. Issue #16 featured the first book-length story, as Winslow battled "The American," aka Tom Toguchi, an American-born Japanese who turned traitor to the U.S. to spy on behalf of his ancestral home. After a rip-roaring four-parter, the American fell off a ship and apparently drowned.

That wasn't the end for him, though. In a retro-war story in issue #38 (September 1946), the American was back to take on Don in a three-parter, having been rescued by the Japanese. It was still a bang-up saga, and a last caption indicated he'd be back for more. In #42 (February 1947), he was. Toguchi was put on trial for war crimes, sentenced to death, and escaped. Don and Red managed to bring him back, but not before Winslow almost died in a quicksand trap. The American made a last appearance in issue #62, in a flashback story that probably took place between issues #38 and 42. The last caption explained, "He paid for his vicious war crimes, and his evil soul plans murder no more!"

In issue #26 (May 1945), the publisher had had to admit that the war was almost over and inserted a nemesis from Don Winslow's past: The Scorpion. No costumed villain was he, but he was a master plotter, did have an army of minions, and was a threat to the U.S.A. and the rest of the world. In flashback, Don recounted their last encounter, in which the Scorpion threatened to poison the Rio Grande and instead fell to his apparent death. Now he was back for a book-lengther (with page lengths shrinking, Fawcett found this an easy way to stretch out the story pages) in which he took over a Navy cruiser, intending to use it to take a weakly defended island as a base. Don and Red nearly lost their lives to him in the case, and Winslow had to be hospitalized in the end. The Scorpion, left on a raft, vowed vengeance on his old enemy.

In the next issue, along with two war stories, Winslow foiled gangsters on a gambling ship. It was a foretaste of postwar programming. The combat cases continued, but *Don Winslow* stirred in more civilian-based adventures, gradually.

Don's next "name" villain turned up in issue #29 (October–November 1945). The Renegade, an ex-con, bank robber, schemer, and ruthless murderer with an "R" branded on his forehead, used stolen money to buy his way into a lifebelt manufacturer. Once in, he killed his partner and used cheaper materials to increase profits. Both Don and Red nearly drowned from using the faulty belts, and trailed and exposed the Renegade. But the villain escaped, as such miscreants do, and returned to wreak further havoc in later issues.

The January 1946 issue (#31) finally admitted the war was over, but there were "Now It Can Be Told"s which had to be cleared out of the inventory. The Renegade and the Scorpion returned for more hijinks. A series of stories built around a gob, Flatbush Foley, who was seeking a career after serving in the Navy, was also strung through various issues. Don Winslow was building a sort of continuity.

Don Winslow #47 (July 1947) introduced Commander Winslow's next and most colorful villain—or villainess: Singapore Sal. Wearing an eye mask and pirate's outfit and wielding a mean sword, Singapore Sal seemed to have stepped out of *Terry and the Pirates*, which was not a bad place for inspiration. In her initial appearance, the pulchritudinous pirate was capturing American ships left and right. Don and Red were called in to investigate, but she captured both of them while posing as a torch singer in a bar. She was a Caucasian version of the Dragon Lady. Don and Red won their freedom and captured her, but she had the last word: "They've got me—now the question is—can they hold me, handsome one?"

They couldn't, and didn't. Singapore Sal came back for several return engagements. A character using her name, who might have been the original Sal without a mask, crossed swords with Lance O'Casey in *Whiz Comics* #109 and 111 (May and July 1949). In fact, she even outlasted Don Winslow himself: AC Comics revived her in *Femforce* #32 (1991) along with a league of Golden Age villains, and she made several more appearances there, most recently in issue #135 (2006).

The Snake, a dope pusher whose elongated body allowed him to slither and constrict like a snake, emerged in issue #50 (October 1947) and returned in #54. Rubberface, another villain, had the ability to disguise himself by distorting his pliable features, and appeared in #55 (March 1948). He later showed up as an aide to the Scorpion. Also in issue #55, Admiral Colby was shown buying a newspaper from Freddy Freeman ... better known as the secret identity of Captain Marvel, Jr. The crossover was never acknowledged.

Don Winslow #66 (March 1951) showed how far Fawcett was willing to go to keep things floating, in that Don and Red encountered aliens from Venus in a flying saucer story. (Captain Midnight was doing the same thing in his Fawcett comic, so it wasn't all that far-fetched.) Three issues later, Fawcett published a three-parter in #69 (September 1951), and called it quits.

That wasn't quite it for Don's comics career. Four years later, Charlton, which was picking up properties from failing companies all over the place on the cheap, reprinted Fawcett's *Don Winslow* #59 in, of all things, *TV Teens* #6 (January 1955). Then they came out with *Don Winslow* #70–73 (March–September 1955). All four issues were reprints. Apparently the sales weren't good enough for Charlton to continue the title, and they deep-sixed the Winslow character. (Also to be considered was the fact that the *Don Winslow* comic strip was finally put to bed on July 30, 1955.) The Charlton series continued with a title change to *Fightin' Navy* and a format change to naval war stories.

Since then, Winslow has been relegated to nostalgic reprints of the comic strip in various places (including one by the Navy in 2018) and of the comic book by AC Comics. He remains unrevived as far as new stories go. Probably that's for the best, as Don Winslow was a creature of his time and belongs there.

Running down the list of a few more entries, *Camera Comics* (#1–9, October 1944–Summer 1946) was a fairly low-quality series about which the most unique thing was that it was published by the U.S. Camera Publishing Corporation. Alongside a bunch of ads for camera products, *Camera* featured the adventures of a bunch of shutterbugs, mostly war photographers in the early days and then crime photogs in the postwar era. The middle 16 pages from issue #2 on were filled with photographs and tips on taking pictures. The adventures of Linda Lens, girl picture-snapper, were a bit more interesting but mostly by contrast. Nothing much developed for *Camera* and after #9, there were no more prints.

Crown Comics was pubbed by McCombs Publishing, ran for 19 issues (#1–19, 1945–July 1949), and was a variety comic whose first issue offered up an Edgar Allan Poe adaptation, a kid humor strip, a funny-animal strip, a secret agent yarn, an adventure story, a war story, and a cop story. The cover, depicting a female ghost rising from a black cat and a corpse, was excellent, possibly drawn by Matt Baker or Alex Blum. It was a scene from the one star strip, *Graves, Ghost Hunter*, probably an offcast Fiction House story.

In the tale, the cover ghost was that of Agnes Harrington, burned as a witch in 1745. She was carrying out her curse on the descendants of the ones who punished her by taking on the form of a cat, then assuming ghost form and killing her prey with poisoned fingernail scratches. Graves had a handy-dandy ghost disintegrator that he used on the vengeful revenant, and she was banished to the beyond. A well-done story, but that was it for Graves.

Issue #2 introed *Mickey Magic*, a kid magician, and *Clue Kelly*, a troubleshooter for an aircraft company, drawn by Blum. *Voodah*, the jungle strip, we've already covered. By issue #4, *Ace of the Newsreels*, aka Ace Williams, debuted in an action-packed story by Matt Baker. He was a newsreel cameraman and his supporting character was

Graves, Ghost Hunter, and a werecat morphing into a beautiful girl. © 1945 Golfing, Inc.

Foggy Gibbons, a female. These features pretty much carried the book through to its end. Jack Kamen and Al Feldstein showed up to aid and abet the art just before shipping out to EC Comics. *Harry Hotspur*, a sword-swinging strip set in old England, had a great cover on issue #8 but nothing else to recommend it.

Crown shifted features faster than a runway model shifts dresses. By issue #9, it debuted *Bryan O'Flynn*, an adventurer who could travel through time by means of a drug; two good strips by Leonard Starr and Frank Bolle, namely *Buckskin,* a very good Colonial-era strip soon retitled *Bart Stewart*, and *Vic Cutter*, a good detective feature; and *Leif the Lucky*, a shamus strip that wasn't nearly so good. The major problem with *Crown Comics* was that you literally couldn't count on what was going to be in the comic you picked up.

Finally, the book settled down to the lineup of Voodah; Vic Cutter; funny-Indian strip *Minnie Soo and Little Ha Ha*; *Buck Farrell*, a seafaring strip that started out lousy and finally got better; *Bart Stewart*; and *Master Marvin*, another kid-humor strip. There were more changes toward the end, including a few one-off Western stories, a two-pager by Bob Powell, and a one-shot appearance of *Dot and Dash*, a boy-girl detective couple by Bolle, but despite the higher quality, time ran out for *Crown Comics* with issue #19 (July 1949). The last issue ran a lot of ads for Harvey Comics, but as far as we know, that company never did anything with the *Crown* features.

In his monumental *Watchmen* series, writer Alan Moore suggested that in a world where superheroes actually existed, comics with other genres might be more popular. He posited that the most popular might be pirate comics. In our own world, there were a few titles in the piracy niche, and some of them were quite tasty indeed.

One of the first was a rather obscure strip tucked away in Magazine Enterprises' *A-1 Comics* #3 (1946). *The Corsair* was drawn and possibly written by Charles M. Quinlan. The title character was one Jonathan Gallant, a farmer come to town who was hired to captain a cargo ship headed for the Caribbean after the owner saw him clobbering two lying sailors in a bar. When pirates attacked the good ship *Silver Spray*, Gallant outfoxed the brigands and defeated them in battle. The Corsair's adventures continued in issues #5-8 and 10 (1946-1947).

Captain Kidd was a two-issue offering from Fox, continuing its numbering from *Dagar, Desert Hawk* (#24 and 25, June and August 1949). Most of the story was true-crime-on-the-high-seas, but Captain Kidd was drawn by Jack Kamen and he was presented as a pirate driven to his role by circumstance. Tom Kidd was depicted as a bondsman, semi-slave, who was lashed by his master for trivialities. He escaped with the help of a friend, signed aboard a ship, got attacked, and was made a galley slave on a pirate vessel. Kidd led a mutiny, overthrew the crew, and was persuaded to become a pirate when his pal pointed out that, as bondsmen, they'd be thrown back into slavery if they turned the ship over to the Crown. He vowed, like Robin Hood, to rob the rich and give to the poor—and, one suspects, himself and his men. The good or bad Captain lasted two issues.

Captain Silver's Log of the Sea Hound, though not a piracy saga per se, was based on the 1942–51 radio show *The Sea Hound* and ran four issues from Avon ([month unknown] 1949–September 1949). With his aides Jerry, Kukai, and Tex, he foiled

The Corsair strikes! © 1946 Compix, Inc.

modern-day pirates and other seagoing villains on his ketch, *The Sea Hound*. It wasn't that bad but, honestly, it wasn't that good.

Quality's *Buccaneers* comic #19–27 (January 1950–May 1951) was one of the best. It took its numbering from *Kid Eternity* and opened with a cover shot of a bare-chested, long-haired hero in torn white shorts and buccaneer boots sword fighting with a more fully clad pirate. To the side, a blonde damsel in a long red dress looked on in concern. The art was by Reed Crandall, and the hero was *Captain Daring*.

Daring and his fat first mate, Patch, washed ashore after their ship crashed in a storm and barged into a duel to decide who was going to command a pirate ship. Taking each contestant on, Daring defeated them both and claimed command of their vessel, the *Revenge*, and soon defeated another brigand, Captain Shark (who looked like a shark) in a battle at sea. A captive governor's daughter was aboard the defeated boat. The good captain took her home to her father and basically blackmailed him into signing a document that gave him the right to defend the isle of Illyria against other pirates. The daughter, Lady Dolores, longed for the day he'd come home. She, her father, Daring, and Patch adventured their way boldly through the end of the title.

The Spanish Main was up next. Lieutenant Dick Warr of the Queen's Navy was called in to deal with pirates, especially the vicious Captain Redhand. Warr cooked up the idea of pretending to assault his commander, fleeing to sea, and posing as a pirate. He signed up with Redhand, fooled him into attacking the commander's island, and blew up the ship he commanded. After bringing in Redhand, Warr made amends with his chief officer and was promoted to captain. *The Spanish Main* continued as an anthology series of seafaring derring-do, through issue #24 (November 1950).

Third in the lineup was *Eric Falcon*, who premiered with a big grin and a sword in hand. He was the son of the late Admiral Falcon, who had left to his heirs—Eric; the admiral's ward, Fortuna Dell; and the bad-guy cousin, Pancras—his castle, a chest, and a sword, with the three of them to decide among themselves who got what. Pancras claimed the chest, Fortuna settled for the castle, and Eric claimed the sword.

The chest held nothing but a "Sorry, Charlie!" kind of note, but the hollow pommel of the sword contained a map to the burial place of the admiral's treasure. Both Eric and, secretly, Pancras learned of the map. Eric fought off a mob of Pancras's men, went to the island where his father's loot was buried, and was trailed by both Pancras and Fortuna, the latter of whom wanted to warn him.

All parties were surprised by the Sea Fox, *another* pirate, who pre-empted them after Eric found the treasure. But our hero outfoxed the Fox, beat him in a duel, gave Pancras part of the treasure, and opted to take the pirate ship and outfit it with a new crew. He was out for adventure, but told Fortuna to wait for him. She said she would. Maybe, in the interim, she joined the same Waiting Ladies Club as Dolores. Falcon made it through the last issue.

The last feature premiered after a short Captain Daring text story. A black-haired, masked bravo was shown dueling with sword and knife against a batch of Barbary pirates. The opening caption read, "The Moslem corsairs were the terror of the seas ... but Black Roger became the terror of the Moslem corsairs!"

The story proper opened with young Roger Randolph, just out of college and proclaimed a lawyer, slugging a bailiff who was trying to grab an orphan, Barty Bewick, to slave off his late father's debt. Then he defended young Barty in court, freeing him from servitude to Lord Willbar, the not-so-nice-guy of the piece. Trouble, naturally, brewed.

Willbar had Roger mugged and shanghaied aboard a ship, along with Barty, to be a slave in American cotton fields. But a craft full of Barbary pirates showed up, and the captain of the slave ship tendered Roger a cutlass for his own defense. While the baddies were attacking the English ship, Roger and Barty snuck aboard the Barbarian ship, freed the European slaves chained to the ship's oars, and led them in an attack. The Barbary baddies were beaten, and the English pirate captain died in battle.

Roger was elected captain of the ship. He donned a mask, went back home as Black Roger, outdueled Lord Willbar, and forced him to sign a document preventing him from raising rent on his land's tenants. After this early example of rent control, Black Roger went back to his ship. "Now, lads, we seek the Barbary pirates, and beat them where we find them!" He sailed on to the last issue.

In *Buccaneers* #24 (November 1950), a new feature took the place of *The Spanish Main*, though the *Main* was still listed on the cover. *Adam Peril, USN* was set in 1801. Lieutenant Peril commanded a frigate, the *Freedom*, and was asked by President Thomas Jefferson to act as a secret agent, head down to New Orleans, and smash up the pirate rings there. Peril was waylaid by a traitor and taken aboard a pirate vessel, but a huge crewman named Tiny decided to fight for America rather than against it, and came to Peril's aid. With his help and that of a girl spy named Anita, they conquered the baddies, commanded the ship, and put out to sea as freebooters to battle pirates. They did so through the final issue.

The Corsair Queen was the last new *Buccaneers* strip, debuting in issue #25 (January 1951). In a sexy two-piece outfit and boots, the title character wielded a cutlass in one hand and a gun in the other, leading a raid on an enemy ship. Joe Millard was the writer and Chuck Winter the artist. The first tale told of how Lila Evans, daughter of the governor of Cathago (wherever *that* was), took to dressing like a "hoyden" and commanding her own ship for the fun of it, whilst swinging a mean sword. She was still a good gal, but when her dad was murdered by the treacherous Lord Merkle, who was in turn killed by his pirate partner Bloody Blake, Lila vowed vengeance. Blake burned down the town of Cathago, but Lila and her aide, Monk, commandeered the freebooters' ship and killed Blake and his men. She vowed to hunt down pirates and bring them to justice. Through issue #27, that's just what she did. Except for some reprints in years to come (and reprints of issues #20 and 23 in IW-Super's *Buccaneer* #1 and 8, 1958), that was the end.

Hillman Comics turns to piracy. © Hillman Periodicals, Inc.

At about the same time, Hillman comics emitted four issues of *Pirates Comics* (#1–4, February–March–September–October 1950), of good quality indeed. Alongside the short stories of corsairs, the title boasted two continuing series: *Alpha, the Slave Pirate* and *Philip Ashton, Boy Pirate Fighter*.

Alpha was a Greek slave in the time of the Romans, one of the guys chained to a seat where he pulled an oar along with scores of others. On a particular sortie in which the shipmaster, Cincanus, wanted to attack Gaul from the sea, the slaves were feeling the lash on their backs when crosscurrents and a squall smashed the ship on hidden rocks. Alpha and his fellows broke free, overcame the slavemaster, and in a battle of chains against swords, beat the Romans. Alpha, now their leader, asked for and got the loyalty of the men. They lured another ship into their hands, freed the slaves, and chained the Romans to their oars. They vowed vengeance against Rome, and became pirates for all four issues. It was a good strip, written by Jack Oleck and drawn by Mike Suchorsky.

Philip Ashton, with Al Ulmer as artist, was set in the times of Columbus. The titular hero was a teenager going to visit his uncle, an advisor to King Ferdinand. Along the way he met with a beauty, Dona Inez, and her bad guy fiancé, Don Grinaldo. The lot of them got captured by a band of Barbary pirates, led by a villain called The Sack. To gain favor, the cowardly Grinaldo bargained with information about a secret entrance to the castle of Philip's uncle. Philip, now a galley slave, busted his oar over the slavemaster's head and freed his fellows. (It was a familiar trope, but what the hey?) There was a battle and Grinaldo was killed by one of Philip's allies, but Dona Inez was still captive, and the Sack traded his life and the lives of his men for the safe return of the girl. Philip got to meet with Ferdinand and Isabella, who were impressed. He figured the affair with the Sack wasn't over, and that was the end of the first story. In the next one, he stopped the Sack from sacking Columbus's ship before his voyage to the new world. The conflict between Philip and the Sack continued till the final issue. As with all the *Pirates Comics* offerings, it was quality stuff.

Avon got into the comics game late in 1945 with their first comic, a one-shot called *Molly O'Day* (#1, February 1945). The Molly story was apparently an inventoried and retitled *Dolly O'Dare* tale from Chesler Comics featuring a female cop. In Avon's action-packed but rather lacking story, she polished off a gang of car thieves. The rest of the stories in the issue were Chesler reprints.

Later, Avon tried an interesting but short-lived take on the sword-and-sandal genre with *Slave Girl Comics* #1 (February 1949), retitled *Slave Girl Princess* with #2 (April 1949). The cover of #1 featured a big pin-up shot of Malu, the titular Slave Girl, in halter and whatever the kind of skirt it is that exposes more leg than it conceals, while Garth, her defender in Roman garb, gutted a surprised guard in the background. Howard Larsen drew the cover and the interior story.

The story began in the present, where redheaded socialite Sandra Worth was introduced to playboy Jeff Garth at a party. He noticed that she was wearing the ancient ring of Ormuz, which gem had the power to let the wearer see the past. With the help of an ancient incantation, Sandra was mentally thrown back 4,000 years to see the adventures of her ancestress, Malu. Jeff's apparent ancestor, a Roman adventurer named Garth, appeared in search of the same ring. Malu, who had been stolen by men of the state of Tammuz as a child, was now a slave girl but was of the royal lineage of Ormuz. She and Garth were sentenced to be killed by lions in an arena, but she found a secret passage and loosed the big cats out into the city. Malu and Garth fled and made their way toward Ormuz, having adventures along the way. At the end of each story, Malu repeated something akin to, "To the end of my days I will be your slave!" They made it to Ormuz, where the king's brother, Malu's uncle, had her sold in the slave market to keep her from threatening his position. Garth bought her back and the two of them reached her father, the King, and engaged her uncle in battle. That was where the vision ended. We came back to the present, and if we wanted to know who won, we'd jolly well have to buy the next issue.

A modern woman gets to be reincarnated as an ancient slave. All in all, it isn't too bad. © Avon Periodicals, Inc.

As it was, in issue #2, uncle Phao lied his way out of trouble, comvincing the King that Malu was not who she claimed to be—it had been 18 years since the King had seen his daughter, after all—and she and Garth were sold into slavery on Phao's galley. Garth freed himself and the slaves, led them in a revolt, and killed Phao. Minutes later, he killed a crewman who was after Malu, and he and the girl were adrift, headed for their next episode. They made it to land and got into more trouble. (Hey, what would the storyline be without it?)

The issue ended on a cliffhanger, but a third Slave Girl story appeared in *Strange Worlds* #3 (June 1951), letting us know that Malu had overthrown her last opponent, the evil queen of Zankhara, and assumed her throne. Garth ruled beside her. But the villainess escaped and made her way to the isle of the Druids, so Garth and Malu had to track her down. In the end, Malu killed her with a crossbow to save Garth, and they made their way back to their kingdom of Zankhara to reign happily ever after. The end.

Another genre of adventure in the Forties, mostly in the postwar era, was espionage. Spies weren't as big as they'd get in the Sixties with the advent of the James Bond movies, but a few of them crept into comics undercover. One of the best espionage-flavored books came from Magazine Enterprises. The cutline on the top of the first issue's cover read, "Thrilling Action!—Grim Suspense!—Crime and Crime-Smashing!—Tales of the F.B.I.!—Scotland Yard—The Northwest Mounties!—Secret Service!" And below that was the title logo of the comic: *Manhunt!*

The first issue opened with a "Story Behind the Cover," which cover featured a masked executioner about to whack a beautiful blonde on a rooftop, while Inspector Kirk of Scotland Yard strove to get there in time to intervene. The two-page text story by Gardner Fox on the inside covers explained the situation, and Kirk got to save the girl from the executioner, who plunged to his death.

In the first comic-strip story, Inspector Ronald Kirk (written by Fox and drawn by Paul Parker) solved a murder involving a fortune stuffed inside a hobbyhorse. It was pretty stereotypical Holmesish stuff but at least was entertaining. Kirk appeared in issues #1–11, 13, and 14 (October 1947–1953) and *Trail Colt* #1 and 2 (July and December 1949), and was reprinted in *Mysteries of Scotland Yard* #1 (1954) and more recently in *A-1 Comics: A Retrospective* #142–143 (February–September 2015).

The star strip of the series came up next. The splash panel depicted a blonde bombshell in a red crossover halter dress and heels, gagged and bound to the bottom of an elevator car. She was *Starr Flagg, Undercover Girl.*

Gardner Fox was the writer and Ogden Whitney the artist on Starr's stories. The heroine herself was a hottie, an American secret agent and a foreign correspondent for a paper called *The Herald*. She ran around in sexy outfits, displayed great detective and scrapping skills, and got

Inspector Kirk brings up the rear and, hopefully, he can stop the axeman's jazz in time to save the heroine. © 1947 Magazine Enterprises.

into more jams than all the perils of Pauline. In her first episode, set in Paris, Starr looked at a portrait of a beautiful woman done by a street artist and detected in the gal's makeup "the diagram of the new Alaskan defense plan for arctic warfare!" She went to the woman's apartment, was grabbed by two male enemy agents, and was indeed bound, gagged, and tied to the bottom of an elevator cage. The villains told her they would shortly cut the cable. After they did, Starr thought, "Guess it's the—*end of me!*"

Not quite. Miss Flagg discovered she could cut her ropes on the frames below the car, swung out, grabbed a pulley cable, and saved herself. Her fellow journalist, Larry, opened a door and saw her. "Hiya, darling," she said. "I have my own way of coming down elevator shafts!"

She tracked down the

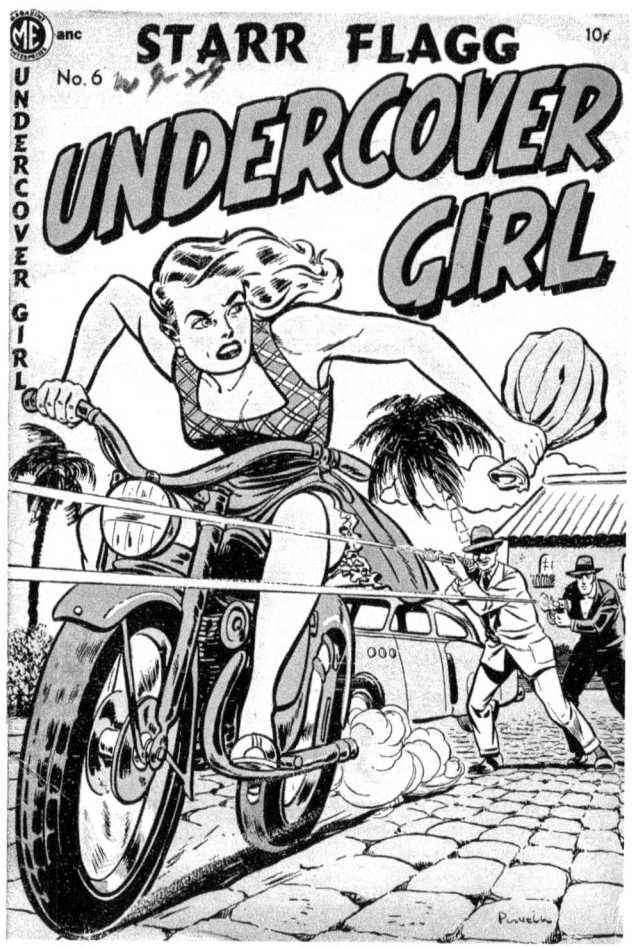

Starr Flagg, U.S. undercover agent, dodges bullets to get a bag of something important into the right hands. © 1953 Magazine Enterprises.

car with the spies who were attempting to escape, caused the vehicle to smash into a wall and burn up the coded picture, and, with the dumbfounded Larry, captured all three of the Commies. They turned the baddies in to the gendarmes, then walked away. Larry asked why they wanted to kill her, when she had told him she just wanted a story from them. "Some people just hate publicity, darling!" she replied, smiling.

That was the way it started. In issue #2 (November 1947), Starr Flagg got a Story Behind the Cover with an Ogden Whitney cover to boot, plus another story in which she got bound and gagged and had to find her way out of a deathtrap. (There was a main plot about atomic spying, too.) In the next issue she fought off some more atom spies while getting in a bunch of bikini shots. She got into her first catfight with a female enemy agent in #5 (February 1948) and followed it with many more. (Fox was always fond of catfights.) Definitely, Starr could handle herself.

The Undercover Girl was featured in *Manhunt* #1–11, 13, and 14 (October 1947– 1953) and *Trail Colt* #1 and 2 (July–December 1949) in original stories. Then came the reprints. *Undercover Girl* ran from issues #5 to 7 (1952–1954) with some terrific covers by Bob Powell. *Red Fox* #15 (1954) reprinted a solo story. AC recycled a couple of Starr stories, and then Boardman Books represented the entire Undercover Girl saga in *A-1 Comics: A Retrospective* #142-143 (2015) and *Undercover Girl: The Complete Adventures of Starr Flagg* (September 2015). She's never appeared in a new story since her first run. We wish she would.

The next strip, *Space Ace*, we've already covered. *Red Fox* was next. He was a Canadian Mountie named Sgt. Jeff Fox, and, like Sgt. Preston, he always got his man. L.B. Cole did an excellent job on the art, and the Fox ran in *Manhunt* #1-11, 13, and 14 (October 1947–1953) and *Trail Colt* #1 and 2 (July–December 1949). He also got a reprint comic named after him (*Red Fox* #15, 1954), but it only offered one Red Fox story. As ever, Boardman books reprinted *Red Fox* in *A-1 Comics: A Retrospective* #142-143 (February–September 2015).

Fallon of the FBI was up next, written by Gardner Fox and drawn by Fred Guardineer and, later, Ogden Whitney. He fought and nabbed a bunch of bank robbers led by one Lady Satan (no, not *that* Lady Satan), saved himself from burning to death, and in general fought the Good Fight. Fallon was, as one might expect, in *Manhunt* #1-11, 13, and 14 (October 1947–1953) and *Trail Colt* #1 and 2 (July–December 1949). He got reprints in *Red Fox* #15 and *Undercover Girl* #7 (both 1954) and all of his stories were reprinted in—yup, you guessed it—*A-1 Comics: A Retrospective* #142-143 (February–September 2015).

Trail Colt, whom we'll cover in our Western chapter, took Space Ace's place in *Manhunt* #8, and that pretty much finished the run. All in all, *Manhunt* was an excellently done comic, and deserves its place in four-color history.

Street & Smith's *Top Secrets* (#1-10, November 1947–July-August 1949) was a book that veered between historical spy and crime stories. When Bob Powell was doing the stories and art, it was pretty good. When he wasn't, it was lousy. The Shadow showed up in an issue (#5, September–October 1948), but, overall, this wasn't a top-notch title.

EC's *International Comics* kicked off in Spring 1947 and, like *Manhunt*, featured a variety of crimebusters and scripting by Gardner Fox. This was a bit before EC's New Trend, which brought about a legendary turn in scripting and art, but all in all, it wasn't bad. The idea was to feature a batch of heroes from different nations, one per strip. America was represented by private eye Van Manhattan, of *Manhattan's Files*.

Van's schtick was that he had a big file, nicknamed "the Coffin," containing cards detailing the history of just about every crook in America. Van was aboard a plane that was hijacked by an old foe, Johnny Dukes, who had just escaped from prison. (This was prescient, way before the plane hijackings of the 1960s.) So, as it turned out, was a girl who thought she was Dukes's sister. Eventually Dukes found out that such was the truth, and he sacrificed his own life to save his sister's life, Van's, and those of everyone else on the plane. It read like one of DC's old "Just a Story" human interest tales, or maybe like a secondhand *Spirit*. Howard Purcell, who had drawn "Just a Story," did the first Manhattan tale. Leo Bachle drew the rest. Van ran through *International Comics* #1-5 (Spring–November–December 1947), then in *International Crime Patrol* #6 (Spring 1948) and *Crime Patrol* #7 (Summer 1948).

Moving on, we find *Igor the Archer* in the issue's second position. In pre–Communist Russia, Igor Rostov was a young man and as able a bowman as William Tell. Count Rostov, his father, was brought up before the Czar on charges of helping a peasant escape jail for theft. When Rostov opined the man was no criminal, just poor, the Czar sympathized by having him stretched on a rack till he acknowledged the Czar's justice—which, of course, he wouldn't do. The ruler ordered that Ivan be brought to him to persuade Count Rostov of the error of his ways.

That proved tough going indeed. Igor, at target practice as ever, learned from his fat sidekick, Boris, that the Czar's men were coming for him. They clobbered the squad of soldiers, rode back to home, and found Rostov's estate in flames, courtesy of Guess Who. The Czar lured both of them into a trap via an archery contest, and Igor got to meet his father shortly before the man died on the rack. With his last breath, Rostov told his son to always fight tyranny: "Crush it, else it crush you." The Czar opted to have Igor hung in public.

Igor and Boris were on the scaffold, hands bound, ready for the noose. But the archer, calling for the overthrow of the Czar, threw himself backward, cut his ropes on a soldier's sword, freed Boris, kicked the Czar off his throne, and made a ladder of arrows on a wall so he and Boris could escape. It was the beginning of Igor's story, and a good one it was, too.

Unlike Van Manhattan, Igor didn't appear in every issue. He showed up in *International Comics* #1, 3, and 5 (Spring–November–December 1947), then in *International Crime Patrol* #6 (Spring 1948) and *Crime Patrol* #8 (Fall 1948).

We'd like to pass over the next feature, but we really can't. *Juan Meatbal* was the third story. It was an ethnic humor bit featuring the aforementioned Juan (as in the song "One Meat Ball"—Google it), a Mexican boy who was the son of Mayor Meatbal. The town he lived in needed to have a fish fry (or, as the caption had it, "Mexican feesh-fry"). There was only one fish in town, so Juan had to go to the "watery coast" and—ahh, skip it. He was in issues #1 and 3 (Spring 1947 and July–August 1947) and that was enough. More than, actually.

The last feature was a goodie. *That's Madelon*, as the strip was called, featured the adventures of a beautiful French photographer for a news mag called *Critique*. She had been a sexy circus acrobat, daughter of another such acrobat, during the Nazi occupation of France. But when her father was shot down in mid-swing by the Germans for sabotaging a troop ship, she became a member of the underground herself, learned how to fight, and became an expert saboteur. After the defeat of the occupiers, to prove she was good enough to become a news photog, she was assigned to get a shot of Bobo, king of the Apaches. (These kind of Apaches weren't Indians, they were French undergrounders.) Along the way, a couple of thieves tried to steal her camera. She cleaned the first one's clock, and the other was so impressed he agreed to bring her to Bobo himself.

Surprise! The thief *was* Bobo himself, and he took her to his lair in the sewers. When a falling-out among thieves occurred, prompted by a Fascist traitor, Madelon and Bobo fought their way to freedom. The effort cost Bobo his life. She got a picture of his last moments and, coming back to *Critique*, ordered an extra print for herself. The last panel was a tip for getting better photographs, which became a standard feature. Madelon made her way through *International Comics* #1–5 (Spring–November–December 1947), *International Crime Patrol* #6 (Spring 1948) and *Crime Patrol* #7 and 9 (Summer–Winter 1948). Fox and Sheldon Moldoff were her creators.

International #2 (Summer 1947) introduced two new features to alternate with Igor and Juan Meatbal. Fox wrote them both. *The Chessmen* were a band of English detectives in the Sherlock Holmes tradition, composed of King (the Holmes figure), Rook (a kid straight from the Baker Street Irregulars), and the Bishop (an old drunk). They solved a murder in a veddy, veddy British manner, and treaded the boards again in issues #4 and 5 (September–October 1947–November–December 1947), in *International Crime Patrol* #6 (Spring 1948), and in *Crime Patrol* #7 (Summer 1948). Lee Ames and Burt Frohman did the art.

Diggy Do and Diggy Don't replaced Juan Meatbal on his off days and, like him, were an ethnic feature with some humor, but they had a serious framework. Kurt Schaffenberger was the artist. Diggy and Diggy were a knockoff of Charlie Chan and Lee "Number One Son" Chan, being a Chinese father-and-son shamus team. In their first *International* appearance (#2, Summer 1947), they got on a case to retrieve the Ruby of Life, a stolen gem intended to be sold for Chinese relief. The traditional dad and the hipster son retrieved the Ruby, and the thief, crazed with fear, fell to his death. It was good for its time. They appeared in issue #4 (September–October 1947) as well.

In *International Comics* #5 (November–December 1947), Gardner Fox pulled out the stops and teamed up Van Manhattan, Igor, the Chessmen, and Madelon in a book-lengther that harkened back to his days writing the *Justice Society of America* stories in *All-Star Comics* (and possibly presaged his later scripting in *Justice League of America*). The story started in Van's episode, continued through Igor's (he was a descendant of the original Igor, thankfully), picked up with the Chessmen, and finished in Madelon's episode. The unit was dubbed the International Patrol, and *International Crime Patrol* was the title of the whole comic in the next issue (#6, Spring 1948).

But it didn't work.

EC was still having trouble finding its legs. With #7 (Summer 1948), the book became *Crime Patrol* and was dedicated to more run-of-the-mill crime stories. *Captain Crime*, the only new feature, made his only appearance in that issue, as a face-scarred veteran who became a cigarette-smoking private eye. He brought in the Field Marshal of Murder, an ex–Nazi villain, in his only exploit. The book burned off the inventory of *International Comics* stories in future issues.

In issue #15 (December 1949–January 1950), the cover teased a horror story "from the *Crypt of Terror!*" inside. The next one (#16, February–March 1950) introduced the Crypt-Keeper, horror host of all horror hosts. By #17 (April–May 1950), EC went the whole hog, renamed the book *The Crypt of Terror* (later *Tales from the Crypt*) and made it an all-horror book. Obviously, it dragged in a lot more cash than its predecessors.

D.S. Publishing's spy offering was *Jeff Jordan, U.S. Agent* (#1, December 1947–January 1948). This one-shot featured the aforementioned Mr. Jordan and it was a

The *International* heroes team up as the International Patrol. Not the Justice Society of America, but they try hard. © 1947 I.C. Publishing Co., Inc., 2022 by EC Publications.

pretty generic tale of an American agent stepping into some Spillane-like stuff while he sought out a batch of stamp counterfeiters. There probably wasn't much reason to continue it for another issue, so they didn't.

In August–September 1949, the American Comics Group published the first issue of *Spy and Counterspy*, which turned into *Spy Hunters* with issue #3 (December

1949–January 1950). The lead feature was *Jonathan Kent, Counterspy*, who, despite his name, was not Superman's foster father. He debuted in hat and trench coat, smoking with the Capitol Building behind him, and relating his origin story. Kent had been a fighter pilot in the war, and in 1946, he volunteered for the American Espionage Service. (The agency was fictitious, but so were S.H.I.E.L.D. and U.N.C.L.E. in days to come.) When a recruiter asked him why he wanted to be a spy, Kent related that, as a kid, he'd gone with his engineer dad to Russia—not identified by name, but a "foreign government with a five-year plan"—and seen upfront the abuses of Communist tyranny. He was out to keep it from happening in America, and they gave him his chance.

Spy and Counterspy: The Cold War comes to comics. © Best Syndicated Features, Inc.

Said chance involved a lot of training in all the spy trade, and Jon Kent bonded with two colleagues, Toby and Gregg. Their first assignment: find a vanished atomic scientist. From there, the trio did much detective work and located their man, now a corpse. The hunt was on for the murderer, who undoubtedly had the atomic secret. Toby was killed by a grenade. Gregg apparently died in the blast. That left Kent, who went to East Berlin, found out his pal Gregg was a traitor and had murdered Toby, and killed him in a fight. After leaving his body in a water tower (which probably poisoned a bunch of people who drank from it!), Kent fell in love with a comely blonde, found out she was really from the other side, got turned over to the Reds, got sprung from jail by the blonde (who decided she was really in love with him), and recovered the atomic secrets. She saved Jon's life and got him to the West Berlin side but was killed in the process. That wrapped up the first case, and was par for the stories to follow. Kent continued through *Spy Hunters* #13 (August–September 1951). Richard Hughes may have been the writer. Charles Sultan was the artist.

A one-shot feature, *Report to the Nation*, followed, with a radio newsman based on Walter Winchell relating a tale of Chinese espionage. Lots of fun swipes at Milt

Caniff's *Terry and the Pirates* lurked within. Then came *Operation: Peril*, with military intelligence ops foiling a neo–Nazi plot to steal an American invention. This one featured the heroic Jerry Lawton, his love interest Phyllis Rogers, and the inventor Professor Barlow. The three characters never came back, but the feature lent its name to *Operation: Peril*, a 16-issue action anthology that ran from October–November 1950 to April–May 1953. The rest of *Spy and Counterspy / Spy Hunters*' pages were filled with non-series spy stories, and the whole effort was pretty good.

Don Fortune Magazine (#1–6, August 1946–1947) was pubbed postwar by the Don Fortune Publishing Company, actually a bunch of Fawcett hands who wanted to try their luck. The story opened with Don Fortune and Andy Jarvis, formerly Marine pilots, discharged and looking for a job in Civilian Land. They stumbled into a hot car ring and clobbered the miscreants. Then they stumbled into an arson ring and got a gig as investigators for an insurance company. Finally, they decided to open their own detective agency. It was pretty good, but the backup, C.C. Beck's *Delecta of the Planets*, was better. This one featured a queen of an alien planet and her fight to save her world from the evil Ardora. Both features ended in the same issue.

Detective Don Fortune and space queen Delecta in the same comic, with art by C.C. Beck. How could you go wrong with that? © 1946 Don Fortune Publishing Co.

Bruce Gentry Comics managed to be published by two outfits within the space of eight issues. Gentry was the star of his own syndicated comic strip, which ran from 1945 to 1951, drawn by Milt Caniff associate Ray Bailey. Late of the Army Air Force, Bruce Gentry ran a small airline in South America and ran into enough trouble and romance to satisfy most *Terry and the Pirates* fans. The first *Bruce Gentry* comic (#1, January 1948) came from Four Star Publications and reprinted the syndicated strips. The next seven (#2–8, November 1948–July 1949) came from Canada's Superior Comics outfit. By issue #4, Jack

Kamen was offering great original stories of Bruce, and they continued till the end. These books are little known now, but they're worth investigating.

Similar was *Brenda Starr*, derived from Dale Messick's classic girl reporter strip. Four Star published the first two issues, numbered #13 and 14 (September 1947–March 1948), which had terrific Kamenesque covers and reprinted syndicated strips inside. Superior took over with issues #3–12 (June 1948–December 1949), and, before long, offered decent and well-illoed crime stories featuring Brenda and her sidekick, Abretha Breeze. Charlton picked it up for a couple of strip reprint issues (#13–14, June–August 1955). In 1963, Dell did a one-shot (*Brenda Starr* #1, October–December 1963) with an original story, and that was it.

Also, two superheroes we managed to miss in our last offerings must be noted here. *A-1 Comics* #8 and 10 (1947) offered *The Masquerader*. Though he didn't wear a costume as such (unless you count the Robin Hood getup he wore in the second story), he was a master of disguise and, as such, used his expertise to foil crooks. His real name was Hank Smith and he was partnered with a beautiful blonde, which probably beats Robin or Bucky.

And *Variety Comics* #1–3 (1944–1946) contained *Captain Valiant*, a red-costumed hero named Bruce Barton who was the understudy to a similarly costumed actor in a Broadway show, *Comic Follies*. When the actor turned up drunk on opening night, Bruce had to sub for him. And when crooks attacked the show for its payroll, he had to put them down, and did. At the end, like the Black Hood, Valiant vowed he would "erase crime from the face of the Earth!" For three issues, as drawn by Marvin Stein, he did just that.

There were, as we've noted, many other Adventurers, mostly backups in anthology titles, but those were the headliners. Not every hero in the Golden Age had to wear a mask or have superpowers, and many of 'em were as readable as the ones who did, or more so.

Once Upon a Time, in the Westerns

Westerns never seem to leave American entertainment. They can fade away for a time, but they never fail to resurge. From the dime novels of the nineteenth century to the pulps of the 1930s, from the silent movie era to blockbusters like *Once Upon a Time in the West* and *Tombstone*, from TV shows like *Gunsmoke* to *Deadwood*, you cannot erase them. Nor should we even try. It is myth, it is morality play, it is glorification of the outlaw, it is justification of the lawman, it is a dramatic form that every American seems to understand. Maybe it's one that the whole world has come to understand.

The cowboys and sheriffs and owlhoots and barmaids and schoolmarms and town tamers all shouldered their way into comics from the start. Our policy for covering Westerns in this volume will be to include the ones which started before 1950, with an exception or two. Westerns may have been *the* biggest action-comic genre during the Fifties. But, as we'll see, there were plenty of hard-ridin' heroes before then.

Indeed, there were sagebrush sagas in the earliest of comics. Dell's *The Funnies* #1 (January 16, 1929) was one of the first serial comics published in America, and it contained a page of *Deadwood Gulch* by Boody Rogers, who would go on to create *Sparky Watts*. DC's *New Fun Comics* #1 (February 1935), their first comic, sported a story of *Jack Woods*, a Western hero, on its cover. He also managed a two-page text story inside, and *Buckskin Jim* by Eugene Koscik followed a little later. At this time, in their genesis, comics tried to look somewhat like a Sunday newspaper comics page with only one or two pages per story. Soon enough, they'd learn how to utilize their pages for fewer, longer stories, but that was still a couple of years away.

Plenty of Western comic strips were reprinted in comic books that did such things, one of the first we know of being a run of *Hairbreadth Harry* starting in *Famous Funnies* #10 (May 1935), but such things are out of our scope. Or maybe out of our range, all things considered. DC continued with the likes of Jack Woods, Buckskin Jim, Loco Luke, and Frank of the Frontier in *New Fun Comics*, renamed *More Fun Comics* with #7 (January 1936), and *Sagebrush 'n' Cactus* in their new book, *New Comics* #1 (January 1936), later to be *New Adventure Comics* and then plain *Adventure Comics*. The Comics Magazine Company offered two 2-page episodes of *Captain Bill of the Rangers* in *The Comics Magazine* V. 1 #1 (May 1936). Most of these and the fillers that followed can be logged in as first efforts, but not much more.

In Dell's *Popular Comics* #4 (May 1936), we got something a bit more notable: *Tom Mix.*

A little background here is necessary. Thomas Hezikiah Mix was very possibly the most important cowboy superstar of his time, and he appeared in about as many media as Tarzan: movies, radio, the circus, Big Little Books, and—oh, yeah—comics. Born in 1880, he learned to ride at an early age in Pennsylvania and worked on a farm while dreaming of joining the circus. He enlisted in the Army during the Spanish-American War but did not go overseas. Later, he rode in the inaugural parade for President Teddy Roosevelt, briefly became a night marshal in Dewey, Oklahoma, and wound up working at the Miller Brothers 101 Ranch, which sported its own traveling Wild West show. (Thank you, Wikipedia!) He roped, rode, and wrangled skillfully enough to catch the eyes of some movie people. That was where it really began.

Mix first hit the film world in 1909's *The Cowboy Millionaire* and proceeded to make 291 movies, ending in 1935 with *The Miracle Rider*, a 15-chapter serial. He and his horse, Tony, captured the hearts of millions of American kids and adults, and he influenced the course of Western movies from that time till this. He had five marriages, got his own radio show in 1933 (Mix, being wounded in the throat by a bullet, couldn't play himself and instead was "impersonated" by actors), was named an honorary Texas Ranger in 1935, and was one of Wyatt Earp's pallbearers in 1929, having met the legendary gunfighter when Earp was a consultant on his early films.

Tom Mix was still alive when his first forays into comic books were made. He died in a car accident on October 12, 1940. Those are the facts. Now for the legend.

Tom and his Straight Shooters from the radio show had appeared in a couple of advertising strips in 1935 that made their way into comics. But his first non-commercial gig was for Dell, so we begin there.

Popular Comics was a book full of reprinted paste-ups from newspaper comics. Tom's first appearance, in issue #4, was only a tad different: a Big Little Book, one of those half-breeds with a page of text on one side and an illustration on the other, was cut up, pasted up, and adapted with captions below the illoes. The BLB was *The Fighting Cowboy*. Leon Morgan did the original text, Hal Arbo provided the art, and Gaylord DuBois did the caption adaptation. (DuBois would later write scads of comics and books, including a 20-year run on *Tarzan*, as we have seen.)

The first story, after presenting a silhouette of Tom and Tony, began with our hero reining up in the town of Snake Prairie, Texas. (Wherever Mix went, the Old West was there.) He was looking for work, but the town seemed a mite ... well ... quiet. "'Doggone,' thought Tom. "Pears like while I'm looking for work, I've run into a mystery.'" And so he had. Tom, "six foot two and lithe as a panther," tied up Tony, went into a local saloon, found out there was a range war between the town founder and an interloper, faced down a card cheat, and rode out to offer his services to the good guys. Colonel White, the founder, hired him. He warned, "But if it's advice you want, here it is: leave here tonight. Dunham's a bad man and a killer."

Tom responded with a smile. "I've been ridin' all over Texas looking for a little excitement. Now I've found it, and I reckon you've got a new cowhand."

That was all that was needed. Tom cleaned up the town and rode off to further cut-up Big Little Book adventures, finishing up his *Popular Comics* run by issue #15 (April 1937). By that time, he'd already jumped to Dell's *The Comics* (#1–5, March–September 1937) as well as *100 Pages of Comics* #101 (1937). Tom then took a little time off and rode back into town in *Crackajack Funnies* #1–18 (June 1938–December 1939). All of this stuff, *all* of it, mind you, was just recycled and adapted Big Little Book material. Tom Mix deserved better. After that, he mounted Tony and headed on over to another territory—to *original* comics.

And those comics were some of his finest ever!

Tom Mix Comics weren't sold on the newsstand. They were sold on the radio. In order to get 'em, you had to send in two box tops from Ralston cereal, which sponsored Tom's show. But kids were used to doing that by then—heck, just about *all* kids' shows on radio had a tear-the-top-off-the-box premium—so that wasn't asking much. What you got was *definitely* worth the trouble.

The first issue, dated September 1940, sported a dynamic cover of Tom astride Tony, both of them busting through the page itself, excellently drawn by Fred Meagher. (Meagher would go on to draw tons of great Western comics, including *Straight Arrow* for Magazine Enterprises in the Fifties.) All of Tom's radio pals were there, including his old pard Wrangler; his ward, Jane; singing cowboy Pecos; Wash, the cook (a Black stereotype, but at least a *nice* Black stereotype); Sheriff Mike Shaw; and, of course, Tony. The first story, a 10-pager entitled "Ghost Canyon," was also by Meagher. A few cowpokes were musing how nobody made it back alive from the titular canyon. Tom Mix laid it on the line: "I have!" The rest of the story told us how he did it. You did *not* doubt Tom Mix.

A fan page for Straight Shooters followed, with a humor strip, *The Fumble Family with Amos Q. Snood*, after that. The latter was straight out of the Sunday-funnies milieu. Amos Q. Snood, in the radio show, was a chiseling lawyer. The Fumbles were, well, about what you'd expect them to be. The feature was written by Stan Schendel and drawn by Charlie Biro, and if we have to tell you who Biro is, you'd better go read the Lev Gleason chapter in *Secondary Superheroes*. Snood got into more slapstick comedy than Three Stooges shorts. Kids have always eaten this up, and the feature balanced out the more serious Tom Mix stories.

The next story featured Jane, Tom's ward, a young teenager, most likely. It dipped into *Little Nemo* territory and concerned Jane's dream adventures, one per night, always picking up the story with the next installment. The tale placed Jane in an ancient kingdom where she had to aid a handsome blond hero named Strongbow, who wore only a bearskin kilt and boots and used a bow and arrow for his weapon. They had to defeat a wizard, Maldred, who had locked up the king of Dream Castle and his daughter. Jane and Strongbow buckled them swashes and saved the monarch and princess, a dream at a time. The tale went on for all twelve issues, and was so humorous, action-packed, and well-drawn and -written that it's a crime nobody has reprinted it yet. But then again, that goes for all of *Tom Mix Comics*.

The issue finished out with another Tom Mix story, "The Gunsight Holdup." The whole book was good, and it was evident why: Ralston-Purina had more money to spend than the average comic book publisher, and they wanted a good product. The kids who ate Ralston cereals to get those box tops couldn't have been disappointed.

The next issue fronted a cover of Tom laying out an armed desperado with one punch, dust billowing up from the ground. Batman couldn't have done it better. Wrangler, Jane, Pecos, and Wash greeted us on the first page, all tall in the saddle (well, maybe a little less tall for Jane) and lifting hands, lassos, or hats to welcome us in. "We tried to make this issue even better than the first," Pecos proclaimed, "so be sure an' tell us just what you think of it!" Inside, we learned that Tony had been horse-napped, and a new Wild West show in town boasted a black horse that nobody could ride. Nobody except Jane, that is, who calmed the critter down. After adding things up, Tom and company deduced the truth: the black horse was Tony with a paint job. The evil Colonel Sutler and his two waddies tried to chase Jane down before she could get Tony to Mix, but the ultra-cowboy shot the guns out of the hands of the badmen and he and Pecos took them down. When Sheriff Mike showed up, Sutler protested they were stealing his horse. Tom mounted Tony, rode him into a river, and emerged with the black dye washed off. All that was left was for Tom to lasso the varmints when they tried to escape, and that was that. To the villain in custody, Tom said, "Lawbreakers always lose, Two-Spot! Straight Shooters always win! It pays to be a Straight Shooter!"

The series continued in this fashion through issue #9. But something happened along the way: Pearl Harbor. Tom Mix couldn't stay out of the conflict, even though he'd been dead for about a year. (Such problems couldn't stop, say, Boris Karloff and Rod Serling from hosting comic stories for Gold Key in the Seventies.) With issue #10 (September 1942), the book was renamed *Tom Mix Commandos Comics*, and on the cover, Tom had traded his cowboy hat and duds for a U.S. Army helmet and uniform. He was tossing Japanese sailors off the deck of a surfaced submarine, and was outnumbered but didn't give a toss about it.

On the inside front cover, we saw a grim picture of Mix in a helmet, with the info that tied in with a hiatus in the radio show: Tom and his buddies were in secret training to become a cowboy commando outfit. Everyone but the underage Jane were signed up to fight the Axis for Uncle Sam. The Japanese were bombing American shores with shells that left no fragments. Quite naturally, G2 called in Tom, who arrived in full cowboy regalia astride Tony. Mix and his crew doffed their cowboy outfits for Army togs, were soon attacked by cloaked and hooded fifth columnists, and then found themselves in combat with the crew of a Japanese sub. Despite being overpowered and captured, the cowboy crew found a way to escape by throwing saltwater on the sub's batteries and producing deadly chlorine gas. Instants before the sub commander could target another American city, the sub crew, blaming him for their danger, rebelled and killed him. Our heroes found gas masks, left through an escape hatch, and swam to safety just before a U.S. battleship sighted the sub and sank same. The mystery shells were explained away as having magnesium casings that quickly burned up after impact. Mix and company then dealt with the gangsterish fifth columnists by boarding a prop plane and forcing their car off a mountain road. The drop was, conveniently, 1,000 feet up. Hopefully, the Axis got the message: *nobody* messed with Tom Mix.

The book lasted two more issues and became outlandish but was still fun: Tom and his cowboy commandos fought off invisible Axis invaders and a horde of flying

Japanese dragons. Things might have been getting desperate by that time, because just about every story and the back cover blurb ended with a plea for kids to send in postcards demanding that *Tom Mix Commandos Comics* be continued. Evidently, it didn't work. With issue #12 (November 1942), the book was gone.

That was the way it stayed for about six years. DC's *Real Fact Comics* #5 (November–December 1946) featured a five-page bio of Mix, including the real fact that he was dead, but that was about it. However, the radio show was still plugging along quite well. (It was ousted in 1943 but came raring back a year later.) The next year, of all things, Tom Mix guest-starred in *Kid Eternity* #5 (Spring 1947) from Quality. The Kid had the power to bring back people from the dead to help him, and Tom Mix, being officially dead, turned up in a puff of smoke to lasso an escaping villain. Kid Eternity sent him back to the sweet by and by after that.

But the postwar superhero bear market was in swing, and one stock that came in bullish was Western comics. Accordingly, Fawcett, publisher of *Captain Marvel*, dealt Tom Mix a new hand.

Tom Mix switches to Fawcett, with plenty of photograph covers and well-drawn stories to come. © 1947 Fawcett Publications, Inc.

Tom Mix Western #1 (January 1948) debuted with a recolored cover photo of Tom brandishing a six-shooter and giving us a tight smile. Most Fawcetts, and indeed most Western comics based on film stars, went with photo covers if they could. Inside, artists Carl Pfeufer and John Jordan, who would do just about all of Fawcett's Mix stories, presented four tales of Mix, starting with one where he proved his cowboy prowess at a Wild West show. Two outlaws conked him on the head and stole a diamond belt he was supposed to be awarded. But as soon as he came to, Mix trailed the owlhoots, jumped them from above, pulled both off their horses, and clouted them both out in two panels. Pfeufer's action endings were always worth the price of reading the rest of the story.

Of Tom's supporting cast, Sheriff Mike Shaw turned up regularly, but Jane and her fellow ward Johnny (who never appeared in comics), Wrangler, Pecos, and Wash were absent. The focus was to be on Mix alone. The radio show was winding down and in 1950 it ceased, with an announcer telling us that Tom Mix would never be forgotten.

That did not inhibit his comics career. At least, not immediately. Tom rode through issue #61 of *Tom Mix Western* (May 1953), kept Mary Marvel company in *Wow Comics* #65–69 (April–August 1948), hung with it when it was retitled *Real Western Hero* (#70–75, September 1948–February 1949), and rode it out when it was retitled *Western Hero* (#76–112, March 1949–March 1952). He also took up residence in Captain Marvel, Jr.'s *Master Comics* (#95–133, September 1948–April 1953). For good measure, he also guest-starred in actor Richard Conte's biography in Ziff-Davis's *Famous Stars* #4 (May–June 1951). Then Tom Mix's Fawcett run came to an end, because Fawcett Comics itself came to an end. DC's lawsuit against them, claiming Captain Marvel was plagiarized from Superman, took its toll.

But Charlton, which picked up tons of features from failing comic companies at the time, took up Tom's option. He found a spot in *Six-Gun Heroes* #27 (June–July 1954) with what may have been a remaindered Fawcett story, and continued with Fawcett reprints through issue #35 (March 1956). He also popped up in Charlton's *Cowboy Western* #53–54 (February–April 1955). And that was the end of Tom Mix's career in comics.

Almost.

In 1982, the Straight Shooters at Ralston-Purina put out a small giveaway comic, *Tom Mix and the Taking of Grizzly Greb*, which was stuffed inside boxes of Ralston cereals. It was possibly scripted by radio-show expert Jim Harmon and definitely drawn by Alex Toth, and was adapted from a story in *Tom Mix Comics* #9. Pecos, Wrangler, Tony, and Jane were back, and it was a quality undertaking for all its small size.

Six years later, Bill Black, the cowboy-lovin' publisher of AC Comics, brought back Mix for a bunch of Fawcett reprints. He appeared in *Great American Western* #3 and 4 (1988–1989), *Tom Mix Western* #1 and 2 (1988–1989), *Cliffhanger Comics* #2 (1989), *Tom Mix Holiday Album* #1 (1990), *Western Movie Hero* #1 (2000), and, finally, *Best of the West* #33, 38, and 55 (2002–2006). As of this writing, that's where it stands. Is Tom Mix, at long last, dead? Physically, yes. In comics? Only time will tell, as the saying goes.

One year after Tom Mix's first comics story appearance, the Comics Magazine Corporation, later Centaur, came out with the first comic regularly devoted to cowboy tales: *Western Picture Stories*. It ran four issues (#1–4, February–June 1937) and is notable for that and for some Jurassic-era work from Will Eisner. Issue #1 opened with a fairly well-drawn tale of a settler, his daughter, and a good-guy Indian beset by a white renegade and bad-guy Indians. After the inevitable gunplay, the good Indian stabbed the white bad guy to death. Not a bad start, really.

Later came one of comics' first original masked heroes, *The Phantom of the Hills*. The Phantom, wearing a bandanna over his lower face and a pulled-down 10-gallon hat, played Robin Hood and stopped a gang of thieves from stealing a gold mine from a family. Swift shooting and rolled-down boulders took care of most of the gang. When the gang leader faced off with the Phantom, he found his gun was out of bullets. The Phantom set him straight: "Five years ago you shot down a youngster in cold blood—That kid was my brother—Now at last I've caught up with you! I could easily finish you as you did my brother—but I'm goin' to give you a fighting chance!"

With that, the Phantom threw down his gun belt, faced off hand-to-hand with the villain, and knocked him down. The baddie snuck one of the Phantom's guns from the belt and tried to shoot him. The hero fell flat on his belly, grabbed the other gun, and shot the sidewinder to death. The last panel showed the rightful claim owners exuberant with a copy of the map to the gold mine and a note from the Phantom of the Hills.

Possibly the first Western comics anthology, *Western Picture Stories*. © 1937 Comics Magazine Co.

The Phantom lasted through issue #3 (April 1937). Back in issue #1, Wild Bill Eisner offered up a story of *Wild Tex Martin*, a blond ranch hand who was mighty good with his gun, as he needed to be. The first tale pitted cattlemen against sheepmen, with the cattlemen being on the side of right. (You could tell because the corrupt sheriff wore a black hat.) Turns out the sheriff was really Cactus Kirby, the murderer of Tex's dad. Tex got made a deputy marshal by the head of an Army garrison and went to find the killer's trail. He had to foil two deadly traps and take out two thugs along the way, but he caught Kirby running for the border. The hero proceeded to knock him off his horse, un-gun him, un-knife him, and knock him out. He brought Kirby back to justice, a rope around his wrists and walking behind Tex's horse. (Considering what horses inevitably do, that was probably an added punishment.) The citizens elected Tex Martin their new sheriff. Tex also made it to issue #3.

The book was filled out with the likes of *Tex Maverick, Windy Parks, Matt Crawford, Buck Bush, Sauerkraut Bill and Spareribs, Tom Brent, Tumbleweeds, Lobo-Dog,* and a batch of generic Western stories. It may not have lasted long—few Centaur comics did—but it was the first.

Dell filled their hand in April 1937 with a one-shot, *Western Action Thrillers*. On the cover, it had a cowboy pointing a smoking gun at us. In the other hand, he held a boy, whom he was presumably protecting. It was 100 pages long and featured tales

Dell gets into the act with *Western Action Thrillers*. © 1937 Dell Publishing Co.

of Buffalo Bill, the Texas Kid, Laramie Joe, Rimrock O'Reilly, Two-Gun Thompson, and Wild West Bill. All the stories were set up like the interior of a Big Little Book, with several illustrations per page accompanying captions under each of them. 'Nuff said, pardner.

DC started out with one- to four-page stories that continued once per month. *More Fun* continued the forgettable adventures of Jack Woods up to issue #35 (September 1938). In the next issue (#36, October 1938), the *Masked Ranger* saddled up. It was drawn well enough by Jim Chambers, and if they missed any strokes from the *Lone Ranger*, it must have been because they weren't trying hard enough: "The founding hoofs of a fiery horse! It's the Masked Ranger—Star and Pedro, riding to match guns and wits with the ruthless Night Raiders. This unique trio, righting wrongs and bringing criminals to justice, strikes without warning then vanishes unrewarded and unthanked."

In his first episode, the Ranger, on his brown horse, Star, saved a wounded man who had been attacked by the same Night Raiders, found out the rannies (top cowboys or ranch hands) had stolen a map to a gold mine (making you wonder how many gold mines there really were, back in those days), and got on their trail. With the help of his aide, Pedro, the Masked Ranger captured the Raiders by issue #38 (December 1938). He was the lead feature in *More Fun*, and he lasted till issue #41 (March 1939).

Detective Comics offered *Buck Marshall, Range Detective* in issues #1–36 (March 1937–February 1940). It ran in black and white, was scripted and drawn by Homer Fleming, and was pretty average for its time. Buck backed out around the tenth appearance of Batman, and it's doubtful anybody noticed.

In *Action Comics*, home of Superman, *Chuck Dawson* held forth from issue #1 to 22 (May 1938–March 1940). Another Homer Fleming creation, Chuck also started out in black and white. His father was killed in "a bloody Texas range war," and after reaching his maturity, Chuck came back to get the waddies of the 4-G Ranch. He graduated to red, white, and black colors in issue #8 (January 1939) and was so dull you could probably be forgiven for cheering on the bad guys.

Something much better turned up in *Action Comics* #42: *The Vigilante*. A cross between a masked superhero and an Old West cowboy hero, the Vig's first page, rendered excellently by Mort Meskin, showed the Stetson-hatted, bandanna-masked, Western-outfitted hero fighting off four modern gangsters, lassoing one behind his back! The intro copy went like this: "From across the Western plains and into the streamlined East flashes a mystery rider symbolic of the spirit of frontier America—The Vigilante—heroic champion of law and order, who battles twentieth century criminals with weapons of the range in a ceaseless one-man stampede again all lawlessness! Follow the victory trail of the Vigilante as he rounds up Public Enemy Number 1 with smoking six-guns and twirling lariat—"

If that wasn't enough to get your pulse pounding, you were probably never a kid who watched Westerns at a Saturday morning matinee. Mort Weisinger created and wrote the character. The Vigilante, already in operation by the time of this story, was on hand to watch the execution of Killer Kelly, a murderer he had brought to justice. Before taking the hot seat, Kelly swore to the Vig that he would return from the

**Mort Weisinger and Mort Meskin produce the modern-day Western hero, the Vigilante.
© DC Comics.**

grave and get him. He did pretty much that, as a doctor whom Kelly had threatened reduced the current so that the crook was able to survive the shock. Kelly went on to graphically shoot down a victim with a Tommy gun during a bank robbery. "A cool hundred grand!" he gloated. "Not bad for a dead guy!"

The scene switched to a local rodeo, where Greg Sanders, a singing cowboy and radio star, was posing for pictures and protesting mildly that his publicity people were building him up too much as a cowboy hero. He saved folks from a runaway steer by roping it a few panels later, so his flacks might be pardoned for all that. After meeting with "blues singer" Betty Stuart, the strip ingenue, Greg learned that Kelly's fingerprints had been found at the bank he robbed. He ducked out, and Betty mused, "If only he weren't such a phoney, I could care a lot for him. But I'll bet he's never been out of this state!"

At his home, Greg Sanders changed into his Vigilante duds, and mused that he had to take in Kelly dead or alive. Then we finally got an origin flashback: "Born in Wyoming, Greg Sanders inherited the sterling qualities of his grandfather, Indian fighter and stalwart frontiersman—" Granddad Sanders was shown gunning down a couple of Indians. "The son of a fearless county sheriff, young Greg Sanders learned the law of the range … to bring to justice those engaged in corrupt practices…." Sanders *père* was depicted busting up a rustler's mob with his two six-guns. "Years later, his father killed by a band of stagecoach bandits, Greg Sanders vows to follow his family tradition and uses his heritage to become The Vigilante, nemesis of all crime from border to border!"

It was kinda strange to contemplate Sanders, Sr., being gunned down by stagecoach robbers in the early twentieth century, but—what the hey—kids didn't care about such things back then, and maybe they still don't. In the next panel, we saw Greg in cowboy regalia, with a guitar, in a radio studio, singing "Home on the Range" with a trio of cuties hanging on his every syllable. (The illo of an open-mouthed Greg with a guitar looks uncannily like the photo of Elvis on the cover of his first album, *Elvis Presley*, released in 1956.)

Anyway, we picked up the trail of the story on the next page, where the Vigilante attended a masked ball disguised as himself. Inevitably, Killer Kelly showed up to rob the soiree, and turned to see the guy dressed as his archfoe: "Hah! Don't you wish you really were the Vigilante!"

A panel later, Kelly found his wrists encircled by the Vig's rope. "Good gravy! He *is* the Vigilante!"

The Vig used his rope to lasso Kelly's confederates, but the badman grabbed Betty Stuart and used her as a shield for his escape. He made a getaway in a stolen car, leading the cowboy crusader to leap onto the running board of a taxi and give chase. That didn't work out so well: Kelly bopped him with the flat of his sword, kayoed him, and took him prisoner.

After the Vigilante awoke, Kelly explained how he had survived the chair and left his foe to be gassed to death from a ceiling nozzle. (The Vigilante was unmasked by this point and remained so for a while, leading one to wonder why Kelly didn't boast of knowing the Vig's secret identity. Maybe he just didn't care.) But he'd tied the Vig with leather straps and left a bucket of water conveniently in the room. The Vigilante soaked his bonds in the bucket, causing the rawhide to loosen up, and freed himself. Still in danger of being gassed to death, the hero ignited the vapors with a lighted match, clobbered a hood that came in to check on him, and corralled Kelly and his gang during another robbery. He roped them all and threw them through a window, letting them land safely (?) on a bunch of high wires, from which supposedly the cops picked them up. Later, as Greg Sanders, he signed a bunch of autographs for female admirers, while Betty looked on and thought, "Just a drugstore cowboy! Why can't he be like the Vigilante?"

Mort Weisinger had a habit of keeping his creations alive as long as he could, so the Vigilante ended up with a comfortable berth in *Action* for a good long while. (With *Superman* as a lead feature, the book wasn't ever *near* cancellation.) The Vig went on through issue #198 (November 1954), until he was replaced by Tommy Tomorrow. He also served as a member of an actual DC super-team, the Seven Soldiers of Victory, alongside the Green Arrow and Speedy, the Crimson Avenger, the Shining Knight, and the Star-Spangled Kid and Stripesy in *Leading Comics* #1-14 (Winter 1941–Winter 1944). (Ages later, someone at DC found an old Seven Soldiers script and had it drawn up for *Adventure Comics* #438–443 [March–April 1975–January–February 1976].)

The movies even gave the Vig his shot at fame. Probably because it was a lot easier to film a masked Western hero than a flying superguy, the Vigilante helmed his own movie serial in 1947. Ralph Byrd played the Vigilante and did some singing as Greg Sanders. And why not? He also dusted a lot of crooks' jaws. A souvenir edition of *Action Comics* with an original Vigilante story in it was given away at the premiere, and it remains one of the scarcest DC collectibles of all. Finally, *Real Fact Comics* #10 (September–October 1947) gave readers a look at how a movie serial was made. If you've been paying attention, you don't have to guess which serial they featured.

Soon enough, the Vigilante took up a motor scooter in place of a horse, and gained two sidekicks—first, the wizened Westerner Billy Gunn, then Stuff, the Chinatown Kid. He also picked up some recurring villains: the Dummy, the Rainbow Man, and the Fiddler. He also managed a berth in *Western Comics* #1-4 (January–February 1948–July–August 1948). But attrition comes to all heroes, and with a story titled "Stand-In for the Prairie Troubadour" (*Action Comics* #198, November 1954), the Vigilante hung up his spurs.

But not forever. Sixteen years later, after a "Fact File" feature in DC Comics which was a bio piece on the hero, the Vigilante was revived in a guest-shot in *Justice League of America* #78-79 (February–March 1970), helping Superman, Batman and company fight an invasion force of polluting aliens. (Literally. The aliens were dumping pollutants in water and air.) After that, the Vigilante made scattered appearances through the Seventies as a guest star and in solo stories, some of the latter drawn nicely by Gray Morrow. In 1983, his name was stolen for a Punisher–influenced killer hero in the early Eighties, but the latter character, thankfully, died. (Said "hero" was replaced by a female Vigilante later on.) Writer Roy Thomas kept the original Vigilante on deck throughout the Eighties in *All-Star Squadron* and *Young All-Stars*. The Vig showed up for a guest-shot in *El Diablo* #12 (August 1990) and then got a retro-series, *Vigilante: City Lights, Prairie Justice* (#1-4, November 1995–February 1996). Since then, he's made appearances in other comics, most notably *Stars and S.T.R.I.P.E.* and *Justice Society of America*. It's hard to tell where the Vigilante has made his last showing as of this writing—possibly in a cameo in a 2016 *Justice League* giveaway comic—but most likely DC will find some employment for him in the future.

There were other DC Western stars, including Dale Evans and Hopalong

Cassidy, whom we'll treat later on. But there were a few more that were originals and debuted before our cutoff date of 1950. They started in 1948 and ran on through 1961, and the first sign of change was the introduction of a brand-new title, called, appropriately, *Western Comics* (#1, January–February 1948).

The first cover, by Howard Sherman, got things running with an old-fashioned stagecoach robbery, with a rifle-toting lawman on the buckboard shooting at two masked bandits and a damsel in distress showing her face in a window. The lawman in question was Jimmy Sawyer, the *Cowboy Marshal*.

Ed Smalle was the artist on the story, and Marshal Sawyer arrived in town in favor of going on vacation to help his brother on the ranch. His boss had a different idea. A bunch of bandits were holding up stagecoaches near the town of Gila Gap, and somebody had to go out there and shoot some trouble. And bad guys. Big Ed Keeler, the town boss and bully, was behind the wrongdoings. Jimmy Sawyer's job: go get him.

After almost being shot down by a crooked sheriff on the way, Sawyer made it into town, had to confirm his good intentions while holding a gun on a crowd from a saloon, and faced down a phony marshal who backed out of a gunfight. Then he knocked down the crooked sheriff. *Then* he was introduced to Big Jim Keeler. After proving Keeler was guilty of ambushing him, Sawyer roped him off the back of his horse. And, after taking his man in, Sawyer waved goodbye to his chief and headed off to his brother's ranch.

Being that this was DC, the Numero Uno of the comics field, the art and writing were better than most. *Cowboy Marshal* lasted through issue #42 (November–December 1953) and then was put out to pasture. Following up was the second feature, *Rodeo Rick*.

Rick's first story was drawn by Howie Post, and the first page showed him astride two separate horses, shooting off two separate guns, putting holes in a bunch of coins that were falling through the air. He and his horse, Comet, were partners in a travelling rodeo show, doing stunts for the people's delight and getting into a bunch of trouble with crooks on the side. Immediately he solved a murder on a ranch and kept a baddie from foreclosing on the place, just by noticing a unique horseshoe print on the dead man's body. He defeated the evildoers in a shootout, and busted a bronc just for good measure. *Rodeo Rick* rode on through issue #69 (May–June 1958), missing issues #28–30, 38, and 68—a good ride by anyone's standards.

After a well-drawn and contemporary-set Vigilante tale, the *Wyoming Kid* was introduced. AKA Johnny Jones, his trademarks were a red shirt, a yellow bandanna, and art by Howard Sherman. On his splash panel, he was duking it out with an opponent, and an opening caption asked why he turned his back on the law. The story was sure to tell us.

As it was, the Wyoming Kid broke an old friend out of jail, but not to see him go free. Instead, he wanted him to confess to a greater charge than he'd been sent up for: murder. He got the man to 'fess up, then apparently got beaten in a furious fistfight. But that was just a ruse, and when the dastard tried to do Johnny in with his own gun, he found that it was unloaded. The Kid downed his foe with a powerful blow, revealed a sheriff nearby who had heard the whole thing, and took him in.

In issue #8 (March–April 1949) we got "The Origin of the Wyoming Kid!" It developed that the Kid's real name was Bill Polk, that he was a sheepman's son, and that (as we all knew) sheep herders and cattlemen were at cold war with each other in the Old West. He grew up learning to fight, ride, shoot, and rope. Then, one day, a sheep-hatin' rancher came to the territory, found Bill's dad had been using the water for his sheep, and warned him to stop. That didn't go down well. Bill and his father ended up fighting the rancher's gunnies, and his dad got dry-gulched one day. Everyone, including Bill, suspected the rancher, Mallon. But the young gunhawk determined that another man had taken his father's life, saved Mallon, and gained his friendship. He also gained a quest: to hunt down Hoke Claggett, the man who had really killed his father, and bring him to justice.

The Kid was lucky enough to cadge a berth in *World's Finest Comics* for a time. In his first story there (#42, September–October 1949), he shared the cover with Superman, Batman, and Robin, and finally found his father's killer. The problem was, Hoke Claggett knew about his presence in town before the Kid knew about his. The villain baited an elaborate trap and frameup, but the guy in the white hat sprang it and won free. When a bullet headed for the Kid's heart was deflected by Claggett's own lucky piece, the killer gave up and leaped to his death. The score was settled, but the Kid would continue his rambling.

He was in *Western* through issue #85 (January–February 1961) and *World's Finest* through #64 (May–June 1953). He got a reprint in *Super DC Giant* #S-14 (September–October 1970) and a one-page reference in *Who's Who* #26 (April 1987), and then faded back into history.

The Vigilante didn't quite seem to fit in *Western Comics*. He was a modern character, not a denizen of the Old West, after all, and he already had a home in *Action Comics*. So, in issue #5 (September–October 1948), *the Nighthawk* took his place.

Wearing a black Stetson, a black eye mask, a black shirt with a white hawk symbol on it, and pants with huge chaps, the Nighthawk started up astride a log headed down a river, shooting it out with two thieving lumberjacks. That was the opening panel. The story was scripted by Joe Millard and drawn by Charles Paris. The hero of the piece was Hannibal Hawkes, a "fix-it" man who traveled from town to town, with a wagon the size and shape of a very small house drawn by two horses. He moseyed on by a sawmill, saved an old man from a vicious beating by roping one ranny and disarming the lot of them, and got into his first adventure. But not before he wrote his initials in a door, with bullets.

After learning the head bad guy, Ben Plunkett, was a price-gouger, Hannibal Hawkes said goodbye to his new friend, went into the back of his wagon, and emerged as the Nighthawk. And, astride his great black horse, Nightwind, he used fists, guns, gimmicks, and wits to bring Plunkett and his men to bear. Taking a tip from Ben Franklin, he flew a kite to attract lightning to a metal gate and knocked out the bad guys who pushed against it. After that, the old-timer had no problems getting his lumber to a mill.

We never learned the Nighthawk's origin, but that's as may be. He continued on, fixing things and jailing outlaws, until *Western* #76 (July–August 1959). Good talents worked on the strip, including writers Gardner Fox, Alan Brennan, John Broome,

Don Cameron, France Herron, David Wood, and Bryan Talbot. Artists numbered the likes of Gil Kane, Leonard Starr, Ralph Mayo, Ruben Moreira, Charles Paris, and Bruno Premiani. Fans who haven't discovered Nighthawk and other DC Westerns of the time can expect a pleasant ambush of surprise.

In the early Seventies, when DC began digging up its old history with a vengeance, two Nighthawk reprints appeared in *Super DC Giant* #S-14 and S-22 (September–October 1970 and February–March 1971). Then he got several more of them in *Johnny Thunder* #1–3 (February–March–July–August 1973) and *DC Super-Stars* #9 (November 1976). Finally, in 1985, he got a cameo in *Crisis on Infinite Earths* #3 (June 1985). In that issue, he died.

For our next DC feature in *Western Comics*, we have to fade back to 1949—specifically, to *Detective Comics* #151 (September 1949). That was the debut of Pow-Wow Smith, Indian lawman.

Pow-Wow Smith's first story, appropriately called "The Origin of Pow-Wow Smith," was scripted by Don Cameron and drawn by Carmine Infantino, both of whom did a customarily good DC job on it. The strip was set in modern times and concerned a Sioux tribesman named Ohiyesa ("the Winner") who, missing his white friend Jimmy, opted to leave his village and go to college with him. He gained the "Pow-Wow" name when stopping a fight between two white men with his powers of deduction. In this 10-pager, he completed his education, proved himself to his tribesmen, and made ready to use his great observational and detective abilities as a policeman. Once again, Native Americans were treated sympathetically, and *Pow-Wow Smith* ran through *Detective Comics* #202 (December 1953), then switched over to *Western Comics* for #43–85 (January–February 1954–January–February 1961), often taking the cover.

The feature had quality for the whole run. Infantino drew them all, and Ed Herron and Gardner Fox contributed scripts. Pow-Wow got the usual batch of reprints in the 1970s and made a guest appearance in *Detective Comics* #500 (March 1981). Howard Chaykin did an update story on him in *Solo* #4 (June 2005).

Also in 1948, DC pulled another switcheroo. One month, *All-American Comics* was cover-featuring the original Green Lantern. The next month, *All-American Comics* #100 (August 1948) gave the cover to a black-haired, hard-riding cowboy astride a great white horse, menaced by no less than three gunslinging, bandanna-masked outlaws. His name was Johnny Thunder.

He shared the name with the lamebrain hero who had a magic genie named Thunderbolt from the 1940s *Flash Comics*. But that was their only relation.

The Western Johnny's opening story was scripted by Bob Kanigher and drawn classily by Alex Toth, who also did the cover. In that first tale, we were introduced to Sheriff Bill Tane of Mesa City, who had a blond, bespectacled son, John Tane, who was a schoolmaster. Not surprisingly, since this was an Old West story, the sheriff considered his son a wimp. But there was more, as the saying goes, than met the eye. The elder Tane and Kathy Dunbar, the beautiful blonde owner of the Hi-Kathy Ranch, saw all of their ranch hands try and fail to bust Black Lightning, a white bronc with a black lightning bolt pattern on his head. John Tane appeared, only to be scorned by his father. But later ... yeah, later....

...John Tane did ride Black Lightning alone, formed a bond with him, and shot the heck out of five bottles on a fence while riding. Nobody saw them, but Tane had proven his prowess. In a couple more pages, when trouble threatened, John dyed his hair black, put on a cowboy outfit, and jumped astride the horse to stop a cattle drive from disaster. He took down the head baddie with his bare hands in sight of his pa, and Sheriff Tane congratulated him. "Yore guns sound like thunder! Yep—you're a regular *Johnny Thunder!*"

Kathy allowed that Johnny could use Black Lightning all he wanted to, and our hero rode back, to wash the black powder out of his hair and resume his John Tane identity. (Evidently, there was a whole lot of black powder around, because

For the 100th issue of *All-American Comics*, Johnny Thunder arrives and shoves Green Lantern out of the cover spot. © DC Comics.

Johnny never ran low on it for 14 years. Or maybe Mesa City had an absolutely killer makeup department.) Kit, Kathy's little brother and one of John's pupils, was introduced in the last few panels. That was the beginning of Johnny Thunder.

(Much later, DC finally got around to giving us Johnny's origin in *All-Star Western* #108 [August–September 1959]. As a kid, John Tane was torn between the differing points of view of his sheriff father, who wanted to make a man of him, and his mother, who prized education, said "Books are better than bullets!" and steered him toward a teaching career. John did indeed become a teacher, but when his dad was humiliated by outlaws, he opted to help him in a different identity. He took the name of Johnny Thunder while watching a storm brew up, and saved his father from the Clifton Gang. It didn't quite jibe with his first story, but it was 11 years later, and DC probably figured not too many readers were keeping score.)

Kanigher, one of DC's best dramatic writers from the Forties through the Sixties, did an excellent job with the scripting, and Toth matched him again and again on the art. Interestingly enough, an unarmed Johnny faced down an armed baddie in one of his early stories with the words, "You can't kill me, Raze! I'm not a person!

I'm an idea! And you can't shoot an idea!"—which Alan Moore would echo, very closely, in the 1980s in *V for Vendetta*.

Johnny Thunder pushed Green Lantern to the back of the book. By issue #103 (November 1948), the title was converted to *All-American Western*, and GL disappeared completely. The gunslinger with the double identity took over under some great Toth covers, with stories inked by Joe Giella. Johnny got an Indian kid sidekick, Swift Deer, in issue #113 (April–May 1950), and he made several appearances thereafter. He was no rival to Red Ryder's sidekick Little Beaver in longevity, though. (We'll get to them later in this chapter.) Loads of stories ended up with Sheriff Tane disparaging his son to Swift Deer, who always responded, "He fights for justice in his own way!"

And so he did, with Toth drawing panels filled with five-pointed stars when Johnny laid a haymaker. Kathy was later given the last name O'Neil (or O'Neill in some stories—they probably weren't paying attention all that much) and kept on as the strip ingenue, with Swift Deer showing up every few issues, usually when Indian conflicts arose. *All-American Western*'s last issue was #126 (June–July 1952) before it morphed into *All-American Men of War*, joining DC's burgeoning war comics line. But was that the end of Johnny Thunder?

Nope, not by a long shot. The cowboy crusader just moved across to *All-Star Western*, similarly converted from *All-Star Comics*, with issue #67 (October–November 1952), only missing a couple of months in between. Carmine Infantino took the place of Alex Toth as artist, and maintained Johnny Thunder very well, thank you. Mort Drucker rode up to spell Carmine with issue #71 (June–July 1953). Gil Kane took the reins in #86 (December 1955–January 1956) and rode the feature out till the end of the trail, with one issue by Infantino to give him a breather. As a matter of fact, Kane rode it *beyond* the end. But we'll deal with that in a bit. Also, Bob Haney popped up to give Kanigher an issue of relief in #99 (February–March 1958), the only Thunder story in the original run written by another scripter.

But in the new era of 36-page comics, Johnny's page count shrunk a bit, and Swift Deer was absent until issue #73 (October–November 1953). At least Kathy, Sheriff Tane, and a recurring villain named Silk Black stayed around to keep Johnny company. Black Lightning, too, but he was probably under contract.

In issue #106 (April–May 1959), Miss Rhodes arrived, an Eastern gal who played Lois Lane to Johnny's Superman (and, just as scornfully, to John Tane's Clark Kent) and stuck to him harder than flypaper. Johnny was more flustered than a schoolkid at his first dance, but Gil Kane would've had to try mighty hard to draw an ugly woman. She lasted only through issue #107 (June–July 1959). In the next one, Kathy was back, this time with the last name of Brown, and guest-starred in the flashback origin of Johnny Thunder. That was her last appearance, unless she showed up elsewhere under another name.

Finally, *All-Star Western* #117 (February–March 1961) gave us a brand-new recurring character. Kanigher had a habit of giving his heroes roguish women as foils—the Harlequin for Green Lantern, the Thorn for the Flash, and, in 1947, the Black Canary for Johnny Thunder—and, in this issue, he provided Madame .44. She was a redhead in a white outfit and bandanna mask, and she could take the gun off

Johnny's belt with a single shot. On the cover, that's just what she did. And, apparently, she was an outlaw.

In her first saga, she did give Johnny a run for his money. But as for money, she proved somewhat picky in what she stole, robbing only crooks who hid behind the law and taking only enough money to maintain herself and her gang. The story revealed that Wyatt Earp himself had given her the name of Madame .44 after she shot out lamps one night in Tombstone, Arizona, to cover her escape. And, though she got on fine with Johnny Thunder, she told him that she wasn't about to stop fighting for the right her way.

Madame .44 continued on the next couple of covers and was soon revealed as Jeanne Walker, a lady photographer. After sharing two more adventures, Johnny Thunder and the Madame both suspected each other's secret identities. In the last couple of panels of the story in *All-Star Western* #119, John and Jeanne walked toward each other, knowing if either one showed the injuries from a recent fight, they would reveal their double identity. Continued next issue?

Not hardly.

That was the end of *All-Star Western*. DC's superheroes were resurgent, and Kane was better served by his new assignments, *Green Lantern* and *The Atom*. The space age was dawning, TV Westerns were waning, and DC pulled the plug on their last Western comic. (They still had *Tomahawk*, but that was set during Revolutionary War times.) It seemed we would never know what happened to Johnny and the Madame.

Except ... well...

...a couple of decades later, in the back of *DC Comics Presents*, there lurked a continuing feature, "Whatever Happened To...?" This series gave artists and writers the chance to give endings to long-canceled DC heroes. Issue #28 (December 1980) featured "Whatever Happened to Johnny Thunder?" The story was written by *Comics Reader* editor Mike Tiefenbacher and drawn by Gil Kane himself. It commenced right after the last panels of Johnny's last *All-Star Western* story, brought Silk Black back for an encore, and showed Thunder and .44 having to team together to survive. (Silk Black didn't.) The two learned each other's secret I.D.'s, Madame .44 was pardoned by the governor, and John and Jeanne got married. Swift Deer attended the wedding. Pointedly, Kathy didn't. In a framing sequence, the story showed us the two retired adventurers with their son and daughter at home. That was the final wrap-up of the story.

But it wasn't the last appearance of the pistol-packing pair.

In between, Johnny got the usual spate of Seventies reprints, including three issues of his own comic (February–March–July–August 1973). *Secret Origins* #50 (August 1990) offered a brand-new Johnny Thunder story, written by Elliot S. Maggin and drawn by Alan Weiss and Dick Giordano. The story filled in a couple of holes in Johnny's history, including his full name (John Stuart Mill Tane) and his mom's name (Dorothea—her death was shown in flashback). Therein, Johnny got to save Sheriff Tane for the umpteenth time, and he finally revealed his identity to his proud papa. As far as we know, that's Johnny's last appearance.

Madame .44 got to take a curtain call, too. A new incarnation of *All-Star*

Western provided a new incarnation of the Madame, as well (#30–31, June–July 2014). The story straddled the genres of Western, horror, and fantasy, and the Madame who appeared in it was based on the original but not quite the same. Johnny Thunder was not in evidence. This, too, is probably Madame .44's last showing to date.

That's where the matter stands right now, and it's probably better off left that way. We will bid a fond farewell to Johnny Thunder and Madame .44, and proceed on.

Lest anyone think that DC cowboy comics discriminated against the fair sex, *All-American Western* #103 (November 1948) would correct them. The next story after *Johnny Thunder* was *Overland Coach*, and an add-on proclaimed "Starring Tony Barrett." Okay. The splash panel showed us a picture of a great-looking blonde woman driving a stagecoach with one hand and shooting at two gunnies with the other. Where's Tony Barrett?

Aw, wait a minute. You mean…?

Yep. Tony Barrett was a girl!

Antoinette Barrett, Tony for short, was the daughter of the late stagecoach owner, and an experienced driver and shooter to boot. She turned up in the frontier town of Laredo just in time to join a posse against the Laredo Kid. The sheriff turned her down flat. Tony declared she'd just see about that, and she stormed the hideout of the Kid himself, who turned out to be … wait for it … her brother. Although he wasn't! Well, he was her brother, but he had been framed by the real Laredo Kid, and he surrendered to Tony. Later on, the real culprit, a banker named Simms, tricked her, trapped her, kayoed her, and tied her up alongside her brother to be murdered later on.

No real Western gal was gonna take that! Tony upset a lamp, started a fire, burned through her bonds, and freed herself and her brother. Then she engaged in an on-horseback gunfight with Simms, and the dang-fool banker stumbled into his own deathtrap, blowing himself up real good. Later on, the sheriff wanted to deputize Tony. She allowed that she had a stagecoach to run, and anyway, didn't he just say that women weren't meant to be gunslingers?

Overland Coach was drawn by Irwin Hasen and Frank Giacoia initially, then passed into the hands of Gil Kane and Leonard Starr. She ran through *All-American Western* #126 (June–July 1952) and was gone.

The next *All-American Western* feature in issue #103 showed a singing cowboy on the splash panel with the caption, "He comes out of nowhere—to leave a trail of cowboy songs behind him!" He was sitting on a white horse, playing his guitar. He was also leading another white horse, which had three unconscious (well, we *hope* they were unconscious) outlaws draped over its back. His name was Harmony Hayes, and the feature was *Minstrel Maverick*.

The first story, "Sing a Song of Six-Guns!" was set in the town of Red Butte and introed Hayes in a bar, guitar on his back, having a stiff shot of—milk. He told the barkeep his real name was Hank but he got the handle "Harmony" for obvious reasons. The bartender warned him that the Avalanche was coming—"the toughest, shootinest hombre in captivity or out!" Said Avalanche did arrive, aboard a white horse, shooting off two pistols and declaring himself "a cross atween a rattlesnake and a plain catastrophe of nature! Cmon out, somebody, and fight!" If you twigged that the story might not be meant to be taken entirely seriously, you'd probably be right.

The bartender allowed that, monthly, the Avalanche rode in and tore up the town. They spent the rest of the month putting it back together till his next visit. The carpenters there must have been rich. Harmony strode up to Avalanche, said he shouldn't be disturbing people that way, distracted him with a song, and then whomped him in the middle with his guitar. Then he laid him out flat with a punch.

Avalanche was taken to jail, proclaimed to be the Black Rustler, an owlhoot who had been stealing cattle, and was going to be the guest of honor at a necktie party. But Harmony didn't figure him for a crook. He baked a gun in a pie (yes, he did!) and delivered it to him in the jail. When Snake Fenton (the real Black Rustler) and his boys came to the hoosegow to stretch Avalanche's neck, Harmony and Avalanche clobbered them.

Later, at the bar, Harmony and Avalanche shook hands. The barkeep admitted Avalanche was a good boy, except on paydays. The big man declared he'd be good on paydays, too, from then on. Later, Harmony hit the trail again, singing a new song as he rode.

Bernie Krigstein, later of EC Comics fame, did the art on the first story. Irwin Hasen came along for the second. The Minstrel Maverick roamed and rambled on through issue #126 (June–July 1952) and then was lost to history.

The fourth strip in the book was illoed by Joe Kubert and John Giunta and was another goodie: *Foley of the Fighting 5th*. The first panel showed Lt. Dan Foley of the 5th Cavalry, on horse between two mounted Indians, holding a gun on one and knocking the other off his horse with his fist. Foley was fresh out of West Point and rode into a frontier outpost, Fort Desolation, to aid one Colonel Henry. The Colonel opened the gates and bade him get in, to avoid some attacking Indians. "Indians, sir?" he responded. "I didn't see any! You must be mista—"

An arrow knocked the hat off his head. Foley double-timed it into the fort.

Foley soon hooked up with an Indian scout, Wingfoot, who would quickly become a supporting character. So did Terry, Colonel Henry's pretty blonde daughter. The Indians, driven by a medicine man, were losing men with every raid but getting closer to success. Against the brass's wishes, Foley snuck out to get a line on the medicine man, Mighty Owl, who turned out to be a masked renegade white man. The Indians tied the impostor to a stake with a fire at his feet, but Wingfoot performed a spectacular rescue. Foley challenged Mighty Owl to single combat, whipped his butt, and brought him back captive to the fort. Semi-peaceful balance between whites and Indians was restored. For the moment.

Foley fought on through *All-American Western* #126 (June–July 1952) and was transplanted to *All-Star Western* with issue #66 (August–September 1952), where he defended the fort through #115 (October–November 1960). His support troops included writers Irv Werstein, Lee Goldsmith, France Herron, Gardner Fox, John Broome, David Wood, Alvin Schwartz, and David Vern, and artists Irwin Hasen, Carmine Infantino, Sy Barry, Gil Kane, Howard Purcell, Mike Sekowsky, and Jack Kirby.

Jack Kirby??

Yup, tenderfoot, Jack Kirby himself rode in for a Foley story in *All-Star Western* #99 (February–March 1958), did his usual excellent job, and then rode back to his customary haunts. We told you there'd be surprises!

Dan Foley made his last appearance in a reprint in *Super DC Giant* #S-15 (September–October 1970). Nothing is known of him since then, but we can be assured he was discharged with full comic book honors.

Squeezing in just before the end of our 1950 deadline, *Jimmy Wakely* was one of DC's few movie Western comics. Since he was a real person, we will do our usual canned biography.

He was born James Clarence Wakely back on February 16, 1914, in Arkansas, but moved with his family to Oklahoma in 1920. Wakely married Dora Miser on a Friday the 13th in 1935 and, two years later, cashed in on the singing cowboy craze with a group called the Bell Boys, later known in various incarnations as the Jimmy Wakely Trio and Jimmy Wakely and his Saddle Pals. Gene Autry gave them a listen and added them to his *Musical Ranch* radio show. In 1939, Jimmy and the Trio showed up in a Roy Rogers movie, *Saga of Death Valley*. Wakely and his singin' pals, or many times, just Wakely, appeared in a whole buncha Western movies through 1959. He also showed up, guitar in hand, in numerous TV shows through 1961, and held down a number of radio series, mostly musicals. Wakely was on *Grand Ole Opry* and *National Barn Dance*, was a Country Music Hall of Fame songwriter, and released albums through 1970. In 1982, he died of heart failure.

With *Jimmy Wakely* #1 (September–October 1949), DC claimed him for their own.

Alex Toth was the artist of note, with inking from Frank Giacoia and Sy Barry. Jimmy's adventures took place in the present, but that wasn't going to stop anyone from including bandits, six-shooters, roping, and towns and fashions straight out of Sagebrush City. He nabbed a bunch of gold thieves in the first story, saving a carload full of actors along the way. Later issues featured him in more modern settings, such as a radio station where his discs were played, and even some stories guest-starring his son Johnny. It was a pretty good read and lasted all the way to issue #18 (July–August 1952). The usual suspects did their customary great work: writers like Gardner Fox, John Broome, Phil Evans, Paul S. Newman, and Alvin Schwartz, with art from Toth, Gil Kane, Mort Drucker, Irwin Hasen, and Joe Kubert.

In between the Golden and Silver Ages, the DC crew got to hone their work on Westerns, science fiction, war, and—it must be admitted—romance. When the superheroes came back to the fore in the late Fifties, they were well equipped to handle them.

One more feature from *Jimmy Wakely* is worth mentioning: the backup character, *Kit Colby, Girl Sheriff*.

On her first page in issue #1 (September–October 1949), the ravishing red-headed cowgirl was shown leaning against a jail wall and smiling while she shined up her tin star. Two other characters to the right of her were behind bars, and weren't so enthusiastic about it. In the story proper, Judge Colby told an assemblage of citizens that their next sheriff would be chosen by a sharpshooting contest. Two guys drilled the bull's-eye. Then, other bullets rang out and completely surrounded the bullet holes. Judge Colby looked back and saw his daughter, Kit, holding a smoking six-shooter.

As one might expect, the judge would be darned if he'd let a woman compete. But there was no law against it, and Kit (named for Kit Carson) outshot, outrode, and probably out-anything-elsed anyone else in the contests. Unfortunately, a bad guy named Cactus Brand and his boys chose that time to rob the town bank of Moon Bow. After a setback or two, Kit Colby roped, fought, and shot her way to victory over the villains, clobbering three of them at once by dropping a tree trunk on them. It was a fun little feature, and Kit continued through issue #13 (September–October 1951) and then came back for #16–18 (March–April–July–August 1952). Infantino, Kane, Hasen, Kubert, and Frank Giacoia drew her. Just to round things out, Frank Frazetta and Harvey Kurtzman contributed some back features.

Finally, we will go all the way back to 1947 to pick up on the longest continually running DC frontier hero of them all. The cover of *Star Spangled Comics* #69 (June 1947), as usual, featured Robin the Boy Wonder. But the interior pages gave us the first story of a character DC had been trumpeting in ads all over the place for a good month—the frontier fighter from the American Revolution, *Tomahawk*.

The first story was "Flames Along the Frontier," written by Joe Samachson and drawn by Edmond Good. In the splash panel, two whites in buckskin, the adult Thomas Hawk and the boy Dan Hunter, fought off a trio of Indians while a log cabin burned in the background. From there, we transitioned to the next page, which started off the story itself. In Kentucky territory, a singing blue jay betrayed the hiding place of Hawk to some nearby Indians, and an arrow thunked into a tree near him. But he recognized them, shot a bow instead of a man, and revealed himself to them.

Tomahawk, the frontier fighter from the American Revolution, who started in the late Forties and lasted through the early Seventies. © DC Comics.

"'Tis you, Tomahawk! I knew it!" said a smiling brave, raising his hand in greeting.

"Greetings, Black Thunder!" Tomahawk responded. From there, we went into a flashback, telling of how Tom Hawk had come with settlers to the land, wandered too far off, and got captured by Indian warriors. But he saved his captor, Black Thunder, from a moose, and the grateful rescuee adopted him into the tribe and taught him Indian ways, including expertise with the bow and arrow. (So many white men got adopted by Indians in the comics that it was hard to see where any hostilities ever started. Then again, decades later, we did get *Dances with Wolves*…) He also met with a beautiful Indian maiden whose name was Laughing Fawn. She didn't smile much in the story, though.

Anyway, Tom Hawk had been sent down from Virginia by the government to check on an Indian uprising. Since Black Thunder hadn't been uprising and didn't know of any other uprisers, this was suspicious. Tom came upon a burning log cabin set ablaze by some apparent Indians. He quickly gave battle, but was stunned by a gunpowder explosion. When he awoke, he was tied to a doorway inside said burning cabin. Adjacent to him, also tied to the doorway, was a young lad, also in buckskin, name of Dan Hunter. As it was, since log cabins are constructed without nails and Tomahawk was pretty stout, he was able to bring down the house and free them both. Dan said that both his parents were long dead, that his uncle had been killed by the villains, and that he intended to revenge himself on the killers. It was the origin of Tomahawk's Robin.

Dan revealed that, wonder of wonders, the evildoers were not Indians but renegade whites in disguise. Armed with this trope, Tomahawk and Dan brought down the villains, with the help of some Colonial soldiers and Laughing Fawn herself. Black Thunder and his braves joined in, and the impostors were soon captured. That is, the ones that lived.

At the end, Tomahawk told Dan he'd probably want to go back to the settlement. Dan negatived that, saying he had no one to return to. Thus, Tomahawk unofficially adopted him, and the story came to its end.

America was in its postwar ultrapatriotic phase, and the heroes of its past were a big deal back then. Tomahawk invoked the spirit of Davy Crockett and Daniel Boone without having to be tied to a real historical figure. He stayed and thrived.

And thrive he did! Tomahawk and Dan fought redcoats and uprising Indians through *Star Spangled Comics* #130 (July 1952) with forays into *World's Finest Comics* #33–35, 65–88, and 90–101 (March–April–July–August 1948; July–August 1953–June 1957; October 1957–May 1959). *Tomahawk* #1 (September–October 1950) gave our 1776-based hero a bigger stage, and it lasted for a *long* time, winding up its run in issue #140 (May–June 1972). Long after that run, Tomahawk and Dan Hunter appeared in backups in *Unknown Soldier* #262–264 (April–June 1982) and, future-hopping to 1985, had a wild-eyed cameo in *Crisis on Infinite Earths* #5 and 7 (August and October 1985), which led into a crossover in *Fury of Firestorm* #42 (December 1985), in which superheroines Firehawk and Wonder Girl came back to 1776 to help Tomahawk fight the Brits. (If you're confused about that one, you're better off not asking.) Four years later, he guested in *Swamp Thing* #86 (May 1989), when the title character time-regressed into Tomahawk's era. Then, in the modern era, he appeared in *Vertigo Visions: Tomahawk* #1 (July 1988) in a new story, guest-starred through more time-travel in *Superman / Batman* #16 (Late February 2005) and got a four-part story of his own in *All-Star Western* V. 3 #13–16 (December 2012–March 2013). As usual, he had a bunch of reprints along the way.

Tomahawk and Dan met all the celebs of the War of Independence, including Ben Franklin, Thomas Paine, and above all, General George Washington. Through the late Sixties, Fred Ray was his chief artist. Other artists included Bob Brown, Sy Barry, Frank Thorne, Nick Cardy, Bill Ely, Jerry Grandenetti, Jay McArdle, Bruno Premiani, John Severin, Howard Sherman, and Frank Frazetta (yes, *that* Frank Frazetta). As for his writers, Bill Finger, John Broome, Murray Boltinoff, George Kashdan, Don Cameron, Sam Glanzman, Bob Haney, France Herron, Bob Kanigher, Alvin Schwartz, Dick and David Wood, and Carl Wessler numbered among them.

By the early Sixties, management at DC probably figured the old formula had to be jazzed up a bit. So, as Batman had gotten Batwoman and Superman had acquired Supergirl, Tomahawk got Miss Liberty.

Dressed up in a blue tricornered hat, a black wig, an eye mask, a red cape, and star-spangled duds, Miss Liberty might have been a Golden Age heroine come 20 years too late. She was actually blonde nurse Bess Lynn, an American sympathizer who turned up one night to save Tomahawk and Dan from the British and the Indians by throwing lit powder horns at them. She led an underground movement of women patriots, but had to keep her identity a secret to keep the bloody Redcoats from taking revenge on her captive brother in England. She first appeared in *Tomahawk* #81 (July–August 1952) and returned in #84, 88, 101, 106, and 110 (May–June 1967).

Since DC has never had any interest in letting sleeping heroes or heroines lie, she's done guest-shots since then. In *Justice League of America* #159–160 (October–November 1978), she joined the Justice League, the Justice Society, and several other time-lost heroes in fighting the Lord of Time. Miss Liberty was also retrofitted by Roy Thomas into being an ancestress of Liberty Belle in *All-Star Squadron* #45 (May 1985), and then showed up to help DC's Golden Age heroes and time-jolted heroes (yeah, *that* trope again) fight super-villains in "the Crisis" (*All-Star Squadron* #54–55, February–March 1986). She's made cameos since then, but nothing substantial.

Two issues after Miss Liberty showed up, we got a real indication that things were changing, and they would *stay* changed. The first page of *Tomahawk* #83 (November–December 1962) showed us how: Tomahawk led a band of six men, all in buckskin, charging across a field. The cover called them "The G.I.'s of 1775." The story called them *Tomahawk's Rangers*.

Taking some pointers from the DC war comics and probably from *Blackhawk*, Tomahawk had the American brass hand-pick warriors to be trained by him as a fighting unit. They included Big Anvil, Cannonball Calhoun, Long Rifle Morgan, Frenchie Duval, Kaintuck Jones, and a batch of others who probably would've worn red shirts if they'd been on *Star Trek*. After the appropriate training, with Big Anvil as a corporal figure, the Rangers went and stormed Fort Cloud, held by the Brits. Some of the tactics hearkened back—or forward—to D-Day. Others, like Kaintuck's smoke signals, were pure Indian. Anyway, the new troop managed to take the fort against big odds, and a new team was born.

Dan Hunter wasn't out of it yet. He backed Tomahawk in the second story of the issue. But his appearances became fewer and farther between, as it were. To make up for it, the Rangers acquired a teenage recruit, one Pvt. Jud Fuller, nicknamed Brass Buttons, in issue #85 (March–April 1963). Stories got progressively weirder, with Tomahawk and his boys running into a giant Indian (#85), a rip-off of King Kong called King Colosso (#86 and 94, May–June 1963 and July–August 1964), the very large Terrible Tree-Man, who was a transformed Tomahawk himself (#89, November–December 1963), the horrific, green-handed Prisoner in the Pit (a dinosaur; #90, January–February 1964), and a whole host of others. It might not have been all that realistic, but DC had comics to sell, and weird villains on covers probably tapped the curiosity in the brains of preadolescent boys.

Stovepipe, a young Ranger in a top hat, turned up in *Tomahawk* #97 (March–April 1965). Wildcat, a warrior from a community of pacifists, joined a few issues earlier. There were weird transformations, monsters, "name" villains like The Hood, Thunder-Man, and King Cobweb (who commanded an army of giant insects), and other things to make the Revolutionary War as wild and wooly as the comics' versions of World War II. It was crazy, but it was fun!

Bob Brown spelled Fred Ray as artist in issue #103 (March–April 1966) in a story of the Frontier Frankenstein, a gigantic double for the classic monster created by a German scientist working for the British. He was really a transformed Big Anvil and was restored to normal at the end. Ray returned with the next issue and stayed for another, but he'd trade penciling chores with Brown for a while. Either that, or Ray would end up inking him. It worked out, any way they tried it.

The year 1968 brought changes, including some magnificent covers by Neal Adams. Bob Kanigher and Frank Thorne became the new creative team with issue #119 (November–December 1968). Super-villains and Miss Liberty were phased out; more realistic situations and sympathetic portrayals of Native Americans came in. Finally, in *Tomahawk* #131 (December 1970), we got the biggest change of all. The cover logo blared, "Son of Tomahawk."

We slipped a generation into the future, in which Tomahawk was a bald old man still full of vigor, and his son Hawk (Hawk Hawk?) had to be saved when he ran afoul of a ranny called the Judge. Tomahawk's youngish wife, an Indian named Moon Fawn, was introduced, as was Hawk's sweetheart, Angela. The setting was the Old West, and Hawk blazed a trail through issue #140 (May–June 1972). Then, after 24 years, *Tomahawk* was done.

Hawk never came back, but Tomahawk was periodically revived. And, since DC is still up and running and experiments a lot with old characters, he probably will be again sometime. The company had other Western heroes of note, but they'll wait for a future volume.

Backtracking to Centaur for a bit, *Star Comics* V. 1 #12–14 (May–September 1938) offered another pedestrian Western, *Riders of the Golden West*, by Maurice Kashuba. More interesting was the *Phantom Rider*, who started in V. 1 #16 and went to V. 2 #6 (December 1938–July 1939). He wore a purple hood that covered his entire head and went down to his chest, with a green cowboy hat and pants and a yellow shirt. He foiled a mob lynching in the first story by severing a rope with a gunshot. After the real murderer of the piece was caught, the Phantom Rider rode off into the sunset astride his horse, Thunder. The creator was Al Petersen, and if it wasn't as good as *The Lone Ranger*, neither were a dozen or so other knockoffs through the years. The Phantom Rider went on to a one-shot in *Funny Pages* V. 4 #11 (January 1940). His last bow was in *Wham Comics* #1 (November 1940).

Another Centaur Western title started out as *Star Ranger* for its first 12 issues (February 1937–May 1938), was converted into *Cowboy Comics* for issues #13 and 14 (July–August 1938), and finally settled itself as *Star Ranger Funnies* with V. 1 #15 through V. 2 #5 (October 1938–October 1939), 20 issues total. William Allison and a few others provided some good art but the stories were pretty much formula-fed. Still, they must have satisfied a few kids hankering for Westerns. Jack Cole of *Plastic Man* fame offered the funny *Home in the Ozarks*, treading into *Li'l Abner* country (V. 1 #15, V. 2 #1, 3, October 1938–June 1939). George Filchock provided *The Ermine*, a mystery man in buckskin from 1730, who was described as "some mythical scout—feared by the Indians—he's supposed to appear and disappear as if by magic—he kills for the sheer joy of killing—God have mercy on the redskin that crosses his path!" Besides dead Indians, his trademark was an ermine tail he left at the scene of the crime. He showed up in V. 1 #15 and V. 2 #1 and 3–5 (October 1938–October 1939). Then he made a last appearance in *Fantoman* #2 (August 1940) and could be seen as a prototype of DC's Tomahawk.

The Headless Horseman was a fairly unique feature from Martin Filchock, presented on the first page as a cowboy *sans* head, astride a great black pony. After crooks had finished holding up a bank, one bystander exclaimed, "Say! Where's Betty? She's never here when excitement is going on!" Since said excitement

Star Ranger, another four-color oater from Centaur. © 1937 Chesler Publications, Inc.

contained the murder of a cashier, maybe Betty could be excused. Anyway, the Horseman went and rounded up the gang of outlaws single-handedly, exposed a crooked sheriff, and kept an innocent man from being hung. After that, the headless rider and mount went into an abandoned mine they used as a hideout, and the Horseman got out of a "weirdly constructed outfit" to be revealed as—big surprise!—Betty, whose head was in the area where a cowboy's chest should be. The story ran in *Amazing Mystery Funnies* #19 (April 1940). She made an encore appearance in *The Arrow* #2 (November 1940). As one of the first female gunslingers in comics, she deserves a tip of the old Stetson.

Finally, *The Gaucho*, a relative in theme to the Cisco Kid, appeared in both issues of *CMO Comics* (1942), a book that existed to promote products of the Chicago Mail Order Co. on almost every page. He was "a wealthy Argentinan rancher in Montana to study American methods," and he and his sidekick, Sanchez, shot troubles for all of two stories. The writer was probably Richard Hughes, but we have no clue as to who was the artist, and it really wasn't that bad.

There were still a passel of movie cowboys to put in comic books, and most of them would get their chance. From the big stars to the B-stars, comics companies would license the cowboy cadre and splash their faces across books a kid could take home and enjoy every day, not just in Saturday matinees. One of the earliest, known mainly these days from an old Bill Cosby comedy routine, first appeared in Dell's *Crackajack Funnies* #1 (June 1938). His name was Buck Jones.

A little fill-in info here: Buck Jones, real name Charles Frederick Gebhart, was born in Indiana in 1891, enlisted in the Army when 16, and, unlike Tom Mix, actually saw action and was wounded during the Moro Rebellion in the Philippines. After an honorable discharge, a career driving racing cars, another Army enlistment, and another honorable discharge, Buck went to work on a ranch. There he met a woman, Odelle Osborne, a professional horse rider, fell in love with her, and married her while they were working at a Wild West show. He ended up in Los Angeles and got into the movie industry as a stuntman, bit player, and stand-in for … yep, it's true … Tom Mix. Jones made his first picture in 1920, transitioned well into talkies with his rugged voice, and kept making movies into the early Forties. On November 28, 1942, he died along with over 400 others in the infamous Cocoanut Grove fire in Boston.

That never stopped anybody from appearing in comics.

Like Mix, Buck Jones's early comics gigs were cut-up adaptations from Big Little Books. These continued till *Crackajack Funnies* #17 (November 1939). Then, almost a year later, Buck made his first appearance in an original comic story. *Buck Jones, Frontier Marshal* began in *Master Comics* #6 (September–October 1940). His stories started out at eight pages, dropped to seven, and ran through issue #32 (November 4, 1942). Actually, *Frontier Marshal*, featuring a character called Bill Crane, had been in *Master* since issue #1 (March 1940). There was a suitable passing of the torch: Crane suffered a head injury fighting bad guys, and Buck, who had recently moved into the town of Big Savage, brought said baddies to justice. Bill Crane went East to get his injury treated by specialists and to finish college. Before he left, he swore in Buck Jones as marshal, and Buck, on his horse, Streak, hurried off to foil a bank robbery in the last panel. The town was in good hands.

In his final Fawcett panel, Buck bid his pardners farewell and advised them to buy lots of war stamps. Then he left, and if the cover date was accurate, it was an eerie premonition of what happened to him 24 days later. Though he appeared in British and Australian comics after that, Jones was not seen in American comics for another eight years.

When he did, Dell got him back with a contract that pulled him back from the dead.

Buck's new incarnation started with an issue of their showcase comic, *Four Color Comics* #299 (October 1950), with a painted cover by Nicholas Firfires and a 48-page story drawn by Mike Arens. In the movies, as Bill Cosby noted, Buck did ride a horse called Silver, as if daring the Lone Ranger to do something about it. In the comics, the horse was slightly renamed Silver-B, and that seemed to satisfy everybody. Phil Evans may have written this and his other Dell outings. The following year, *Buck Jones* #2 (April–June 1951) appeared, this time with art by *Tarzan*'s Jesse Marsh. The book continued through #8 (October–December 1952), but Dell just wouldn't give up on Buck. They slugged him into several more issues of *Four Color*, finally finishing up with #850 (October 1957).

That *still* wasn't the end of Buck.

Comics of the American West have often gone over better in foreign countries, and Buck Jones continued to appear in Italian, British, Australian, and Swedish comics through 1980, with reprints showing up as late as 2018. Somewhere, on some distant four-color plain, it's safe to assume that Buck Jones still rides.

Doubling back on our trail a bit, with the next issue of *Master Comics* (#33, December 2, 1942), it was obvious why Buck Jones had been given the boot. His successor was more contemporary and an honest-to-goodness phenomenon, and he stayed that way through the late Fifties without a slip. He was Hopalong Cassidy.

Once again, we've got to shovel in a little bit of history. Hopalong Cassidy, originally called "Hop-along Cassidy," originated in a series of prose stories by Clarence Mulford. He saw print in 1904 in the novel *Bar-20* and was a tough and mean kinda coot, with a wooden leg that made him—well—hop along. The movies got hold of the character starting in 1935, with Bill Boyd playing Hopalong. But this version wasn't like Mulford's. Though Hoppy hopped, thanks to being shot in the leg, and though he dressed in black, he was a good man. The strongest drink he took was sarsaparilla, he was as fond of fair play as Popeye, he rode a white horse named Topper, and he usually was accompanied by two pardners, one a kid, the other an old, wizened, and funny guy. One of the kids was played by George Reeves, later to become—you probably already know this one—TV's Superman. One of the old codgers was Gabby Hayes. Robert Mitchum appeared in no fewer than seven Hoppy films.

Altogether there were 66 Hopalong Cassidy movies, ending in 1948. Kids ate them up. When the series ended, Bill Boyd made a bit of a gamble. He bought the rights to his films and took them to NBC TV in 1949. They took off faster than the speediest steed in existence. NBC edited the films down to regular show lengths, Hoppy got put on a bunch of national magazine covers, and several long tons of Hopalong Cassidy merchandise was sold. He was pretty much the Indiana Jones of his time.

Hoppy's comics career started with the aforementioned *Master* #33. Our hero and his pal Mesquite rode into a town named Buffalo Hide, introed by blurbs that branded him "Famous Movie Hero" and "Star of Best-Seller." An opening caption read: "Buffalo Bill Cody! …Wild Bill Hickok! … Famous names out of the romantic Old West! But there is another name that brought terror to badmen—Hopalong Cassidy! Two hard-hitting fists—a flashing form on horseback—a never-missing lariat—and the fastest draw in the whole wild West! Add them all together and you have the law's greatest champion—the outlaw's mightiest foe—Hopalong Cassidy!"

With an intro like that, a story was almost anticlimactic. But Fawcett had pages to fill and bad guys to punish. Hoppy and Mesquite neared a gambling hall run by one Black Bart, who was accused of dealing from the bottom by a patron. Bart repaid the man with a bullet in the shoulder, right in front of his pretty daughter. The law was reluctant to deal with the villain. When Mesquite called Hoppy's attention to it, and he got the lowdown from the girl, our hero's comeback was quick and decisive. "Now don't you fret, little lady. It looks right up our trail."

Hoppy and Mesquite proved their mettle by outshooting and outroping Bart, and Hoppy was soon sworn in as deputy sheriff. He and his pardner invaded the bar, knuckle-dusted and roped Bart's gang, and outdrew Black Bart himself. The bad man called in Mountain Jim, his bouncer, who was about as physically vulnerable as Mongo in *Blazing Saddles*. Hoppy tricked the guy into punching through a wall, and Mesquite caught his hand on the other side and cuffed it to an iron post outside. Then the cowboy crusader tackled Black Bart when the dastard tried to flee, and that finished the fight. The citizens of Buffalo Hide begged Hoppy to stay and be sheriff. Hoppy replied, "I think I'll just hop along!" He rode off with Mesquite, who said, "I reckon there's a lotta other hoomin coyotes around!" There were, too.

Cassidy hung out in *Master Comics* for a spell, all the way to issue #49 (April 1944). In 1943, Fawcett published *Hopalong Cassidy* #1, evidently meant to be a one-shot, with Captain Marvel on the cover in a cowboy hat. "Hopalong's my choice for rootin'-tootin' Wild West action!" the Captain proclaimed, and who were we to disagree? Harry Parkhurst drew the interior. But after his initial *Master* run, Hopalong took some time off till World War II ended and paper quotas were eased. Then he came back with a vengeance.

Hopalong Cassidy #2 (Summer 1946) offered eight Hoppy stories and a number of side features. The book stayed a quarterly until issue #5 (March 1947), when it went monthly. Photo-covers of Bill Boyd as Hopalong replaced drawn ones, and he went back into *Master* with issue #88 (March 1948). He lasted till issue #94 (August 1948), then jumped to *Real Western Hero* #70 (September 1948), titled *Western Hero* with #76 (March 1949). After issue #86 (January 1950), he transferred to a new title, *Six-Gun Heroes,* and stayed there for issues #1–24 (March 1950–January 1954), the last of which was published by Charlton. Dan Spiegle drew a well-done Hoppy comic strip for the newspapers. His success led Fawcett to put out another comic, *Bill Boyd Western*, which featured Boyd himself in more rip-roarin' Western adventures (#1–23, February 1950–January 1952). Hardly anybody at the time rode higher in the saddle than Hopalong Cassidy.

But trouble stalked Hoppy's comic, the kind even a cowboy couldn't conquer. His fate, as well as that of all Fawcett comics, was linked to that of Captain Marvel. And, since Cap had been consistently outselling Superman for years, DC was out to put Fawcett out of business any way they could. They brought suit against Fawcett, claiming the World's Mightiest Mortal was a knock-off of the Man of Steel. When the dust cleared, the House that Captain Marvel Built agreed to give up their comics empire, though they later published *Dennis the Menace* comics and distributed *Archie* titles.

Did Hoppy hang up his spurs? Or was he taken over, like so many other properties, by Charlton?

Shucks, no! DC knew a good property when they saw it, and they made sure Hopalong Cassidy rode on their ranch.

Fawcett's last *Cassidy* issue was #85 (November 1953). His first DC comic was #86 (February 1954). And as good as his Fawcett comic was, his DC title was even better.

Julius Schwartz was the editor, Gil Kane was the artist, and the whole outfit churned out some of the finest Western comics to date. In a couple of years, Schwartz's crew would rework the old superheroes of the Forties into the new champions of the Silver Age with *The Flash, Green Lantern, The Atom, Hawkman, Justice League of America,* and many more. But before that came to pass, they churned out high-quality science fiction and Westerns. And Hoppy's were so well done that, years later, Kane still regarded those stories as some of his best work.

Hoppy hit the end of his trail with issue #135 (May–June 1959). It had been a good long run, and he was entitled to his retirement. Like Buck Jones, Hopalong Cassidy continued his four-color range riding in countries outside the U.S. Thanks to copyright and demand, or lack thereof, not many Cassidy stories have been reprinted, and those by DC had to use an assumed name. But those who can manage to find old *Hopalong Cassidy*s, especially the DC run, are in for an unexpected treat.

One of the most famed cowboy heroes of all wasn't slack in showing up in comics. Like Tom, Buck, and Hoppy, he trailed through a number of publishers and even now, his name can bring back memories of his movie and TV career. He was Gene Autry himself, and he rode into the four-color ranch in 1938.

As famous for his contributions to country music as he is for his many films and TV shows, Gene was born Orvon Grover Autry in 1907, worked on his dad's ranch while in school, and played guitar and sang at dances (and at his job in a telegraph office, which got him fired). Will Rogers himself heard Gene singing, and told him to try it professionally. By 1928 he was singing on a Tulsa, Oklahoma, radio station. By 1929 he had a contract with Columbia Records.

Autry's film career kicked off in 1934 when he and his singin' pardner, Smiley Burnette, were part of a quartet of yodelers in a flick called *In Old Santa Fe*. The next year, he sang and shot his way through a Western / sci-fi serial called *The Phantom Empire*. He teamed with Burnette and then with Pat Buttram, rode his famous horse, Champion, and starred in a long ton of movies, radio shows, and TV shows, along with recording a lot of top-selling songs. (Among them were "Rudolph, the Red-Nosed Reindeer," "Frosty the Snowman," and "Santa Claus Is Coming to Town," which you probably already knew.) Even Champion had a radio show, but he was probably dubbed.

Popular Comics #28 (May 1938) from Dell was the place where Gene first made his comic bookmark. He didn't get the cover, but he did get the lead position in the book with a six-page adaptation of his movie *The Old Barn Dance*. From there he headed out to *The Funnies*, where he rode through a small batch of four-page sagas (#30-35, April–September 1939), some drawn by Al Lewin. After that, Gene eschewed the comic books for a couple of years, but was seen in a newspaper strip by Till Goodan in 1940-41.

And finally, Fawcett, which always seemed to be prowling around for Western stars to sign, brought out *Gene Autry Comics* #1 in December of 1941.

Till Goodan was the artist on the book and Gerald Geraghty the writer, with a cover story titled "The Mark of the Cloven Hoof." The comics were 68-pagers, and contained two long Gene stories with some fillers. The art, especially the Western backgrounds, was worthwhile indeed. The series ran through issue #10 (September 1943), at which time Dell figured out their competitor was making a lot of money with it. They reached out and grabbed the book, and produced issues #11 and 12 (November 1943 and February 1944).

After that, the great Singing Cowboy ran through six issues of *Four Color Comics* (July 1944–March 1946) and one of *March of Comics* (#54, 1946), Western Publishing's giveaway title. Then, in May–June 1946, Dell's *Gene Autry Comics* #1 saw print. Postwar paper availability might have had something to do with it, but there's no telling by now. Jesse Marsh succeeded Goodan as Gene's chief artist. In turn, Nicholas Firfires spelled Jesse, and Dell workhorse Gaylord DuBois wrote many of Gene's stories.

Autry continued through his own title and scattered issues of *March of Comics* for year after year. Not to be neglected, Gene's horse Champion got his own tryout in *Four Color Comics* #319 (1951). This was not uncommon; plenty of cowboy heroes' horses got their own series in the Fifties. Champ appeared in another *Four Color* and then nailed down his own title. *Gene Autry's Champion* debuted with issue #3 (August–October 1951) and ran through #19 (August–October 1955), with great painted covers by Sam Savitt and darned good interior art by Mo Gollub.

Gene himself expanded his horizons into *Western Roundup*, a Dell Giant comic featuring a number of their Western wonders, starting with issue #1 (June 1952). Champion had his own solo story in that issue. Then *Gene Autry Comics* became *Gene Autry and Champion* with #108 (March–April 1956). Apparently the horse had a great agent.

But all balloons must burst, and *Gene Autry and Champion* ended with #121 (January–March 1959). Gene's last *Western Roundup* was #18 (April–June 1957), though Champion made it into the next issue (#19, July–September 1957). Aside from a few reprints in AC Comics, Gene had ridden off into the sunset.

And where Gene Autry rode, could Roy Rogers be far behind?

Apparently, he could. The King of the Cowboys saddled up a little later than Gene, appearing first in Dell's *Four Color Comics* #38 (April 1944). He appeared in 13 issues of *Four Color* in all, so evenly spaced he might as well have had his own title already. (The last one was #177, December 1947.) Then *Roy Rogers Comics* #1 came forth in January 1948, and it by-golly kept coming forth until the last issue,

Roy Rogers and Trigger #145 (September–October 1961). Beyond that, Roy appeared in a couple more issues of *March of Comics* through 1964, and got his own Gold Key one-shot in July 1967. And to wind things up, he was featured in a Hardee's giveaway comic done by AC Comics in 1990, *Fabulous Fun Comics*. Staying power? Roy wrote the book on it.

We'll do our customary history dump here: Roy Rogers was born Leonard Slye on November 5, 1911, ended up learning to ride a horse, sing, and yodel, picked peaches in a California labor camp à la *The Grapes of Wrath*, and started singing with a country group. Eventually it evolved into the Sons of the Pioneers, who were responsible for "Cool Water," "Tumbling Tumbleweeds," and a bunch of other songs. In 1935 he backed up Gene Autry in a movie. When the hunt went out for a new singing cowboy to be an alternative to Autry, Len Slye won the competition, was renamed—you know it—Roy Rogers, and played lead in *Under Western Stars*. He married Dale Evans after the death of his second wife, and went on to a big (and we mean BIG) career in movies and TV. Roy was a great businessman to boot, made appearances in TV shows long after his own program left the air, and even sang and guested in a music video by country star Clint Black in 1991. And if you've ever heard someone sing "Happy Trails to You" when a party was breaking up, you know where they got it from.

He first rode up in a 49-page tale called "Blazing Guns," written by Gaylord DuBois and illoed by one Burris Jenkins. In the first few pages, Roy, astride Trigger, saw a runaway stagecoach, jumped from Trigger to the backs of the fleeing horses, and brought them to heel in a few action panels. Once they were stopped, he discovered a boy within the coach. "My name is Roy Rogers," the hero said. "What happened?"

From there we proceeded into a tale of evildoers trying to run the boy—who actually turned

The King of the Cowboys: Roy Rogers. © 1944 Dell Publishing, Inc., © 2022 Roy Rogers, Inc. By permission of the Roy and Dale Evan Rogers Children's Trust.

out to be a girl in disguise—off of the ranch, which was on land the railroad wanted. Roy ended up helping the crew drive a herd of 3,000 cattle along the Chisholm Trail to Abilene, Kansas, with a stampede and a fire along the way. In the end, Roy engaged the chief bad guy in a terrific fist battle, made the villain beg for mercy, and brought him to justice. The heroine wanted Roy to stay, but he had other plans (and maybe Dale Evans, who wasn't in the book, would've objected). Roy Rogers rode off into the sunset on Trigger, and that ended his debut story, which was pretty good.

Besides DuBois, Kellog Adams, Elizabeth Beecher, and Eric Freiwald wrote for Roy, while John Buscema, Alex Toth, and Dan Spiegle were among his many art-wranglers. As Dell Westerns went, it was a quality book. Trigger got a tryout in *Four Color* #329 (May 1951) and horsed around in his own series, *Roy Rogers' Trigger*, for issues #2–17 (September–November 1951–June–August 1955), before sharing Roy's own comic as a title character. Roy and Trigger also held up their share of *Western Roundup* #1–25 (June 1952–January–March 1959). Dell closed the gate on the ranch in '61, as noted. But Roy made a few pop-up comic appearances for *March of Comics* and Gold Key, and was reprinted a lot by AC Comics. He retired with class.

Now, what of Dale Evans, the Queen of the West?

Well, Dale (born Lucille Wood Smith in 1912 and married to Roy in 1947) did show up on a few cover photos for Roy's comic, but wasn't inside. Then DC Comics signed her onto their outfit and introduced her in a five-page story, "Queen of the Westerns," in *Real Fact Comics* #13 (March–April 1948). Roy wasn't in the story. A few months later, she and her horse, Pal, made their presence known in DC's *Dale Evans Comics* and stayed there for a 24-issue run (September–October 1948–July–August 1952). She was drawn by Max Elkan and had a lot of stories written by Ryerson Johnson. Since

Where Roy went, Dale was sure to follow. © 1948 National Comics Publications, Inc., © 2022 Roy Rogers, Inc. By permission of the Roy and Dale Evan Rogers Children's Trust.

Roy was busy on the Dell ranch, they couldn't guest-star together, but she did refer to him in the letters pages. Dale had a wheelchair-bound Uncle Six as a supporting character, she was drawn right purty by Elkan, and the stories had the usual DC quality. One of the first tales was called "The Spirit of Annie Oakley," and that seemed to sum it up.

Once she was gone from the DC outfit, Dale struck out to join Roy in his home at Dell. Her first solo book there was *Four Color Comics* #479 (July 1953). She appeared in two stories with her partner, Pat Brady, her dog, Bullet, and her horse, Buttermilk. Roy was mentioned but never appeared. She and Roy finally co-starred in a giveaway comic in 1954 for Dodge, the auto company, called *Roy Rogers and the Man from Dodge City*. Then she headed back to Dell for *Four Color* #528 (January 1954) before again getting her own book, *Queen of the West, Dale Evans* #3 (April-June 1954). Hi Mankin and Russ Manning, the latter later to rise to fame as the artist of Magnus, Robot Fighter, and Tarzan, were the artists. The comic ran through issue #22 (January-March 1959), with Dale taking a side trail into *Western Roundup* #11-25 (July-September 1955-January-March 1959). After that, she finally moved into *Roy Rogers and Trigger* as a backup strip (#132-145, July-August 1959-September-October 1961). She got co-billing with Roy in *March of Comics* #221, 236, and 250 (1961-August 1963). Her last original story appearance was with Roy in *Fabulous Fun Comics* #1 (1990), but AC reprinted a few of her and Roy's stories.

Roy died of heart failure in 1998. Dale followed in 2001 from much the same ailment. It'll take a lot to make us forget them.

There was, of course, a fictional character that ranked with the best of the "real" cowboys, and the mention of his name can bring up a familiar theme in the mind, generation after generation. A fiery horse with the speed of light, a cloud of dust, and a hearty "Hi-Yo, Silver!" The Lone Ranger rides again!

The Masked Man's beginnings and career are legendary. He was created by writer Fran Striker, and possibly by radio station boss George W. Trendle, in 1933. His origin went as follows: six Texas Rangers, on the trail of outlaw Butch Cavendish (who, apparently, lacked a Sundance Kid in this milieu), were lured into an ambush and shot to pieces. Five of them died, but a trusty Indian named Tonto found one alive and nursed him back to health. He was the brother of one of the slain Rangers and his true name has been disputed, but these days it's acknowledged his handle was John Reid. When he came to awareness, he asked Tonto what became of his fellows. "You lone Ranger now!" Tonto replied.

John Reid intended to avenge his brother. To conceal his identity, he made a black eye mask from his brother's vest. Tonto, or perhaps Reid himself, dug a sixth grave with the name of John Reid on it. The Lone Ranger, most stalwart of the knights of the West, then brought Cavendish and his mob to justice and continued to fight outlawry and evil on the frontiers of America and elsewhere. He started in radio, all right, but soon enough rode into novels, Big Little Books, movie serials, and just about any place the *William Tell* Overture could be heard.

As the story goes, years later, after all his gang was dead, Cavendish escaped jail and finally engaged the Ranger in a fight to the death. The bad man ended up taking a fatal fall off a cliff. Before Cavendish died, the Ranger unmasked and revealed himself as the sole survivor of the long-ago ambush. Trying and failing to reach his hated foe, Butch Cavendish died.

The Ranger's first venture into comics came in the form of the *Lone Ranger* comic strip in 1938, first written by creator Fran Striker and then by Bob Green and others. Ed Kressy was the first artist, but Charles Flanders replaced him a year later and stayed till the strip concluded in 1971. The Ranger appeared in 1939 in *Large Feature Comic* #7 from Dell, but this was an illustrated text story by Striker, an expanded Big Little Book sort of thing. A promo comic from an ice cream company came out the same year, but we have no info on it.

David McKay Publications, which reprinted tons of King Features Syndicate material, put him incongruously into a title called *Future Comics* #1 (June 1940). The story was reprinted from the comic strip, as would be the subsequent Lone Ranger appearances in McKay's *Feature Book* #21 (July 22, 1940), *King Comics* #52 (August 1940), and *Magic Comics* #17 (December 1940). *Future* died with issue #4 (September 1940), but the Ranger kept on in *King* till probably issue #145 (May 1948), in *Magic* through issue #115 (February 1949), and in *Ace Comics* from #135 to 137 (June–August 1948).

By that time, Dell had gotten their hooks into him.

Four Color Comics #82 (1945) featured the Lone Ranger's Dell debut, an issue made up, again, of comic strip reprints. This continued through the Masked Man's succeeding *Four Color* appearances (#118, 125, 136, 151, and 167, September 1946–October 1947). *The Lone Ranger* #1 finally came out with a cover date of January–February 1948, and the stories were all newspaper strip reprints up through issue #37 (July 1951). Finally, with the next issue (#38, August 1951), Paul S. Newman wrote and Tom Gill drew "The Ghost Gang," the Ranger's first original story in comics. It was action-packed, the art was decent, and he almost seemed like a frontier Batman. From there on in, the Lone Ranger took the path of all-new stories in the Dell run. The fact that he'd been appearing in a hit TV show since 1949 couldn't have hurt things.

Like Trigger and Champion, his horse, Silver, got his own well-drawn comic, starting with a *Four Color* tryout in issue #369 (January 1952), featuring his origin and guest-starring the Ranger, and #392 (April 1952), which continued with tales of his early years. After that, *The Lone Ranger's Famous Horse Hi-Yo Silver*, a title almost long enough to bring down the comic with its weight, ran from #3–36 (July–September 1952–October–December 1960).

Tonto, though a sidekick, wasn't about to be left out. *Four Color* #312 (January 1951) was his first solo comic, and he didn't need another tryout, putting him several issues up on his Kemosabe. *Tonto* ran swiftly from issues #2 to 33 (August 1951–November 1958 / January 1959), with art by Jon Small and Alberto Giolitti.

The Ranger also maintained his own 100-page giant comic, *The Lone Ranger's Western Treasury* (which changed to *The Lone Ranger's Golden West* with the third issue) from #1 to 3 (September 1953–August 1955). *The Lone Ranger Movie Story* #1 (March 1956) was another 100-pager, adapting the then-current movie and retelling the origins of the Ranger, Tonto, and Silver. Even when he appeared in flashback before his Lone Ranger days, John Reid's face was *never* shown. His first *March of*

Comics, #165, came out in December 1957. Several others followed in the series. Also, he appeared in numerous comic giveaways from merchandisers that wanted to hitch their wagon to his franchise, from around 1939 all the way to 1978.

Newman and Gill continued with *The Lone Ranger* until the last Dell issue, #145 (May–July 1962). Shortly after that, thanks to Dell's disastrous move of inflating their per-issue price from 12 cents to (gasp!) 15 cents, the company lost just about all their licensed properties. The Ranger, sadly, was among them.

But he wasn't off the trail for long. Gold Key, Dell's supplanters, published *Lone Ranger* #1 in September 1964. It commenced with reprints from the Dell series, but at least the Ranger was back. The reprints continued until issue #8 (October 1967), when Tom Gill stepped in for a new five-page Lone Ranger story. After that, Gill continued with an original story per issue through #12 (October 1968), then the book continued as all-reprint, except for non–Ranger filler. But *The Lone Ranger* #22 (September 1975) finally offered an all-new issue with two stories drawn by José Delbo. Paul Newman returned soon after as writer, with Frank Bolle stepping in as artist for one issue, #26 (September 1976). It looked like the Lone Ranger was in good hands again.

Unfortunately, that wasn't the case. *The Lone Ranger* #28 (March 1977), with art by Don Heck, was his last. Heroic Westerns had been replaced by the savage Clint Eastwood variety, and the only Western hero thriving in comics was Jonah Hex. Gold Key, later Western, wasn't doing so hot themselves at the time, and only the most devoted fans noticed when the Ranger's comic was cancelled.

That wasn't quite the end, though. Several attempts (and we do mean "attempts") over the years were made to bring the Lone Ranger back in movies, but they failed to live up to the ultraheroic image Clayton Moore had given us with his 1949–1957 TV show, and they busted. In comics, Topps, who were all about licensing properties in their short existence, brought out a four-issue *Lone Ranger and Tonto* series (August–November 1994). Joe Lansdale, Tim Truman, and Rick Magyar did the honors. But thanks to an ill-advised personality conflict between the Ranger and Tonto, the series didn't go over well.

In 2006, a five-page preview story in *Highlander* #0 (July 2006) from Dynamite previewed their upcoming *Lone Ranger* revival. Their *Lone Ranger* series commenced a few months later with scripts from Brett Matthews and art by Sergio Carello. It lasted a respectable 25 issues (September 2006–May 2011). A four-issue spinoff, *The Lone Ranger and Tonto*, spanned March 2008–December 2010. Finally, Dynamite teamed the Ranger with Zorro in *The Lone Ranger and Zorro: The Death of Zorro* #1–5 (March–June 2011). Zorro died. The Ranger didn't. They've published several Lone Ranger series since then, including a *Lone Ranger–Green Hornet* crossover that linked the Ranger with his famous great-nephew, and they don't show much sign of stopping. There is hope.

As long as folks can access the old radio shows, the old TV shows, the old movies, and yes, the old comics, the Lone Ranger will keep up his ride for justice.

Most of the rest of Dell's Western input began in 1950 or afterward. But are there any other tall-in-the-saddle guys left to cover from that company? You betchum, Red Ryder!

The red-haired range rider is mostly forgotten today, but in his time, roughly from 1938 to 1965, he was one of the biggest Western comic strip stars around. Stephen Slesinger wrote and Fred Harman drew his earliest newspaper strips. Harman had created a similar strip, *Bronc Peeler*, a few years later, which tanked. With the help of Slesinger, a marketing genius, Harman hit the big time and stayed there.

The strip featured the adventures of the red-headed, red-shirted Red, his Indian kid sidekick, Little Beaver, his girlfriend, Beth Wilder, his enemy, Ace Hanlon, and his horse, Thunder. His era was the 1890s and he lived on the Painted Valley Ranch with the Duchess, his aunt. Red and Little Beaver got into trouble almost as much as the Lone Ranger, and handled it just as courageously. Since newspaper strip reprints were still very much a thing in contemporary comics, it's not surprising that Red sashayed into *Crackajack Comics* from Whitman with issue #9 (March 1939), on which he took the cover. The stories were, of course, reprinted from the comic strips, and he hung on there till issue #35 (May 1941), with a stop-off for a text story in *The Funnies* #30 (April 1939), his first Dell appearance. Slesinger had done a deal with, among other clients, the Daisy BB Rifle company, and Red Ryder was soon plastered all over the back covers of a whole bunch of different companies' books, telling kids why they should beg their parents for a Daisy BB Rifle. Daisy continues manufacturing said rifles to this very day.

Slesinger's Hawley Publications outfit published the first issue of *Red Ryder Comics* in September 1940 with a 65-page collection of reprints that featured Little Beaver's origin. Red skipped the next issue, which was called *Hi-Spot Comics* and featured an adaptation of Edgar Rice Burroughs's David Innes of Pellucidar. But he was back for the next one, and stayed for two more with Hawley (#3–5, August–December 1941). Then Dell took over, and Red thrived on their ranch.

Red Ryder #6 (April 1942) featured a cover scene of a campfire with Red, Little Beaver, and his newspaper co-stars Wash Tubbs, Captain Easy, and King of the Royal Mounted parked around it. It was telling that they were all meeting at *his* place. A batch of other strip characters—Alley Oop, Boots, Yanks in the RAF, Herky, Myra North, Freckles, and Dan Dunn—shared the interior as well. But Red Ryder took the lead with a 12-page reprint story, and he doubtless made sure that everybody else knew it.

Things continued pretty much that way, with the back features changing a bit, until *Red Ryder Comics* #47 (June 1947). With that number, original stories of Red and Little Beaver began. They saved a captured schoolmarm and busted a bunch of bank robbers in the first story. The rest of the issue was filled by a *King of the Royal Mounted* reprint, a Little Beaver text story, another Red tale in which he tried to teach a young boy horsemanship, a feature called *The Kiyote Kids*, and a funny-animal Western by Dan Gormley named *Panamint Patty*. Like the Lone Ranger, Red Ryder had chosen an original story path. He continued as such through the rest of the comic's run.

Though Red's horse, Thunder, never got his own comic, and probably had to endure the snobbery of Silver, Trigger, and Champion for such, Little Beaver was a bit more successful. He appeared in a string of *Four Color* tryouts starting with #211 (January 1949). After four more tryouts, he got his own comic. *Little Beaver* ran for issues #3–8 (we don't try to explain Dell numbering here! October–December 1951–January–March 1953). He then returned to *Four Color* for seven more issues between #483 and 870 (July 1953–January 1958). All this time, he had his own solo feature in Red's own book. Like a lot of sidekicks, he made out about as well as his mentor.

Besides DuBois, Kellog Adams, Paul S. Newman, Robert Ryder, and Phil Evans scripted some of Red's adventures. Artists in his bunkhouse included Pete Alvarado, Dick Calkins, John Hampton, and Bill Lignante. Sam Savitt produced some impressive cover paintings, as he did for the rest of Dell's Western line.

The series changed to *Red Ryder Ranch Magazine* with #145 (October–November 1955) and then to *Red Ryder Ranch Comics* in issue #149 (October–November 1956). By that time, cover photos from Red's then-current TV show shared space with painted illustrations. Then, with issue #151 (April–June 1957), Red and Little Beaver hung it up. The comic strip had about seven years to go. But in comics, the bloom was off Red's rose. He managed another appearance in *Four Color Comics* (#916, July 1958), either an attempt at bolstering interest in a revival or a burnoff of an inventoried issue, but that was it. No matter. Whenever a kid saw the Daisy ad on the back of a comic, he knew Red Ryder existed, though he may not have known more than that.

Finally, note should be taken of the *Zane Grey* series from Dell. These were adaptations of the famed Western author's novels, a lot of them written by Gaylord DuBois and drawn by Albert Micale. Grey had 32 such books turned into comics in the *Four Color* series, beginning with #197 (September 1948, "Spirit of the Border") and ending with #996 (June–August 1959, "Stories of the Old West"). In between there, *Zane Grey's Stories of the West* adapted 13 more (#27–39, September–November 1955–September–November 1958). *Four Color* #996 was reprinted by Gold Key as a one-shot, *Zane Grey's Stories of the West* #1 (November 1964), and that's where it ended.

There were lots of other occupants of the Fawcett corral. The earliest of them debuted in *Whiz Comics* #2 (February 1940), a little bit after Captain Marvel, and he lasted almost as long. Golden Arrow was his name.

Bill Parker, who created the Big Red Cheese with C.C. Beck, and Pete Costanza, who drew a whole bunch of his stories, were Golden Arrow's creators. As far as origins went, the Arrow's was pretty good. A few years before World War I, Prof. Paul Parsons perfected a lighter-than-air, non-flammable gas which he intended to sell to the Army. He built a huge balloon, filled it with the gas, and loaded himself, his wife, Gloria, and his three-year-old son, Roger, into the gondola below it for a cross-country flight as a demonstration. An "outlaw ex-munitions maker," Brand Braddock, saw the balloon overhead, lusted for the formula for the gas, and had a couple of his men shoot it down. The professor and his wife were killed on impact when the balloon dropped.

Roger wasn't.

A mountain lion saw him, picked him up in his jaws, and carried him off. An old prospector, Nugget Ned, saw the big cat, shot him, and rescued the toddler. Later, Ned saw the Braddock bunch burying the Parsonses and their balloon. Fearing reprisal, he vowed to raise the boy himself.

Roger's raising went pretty well. He could wrestle a bear cub, catch a running antelope, and see fish in a pool a thousand feet below the surface. But he was best with the bow and arrow, and was an uncanny shot with it. Ned gave him gold to fashion arrowheads with, and the nearby Indians called him Golden Arrow. He later tamed a great white stallion and named him White Wind. The horse would be his companion through all his stories.

When Roger reached maturity, Ned died of a heart attack, but not before relating to him the story of his parents' deaths and the name of the man responsible. Golden Arrow stormed the Braddock manse, took back his father's formula, defeated Brand Braddock and his sons, and gave the formula to the Army. The last panel showed him astride White Wind, looking into the sunset. End of story.

Golden Arrow's shafts best a badman's gun. © 1942 Fawcett Publications, Inc.

Golden Arrow lived in the present, but his stories always hearkened back to the Old West. If his creators sometimes forgot he was in the twentieth century, that can be forgiven. He clashed with the Braddocks again in the next issue. By #3 (April 1940), a bandit killed Brand Braddock with one of the Arrow's gold-headed shafts and framed him for murder. The hero escaped and caught the real killer, but Bronk and Brute Braddock, Brand's no-good sons, weren't mollified.

The Braddocks continued to bedevil Golden Arrow in succeeding issues, but their pretty niece, Carol Braddock, arrived in *Whiz* #5 (June 1940), and, since she'd inherit the ranch on her 21st birthday, promptly became a murder target for her uncles. Golden Arrow killed a mountain lion that menaced her and then saved her from falling to her death. "When I was twenty-one I was going to give [the Braddocks] each a third interest in my gold mine!" Carol said. "But now I think I'll have all the ore made into golden arrows!"

If that wasn't a cue that a love interest was in the making, we don't know our comic books.

Carol carried on through *Whiz Comics* #25 (December 26, 1941) as a supporting character. Bronk and Brute only made it to issue #8 (September 1940), in which they were unceremoniously shipped off to jail. That was okay. There was a passel more bad guys for Golden Arrow to deal with. He dealt with them through issue #154 (April 1953) and appeared in seven issues of his own comic from 1942 to Spring 1947, plus single stories in *America's Greatest Comics* #8 (Summer 1943) and *All Hero Comics* #1 (May 17, 1943). He was also found in a giveaway issue of *Whiz* that was taped to Wheaties cereal boxes in 1947. On top of that, he cameoed in a number of Captain Marvel stories along with the rest of Fawcett's hero crew. Since he wasn't the Captain himself, Charlton Comics had no qualms about picking him up in 1954 for a few issues of *Cowboy Western* (#48–51, 57, Spring 1954–October 1955), *Tex Ritter Western* #27 (February 1955), and *Range Busters* #10 (September 1955). Except for a few scattered reprints from DC and AC Comics, that was his last hurrah.

Lucky Lawton, another Western guy, appeared in Fawcett's *Slam-Bang Comics* #1–7 (March–September 1940) and *Wow Comics* #1 (Winter 1940–41) and was pretty forgettable, so let's forget him. Instead, we'll try to check out a few more Fawcett movie cowboys who started before 1950. There were, of course, no lack of steel-jawed heroes, good with their brain, their fists, and their gun.

And then there was Gabby Hayes.

Gabby, whose real name was George Hayes, was born in 1885, ran away from home at age 17, became a successful vaudeville star, got married, and lost his considerable fortune in the 1929 stock crash. His wife urged him to try his luck in cinema. They moved to Los Angeles, and it worked: he got movie roles almost immediately. After playing characters ranging from leading men to villains, George Hayes found his niche as the bearded, humorous, dad-gummit-saying old-codger sidekick of Hopalong Cassidy from 1935 to 1939, and then moved over to Republic, where he gained the name Gabby Whittaker and played opposite Roy Rogers, John Wayne, Randolph Scott, Gene Autry, and Wild Bill Elliott. He made his last movie in 1950, moved to TV for his own show through 1956, and was funny.

He also had his own comic book.

The first Gabby Hayes story was in Fawcett's *Real Western Hero* #71 (October 1948), was entitled "The Kayo Cookies," and opened with an action shot of Gabby trying to sneak some cookies out of the kitchen at the Bar Nothing Ranch. He was interrupted by one Aunt Hester, who told him that a no-good bear hunter, Grizzly Gus, had stolen a saddle that Gabby had paid two hundred simoleons for. Gabby threw his hat on the ground, hollered "Ding bust it!," mounted his horse, Corker, and rode into town. As he left, Hester confided she'd mixed in some knockout drugs in the batch of cookies which she intended to use on an ailing steer. The rest of the story proceeded about as expected: Gabby disguised himself with a bear skin, encountered Grizzly Gus, and was going to be skinned by him. He stalled his enemy by offering him some cookies, then closed with him in possibly-mortal-if-it-went-through combat. Gabby swung a mighty roundhouse punch. Grizzly Gus fell over like a patient anesthetized on a table. The sheriff, a little less than Johnny-on-the-spot, saw it, and when his partner proclaimed Gabby ferocious, the hero replied, "Reckon I am, son! Reckon I am!" He rode back with his new saddle in hand, or at least on Corker. The first awe-inspiring adventure of Gabby Hayes had concluded.

A month later, *Gabby Hayes Western* #1 appeared (November 1948), and things continued in the same vein. The comic continued in Fawcett's hands through issue #50 (January 1953) and then fell into the grip of Charlton, which kept it going as *Gabby Hayes* #51–59 (December 1954–January 1957). In between, Toby Comics, which was owned by *Li'l Abner* creator Al Capp, did one issue of *Gabby Hayes Western* (#1, December 1953). He also appeared in five little bitty giveaways from Quaker Oats in 1951, like a lot of Western good guys. Gabby's *Western Hero* gig lasted till #112 (March 1952). He also occupied a spot in Fawcett's *Monte Hale Western* #34–80 (March 1949–January 1953). Charlton took command of *Monte Hale* after that and Gabby kept his gig from #83–86 (February–August 1955). After that, the ding-busted old codger called it quits. Gabby Hayes died in 1969. Otto Binder, Rod Reed, and Irwin Schoffman pounded the typewriter for him, and Jack Binder, Clem Weisbacker, Leonard Frank, and Marc Swayze were among his artists.

AC Comics, as might be expected, reprinted three Gabby stories in 1989 and one in 1999. Since then, he has vanished from the comics.

Monte Hale Western also started off in 1948. He saddled up in *Real Western Hero* #70 (September 1948), just one issue earlier than Gabby. Really, his book wasn't half bad, though he's pretty much forgotten today.

Monte, born Samuel Buren Ely in 1919, followed a familiar career path: he learned to play guitar and sing, ran away from home, and got into radio and stage shows as a singing cowboy. He became a member of the band in the Stars Over Texas bond drive, encountered some Western movie stars, and was recommended to Republic Pictures. There he made pictures for about seven years, though his movie career cooled down when TV Westerns started horning in on the movies. But Fawcett and others were looking for more movie cowhands to put in comics, and Monte was one of the ones they chose. He was 6 foot 5 in height and more than once was referred to as "the giant cowboy."

In his first story, Monte found his sleep disturbed by a bank robbery and vowed to go after the robber, a dastard called the Coyote. He proved his bona fides by outfighting a bully during the first few pages, then got down to business with his horse, Pardner. The Coyote proved to be a deadly fellow indeed, threatening to let two posse members whom he had roped fall to their deaths. Monte shot a knife out of the killer's hand, but soon found himself kayoed by the Coyote, tied sitting up to his horse, and sent back toward the posse to be shot down by mistake. (The baddie could have done the job himself, but figured it'd be more artistic to let Monte's allies do the job themselves. Hopefully, he learned a lesson from the outcome. Or maybe he was just too lazy.) Monte awakened in time to grab the horse's reins with his teeth and halted the nag. Anyway, he was freed by his allies and went on to trick the Coyote into emptying his gun. Then, with two good punches, he laid the villain low. When he returned to San Pedro, the folks offered him the job of town marshal. He declined in favor of going back to bed.

Monte Hale had an itchy foot, hardly ever stayed in the same place per story, and was soon named a U.S. marshal. He battled bad guys in *Monte Hale Western* #29 (converted from *Mary Marvel*) through #82 (October 1948–June 1953), and had a side gig in *Real Western Hero* #70–75 (September 1948–February 1949), renamed *Western Hero* and running for issues #76–112 (March 1949–March 1952). He also extended his booking into *Six-Gun Heroes* #18–22 (January–September 1953). A number of his movies were adapted into comics as well. Carl Pfeufer, Leonard Frank, Edmond Good, Pete Riss, and Bob Laughlin were among the guys who limned his adventures, and Paul S. Newman, Bill Woolfolk, and Irwin Schoffman wrote them.

He also managed a recurring villain, the Undertaker. Said villain turned up first in *Monte Hale Western* #30 (November 1948), dressed all in black with an expression borrowed from a bill collector, and digging a hole in a town street for a nearby coffin with Monte Hale's name on it. The Undertaker was said to be the deadliest man in the West, a hired gun who was hired by a political boss to stop Monte from running interference against his plans. With a sneer on his face that would have given the Lone Ranger pause, the Undertaker had come into town, went to a carpenter's shop, and ordered up a coffin for Monte.

In a midnight showdown, the Undertaker appeared to have gunned Monte down. He placed his victim in the coffin and, the next morning, led a funeral procession to a newly dug grave. But Monte Hale himself emerged from the six-foot-deep hole before the coffin could occupy it! The corpse in the casket was one of the boss's own gunnies, and Monte outdrew the man in black. As Hale was preparing to walk the politician to jail, someone noted that the Undertaker was just shot in the shoulder. "He'll live to face the hangman!"

Actually, he'd live to face Monte Hale again. The Undertaker returned in issue #34 (March 1949), this time known as the Gravedigger. (The reason for the name change is unknown, unless Quality's Doll Man informed them that *he* had a foe named the Undertaker, too.) This time, the black-clad bad guy was being paid by a crook on trial to terrorize a judge and anyone who might serve on a jury trying him. Monte struck back and, with the help of a couple of disguises, captured the Gravedigger and his employer. In the next issue (#35, April 1949), the Gravedigger figured that in union there was strength, and teamed up with the Gopher and the Coyote to put Monte six feet under. As usual, it didn't work; the Gravedigger should have shelled out some dough to the writer and artists. He escaped the hangman in issue #38 (July 1949) and locked Monte in a coffin, but the hero unscrewed the hinges of it with his badge and corralled his enemy again.

The Gravedigger came back in issues #40 (September 1949), 51 (August 1950), 56 (January 1951), 59 (April 1951), 65 (October 1951), and 77 (October 1952). In the last of these, the villain was apparently blown to pieces by a dynamite blast. Monte allowed that the Gravedigger might not really be dead, but he never came back, so we'll take that as a finale.

Hale's second great recurring foe showed his face in *Western Hero* #89 (April 1950): the Minstrel Man. Actually, the real minstrel man of that story was an innocent entertainer in clownish face-paint, a big fake nose, and patched clothing. He plunked a banjo and sang ditties, but he also seemed to be involved in local crime. Monte exposed the villainous Minstrel Man as the original's manager and took him to the hoosegow. The bad-guy Minstrel Man returned in issues #91 (June 1950) and

98 (January 1951), then in *Monte Hale Western* #58 (March 1951) and #66 (November 1951).

Monte also crossed swords or guns with the Wolfman (issues #33 and 40), the Pueblo Kid (#37, June 1949), and Mr. Law (#39, August 1949), among others. The Coyote and the Gopher also made encore appearances. In one prophetic tale, Monte encountered the proto-women's libbers of Skirt Ranch ("Cowgirl Courage," #38, July 1949). They ran their own ranch and wouldn't allow men on it, in a sagebrush version of Paradise Island. Monte had to dress up in drag as "Lucy Hale" to help them out. Hopefully, he got that out of his system in a short time.

Then Fawcett went to Boot Hill, and Monte signed up with the Charlton Ranch.

Monte Hale Western jogged along for issues #83–88 (February 1955–January 1956), with Monte also appearing in *Cowboy Western* #55–56 (June–August 1955). All of Monte's stories for Charlton were Fawcett reprints. Then Monte and Pardner found a way to leave the stage. He was a favorite of AC Comics, though, and they reprinted a bunch of his stories from 1999 to 2006. After that, even the reprints ended.

Then came *Rocky Lane*. He barely squeaks in under our pre–1950 criterion, but his comic did start in 1949, so he gets covered. Stand back and give us room for another history.

To begin with, Rocky was born Harry Leonard Albershardt in 1909 and, quite frankly, we think a Western hero named Rocky Albershardt would have been kinda interesting. He had been a stage actor and model by the time Fox Corporation glommed onto him and starred him in his first movie in 1929. Shortly thereafter he jumped to Warner Brothers, jumped back to Fox, went to Republic, and made a whole bunch of pictures through 1966, mostly Westerns. Lane starred as *King of the Royal Mounted* in a 12-part Saturday morning serial, made several other well-received Mountie films, starred as Red Ryder in seven films in the Forties, then went on to play a cowboy named after himself ... well, after Rocky Lane, anyway. He made a lot of those movies, with his trusty horse, Black Jack, beside him, or underneath him, as it were, and, in the early Sixties, became the voice of Mister Ed. In 1973, Lane died of cancer.

Rocky's first comic book appearance was in, quite logically, *Rocky Lane Western* #1 (May 1949). He maintained this title through issue #55 (January 1954), after which he jumped to Charlton with most of his Fawcett buddies. They extended his run from #56–87 (February 1954–November 1959), a successful run by anybody's standards. He did appear in some Fawcett adaptations of his movies, but the first time he ventured properly out of his own comic was in *Six-Gun Heroes*, where he stayed from issues #2–23 (May 1950–November 1953) and then worked under the Charlton banner for issues #24–55 (January 1954–February 1960). He also showed up for work in Charlton's *Cowboy Western* #48–50, 52 (Spring–December 1954), *Masked Raider* #3, 22, and 24 (October 1955–June 1960), *Sheriff of Tombstone* #7 (January 1960), *Outlaws of the West* #23 (January 1960), *Wyatt Earp, Frontier Marshal* #28 (January 1960), *Black Fury* #25 (July 1960), and *Cheyenne Kid* #24 (September 1960), his last hurrah.

Black Jack, who probably wanted equal time, lasted a bit longer than Rocky. The first solo Black Jack story appeared in *Cowboy Western* #52 (December 1954). After enough time waiting for a solo title booking, he got a regular gig in *Rocky Lane's Black Jack* #20–30 (November 1957–November 1959). After that, he jumped from title to title like someone had put a burr under his saddle: *Billy the Kid* #21 (March 1960), *Masked Raider* #23 (April 1960), *Texas Rangers in Action* #21 (April 1960), *Outlaws of the West* #25 (May 1960), *Kid Montana* #23 and 27 (June 1960 and February 1961), *Sheriff of Tombstone* #12 (November 1960), *Lash Larue Western* #81 (December 1960), *Wyatt Earp, Frontier Marshal* #34 (January 1961), and *Cheyenne Kid* #27 (March 1961), Black Jack's last showing. He outlasted his mentor. Not even Silver, Champion, or Trigger could boast that. Also, Charlton gave him a last reprinting in *Gunfighters* #78 (April 1983). That, folks, is a horse with staying power.

Anyway, in Rocky's first story, marauding Comanches were wiping out wagon trains and the governor of Texas sent out a summons for able men to become marshals for secret duty, known only to comics readers. Rocky Lane rode by a poster for such nailed to a tree, halted Black Jack, and read it. "So they're looking for marshals for secret duty, Black Jack! Doggoned if that job isn't just to my taste!"

The governor himself, passing by coincidence in a stagecoach, noticed Rocky's horsemanship, stopped, and offered him a job. Lane, not knowing the job he was offered was the one he was looking for, declined and went on his way to Austin. But on the way, both parties came upon a band of Indians attacking a wagon train. Rocky went into action with rope, pistol, and Black Jack, and put the attackers to flight. Rocky got offered the job again, rejected it again, and went to Austin. There, he passed a shootin' test and was told he had to wait two weeks to see if he got the job. Since he had the time to spare, Rocky foiled the plans of a white renegade to help the Comanches trap another wagon train, beat the heck out of the baddie, and defeated the Indian chief in a hand-to-hand battle. Then he brought his captive back to Austin, where the wagoneers, the renegade, and the governor had convened. The governor finally had the chance to explain what job he was offering, and Rocky took it. He also released the chief, who, admittedly, had been bamboozled by the villain of the piece.

Except for a Slim Pickens Western funny, that was the end of the issue. Rocky continued as such through the end of his run, with the likes of Otto Binder, Ken Fitch, Bill Woolfolk, and Irwin Schoffman on scripts and Stan Campbell, George Evans, Frank Doyle, Ernie Hart, Dick Giordano, John Severin, and Syd Shores on art. As for Black Jack, he used most of the same artists, plus one additional: Steve Ditko. So the feature wasn't lacking for talent.

Decades after the last Charlton stories, AC Comics took up the reprinter's burden and republished an old Rocky Lane story in *Great American Western* #1 (1987). Further scattered reprints followed, including two issues of *Rocky Lane Western* (1989 and 2000) and a semi-regular spot in *Best of the West*. Their last Rocky reprint to date was in *Best of the West* #68 (2008). But Steve Ditko's Black Jack stories got reprinted in Fantagraphics' *Steve Ditko Archives* #6 (April 2016). At this writing, that's where matters stand.

Also in 1949, another prairie Paladin appeared. Actually, he might have been an influence on Indiana Jones, given his choice of weaponry. He was the Man in Black before Johnny Cash, and he lasted a long, long time in comics. His handle? Lash LaRue.

We're in for another history dump, so here goes. Alfred LaRue was born in 1917, moved to California with his parents, and was originally screen tested by Warner Brothers but was rejected because he looked too much like Humphrey Bogart, which for some reason was seen back then as a detriment. He made a few screen appearances and then was cast as the Cheyenne Kid (later the namesake of another Charlton cowboy) in a Western. The part called for an expert with the whip, so Al LaRue bought a couple of whips and, according to him, "beat the hell" out of himself learning to use them. But he learned. The newly named Lash LaRue brandished an 18-foot whip, dressed all in black, and used his weapon to snap guns out of the hands of baddies. With that kind of skill and with that kind of image, Lash LaRue became a star. Much later, he'd teach the same skills to Harrison Ford, who had signed up to play a part called Indiana Jones in an obscure flick called *Raiders of the Lost Ark*.

Anyway, Lash's career was still in its prime when Fawcett brought out the first issue of *Lash LaRue Western* #1 (Summer 1949). He did look an awful lot like Bogie on the cover (and Bogie had played an outlaw named Whip McCord in *Oklahoma City*, himself), and he was smiling, but somehow you knew you probably didn't want to cross him. The first story was called "The Range Riders of Destruction." Even though Lash, called a "roving marshal," wasn't in black, he showed his stuff well in the first two pages. A bandit on a hillside was covering himself with a deadly array of gunfire. Risking his life, Lash leaped onto a boulder above him, showed himself to the owlhoot, and whipped the gun out of his quarry's hands with one SNAP! Then he jumped down onto the fleeing crook and knocked him out with one punch. Lash had proven his bona fides.

One fun factoid about the series: Lash had a twin brother, the Frontier Phantom. All we knew about him is that he was wilder than Lash, who called him "Frontier," and he was naturally mistaken for the hero in his first story (issue #6, July 1950). This was taken from Lash's movie series, in which he played both himself and his identical twin in two movies. The Phantom reappeared in *Lash LaRue Western* #21 and 29 (October 1951 and June 1952), with a reprint in issue #57 (September 1955).

Lash LaRue Western carried on with Fawcett through issue #46 (January 1954), making that issue one of the final books published by Fawcett. Charlton took it up without a slip and published #47–84 (March–April 1954–June 1961). He also whipped through *Fawcett Movie Comic* #8 (December 1950) and *Six-Gun Heroes* #5–23 (November 1950–November 1953) before Charlton picked the latter title up and ran from issues #24–64 (January 1954–August 1961). Lash laid low for 19 years, then a shortly revived Charlton reprinted him in *Gunfighters* #58, 61, 68, and 70 (January 1980–September 1981). Finally, AC Comics got him in their sights, and reprinted him first in *Great American Western* #4 (1989), then in *Lash LaRue* #1 and *Lash LaRue Annual* #1, both in 1990. He got reprinted a small batch of times more by AC, finishing up with *Best of the West* #69 (2008). That seemed to prove it was not too late to whip it.

Paul S. Newman, Irwin Schoffman, Ernie Hart, and Ken Fitch were among Lash's writers, and Sam Citron, Frank Doyle, Bob Powell, George Tuska, John Belfi,

Stan Campbell, Bill Molno, Doug Wildey, Maurice Whitman, and Rocco Mastroserio drew the pictures. With that, we leave Fawcett for a later time, and head on to other routes.

Quality Comics, which usually had better art and writing than a lot of the competition, offered Westerns that lived up to their name. George Brenner's *Lone Star Rider* (*Smash Comics* #2, September 1939) may have been their first. He mixed the Lone Ranger cliché with the other cliché of having his parents killed by desperadoes and vowing revenge. One issue was all he got.

The Fargo Kid (*Feature Comics* #47–63, August 1941–December 1942) was pretty generic but at least had decent art from Alex Koda. But for the most part, Quality left the genre alone until the late Forties, when superhero sales were dropping off and they converted their omnibus titles from the costumed guys to other genres.

Jeb Rivers wasn't strictly speaking a Western, but it was set in the same milieu, and it was neatly done indeed. As one might expect, Jeb was the pilot of a riverboat down South, and his origin of sorts came in *Hit Comics* #61 (November 1949). The art was by Reed Crandall, and Jeb Rivers himself was a mysterious drifter who had experience in piloting a boat and plenty of experience with his fists. He also had a kid sidekick named Catfish, whom he brought aboard the good ship *Paragon* with him when he needed transport quickly to St. Louis. Said ship, captained by Lucius Pelham and piloted by his pretty daughter, Marnie, was in a race against another boat from New Orleans to Saint Looie, and a crooked gambler aboard, one Gooler, was out to make sure he lost. Jeb beat the bejabbers out of the bad guy, steered the *Paragon* away from destruction, and helped the captain win the bet by miles.

After that, in the next story, Jeb revealed, "I can pilot a river boat—teach a school or edit a paper—a good shot and a swordsman—Once I fought a draw

Jeb Rivers pilots his riverboat into adventure. © 1949 Comic Magazines.

in Cincinnati with the British bare-knuckle champion!" In that story, he and Catfish went underground to break up the plot of a tyrant named Thraill to make himself emperor of the United States. An Army officer wanted Jeb to go to Washington to get the president's thanks, but he went back with his kid partner to the *Paragon*. Guess you always go where your heart is. Jeb settled in for more two-fisted adventure. But *Hit* died with issue #65 (July 1950). Jeb caught a ride in *Doll Man* #32–34 (February–June 1951) and, hopefully, made a family afterward with Marnie and Catfish.

In 1949, Quality finally got on the bandwagon or the stagecoach with *Crack Western*, continuing its numbering from *Crack Comics*. It opened with issue #63 (November 1949), went to #84 (May 1953), and thereafter gave its space to *Jonesy*, a teen humor comic. *Crack Western* was an above-average Western comic, thanks to its exceptional art and the usual Quality snappy scripting. The first cover depicted a green-shirted cowboy astride a speeding horse, trying to race a wagon full of explosives downhill before it reached a passing railroad train. That was our intro to Arizona Raines.

Actually, Arizona Raines started as Arizona *Ames* and was written, drawn, and lettered by Paul Gustavson, one of Quality's aces. The first story introed us to a red-shirted Arizona and his kid sidekick, Spurs, who was running lickety-split from a horrible noise he'd never heard before—a railroad whistle. In a storyline that may seem familiar, the beautiful blonde Kathy Dale owned said railroad and was racing rival Mike Bates to get through a narrow pass in the foothills to some silver mines. If Bates won, said she, he'd "strangle" the mines with high rates. Arizona, like most cowboys, was happy to help a damsel in distress. When Bates sent the cover-pictured wagon full of dynamite toward the oncoming train, Arizona and his horse, Thunder, got ahead of it, lassoed it, and

Arizona Ames, later Raines, races a death-wagon to save a train. © 1949 Comic Magazines

pulled it across the tracks before the train could get there, with instants to spare. Then they hit the dirt before they could get blown up real good.

Arizona and Spurs, who complained all the way about not being allowed a gun and insisted that his mentor fall in love with Kathy, foiled the plans of the villains in the end. Our hero collected a great smooch from Miss Dale and then had to ride off. Spurs complained, "Aw, sometimes I think Arizona Ames ain't got good sense!" That was it for story #1.

Plumb shy of women, Arizona moved on from town to town when a pretty miss threatened to settle him down after a hard day of owlhoot-punchin' and straight shootin'. He changed his handle to Arizona Raines by issue #66 (May 1950) and continued his wandering saga. Spurs did eventually get his gun and use it in the fracases he and Arizona got into, which, when the comic expanded to 52 pages, was twice an issue. But they came to the end of the trail after 22 stories.

Two-Gun Lil, Quality's answer to Annie Oakley, debuted one story later. She was the beautiful blonde daughter of Sheriff Sam Peters, who taught her how to use a shootin' iron as good as any man. Joe Millard wrote the first story and Charles Sultan drew it, and the splash panel showed what looked to be a 30-foot Lil Peters with two smoking guns, frightening all the bad men out of Sage City. The story opened with Lil in Boston, where she had gone to school at her dad's insistence. She went to a charity carnival, grabbed two guns at a shooting gallery, and knocked a passel of targets off their shelves. A few panels later, she was in tears when she learned from a telegram that her daddy had been killed by a bushwhacker. Looking at her two .44's, she said, "These are my friends now ... and they're going to help me pay back the buzzard who bushwhacked you! That's a promise!"

Lil hooked up with Deputy Bob Cross as soon as she alighted from the stagecoach and soon learned that gambler Garson Cade was behind her father's murder. Two rannies in Cade's employ overpowered her, tied her up in a hotel room, and left her there with a pack of dynamite and a burning fuse. "These men always figure a gal will be too paralyzed with fright to use her head!" muttered Lil. She used her tied feet to grasp the dynamite and threw it through a window to explode on the street below. Then she donned a red fringed dress, boots, gloves, vest, cowboy hat and—oh, yes—a gunbelt and two hoglegs. Lil proceeded to invade a saloon where Cade and his boys were hiding out, shot down a chandelier over them (it's a wonder they even *made* those things, except to shoot down), and worked a confession out of the bad guys. By the last panel, Lil had been drafted to run for sheriff of Sage City. By the next issue, she was off to the town of Perdita, took on the job of marshal, and did similar duties to similar owlhoots. Then she rode off. The Western wildcat did her work throughout the run of *Crack Western*.

Dead Canyon Days, an echo of radio's *Death Valley Days*, concerned itself with one Captain Tom Lance, who left General Lee's Confederate Army after the war to become a newspaperman way out West. He ended up slinging ink in the aforementioned Dead Canyon after helping Ben Nolan and his lovely, rifle-toting granddaughter Sue repel some gunnies in the employ of Bat Ellery. Naturally, Bat wasn't hot on such doings, and ended up challenging Tom to a duel—one which Tom, who wasn't a fast-draw artist, was bound to lose. But Lance turned the tide by riding in on a horse and doing his shooting while mounted, putting Bat and his boys to flight. Thereafter, the new Dead Canyon press thrived. Future issues featured a rotating cast of characters. Reed Crandall was in charge of the art for the first few issues and some thereafter, and did a tolerable great job. The feature ended with issue #69 (November 1950).

Bob Allen, Frontier Marshal, was the next up, and was drawn by Harry Anderson. He helped save a gold mine owner and (again) his pretty daughter from (again) a rival who was intent on wrecking the flume by which they sent out their gold. Our hero won through in the end, but it was really a pretty average strip, though it improved somewhat in later issues. Bernie Krigstein and Reed Crandall did some of the stories.

By issue #66, *Crack Western* boasted a photo cover of somebody trying to look like Arizona Raines protecting a woman behind him, his two six-shooters drawn. Or maybe they weren't. Anyway, the B-Western players were Bill Williams and Jane Nigh. A lot of comics were going for photo covers back then, and Quality must have figured it might help. Famed movie cowboy Randolph Scott fronted issue #67 (July 1950), in a still from *The Nevadan*. Issues #68, 72, and 73 also bore photo covers, but all the rest were drawn, and drawn quite well.

Issue #70 (January 1951) replaced *Dead Canyon Days* with *The Whip*, a masked hero who matched his leather weapon against enemy guns and won every time. He was one Johnny Lash, a kid whose pioneer parents had been killed by phony "Indians" who robbed their covered wagon. Johnny grabbed his father's rifle, shot down two of the faux redskins, and drove the rest off, vowing to find them and bring them to justice. He was taken in by Pedro Gonzalez, a whip-wielding stage driver, who taught him the use of the weapon. The text admitted, "Johnny

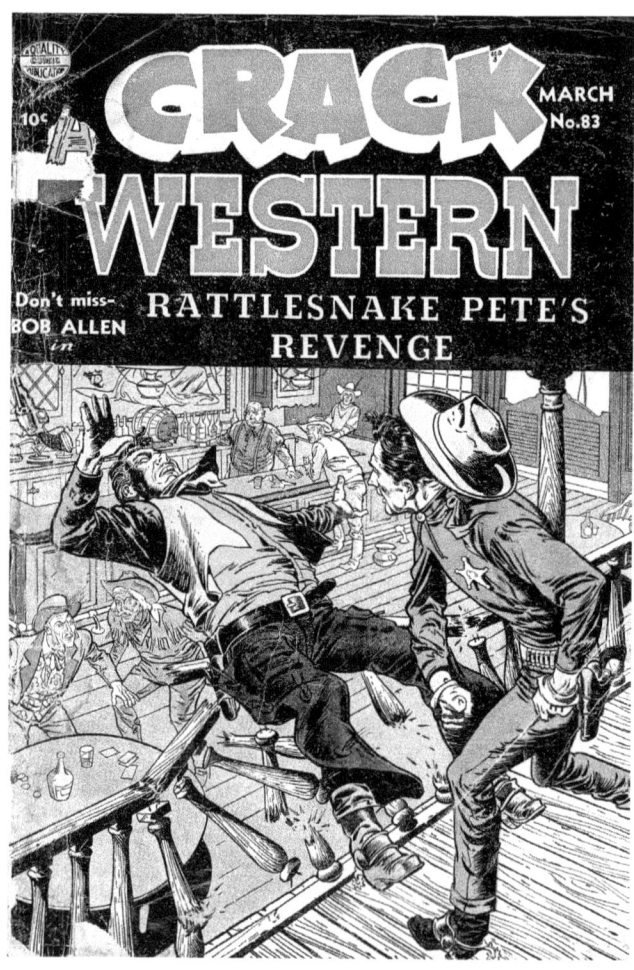

Bob Allen belts a badman. © 1953 Comic Magazines

was good with a gun, but it never suited him like the whip!"

Johnny grew up and became not only an expert whip man, but Pedro's stage-driving partner. Unfortunately, Pedro himself got shot by desperadoes, and Lash recognized their ringleader's laugh as that of the man who had killed his parents. In a Batman-like move, Johnny saddled his dark horse, Diablo, went home, donned an outfit complete with mask which he'd been holding onto for two years, and rode back into town to seek vengeance. The Whip lashed the devil out of the villain's gang, confronted the killer himself, and revealed his identity to him. Whether the Whip killed his foe or not was left to our imagination. The story cut to a panel of the Whip aboard Diablo, riding into the distance. Reed Crandall, again, was the artist. The Whip continued till *Crack Western*'s last issue.

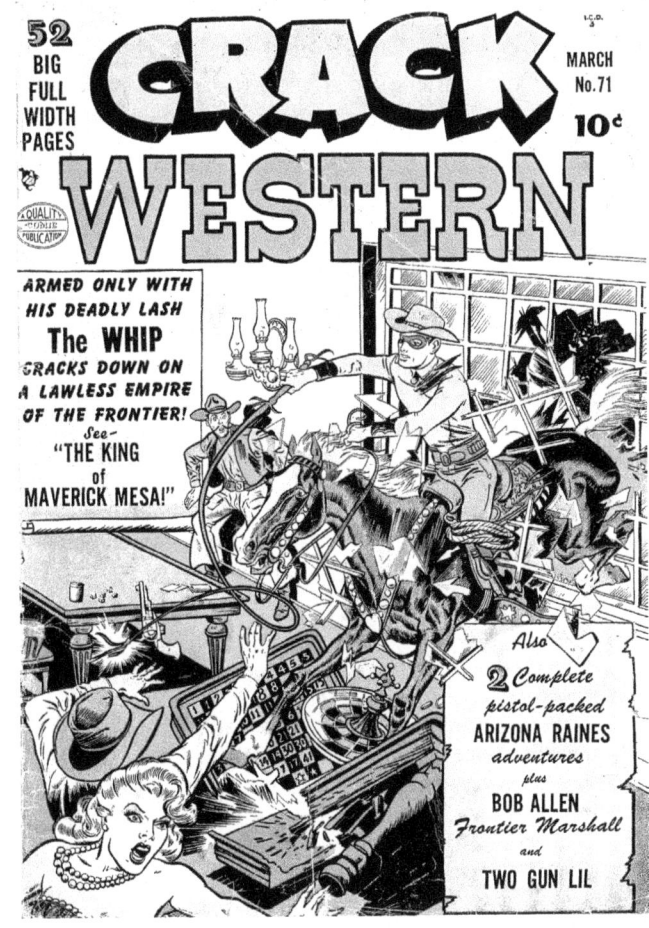

The poor man's Zorro: the Whip. © 1951 Comic Magazines

But all good comics (mostly) must come to an end, and Arizona Raines, Two-Gun Lil, Bob Allen, and the Whip made their final bows in *Crack Western* #84 (May 1953). Three years later, Quality followed it into Boot Hill.

Fox Comics made their first comics foray with *Wonder Comics* #1 (May 1939), and their Western filler was *Tex Dawson*. His first story was probably done by Will Eisner under the name of "Leon Spuds." (Hey, there are only so many good pseudonyms out there, y'know what I mean?) It was pretty much a rerun of his Wild Tex Martin story from *Western Picture Stories* #1. Eisner might have written the next story, but Munson Paddock hired on as chief art hand, and would remain there for some time. Tex was given the last name of Maxon in that story and kept the handle. The book was retitled *Wonderworld Comics* with issue #3 (July 1939) and by issue #10 (February 1940) Tex retitled himself as the Phantom Ranger. Why he called himself that is undetermined, because he didn't wear a mask or costume. But by the next story, he was the Phantom Rider, or maybe Ranger, since his name kept changing in the text. In this one (#11, March 1940), he wore a flowing black costume like a judge's robes, had a black hat and a red mask, and thwarted outlaws in pages that could have as few as three panels. He lasted through issue #27 (July 1941). It's hard to see why.

Mystery Men Comics #1 (August 1939) gave us *The Waco Kid*, decently drawn by Art Peddy, and it ran through issue #3 (October 1939). *Weird Comics* #17–20 (August 1941–January 1942) offered *The Black Rider*, a quasi-Western set in the modern day, in which a black-clad rider on a black horse took a bandit's black mask and stopped car-driving crooks from taking over a mine. When he took his leave of the female lead, she asked for his name. "Just call me—the Black Rider!" he declared. Pierce Rice drew it and it was a passable feature.

When Victor Fox returned to comics publishing after the war, his major "contribution" to the genre was *Western Outlaws*, a title that ran from issues #17 to 21 (September 1948–May 1949). Jack Kamen, Al Feldstein, A.C. Hollingsworth, and others worked on this "Western true crime" title, and Jack and Al were probably glad when they escaped to EC Comics a little while later. *Western Killers* (#60–64, September 1948–May 1949), *Western Thrillers* (#1–6, August 1948–June 1949), and *Western True Crime* (#15, 16, V. 2 #3–6, August 1948–June 1949) followed the same pattern.

On to Harvey, or, more precisely, its predecessor Brookwood, which published the first 11 issues of *Speed Comics*. The first six issues (October 1939–March 1940) gave us *Texas Tyler*, drawn by Walter Frehm. Texas stopped a shootout in a bar on his first page and, with his pard Baldy, cleaned up the bad guys in town and then rode off. The end. The rest of his stories were much like this.

But in 1949, Harvey came up with something better, though the stories were awfully short and hidden in the back of *Kerry Drake Detective Magazine*. The first one, in issue #12 (January 1949), was introduced like this: "What can a girl do in the Wild West against desperate bandits, you say? Well … any girl … perhaps nothing! But Kitty Carson? That's another story!"

The opening caption went on to tell us that Kitty's dad, apparently the town sheriff, had been killed by rustlers. She "inherited" the job by cleaning up "that mess" (and we never knew exactly *how* she cleaned it up, but she apparently did a great job) and kept the town peaceable with her twin six-shooters. We're referring to her guns, guys.

Bob Powell was the writer and artist and, though Kitty's stories never exceeded four pages and shrank down to slightly less than two, he made them worth wading through the book for. In the first tale, a ranny named Drop Crandall had robbed a stage and taken two hostages with his two compatriots. Kitty was informed, rode out after them, shot two of the owlhoots down (one, while dangling off the side of her horse), and accidentally hung the last one when she roped his neck, the lasso broke, and it caught on a branch. The hostages, a doctor and his sister, were free. But the doc insisted on having dinner with Kitty, so he may not have intended to stay that way. Kitty kept sheriffin' until issue #20 (June 1950). AC reprinted a batch of her adventures in *America's Greatest Comics*, *Best of the West*, and other comics in the '90s and '00s.

Harvey was known for one of the greatest Western comics of all time later on. But since it began after 1950, we'll have to tease you with the information and save it for another volume! Let's move on.

In 1939, Martin Goodman decided to extend his pulp magazine empire into the comic book field, and produced *Marvel Comics* #1 (October 1939), containing the Human Torch, Sub-Mariner, Ka-Zar, and the Angel. It also housed *The Masked Raider*, Marvel's first Western hero. His name was Jim Gardley, he was framed for a crime he didn't commit, and he escaped jail and rode to freedom in the hills. Intent on freeing the town from its corrupt boss, Brunder (there were hardly any Western towns with upright bosses, apparently), Gardley tamed a swift white horse he named Lightning and wrapped a black bandanna about his head to conceal his face. "I, Jim Gardley, hereby make a solemn vow to forever fight the lawless ... bring justice to the oppressed, and help the poor—to this end, I, *the Masked Raider*, dedicate my life to this oath!" It was a comic book origin story if we ever saw one. With the help of the encouraged sheriff and the townspeople, the Raider brought the Brunder Gang to justice. Al Anders drew the story. The Masked Raider carried on through *Marvel Mystery Comics* #12 (October 1940).

The company, which started as Timely (and sometimes Marvel), changed its name to Atlas in the Fifties and reverted to Marvel in the Sixties. They became converts to Westernism big-time circa 1948 when the bottom started dropping out of the superhero market.

And the first entry of all that were to come was *Two-Gun Kid*.

The debut issue, *Two-Gun Kid* #1 (March 1948), showed a blond, black-clad cowboy astride a black horse, saving an old gent from a noose and from a trio of masked bandits. The cover and both Two-Gun Kid stories inside were drawn by Syd Shores, who had done great work on *Captain America* (and would do so as an inker in the late Sixties). On the first page of his first tale, the Kid looked to be about 50 feet tall, scowling and

Marvel's hard-ridin', fast-shootin', justice-lovin' hero, the original Two-Gun Kid. © 1948 Marvel Comics, Inc. and © 2022 Marvel Publications. Used with permission.

shooting off both his guns as he rode his horse, Cyclone, who was white in color, scattering civilians who were the size of Lilliputians. Truthfully, this was symbolism. Giant-Man was a long way in the future.

In his opening tale, the Kid, whose name was eventually revealed as Clay Harder, rode into the town of Sundown, Arizona, singing a cappella (he either forgot his guitar or left it home) about how he was the Two-Gun Kid, but he wished he had four guns, because he liked to fight. Once he got into town, he ran into trouble with the city bully, one Brett Dawson. After ordering a glass of milk (which, in the Old West, probably would have gotten him killed as fast as a shootout), the Kid was accosted by Dawson. After taking a slap, he disarmed the bad guy with a kicked table and proceeded to whomp the ever-lovin' dog out of the guy, shoving him down a bartop for good measure. It turned out that Dawson had mortgages on everybody's land, and the townspeople were afraid to go against him. When even Dawson's girlfriend turned on him, he decided to throw her to her death for impertinence. The Kid showed up in time, lassoed the girl to keep her safe, and let Dawson fall to his much-desired demise. Then he rode off, waving to the girl.

The script was pretty standard but Shores's art was decent and it set the tone for the series. The Two-Gun Kid meandered through another script in that issue and three more in the next (June 1948). It took a long time for Marvel, or Timely, or Atlas, to get to his origin, but they finally did so in *Two-Gun Kid* #36 (April 1957).

The Kid's father, Frank Harder, had been a sheriff in the town of Mesquite. He'd met a woman named Milly, who was an Easterner, and married her. Milly had little taste for gunplay, so after Clay was born, sharp-shootin' Frank put away his gun, moved to a farm in Kansas, and raised crops and his family.

The problem was, Clay, as a child, found his dad's gun stashed in a potato cellar. He also found out he was an expert shot with it. One could predict the way the story was going: Frank made Clay swear off using the gun. But that same day, the people of Mesquite asked Frank to take over the job of sheriffing, and Frank, not by any means a rich man, took it.

Inevitably, outlaws came: the three Corbett brothers, late of Quantrill's Raiders. They demanded supplies. When Frank Harder demurred, they shot him down in front of his son. Milly, watching from horseback, was thrown to her death from a spooked horse. When young Clay got to his dying father's side, Frank told him, "I give you back your promise! There can be no peace while evil rides! Take my guns! Use them to bring peace to this troubled land!"

And, taking up his father's gun and one dropped by the Corbetts, Clay Harder swore to do just that. Years later, he ran into the Corbetts in the town of Carbonville, honored his dad's memory by just shooting the guns out of their hands instead of shooting them dead, and turned them over to the law. As in most retro origin stories, the tale had come full circle.

Never one to leave sleeping origin stories alone, Stan Lee and Al Hartley brought us "Origin of the Two-Gun Kid" in issue #48 (June 1959). This was a totally different take on his beginnings. The tale revealed that Clay Harder had left home when he was just a kid (a *little* kid, that is) and came to Sundown, Arizona (the site of his first adventure in issue #1), where he was bullied by one Bull Yeager, the kind of punk whose descendants would steal lunch money from other kids in school. He made his way to the Circle-H Ranch, where his dad, Seth, lived. The elder Harder was now a cripple, but had made Clay promise never to take up the gun again (a noble cliché about to be shattered, as usual). Bull Yeager wanted his ranch. Bull Yeager proceeded to kill Seth, and handed Clay a shovel to bury his dad with.

With that, Clay Harder figured his vow was no longer active. When Yeager and his men reappeared, Clay shot the guns out of Yeager's hands and captured his gunnies. Then he challenged the villain to a hand-to-hand battle. It ended when Yeager tried to force Clay Harder into the well, and Clay threw him in instead. The bad man did not come up.

The sheriff, upon learning what had happened, told Clay, "You're a regular two-gun kid!" And so he was. After selling the ranch, he lit out for the prairies. And thus, for the second time, a legend was born.

In #52 (February 1960), they did it *again*. With superior John Severin art and Stan Lee scripting, the origin from #48 got another run-through. The only change, besides the art, was that Bull Yeager was pulled out of the well and delivered to the law. He probably should have been left in it.

And in issue #58 (February 1961) ... yep, you guessed it. The Kid had a new artist—Jack Kirby himself!—so they had to run through the origin again. The art was fantastic. The script was the same, except this time, the Kid and Bull fought on the edge of a cliff, and Bull fell to his death. This time, we think it was permanent. That's just our opinion, mind you.

Most of the stories were pretty formulaic, with the Kid riding into a town, finding trouble, dealing with said trouble, and riding out. But in issue #7 (April 1949), he got a sidekick. Two-Gun came upon a child crying near a river. Inquiring why the boy was weeping, he was informed, "I'm goin' to run away and be like the Two-Gun Kid, that's what I'm goin' to do!"

After introducing himself to the appropriately startled boy, the Kid was covered with hero worship. Nonetheless, he insisted on setting the lad back on his pony and taking him back to town. The boy, whose name was Rusty Randolph, explained that his dad had been killed by accident. "He accidentally took somebody else's cows, an' they accidentally caught him and shot him—so it was kinda like an accident!" Indeed.

Well, the Kid took the kid back to school, which was run by a pretty belle named Miss Kitty. But a gang of toughs came up and swore that Rusty, being the son of a rustler, had no right to readin', writin', or 'rithmatic. Thus, the Kid had to defend Rusty, and defend him he did, with both guns and a lot of fisticuffs. Two-Gun himself got a shiner and some bruises, and he was about to celebrate his victory when Miss Kitty informed him that one of the bullies was her husband. She asked him to leave in no uncertain terms. And, when he was a few miles down the trail, the Two-Gun Kid turned and saw Rusty on his horse, following. Looking at the reader, Two-Gun said, "What's the use? I give up!" Rusty accompanied him for a number of stories.

For some reason, possibly sales, *Two-Gun Kid* was suspended with issue #10 (November 1949). A couple of stories ran in *Wild Western* #11 and 12 (June–September 1950), but for three years, that was it. Then a single Two-Gun tale appeared in

Black Rider #19 (November 1953). A month later, *Two-Gun Kid* #11 (December 1953) signified his return to the stands, and he kept a steady pace after that.

Two-Gun's scripting and art improved as time went on. By the mid-1950s, he was starring in classic tales with John Severin's equally classic art. Marvel scripting wasn't as polished or erudite as DC's, and it might be formula-fed, but it was still a lotta fun.

The Two-Gun Kid and Cyclone wound their way through *Two-Gun Kid* #1–59 (March 1948–April 1961), *Wild West* #1 and 2 (Spring–July 1948), *Wild Western* #3–12, 34–39, 41 and 42 (September 1948–March 1955), *Kid Colt* #2 (October 1948), *All-Western Winners* #2–4 (Winter 1948–April 1949), *Blaze Carson* #4 (March 1949), *Western Winners* #5–6 (June–August 1949), *Best Western* #58 and 59 (June–August 1949), *Black Rider* #19–23 (November 1953–June 1954), and *Gunsmoke Western* #57–63 (March 1960–March 1961). Besides Syd Shores, Chu Hing, Chuck Miller, John Severin, Jack Kirby, George Tuska, Dick Ayers, Matt Baker, Joe Maneely, Alex Blum, Fred Kida, Bob Forgione, and Bob Fujitani's art kept him on the path. Stan Lee, Don Rico, Paul S. Newman, Joe Gill, and unheralded others wrote his scripts. Then, in 1961, after dealing with a baddie named Wolf Waco in the first story of *Two-Gun Kid* #59 (April 1961) and a couple of ne'er-do-wells in the second, with writing by Stan Lee and art by Kirby and Ayers, he vanished.

And, in 1962, he reappeared, more or less.

Two-Gun Kid #60 (November 1962), under a Jack Kirby cover, presented a new, masked Western crusader by the same name. This Mark II Two-Gun Kid was secretly Matt Hawk, a lawyer. Stan Lee and Kirby crafted a tale of how he came to the West a dude, got trained in gunplay and fisticuffs by an old codger, and created another identity for himself. "Back east I remember reading about a fictitious gunfighter called the Two-Gun Kid! I don't know whatever happened to him, but I think I'll borrow the name." The original never showed up to take it back, and Matt Hawk went on to a good long run.

In the first *Two-Gun Kid* issue, there was a fairly nice backup dubbed *The Sheriff*. The unnamed lawman and his deputy, Rusty, dealt with a nasty guy named Bat Miller, who beat his horse out of sheer cussedness. Out of sheer righteousness, the Sheriff belted Bat and thus enraged him. The ornery fella decided later to bait the Sheriff by holding up a bank and making a getaway. He had no such luck: his horse wouldn't have anything to do with Bat, and left him for capture. In a later story, we learned that the Sheriff's first name was Al, and that he'd been married to a woman named Jane who died of an unnamed illness. He showed his tin star in *Two-Gun Kid* #1–3 (March–August 1948), *Tex Morgan* #1 (August 1948), *Kid Colt* #1 (August 1948), and *Wild Western* #3 (September 1948).

Probably he continued as Blaze Carson, another sheriff who looked mightily like him. Given that "Blaze" might be a nickname, and most likely was, it's not too hard to connect the two. He got his own comic, which ran for five issues (September 1948–June 1949) and did side stints in *Tex Taylor* #1–2, 4–6 (September 1948–July 1949), *Two-Gun Kid* #4, 7–9 (October 1948–August 1949), *Wild Western* #5–7 (January–May 1949), *Tex Morgan* #5 and 6 (May–July 1949), and *Kid Colt, Outlaw* #5 (May 1949). Truthfully, we'll bet nobody noticed when he left.

In the late Forties, Timely Comics always seemed to have a glamour girl hanging around somewhere to boost sales, à la Namora in *Sub-Mariner*, Golden Girl in *Captain America*, and Sun Girl in *The Human Torch*. Annie Oakley was the Western version of that.

Annie's initial comic run was part Western, part glamour, part comedy, and we'll leave you to judge what percentage each part played. Her first cover (*Annie Oakley* #1, Spring 1948) showed her sashaying down the street in a slit skirt, smoking rifle slung under her arm, walking away from a house wall in which she'd shot a silhouette of a cowboy, complete with hat, in bullets. Six guys recoiled in terror. Annie mused, "I wonder why the men in this town shy away from me the way they do?" A hint, Annie: it wasn't because of your lace-up-in-front blouse or your half-unbuttoned skirt.

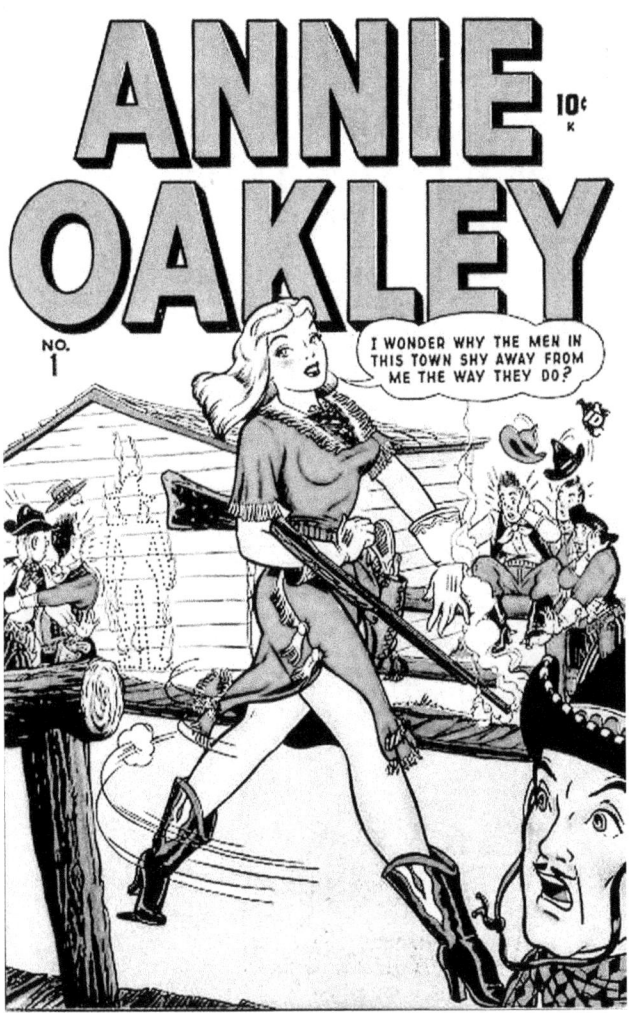

Annie Oakley, Western heroine and part-time pin-up gal. © 1948 Manvis Publications, Inc. and © 2022 Marvel Publications. Used with permission.

The first story, except for the setting and gunplay, could've come from a *Millie the Model* offering. The Barr-X Ranch needed a new cowhand. Mr. Barr, owner of said ranch, told his beauty-queen secretary, Sally, about it. A second or two later, Tex Collins, Barr's majordomo, entered and said that a cowhand had been found. Of course, it was Annie, riding up on a white horse. This pleased Sally not at all, and she tried to torpedo Annie's chances. But a page or two later, Annie took care of a wild bull, and she proved her credentials. Sally, who had fainted before, refainted upon hearing it.

With variations, this was pretty much the way Annie's stories ran in her first Timely incarnation. *Annie Oakley* lasted all of four issues (Spring 1948– November 1948) and the curvaceous cowgirl also fit into *Two-Gun Kid* #3 (August 1948), *Tessie the*

Typist #19 (December 1948), *Millie the Model* #15 and 16 (December 1948–February 1949), and *Nellie the Nurse* #17 (February 1949). She didn't last very long and, probably, nobody expected her to. Chris Rule may have done the art and Mickey Klar Marks, a female scripter, wrote at least one and possibly other stories.

But that wasn't the end of Annie. Since she was a historical figure, she was up for grabs, and Timely (now Atlas) grabbed her again in 1955. This time they played it straight. Annie was now set in the Old West, in Buena Vista (the state she was in wasn't certain), and was the hard-ridin', straight-shootin', sure-ropin' daughter of Mr. Oakley, owner of a ranch. She introduced herself by bringing in three bandits. The local sheriff fell in love with her at first sight, and Annie reciprocated. Later, after triumphing in all the events in a local rodeo and saving the sheriff from more banditos, she expected a kiss. Instead, unmanned by her prowess, he gave her a bag of cash. Mr. Oakley later said to his tearful daughter, "You didn't win, Annie dear … you lost!"

Still, Annie was up for a bunch more entertaining adventures, all of them illustrated by Ross Andru and Mike Esposito, and written by Hank Chapman. The new *Annie Oakley* series ran from issues #5–11 (June 1955–June 1956) and spilled over into solo stories in *Wild Western* #46 and 47 (December 1955–January 1956). Of course, there was one more tale to reckon with: in *Wyatt Earp* #5 (July 1956), there was an ultra-rare Western crossover: "The Day Marshall Earp Met Annie Oakley!"

In this tale, Annie (who allowed her real name was "Annie Mozee") saved Wyatt from the Barker Brothers gang, noted she was already in Buffalo Bill's Wild West show, and teamed up with him to bring the Barkers down. Then she rode away, and Wyatt mused, "I'll never forget that gal!" Neither will we.

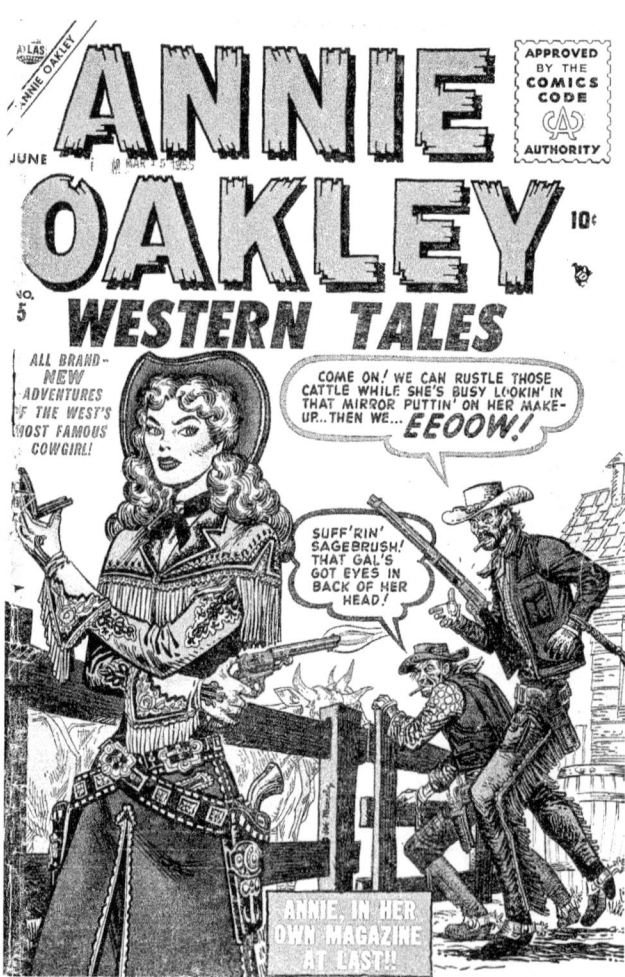

Nobody backshoots the Mark II Annie Oakley! © 1955 Current Detective Stories Inc. and © 2022 Marvel Publications. Used with permission.

Annie turned up in the hands of various other publishers through the years, but she only returned to Marvel as a "kicker" in various Western stories. *Ringo Kid* #10 (February 1956), which was published during Annie's Atlas run, gave us a Stan Lee–Al Williamson story, "Stranger in Town," in which a buckskin-clad Annie drove a punk named Reb Duncon out of town. In *Rawhide Kid* #44 (February 1965), a backup story written by Larry Lieber featured an Old West blonde beauty spooning with her swain, Frank. A band of bad guys showed up to menace them, but the blonde's superior shooting saved the day. At the end, she was revealed to be Annie Oakley.

Much later, in *Rawhide Kid* V. 2 #2 (September 1985), an aging Rawhide hooked up with Buffalo Bill's Wild West show and got a big hug from a black-haired Annie Oakley, who revealed they'd ridden shotgun on a stagecoach in the past. He had to make an escape from Pinkerton agents and she covered him while he did so. Finally, in a four-issue story arc set chronologically earlier than the previous tale but published in 2010, Annie, still black-haired, was drawn as a sex bomb and teamed up with the Kid and several other Marvel Westerners for a new adventure (*Rawhide Kid* V. 4 #1–4, August–November 2010).

Were all, or even some, of these appearances by the same gal? It's possible, but subjective. We have our doubts, especially about the last one.

The next Timely Western comic was *Wild West*. It was their first Western anthology, and the Two-Gun Kid was the headliner. But it also introduced two new characters, Arizona Annie and Tex Taylor.

Arizona Annie was, thematically, between Annie Oakley's 1940s and 1950s versions. She was a pretty Western gal with great sharpshooting ability, but she used her beauty as a weapon against bad guys. Annie rode the range with a partner named Slim Smith. While getting her horse shoed by a blacksmith who hated women, she was on the scene when a trio of bandits robbed the 'smith of a bag of gold. Annie pretended to fall for one of the crooks, rode off with them, and clobbered them one by one. After she rode back in with the gold and the bad guys in tow, the smith changed his ways and gave free shoeings to any woman in town. Arizona Annie had a fairly short run, in *Wild West* #1 and 2 (Spring–July 1948), *Wild Western* #3 and 4 (September–November 1948), *Two-Gun Kid* #5 (December 1948), and *Tex Morgan* #3 (December 1948).

Tex Taylor had a bit more luck. In a 10-page origin story, the black-clad cowboy rode into Wishbone, Texas, fresh from "the war" (possibly the Civil War), and looking for an hombre named Calhoun, who was the sheriff of the town. Calhoun proved to be crookeder than a dog's hind leg, and, when confronted by Tex, who wanted info on his father's death, got shot to death by a sniper. Tex was framed for the murder and the town mayor heard his origin story: the cowboy's father had a spread down in Whispering Valley and refused to pay protection money to Calhoun. While Tex was in the army, Calhoun had been elected sheriff, and afterward forced the elder Taylor to sell out to him. In between that and Tex's return, the elder Taylor had died. Tex suspected murder, but was convicted of Calhoun's killing by a kangaroo court. He escaped, exposed the mayor as the real murderer, and killed him in battle. In the last panel, Tex rode off, intending to clear himself with the law and finance himself with gold deposits found on his father's ranch. "I'll have enough to spend the rest of my life hunting down varmints like the mayor—and *destroying* them!"

So saying, Tex destroyed his way through *Wild West* #1 and 2 (Spring–July 1948), *Wild Western* #3–11 (September 1948–June 1950), *Tex Taylor* #1–9 (September 1948–February 1950), *Blaze Carson* #1 and 5 (September 1948–June 1949), *Tex Morgan* #2, 6, 7, and 9 (October 1948–February 1950—Timely boasted a lot of Texes), *Two-Gun Kid* #6 (February 1949), and *Kid Colt Outlaw* #4 and 6 (February–July 1949). It was a healthy run at the time, but he's little remembered today. Bill Walsh, Pierce Rice, Chu Hing, and John Buscema were among his artists.

Then, in August 1948, a character who would last from Timely through Atlas to Marvel debuted, destined to become Marvel's longest continually published Western hero of all. This was the first issue of *Kid Colt*.

Kid Colt, subtitled *Hero of the West* (the *Outlaw* didn't show on the cover till issue #3), bore a cover with a red-headed Colt (turned blond on the inside, and forevermore) blazing away with his two Colt pistols at unseen foes, while a sheriff behind him told him to hold on while he came to help. The story within, "Hot Lead for Crooked Lawmen," started a run that would last 30 years. It was familiar, true enough, but it worked.

Briefly: Blaine Colt, son of a rancher in the town of Purgatory, came upon a corrupt deputy, Lash Larribee, beating Gabby, the old hand of the Bar-C Ranch, mercilessly with a whip. Blaine wore no gun—he had a rep of being too scared to—but he barged in and socked Larribee in the jaw. The bad man responded by lashing Colt over and over again, till Sheriff Yates, even more corrupt than Larribee, told him to lay off.

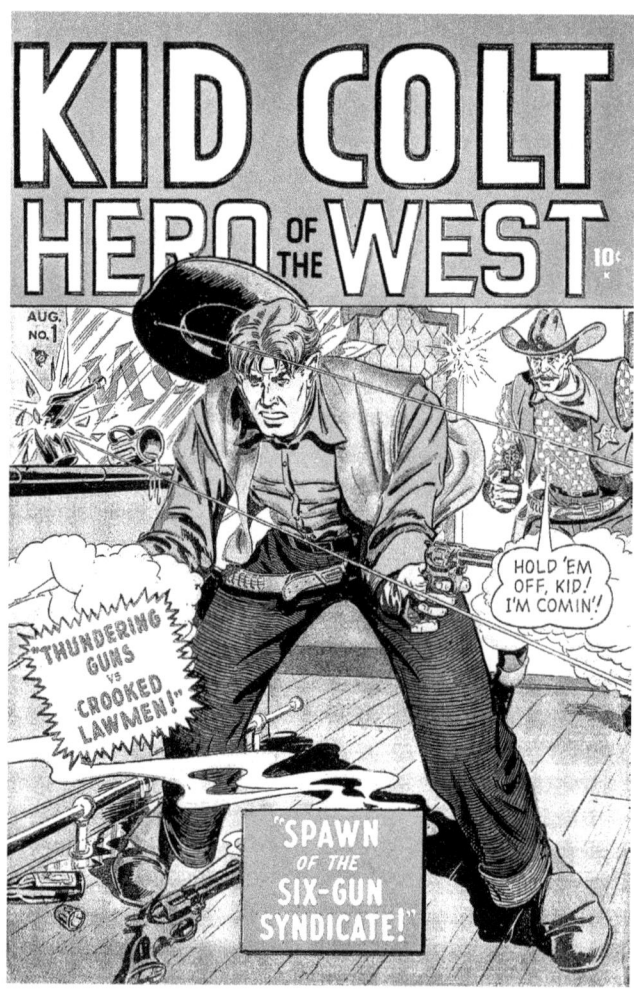

Kid Colt, hero of the West, soon to become Kid Colt Outlaw and go blonde. © 1948 Leading Comic Corp. and © 2022 Marvel Publications. Used with permission.

Gabby got Blaine Colt back to the ranch, where they told the elder Colt what had happened. Instead of getting mad at Larribee, Colt père disparaged his son for not having the guts to wear guns and call the scumbag out.

Later, on the trail with Gabby, Colt snatched a gun from him and drilled a rattlesnake in their path with deadly speed and accuracy. "Whew! Now I get it," Gabby said. "With yore temper and six-gun speed, you'd end up killin' somebody if you wore guns!" Blaine agreed with that, and they went to the line camp.

And the next morning, Sheriff Yates burst in with a buffalo gun and accused Colt of murdering his father. Gabby and the kid gave battle, but Yates and Larribee brought them in. The Sheriff claimed that Old Man Colt lost the ranch to him in a poker game just before his murder. Gabby busted Colt out of jail, both of them visited the mortician's office, and they learned that Colt's father had really been shot to death—by a buffalo gun.

With that, Colt buckled on his dad's gunbelt and started a new phase of life. Gabby brought up Colt's favorite horse, the Steeldust Stallion (later shortened to just Steel), and the Sheriff showed up just in time to confess his evil deed and to dare the Kid to draw down on him. Colt did just that, shooting the Sheriff straight through the heart, killing him on the spot.

Lash Larribee, meanwhile, had shot Gabby and was beating him with his whip while he died. Colt came after him, but Lash dealt him a whip-blow across the eyes. Colt wasn't quite blinded, though. He shot Lash in the hand, took his whip, and proceeded to give the dastard some of his own medicine. Larribee went down, possibly beaten to death. Then Colt, seeing a posse coming for him in the near distance, mounted Steel, riding off to wherever he could hide.

It was not a pretty story. But it was the origin of Kid Colt.

Later on, other stories would do revisions on the Kid's origin. In *Kid Colt, Outlaw* #11 (October 1950), the story was basically retold, but Colt told Gabby about his brother, Slim Colt, who tried to make a name for himself as a gunslinger and got shot in the back ... a bit of a prescient fate, as we'll learn later. Gabby was given the last name of Barnes, Sheriff Yates shot both him and Lash, and Kid Colt knocked Yates off a cliff in a hand-to-hand battle. All things considered, we still prefer the earlier version.

Issue #79 (July 1958) set Colt's hometown in Wyoming, renamed it Abiline, gave the elder Colt's name as Dan, and made Lash Larribee a gun-toting gangster who wanted to force Dan Colt to join his protection racket. Later, alone, Dan Colt stood against Larribee in a gunfight and lost. Furiously, Kid Colt strapped on guns, challenged Larribee to another gun-duel, and killed him. Gabby, who in this story died of a heart attack, asked Colt not to run, but the Kid chose the outlaw path. Sheriff Yates never showed up, at least not in his villainous role. The Comics Code had a lot to do with the toning-down. Stan Lee wrote the story and Jack Keller drew it.

Gunsmoke Western #72 (September 1962) did another riff on the origin, with Lee and Keller reprising themselves. In this one, Larribee had his lash back, Gabby was renamed Jeb, and the rest of the story pretty much duplicated the one in *Kid Colt, Outlaw* #79. A couple of stories in the early Sixties attempted to give us a look at Kid Colt when he was a teenager, in *Kid Colt, Outlaw* #99, 102, and 107 (July

1961–November 1962), but they pretty much violated the origin continuity, so they can be banished from the canon.

Out of the canon, too, was the story in *Kid Colt, Outlaw* #39 (July 1954), in which the Kid related his "origin story" to a youth who was contemplating the outlaw road himself. (Kid Colt discouraged so many teenagers from becoming outlaws that they probably formed their own glee club.) In this story, Colt said he was in school in the East when a hired killer shot his father, named *William* Colt, in the back. The Kid's mother showed up for the first and only time in this story, discouraging Blaine Colt from becoming a gunhawk, but he practiced with his six-shooters and then confronted the killer, Markson, in a bar. Markson refused to be taken in for trial, so he faced the guns of Kid Colt, but only for a short time. The Kid killed him before he could reach his weapons. After that, of course, he shot the guns out of the hands of two of Markson's men, and then began his eternal outlaw life. Of course, the Kid could have been making it up, and maybe he was. But after helping Colt in battle, the young man promised to walk the straight and narrow.

Bill Walsh and Chu Hing probably did the art on issue #1 and the other Kid Colt stories in the book. Ernie Hart wrote the first Kid Colt story and most of the rest through issue #8. Leon Lazarus, Paul Newman, Joe Gill, and Carl Wessler were among his earliest writers. Artists from the late Forties through the Fifties included Russ Heath, Pete Tumlinson, Dick Ayers, Mike Sekowsky, Gene Colan, Reed Crandall, Joe Kubert, and Joe Maneely. The art wasn't as polished as a DC offering, but it was considerably gutsier.

In the early days, the Kid didn't shy away from killing. But only the bad guys bit the dust. He didn't murder as many men as, say, Jonah Hex, but if a story went down without one baddie getting salivated, it wasn't for lack of trying. This was the time before the Comics Code, and DC notwithstanding, Western fans expected their heroes to shoot down the bad guys. And Kid Colt did.

Tracking down the Kid's appearances is going to be like rounding up a herd of stampeding cattle, but we'll give it a go. Besides *Kid Colt, Outlaw* #1–229 (August 1948–April 1979), he turned up in *Wild Western* #4–9, 11, 20–57 (November 1948–September 1957), *All-Western Winners* #2–4 (Winter 1948–April 1949), *Western Winners* #5 and 6 (June–August 1949), *Best Western* #58 and 59 (June–August 1949), *Two-Gun Kid* #10, 14–20 (November 1949–January 1955), *Two-Gun Western* #8–14 (June 1951–June 1952), *Black Rider* #26, 27 (January–March 1955), *Gunsmoke Western* #32–77 (December 1955–July 1963), *Giant-Size Kid Colt* #1–3 (January–July 1975), *Blaze of Glory* #1–4 (February–March 2000), *Marvel Westerns: Kid Colt and the Arizona Girl* #1 (September 2006), *Kid Colt One-Shot* #1 (September 2009), and a ton and a half of guest appearances which we'll cover later. He also showed his face and guns in a mini-comic for Wisco-Klarer called *Kid Colt: He Lived by His Guns!* It was a reprint from an early *Colt*.

The Comics Code came in with *Kid Colt, Outlaw* #46 (March 1955) and, as bid by Dr. Wertham, Colt did a lot less killing and a lot more shooting of guns out of rannies' hands. No matter; the usual three short stories per issue were still action-filled. But by issue #77 (March 1958), Stan Lee was writing the stories. Changes were in the wind. The next issue (May 1958) introduced the long-running character Sam Hawk,

Manhunter, who was sworn to bring the Kid in alive. He appeared in a brace of issues, but he never nabbed Kid Colt for long.

Real Western figures began appearing in the stories, just as they did in TV Westerns of the time. Jesse James turned up in issues #82 and 101 (January 1959 and November 1961), Johnny Ringo in #84 and 101 (May 1959 and November 1961), and John Wesley Hardin in #126 (January 1966); Billy the Kid showed up in *Gunsmoke Western* #71 (July 1962). In *Gunsmoke Western* #61 (November 1960), the ultimate real-world crossover happened: Kid Colt met with President Abraham Lincoln, who promised him a pardon if he'd clean up the town of Gila Pass. He did. But in the interim, Lincoln made his fateful visit to Ford's Theatre, and the Kid had to remain an outlaw.

Stories gradually lengthened. *Kid Colt, Outlaw* #94 (November 1960) featured the Kid's first 13-page tale. By #111 (July 1963), the story page count went up to 18. Jack Kirby, newly returned, started doing the covers. The Kid, who previously had killed about as many bad guys as the Shadow, refrained from murder. Covers were festooned with blurbs and word balloons. Colt's first "name" villain, the Gun Wizard, showed up in issue #90 (May 1960) and was followed by a batch of others. Iron Mask, the Scorpion, Doctor Danger, the members of the Circus of Crime ... Kid Colt had almost as many super-villains as Spider-Man.

In short, though the Fantastic Four were still a year or so in the future, Stan Lee was molding Kid Colt into more of a superhero figure. And it showed! In issue #107 (November 1962), the Kid faced "The Giant Monster of Gila Valley," who turned out to be an honest-to-gunsmoke alien from outer space! *Gunsmoke Western* #73 (November 1962) featured a robot, designed by a bank-robbing scientist, explicitly made to outdraw Kid Colt. Thankfully, this sort of stuff stopped before the Kid ended up on Mars or some such territory.

In issue #121 (March 1965), Colt had his very first Western–hero crossover when he met the Mark II Rawhide Kid. They overcame their mutual differences long enough to team up against Iron Mask, and they parted friends. Not to be outdone, the law-abiding Mark II Two-Gun Kid popped up in issue #125 (November 1965) to try and bring Colt in, but ended up fighting side-by-side with him against a crooked politician's gang. Stan quit scripting with issue #123 (September 1965). His place was taken by Al Hartley, Larry Lieber, Roy Thomas, Gary Friedrich, Steve Skeates, Sol Brodsky, Ron Whyte, and others. Jack Keller maintained the Kid's art, as ever.

Finally, in #134 (May 1967), writer Denny O'Neil and artist Herb Trimpe did the first post–Keller issue, and various hands continued the Kid's saga. Issue #140 (November 1969) featured the last original Kid Colt stories in his own book. Did that slow him down?

Shucks, no!

The Kid continued as a reprint book, year after year, finally hanging it up with *Kid Colt, Outlaw* #229 (April 1979). Along the way he appeared in new stories in *Giant-Size Kid Colt* #1–3 (January–July 1975), pairing Colt with the Rawhide Kid in #1 and the Night Rider in issue #3, with solo tales of the Kid in #2. And that wasn't the end.

Since time-travel has never been a problem in Marvel Comics, Kid Colt teamed with the Two-Gun Kid, the Rawhide Kid, the Night Rider, the Ringo Kid, and the Avengers (that's right—the Avengers!) in a chrono-crossover in *Avengers* #142 and 143 (December 1975–January 1976) to fight their future-based enemy, Kang the Conqueror. It actually worked out well, to boot. Since then, the Kid has appeared in a number of time-lost crossovers with various Marvel heroes. They probably just wanted to have their picture taken with him.

At long last, Kid Colt came to an ending of sorts. *Blaze of Glory*, a four-issue mini-series (February–March 2000) teamed him with the Two-Gun Kid, the Rawhide Kid, and a bunch of other Western heroes in another retro series. And in issue #4, Kid Colt, misnamed "Johnny" and not looking like his former self in features or costume, died in battle.

Shot in the back.

His assassin was dispatched moments later by one Caleb Hammer, but it didn't make it any more pleasant.

Again, that wasn't the end.

Six years later, *Marvel Westerns: Kid Colt and the Arizona Girl* #1 (September 2006) featured a tale set well before *Blaze of Glory*. Therein, the Kid teamed with a heroine called the Arizona Girl to fight a town full of—wait for it—Skrulls. (For those not in the know, the Skrulls are a shape-changing race of aliens first seen in *Fantastic Four* #2 [January 1962], and now a mainstay of the modern Marvel Universe.) Well, let's face it: by 2006, the Kid had to do *something* to amp up his act.

There will undoubtedly be more short-lived Kid Colt stories and superhero crossovers in the future. But for now, we will tip our Stetson to a character who, like Superman, Batman, Wonder Woman, and Blackhawk, bridged the Golden and Silver Ages without missing a month. As long as there is a Marvel Comics, Kid Colt will never die.

(A completist would probably note that a horse-human hybrid named "Kid Colt" appeared in modern Marvel comics, but I'm not nearly that much of a completist.)

There were other oaters that Marvel started before 1950. *Tex Morgan* #1 appeared in August 1948. Morgan was a too-tall cowboy who came back to Mesquite, Texas, from the East, where his mom had sent him to get away from guns. He put on a pair of six-shooters to kill the man who had shot his dad, and that started the whole thing running. Morgan did his thing in *Tex Morgan* #1–9 (August 1948–February 1950), *Wild Western* #3, 4, 6, 7, 9, and 11 (September 1948–June 1950), *Blaze Carson* #2 and 3 (November 1948–January 1949), *Kid Colt, Outlaw* #3 (December 1948), and a two-page text story in *Western Outlaws and Sheriffs* #65 (February 1951). He had an Indian sidekick named Lobo and a horse named Lightning, and undoubtedly died of poor circulation.

The Black Rider fared a lot better. He showed up beside Kid Colt and the Two-Gun Kid on the cover of *All-Western Winners* #2 (Winter 1948), dressed in black with a black face-mask to boot, wielding a whip, and riding a white horse. This was the start of a feature that would last a good 11 years, and beyond. And it was pretty darned good.

"The Syndicate of Six-Gun Terror" gave us his origin. In Jefferson County,

Texas, at a time roughly defined as before the Texas Republic joined the USA proper, a teenage gunslinger called the Cactus Kid rode into town and entered the Last Chance Saloon, not knowing it was the watering hole of the Davis Gang, a murderous bunch who were terrorizing the territory. A few gunshots later, the sole survivor walked out of the place: the Kid himself. One wonders if he ever got his drink.

A month later, the governor of Texas himself summoned the Cactus Kid to the capital and gave him a pardon for his past crimes thanks to his recent crime of killing the Davis bunch. Respectfully, the Kid gave his name as Matthew Masters and his age as 17.

"Son, you have your whole life before you! To go on as you were could lead to nothing but outlawry, disaster and death! He who lives by the gun, shall die by the gun! Now, how can I serve you?" asked the governor.

"Well, sir, I've killed and wounded many men!" the Kid answered. "I'd like mighty well to study doctorin' so I could learn to cure instead of kill!"

The governor gave him his blessing, and informed the Cactus Kid that he would begin his journey east in the morning. One scene-change later, an adult Matthew Masters in a green gabardine suit and cowboy hat rode into the town of Leadville, nailed up a sign advertising his services as a doctor, and began his career a couple of moments later. A horse-drawn wagon pulled up, driven by a beautiful blonde named Marie Lathrop and carrying her rheumatic rancher dad, Jim, and a gunshot ranch hand named Charlie. They named Blast Bennett, a badman, as the culprit, and said he was forcing all the ranchers in the area *out* of the area to take it over.

It was origin time!

While Doc Masters was working on his patient, the stubble-bearded Blast

Marvel's masked man of the Wild West, the Black Rider. © 1949 Current Detective Stories Inc. and © 2022 Marvel Publications. Used with permission.

Bennett himself sauntered into the place, demanded that Marie marry him, and shot the cowhand dead while the latter was on the operating table. Then he left, and Jim Lathrop bade Masters take his gun, but the doctor refused. He would not go back to his gunslinging ways. So Lathrop himself went out and was shot by Bennett. The old man was wounded, but not killed. Marie yelled at Matt Masters for being a coward and took her dad back to the ranch to recover.

That night, Matt went through hell, driven by his need to do justice and his fear of reverting to the Cactus Kid. But, when a bystander told him that the Bennett gang was headed for the Lathrop spread to finish up business, Matthew Masters made his decision. He snuck into a general store, grabbed some black clothes and material, and fashioned himself a handkerchief mask. "I entered here as meek little Doctor Matthew Masters, the tenderfoot who is afraid of guns.... I *leave* as the *Black Rider, panther of the plains!*"

Then he boarded his white horse, Satan, charged off to the Lathrop ranch, and, as the Black Rider, rushed the Bennett bunch with both cannons blazing. Bennett himself managed to reach the ranch house, snatch Marie, and make off with her. The Black Rider got on his trail, knocked both Bennett and Marie off Bennett's horse, and faced off with his foe in a gun duel. A few seconds later, Bennett was dead.

Marie, allowing she would have killed herself rather than be taken by Bennett, thanked the Rider, who bowed with courtesy. The Rider said he would send Doc Masters back to tend to the wounded. When the girl dissed Masters, the Rider defended his alter ego, and rode away. It was the good old Superman–Lois Lane–Clark Kent triangle again. At story's end, the Black Rider rode past Marie and threw her a rose. The gal was in love, but with the wrong identity.

The tale was retold in *Black Rider* #10 (September 1950). Syd Shores and Joe Maneely did the art, and a few details were added. In this version, we learned that Davis's first name was Luke, and that he and his gang had raided the Masters ranch and killed Matt's parents. The boy swore to avenge their deaths, and soon became the Cactus Kid. That made his entry into the saloon a deliberate act, and he turned himself over to the authorities after the battle. The shot cowhand was named Charlie Maddock, and Blast Bennett was renamed Blast Burrows. Outside of that, the story was pretty much the same.

Another version came up in *Black Rider Rides Again* #1 (September 1957). This time Jack Kirby was the artist, and he pretty much redid the story from *Black Rider* #10 without many additions. In this one, however, the Rider wore a black eye mask instead of a hanky mask and just kayoed Blast and shot the guns out of the bad guys' hands. We tend to believe the original. A final flashback origin in *Strange Westerns* #1 (October 2006) gave Matt's parents the names of Ned and Jezebel, violated the original by saying that Matt's mother had died in childbirth (though it's possible Ned remarried before his death), and featured scripting by Steve Englehart and art by Marshall Rogers. Somehow, they tied it all in with the Ancient One and Doctor Strange.

Be that as it may, Black Rider next appeared in a five-page short in *Wild Western* #5 (January 1949), in which Bobby, Marie's nephew, was introduced. He was a toddler in this story, but quickly grew into a young boy in his next showing (*All-Western*

Winners #3, February 1949). In that tale, Bobby secretly watched Doc Masters change into the Black Rider and immediately became his confidante. Marie kept dissing Masters and lusting for the Rider.

The Rider's shoot-'em-ups continued for a long time. Altogether, he was in *All-Western Winners* #2–4 (Winter 1948–April 1949), *Wild Western* #5, 8, 12–19, 32–43, 45, and 50 (January 1949–July 1956), *Best Western* #58 and 59 (June–August 1949), *Western Winners* #5 and 6 (June–August 1949), *Rex Hart* #6 (August 1949), *Two-Gun Kid* #9, 11, and 12 (August 1949–February 1954), *Black Rider* #9–27 (June 1950–March 1955), *Whip Wilson* #11 (September 1950), *Two-Gun Western* #13 and 14 (April–June 1952), *Western Outlaws and Sheriffs* #73 (June 1952), *3-D Tales of the West* #1 (January 1954), *Kid Colt, Outlaw* #33–45, 74, and 86 (January 1954–September 1959), *Outlaw Kid* #1 and 2 (September–November 1954), *Ringo Kid* #2 (October 1954), *Western Tales of Black Rider* #28–31 (May–November 1955), *Two-Gun Western* V. 2 #5 (July 1956), *Gunsmoke Western* #36, 47, and 51 (August 1956–March 1959), and *Black Rider Rides Again* #1 (September 1957). If anything, publisher Martin Goodman believed in cross-pollination.

That was the end of the Black Rider for over a decade. But, given Marvel's (and everyone else's) propensity for recycling their old stuff, it wasn't the end. A Black Rider story was reprinted in *Kid Colt, Outlaw* #143 (February 1970). With his name relettered as the *Black Mask*, so not to conflict with the Ghost Rider in the front of the book, the Black Rider reappeared in *Western Gunfighters* #3–7 in reprints (December 1970–January 1972). Then, when the Ghost Rider exited, the Black Rider reclaimed his old name and continued in reprints for issues #8–16 (April 1972–July 1973) and finished his reprint run in *Two-Gun Kid* #117 (April 1974).

As you might guess, that *still* wasn't the end.

In March 2006, as noted earlier, when Marvel started exhuming their cowboy heroes for another run, Steve Englehart and Marshall Rogers collaborated on a new Black Rider story for *Marvel Westerns: Strange Westerns Starring the Black Rider* #1 (no lie; that was really the title!). Englehart renamed the hero Morris Masters for some reason. He came to New York to see a doctor for his horse, met his aunt and uncle, learned some unfavorable family history, and finally it was revealed that he came there to seek revenge for a dead Chinese prostitute. The Black Rider was aided by an Asian called Yao, found out his aunt and uncle were running a ring of Chinese hookers to Texas, and dealt out justice as only he could. With a flash-forward to the present, we learned that Yao was really the Ancient One, mentor of Doctor Strange.

Lastly, the Black Rider cameoed in the time-travel saga *Avengers Forever* (#5, April 1999) and showed up on a couple of pages in *Marvel 1000* (October 2019), his last appearance to date. But we wouldn't be surprised if the man in black shows his masked face again in the future.

Just about the last Western feature in 1949 from Marvel was *Rex Hart*, whom they apparently tried to pass off as a movie cowboy with photo covers and the billing, "Your famous Western star!" He was a ranch foreman and, although he usually had good art by Syd Shores and Russ Heath, there wasn't really anything special about him. That's probably why he only lasted three issues (#6–8, August 1949–February 1950).

Of course, Marvel (or Timely, or Atlas, whatever name they were using at the time) put out a long ton of Westerns after 1950, well into the Seventies. But they'll have to wait for a future volume. We have enough on our plate with the Forties, already. On to MLJ comics.

MLJ's first publication, *Blue Ribbon Comics*, shoveled in *Buck Stacy* in the first two issues (November–December 1939). He was a "young range detective" hired to find some cattle thieves. W.M. Allison was the artist and did a good job on the characters, but they all seemed as stiff as pokers. The story was in black, white, and red, and continued through issue #2, then was dropped.

Nevada Jones, Quick-Trigger Man held forth in *Zip Comics* #1–25 (February 1940–April 1942). He was another "range detective" who saved a girl's ranch from some Mexican raiders (who were repeatedly called "greasers" in the story). Nevada had better action than Buck Stacy, but by the second issue, he was framed for (again) a crime he didn't do, escaped into the hills (again), put on a mask to disguise himself (again), and fought bad guys as the Quick-Trigger Man. He came upon a wounded Mexican called Little Joe, who had been injured by the same guys who framed him. Tellingly, he didn't call Little Joe "greaser." The two of them went after the bad man who killed Little Joe's boss, and Little Joe shot him to death over the protests of Nevada. That was that. It became a fairly decent strip and greased its way along the next two years.

Moving on to Nedor, also known as Better, Standard, or Pines, their first publication, *Thrilling Comics*, offered *Rio Kid*. The first caption told us, "The Rio Kid rides on his eternal quest for adventure!" There were so many comics cowboys doing the same, they were bound to have a lodge somewhere. He saved a girl and her horse from a snake, was rewarded with a job, had to ride the toughest Cayuse and fight the toughest man in the outfit to get it, and did both. But the outfit was being rustled, a competitor wanted their land, and the tough guy Rio beat wanted vengeance. As it was, Rio sent a summons for some friends of his who were more or less a prairie version of the Justice Society, and they helped him take care of the bad guys. This was a relief from the lone cowboy who could crush all opposition by himself. Rio rode from *Thrilling* #2 to 29 (March 1940–August 1942), missing three issues along the way.

Exciting Comics #1 (April 1940) debuted the Western filler strip *Jim Hatfield, Texas Ranger*. The first two panels of the intro story showed us pictures of two rival trains being dynamited by their competitors. Jim was called in to stop the railroad war, and managed to do so in eight action-packed pages. He skipped the next issue, but returned for #3–21 (June 1940–August 1942), missing #17 and 20 along the way.

The Masked Rider, in *Startling Comics* #1–17 (June 1940–October 1942), was another Lone Ranger clone. The origin was pretty much fill-in-the-blank: Bronc Randall came home to his uncle's ranch after two years on the rodeo circuit, found his uncle dying, got creased by a bullet, and found a bad guy had the deed to the ranch. To set things right, he donned a mask and became—you guessed it—the Masked Rider. The man in the mask conquered the villains and forced a confession at gunpoint from their leader. No Miranda rights back then. The art was decent for its time, being done by John Daly. That was pretty much it for Nedor's initial Western strips.

But in 1947, with superheroes starting to wane, Nedor hedged their bets with their first Western title, which was *Broncho Bill*. This title went from issue #5 to 16 (December 1947–December 1950) and consisted of repackaged comic strips of the title character by Harry O'Neill. The stories had new splash panels and titles pasted onto them, and that was pretty much that. Actually, Bill had been reprinted in comic books since *Tip Top Comics* #1 (April 1936) and saw his last appearance in *Tip Top* #170 (September–October 1951). But it did well enough for Nedor to consider doing their own Westerns.

With *Thrilling Comics* #72 (June 1949), the jungle queen Princess Pantha was nudged off the cover by Alex Schomburg's illo of two buckaroos flanking a filly (a girl, not a horse), all of them apparently waiting for a train to New York. The big guy on the left was Buck Ranger, who took the lead position in the book immediately. His buddy was Chico Charlie, and there ain't no telling who the girl was. But the story was in the capable artistic hands of Ruben Moreira and it was a winner. Buck, on the splash page, buried his fist in the gut of an owlhoot while Charlie jumped up and cheered.

Described as a "cowboy detective" who worked for the Cattlemen's League, Buck and his sidekick Charlie rode into the town of Lansdale to touch base before heading out again. As is inevitable in Westerns, there was trouble brewing. They walked into headman Jim Bracken's office and interrupted a conversation in which Bracken described to a visitor named Jepson that Buck was the best undercover agent the League ever had. Buck informed Bracken that he and Charlie were quitting, out to travel the West. But Bracken shamed him into just one more job, to stop a range war that would leave a lot of people homeless or dead.

It happened that League member Race Marlow wanted to drive a bunch

Buck Ranger, Chico Charlie, and friend. © 1949 Standard Magazines, Inc.

of nesters off his land, and wasn't particular how he did it. "All right, Bracken, I'll do it!" snapped Buck. "We can't afford another range war! But this is my last job for you!"

Yeah, right.

Buck traded fisticuffs with Marlow after the latter had a nester's house burned down, and came out on top. Charlie shot the gun out of the hand of a guy who had the drop on Buck. Our hero tried to persuade Marlow to leave the nesters alone, but the man had other ideas. He rode back to his ranch, picked up his pretty daughter, Gale, and declared his intention to burn out all the nesters. It turned out that Jepson and Gale had feelings for each other, but Marlow intended to beat those feelings out of him, along with anything else that came with them.

Buck intervened, telling Marlow, "You're not going to beat up anyone! And you're going to answer to the law!" Marlow attacked, but Buck and Charlie put him back on his heels. A fight between nesters and Marlow's minions was barely staved off, but Gale was nearly killed when her horse stampeded through a store window. Seeing his injured daughter, Marlow came to his senses, and said, "The nesters have got as much right to the land as I have … and I'll make up to 'em what they've lost!"

Standard's Billy West gets his own comic. He's the guy on his knees. © 1949 Standard Magazines, Inc.

Gale and Jepson declared their intention to get married, and Buck and Charlie declared their intention to move on. That finished the first story, and it was a good 'un.

Buck Ranger held the cover through *Thrilling*'s last issue, #80 (April 1951). The book steadily converted to Westerns in its limited time. *Billy West* moved in with #75 (January 1950) and helped Buck finish out the run. But Billy actually debuted before Buck, so we must turn back on the trail.

Billy West #1 (April 1949) started with a 20-page story of Billy, a blond guy in a cowboy hat (what else?), riding into his hometown of Lone Creek, Wyoming, after spending three years at school in the East. A band of crooks tried to rob the coach, but they'd picked the wrong day for their doings. Billy grabbed his guns and salivated the baddies. After that, he was met in town by an old coot named Uncle Dan'l, a beautiful gal ranch owner named Molly Sage, and her kid sister, Julie, all of whom were—you guessed it—trying to save their ranch from rustlers. Molly proved her worth: when rustler Bull Jason tried to put the moves on her, she pulled out a whip and lashed him. Thankfully, he wasn't kinky enough to appreciate it.

When Bull had words with Uncle Dan'l and knocked him down, Billy stepped up and two-handedly knocked the bejabbers out of Bull and his boys. Battle was joined. The three bad guys ended up in a horse trough. Dan'l introed Billy to Julie and her brother, Snubby, and revealed that the Sages' dad had been cheated out of money in a poker game by Bull and shortly afterward was shot in the back. It took a lot of action, but eventually Billy defeated and captured Bull, the kids recovered a document proving the bad guy's perfidy, and all was well. Billy was made a hand on Molly's ranch, and we all knew what was coming.

In the second story, Uncle Dan'l spun a story for Snubby and Julie of how he saved an orphaned kid from Indian raiders, learned that his name was Billy, and gave him the surname of West. There was more to it, including the bit about how the kid converted Dan'l from an outlaw into an honest working man, but the gist of it was that Billy grew up to be a fine Western hero. In future issues, Dan'l would continue Billy's origin story, up to the point where he first appeared in issue #1.

On top of that, Nedor offered membership in a Billy West Cowboy Club. For 15 cents "to cover mailing," you got a silvered ring with a picture of Billy West on it, a membership in the club, a copy of the Billy West Secret Code, and a picture of Billy West himself. No true fan could ask for less.

John Celardo, who later drew the *Tarzan* newspaper strip, handled most of the Billy West stories decently. Badmen were always trying to rustle the cattle of the Blue Sage Ranch and make off with Stubby and Julie, or even Dan'l and Molly, but our hero prevailed in every story.

By issue #3, Rhoda Trail, another pistol-packin' female, drew her rifle and put down some night riders in a story well-drawn by Ruben Moreira. She stayed through issue #9 and was a welcome addition to the girl gunslinger genre. When someone asked her, "Why is a pretty girl like you lookin' for a ruckus? You ought to be home baking biscuits!" she retorted, "I'll bake some for you with coyote poison in them." She soon gained a love interest named Slim. That didn't stop her from snaring outlaws. *Rhoda Trail* lasted through issue #9.

Also, Buck Ranger himself appeared in backups in issues #5, 8, and 9 (February 1950–February 1951) and *America's Best Comics* #31 (July 1949). Billy West shortened his mag's title to *Bill West* with issue #10 (February 1952). He picked up an Indian kid sidekick called Little Fox along the way, but that was his last issue. Undoubtedly, he married Miss Molly and settled down to a little quieter life on the ranch.

With the exception of the romance title *Western Hearts*, that pretty much does it for Nedor's frontier fracases. A new upstart company, Avon, which published a lot of paperbacks and a good deal of quality comics, was about to try their hand at the genre. Their initial effort was an interesting seven-issue series called *Cow Puncher*.

Though nobody, thankfully, was shown actually punching a cow, there was a lot of Western action in the book. The cover of issue #1 (January 1947) showed a horseman aiming his rifle back at a band of pursuers, all of whom were probably picking on the wrong guy. The character depicted was Clint Cortland, *The Texas Ranger*.

Whoever drew the cover did a lot better job than the artist who did the story, but it was well-written enough for a pass. Maybe. On the first page, Clint (who would later be named Cal) crouched behind his dead horse and attempted to hold off a squad of attacking Comanche. He was saved in time by the cavalry, who had been summoned by his Indian friend and partner, Pronto. (Please … hold your giggles.) It turned out that a white opportunist had been selling guns to the Comanches. The gun runner was exposed as a renegade Ranger, and Pronto helped Clint disguise himself as an Indian well enough to infiltrate the tribe. In the end, the traitor got burned at the stake by the tribe, Clint was saved from death by Pronto, and Clint himself shot the hostile chieftain. It wasn't perfect, but it was a start.

The next issue was a humor bit, as a short, fat amateur called Pill Peters, who had somehow gotten into the Rangers, tried to help out Cal and Pronto. He couldn't hit the proverbial broad side of a barn with a six-shooter, but somehow managed to bring in an entire gang by himself. It was a reasonably funny story. Then Al Ulmer stepped in with issue #3 (1947) and did a major quality overhaul on the art. The script may have been by Henry Kuttner. In this issue, Cal Cortland took on a bunch of glowing outlaws called the Fiery Riders and defeated them. Ulmer continued on the feature through issue #7 (1949).

Alabam, the best strip in the book, only lasted two issues. But it featured the primal work of Joe Kubert, one of comics' true artistic masters. On the splash, a two-gunning Alabam, in black outfit, badge, and Stetson, faced off with a mustachioed bad man while a grieving widow sprawled across her husband's grave. The caption read: "*Broken Creek* was a cemetery for sheriffs! There was something deadly for the law in its atmosphere until *Alabam* rode into town, each palm resting on a gunbutt! But who knows how Alabam's battle would have turned out if not for a SPLIT-SECOND STAND-IN!"

The story opened at the Paradise Bar, where one Mike Mantee, the villain of the piece, finished off his morning by shooting a guy who was winning too much from him in cards. Sheriff John Hyler, 51 years of age, came to take Mantee to the hoosegow. Mantee outdrew him, shot him in the gut, and killed him. Stumbling upon the scene, Hilda, the sheriff's wife, drew his gun from his holster and tried to administer justice to the killer, but got shot in the hand. Sobbing, she vowed revenge.

Shortly after that, as mail ran in those days, Alabam himself, a Texas cowboy, got a letter from Hilda, who was his aunt. She explained the situation, and Alabam betook himself to Broken Creek. There he put on his dead uncle's tin star and promised Hilda that Mantee would face justice. She wanted him to shoot the killer down on the spot, but he refused, saying, "I intend to ask my questions before I shoot, not after!"

When Mantee got wind of what was happening, Alabam had to slug and shoot his way into the Paradise Bar, and did just that. He then ordered Mantee to throw down his guns and come peacefully, but the murderer did neither. At that point Aunt Hilda appeared and started slapping the hell out of Mantee, daring him to draw his gun. He did, and dropped her on the spot. Finally forced to action like Hamlet, Alabam quickly perforated Mantee. The killer fell dead to the barroom floor. For his part, Alabam carried his deceased aunt from the place, muttering, "You're happy now with uncle John, aren't you?" He buried her beside the sheriff and vowed to be as good a law keeper as John Hyler himself. *Alabam* was an excellent strip, but it only went another issue.

Kit West followed, featuring a glamour-girl frontierswoman in a very short skirt, a laced-open shirt, and red boots, armed with a Kentucky long rifle. On the first splash, she was threatened by a symbolically huge snake while she stood over a dead Indian. She was pretty, all right, but she was a darned tough mama.

Fade in on a council of the Wyandotte tribe, who, understandably, were hacked off by the inroads the whites were making into their territory. Spitting Snake, the chief, declared, "Our lands must run red with the blood of the invader!" Kit watched in hiding from a tree, trying to get all the info she could. A scouting party saw her, and Little Snake, the chief's son, sent an arrow through her leg. Kit was hurt and bleeding, but that didn't stop her from shooting and clubbing at her attackers. In a fight to the death with Little Snake, she killed him with his own tomahawk. *Then* she took out the arrow.

Presenting Kit West, glamorous gun-girl. © 1948 Avon Comics, Inc.

Spitting Snake took it upon himself to finish the vendetta. He kayoed Kit, tied her to a tree, slapped her awake, and promised to torture her with thrown tomahawks until she died. Spotting a real snake on the ground, Kit tricked her enemy into stepping back within range of the reptile. The snake, possibly a copperhead, chomped him in the leg. Enraged, the dying Spitting Snake lunged at her. She kicked him in the chin, then sawed herself free. The copperhead took up a perch on Spitting Snake's body.

Kit skipped the next

issue but came back for #3–7 (1947–1949). A number of artists handled her, including Gus Schrotter, John Forte, and Jill Elgin. Howard Larsen did her last story. In issue #3, she defended Indian captives against their white captors and related what might have been her origin. She had been a girl in Kentucky when attacking Indians killed her brother and sister before her eyes and then murdered her parents. The young Kit was tied to a stake and put in the tent of one Broken-Face, who said he would burn her at the stake after having his "amusement" with her, and the look on his face didn't leave much doubt as to how he would amuse himself. But a sympathetic Indian girl bonked Broken-Face on the head, freed Kit, and was killed for her merciful action by Broken-Face's tomahawk. Kit West grabbed the tomahawk, threw it back, and killed Broken-Face. Then she cradled the dead body of the girl who had saved her life.

The story convinced the settlers to be more humane to the Indians. Afterward, a guy took her aside and said he'd seen her folks alive and well in Boston a week ago. Smiling, she told him, "Sometimes a little white lie keeps people white in their hearts!" Okay.

The Fighting Parson was the last offering in *Cow Puncher* #1, with an impressive splash page by Jon Small as "Jack Ross." The opening caption explained, "John Watkins came to the Western frontier to preach a great message, but the reply to that message was too frequently enclosed in steel jackets full of deadly lead! And so John Watkins became the Fighting Parson, the strangest figure in the West! And his blazing six-shooters pumped terror into the most evil hearts...." They probably pumped something more than terror there, too.

The tale commenced with the hanging of a murderer named Claude Piper. Mr. Piper had three equally criminal brothers who were sworn to revenge him. They caught up to the sheriff while he was attending church services run by John Watkins, proceeded to shoot the pastor in the arm, and murdered the sheriff none too cleanly in cold blood. After the Pipers rode off, Watkins cradled the sheriff's body and vowed, "From now on I'm packing guns—and I'm not taking them off till the West's safe from snakes like the Pipers!"

True to his word, the parson bought a pair of guns, trained with them till he was a crack shot, then confronted the Pipers when they returned to town to rob a bank. He shot two of them down, took out the third with his fists, and was there for the hanging. The last Piper's final words were to curse the sheriff. "God rest his soul," the Fighting Parson said, as the trap was sprung and Piper exited the Earth. After another adventure in the next issue, the Parson exited comics, except for reprints.

Boots Bradley spelled *Kit West* in *Cow Puncher* #2 (September 1947). She is probably more famous for the Jack Kamen cover showing her bound to a stake while a cowboy hero stopped an outlaw from branding her with a hot iron. Inside, she took up the last story slot. Steve Webb and John Forte were the artists, and Boots herself was a "rootin', shootin', cactus beauty" who owned a ranch, cussed up a storm, and wasn't shy about taking on bad guys. In this one, she saved a male schoolteacher from ranch rival Ratler Flint and pitched a little woo with him on the way home. That was her only story, but Avon recycled it a bit, as they were wont to do.

Anthology stories and a Mountie series, *Knight of the North*, filled out the rest of the books. *Cow Puncher* was an unsettled series, but impressive nonetheless.

Avon produced *Wild Bill Hickok* #1 in September–October 1949. He lasted a good 28 issues, up through May–June of 1956, and was one of Avon's longest-lived titles. So, we shall examine it.

The bare facts about Wild Bill: He was born James Butler Hickok in 1837 in Illinois. After thinking he'd killed a man named James Hudson in a fight (Hudson, in turn, thought he'd killed Hickok), he lit out at age 18 for the Kansas Territory, joined a vigilante group, met a young Buffalo Bill Cody, and became a stagecoach driver. Later he joined the Union Army during the Civil War. There were other major doings in his life, including gun duels, work as a marshal, an attempt to arrest John Wesley Hardin, a possible marriage to Calamity Jane (Martha Jane Cannary), and a batch of other famous doings which can be accessed through biographies or articles. Wild Bill Hickok led an action-packed life, all right, and ended up shot dead by Jack McCall in a poker game. (The incident was copied ages later for the death of Jonah Hex.)

The tales in *Wild Bill Hickok* sugar-coated his history a bit to remove some of the rough spots. Nonetheless, they were pretty fair Western comic stories. The cover of issue #1, by Graham Ingels, showed a buckskin-shirted Bill and a busty blonde aboard a stagecoach, said blonde holding the reins, while Bill, his face turned away from the readers (he might have been Milton Berle, for all we knew), blazed away at attacking Indians with his two six-shooters. In a Story Behind the Cover, the shooter wasn't identified as Bill Hickok at all. But the blonde was. She was said to be Calamity Jane.

Jimmy Thompson, a darned good comics artist with work on DC's Robotman and Timely's Human Torch to prove it, was the artist. The splash page

Boots Bradley braves branding. And that's *Boots*, pardner.
© 1947 Avon Comics, Inc.

showed Bill going mano a mano with a knife against a bear while a stagecoach driver brandished a shotgun and a lady in a hoop skirt looked on in terror. The story, "The McCallan Gang Fight," related Wild Bill's birth ("Got as much blonde hair as a girl!"—actually, Bill was probably a redhead), his skill as a boy with a rifle, his tutelage from the Indian Grey Eagle, his travel West at age 18 (the fight with James Hudson was excised), a victory in a shooting contest, a gun battle with an owlhoot named Don McCallan (actually David Colbert McCanles), his successful career as a shoot-from-the-hip stagecoach driver, the battle with the bear (which really happened, and took him four months from which to recover), and a final encounter with the vengeful McCallan and his gang, in which Hickok killed McCallan and all of his men. This took 10 pages. Back in those days, comics got things done *fast*.

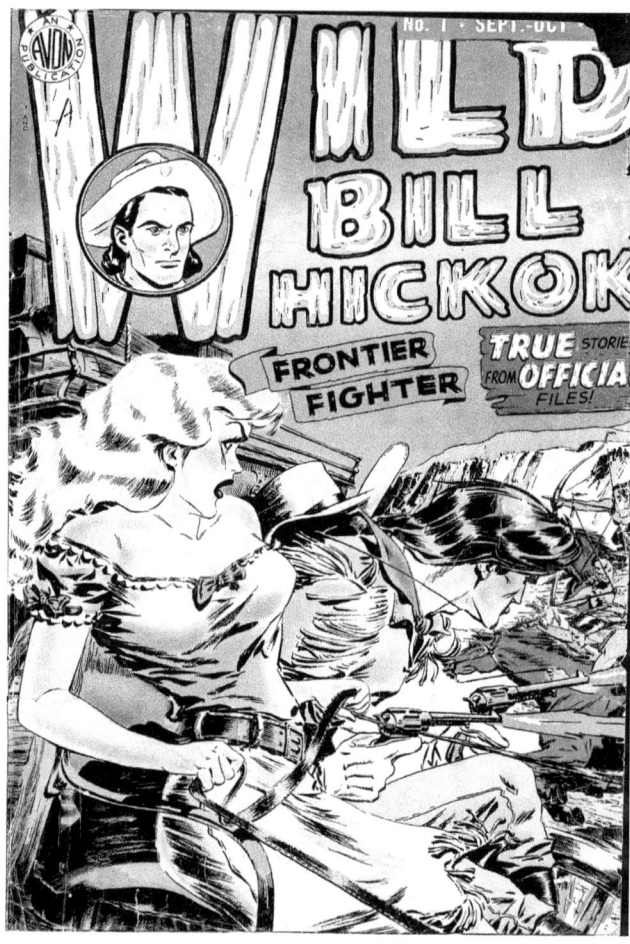

With a Graham Ingels cover, Wild Bill Hickok begins a fairly long and well-drawn run at Avon. © 1949 Avon Periodicals, Inc.

Paul S. Newman may have written the story. In the second tale, Wild Bill and Buffalo Bill teamed with General George Custer to fight off a band of attacking Indians. The comics might have stretched the truth a bit, but, as another Western character might say, they were printing the legend.

Howard Larsen took over from Thompson with issue #3. Art Peddy also contributed to a story or two. Bill's hair color shifted from a dark shade to blond, as long as the real Hickok's but minus his mustache and beard. There were lots of incidents in Hickok's life to weave into stories. Somehow, though, he never encountered Jack McCall.

Covers were usually superb, either painted ones or line drawings by Everett Raymond Kinstler. Also, Kinstler provided excellent black-and-white intro pages on the inside front covers, a touch Avon was known for. And the comic went on. Also,

Wild Bill made a foray into Avon's *Blazing Six-Guns* #1 (December 1952), in a story also drawn by Larsen.

Around issue #16 (December 1953–January 1954), reprints from earlier issues crept in, and later issues were usually all-reprint. Avon, possibly prompted by the Wertham crusade, was preparing to jettison their comics experiment. In issue #23 (May–June 1955), a new Wild Bill story by Bob McCarty and Kinstler appeared. Then Kinstler followed up in the next issue (#24, August–September 1955) with a six-page Hickok story of his own. The two artists managed a new story per issue till the last (#28, May–June 1956). Like his namesake, the comic book Wild Bill Hickok passed into history. At least the Avon version; the Wild Bill Hickok of Charlton Comics, which began before Avon's version, lasted well past it through 1961. Hickok also showed up in a battery of stories from other publishers, usually as a guest star or in an isolated story.

But the Avon version didn't quite die. Israel Waldman, mastermind of IW-Super Comics and the later Skywald, saw to that. In 1958, *Wild Bill Hickok* #1 appeared, reprinting Avon's issue #20, which was itself reprints from other issues. Issues #10–12 followed in 1963–64, reprinting other Avons. All of this, of course, was without permission, but Avon didn't seem to give a big, big D. Seven years later, *Blazing Six-Guns* #2 (April 1971) reprinted a Hickok story from Avon's issue #5. In 1997, DC used Wild Bill as a recurring character in their maxi-series *The Kents*, about Superman's adoptive ancestors. That may be the last of his appearances in comics, but frankly, we doubt it. Avon produced other Western series and one-shots, but they all began in 1950 or afterward.

D.S. Publishing and P.L. Publishing seemed to be the same outfit, maybe branded over like rustlers do stolen cattle, and their main cowboy offering was *Tex Farrell*.

The first and only issue of *Tex Farrell* was from D.S. and was dated March–April 1948, with a Sheldon Moldoff cover of our man Tex jumping off a horse on a bluff toward two outlaws who didn't seem to appreciate the move. He was dubbed the Pride of the Wild West and apparently proved it on the first page by charging in on horseback against a force of Indians attacking Fort Sagamore. He shot one in the forehead with his right-hand gun. We weren't exactly sure what he was aiming at with his left-hand gun, but presumably he hit it.

Tex, a blond guy, had enough of a rep to scare two Indians whom he met before the big massacre and knock them both out. Most of the soldiers in Fort Sagamore were down with food poisoning—after living on army chow, that must have been *some* poisoning—and Tex helped man the fort against the attackers. Honestly, the story wasn't good enough to waste much more space on it. Tex Farrell reappeared in P.L.'s *Western Frontier* #2 and 3 (July–August–October 1951), but we're not really sure why.

D.S. also put out a modern-type western, *Breeze Lawson, Sky Sheriff* (#1, Summer 1948), in which the hero was a present-day sheriff who tracked down crooks in an airplane. More or less, it was a knockoff of radio's (and later, TV's) *Sky King*, and it was drawn by Edmond Good. So much for that.

We'll move on now to Lev Gleason, who had a few things to say about the genre and said 'em in two danged-good comics titles: *Desperado* and *Black Diamond Western*.

Desperado, in some ways, was an outgrowth of Gleason's successful *Crime Does Not Pay* and *Crime and Punishment*. Writer-editors Charlie Biro and Bob Wood had been presenting crimes and criminals in both those titles for years. When they judged it time to hitch their wagon to Westerns, they just transferred their "true crime" techniques to the sagebrush set. *Desperado* #1 (June 1948)—or "Desperado *Desperado* DESPERADO," as the logo would have it—bore a cover featuring an outlaw drinking the last swig of water from another man's canteen in the desert. He had a gun pointed at the man's throat, and his victim was emptying a whole bag of gold nuggets against his chest, trying in vain to buy one last sip. That was the way it started.

The first story, entitled "Joe Slade," opened with a shot of some famous outlaws' gravestones in Boot Hill and was narrated—no lie—by a gun. Really. It was akin to a gimmick Bob Kanigher used for his DC war comics later on, with talking soldiers' helmets and such. But the revolver's monologue went thusly: "I was forged into shape in a Tucson blacksmith shop! Hank Beardsley, the master gunsmith, had a lot of trouble boring my barrel! He broke two drills on it and cursed me till he was blue in the face! Hank wasn't the last! Hundreds of men cursed me, with red foam bubbling from their lungs that I had blasted to bits! I was tough and hard! I had to be! I was probably fired more times than a dozen six-guns put together! My history is the history of the West—when the redmen were mighty and justice was unknown! Your right to live depended only upon how fast you drew! I was destined to be used by the lightning trigger fingered Joe Slade! But many an hombre who took the last trail, might have lasted a bit longer, if they had me weighing down their gunbelts! Men like Billy the Kid, Jesse James, Sam Bass, and the rest of the names you see chiseled above rotting bones!"

Desperado Desperado DESPERADO, the first Western comic by Charlie Biro *Charlie Biro* CHARLIE BIRO! © 1948 Lev Gleason Publications.

The gun did the narration for the entire 13-page story. Joe Slade was indeed a killer from the West, one whom Mark Twain himself briefly met during one of his travels. The gun which he claimed took two lives before he got it, when a widowed woman killed her husband's murderers. Once Slade got it from a pawn shop, he put it to far deadlier use. In the space of 13 pages, he committed 18 murders. He was finally hung and the gun thrown in his grave with him. "I feel only disgust for you, villain of villains!" the weapon finished. It was a heck of a start, and the blood had just started flowing.

Sam Bass, a train robber, and Bill Longley, who killed two cavalrymen, finished up the issue. An unidentified pencil-and-ink team, Al Bare and Fred Guardineer, were the artists. It was *Crime Does Not Pay* in Stetsons and boots, and it probably should've worked. Maybe it did. But after eight more issues of kill-crazy outlaws, whose tales could be told by a gallows, a tin star, a silver dollar, or an ace of spades, Lev Gleason decided it was time for a change. So...

...with issue #9 (March 1949), the book became *Black Diamond Western*, and changed aplenty.

Instead of being the Western version of *Crime Does Not Pay*, *Black Diamond Western* was more akin to *Boy Comics* or *Daredevil*. The first cover showed a masked, yellow-shirted cowboy astride a Palomino horse, waving to the people of a town called Junction. He had posted a note to them on a tree with a big knife to hold it there, declaring that they didn't have to worry anymore and he was the new self-appointed marshal of the territory. That was the way *the Black Diamond* introduced himself.

It took 18 pages to tell his origin story, and it was a whangdoodle of one, a worthy companion to the one

The long-running *Black Diamond* series takes up where *Desperado* left off. © 1949 Lev Gleason Publications.

Biro had concocted for Daredevil. William Overgard drew it, and it faded in with a scene of a white renegade named Hawkins urging a bunch of Indian warriors to attack a train bringing white men in to despoil their land. Hawkins's motives were less than praiseworthy. To an underling, he confided, "The more settlers that die, the fewer trappers that will dare to come out here, and the more my furs will be worth!"

As expected, the Indians attacked the train and proceeded to massacre everyone they could get their hands on. One they couldn't was a blond-haired boy who was concealed by his mother in a trunk. The braves and Hawkins boarded the train and rode it all the way to the brand-new town of Junction, where they commenced even more killing. A newspaperman named Lloyd Vale was on hand, and lent his hand to fight the Indians. But he was struck down and choked half to death by Hawkins, who lost one thing in the process—a black diamond ring he had been given by Chief Thundercloud as a token of friendship. When Vale awakened hours later among the corpses, he found the ring in his hand, heard the cries of the kid inside the trunk, and freed the boy. As it was, Lloyd Vale ended up adopting the boy, marrying a woman he'd fallen in love with, and settling down in Junction.

The boy's name was Bob, and he joined his dad, Lloyd, his mom, Martha, and his half-sister, Patricia, on the ranch Lloyd founded. Bob bonded with a Palomino colt who subsequently saved his life from a mountain lion. From his father, he learned of the renegade who had worn the black diamond ring. But times were tough, as they tend to be, and Lloyd had to sell his horses just to keep their homestead alive.

Bob Vale sadly took his colt to the buyer, who, wonder of wonders, was Hawkins. He recognized the dastard from his father's description, Hawkins recognized the black diamond ring Lloyd had given to Bob, and both men promptly put two and two together. It ended up with Hawkins murdering Lloyd Vale and Bob being framed by Hawkins for murder, and put in jail.

That was enough for an origin, and that's what happened.

The Palomino came to the jailed Bob with a coil of rope, which the 21-year-old youth used to allow his mount to pull the bars off the wooden jail's wall. After that, Bob warned Pat against going to the sheriff to clear his name, for fear Hawkins would kill her. And after *that*, Hawkins got a note pinned to a knife thrown through a window, warning him his hours were numbered, and signed, "The Black Diamond."

Later that night, a figure in a black hat and eye mask, purple pants, and a yellow jacket with a black diamond on the chest clambered up to Hawkins's bedroom, overcame the gangster, lured in his three confederates one at a time, and clobbered them all. Then he delivered the gang in a wagon to the local Western Union, where a telegraph message summoned the U.S. Marshal for the territory. Hawkins, "with a little persuasion," signed a confession by the time Marshal Bonner got there. Black Diamond collected $10,000 in reward money, enough to bail the ranch out of trouble. He was also offered the job of marshal for the territory of Junction. On the condition he'd never have to unmask or reveal his true name (though his Palomino would seem to be a dead giveaway), Black Diamond accepted. And, with a teaser for next month's story, that was the way the tale ended.

The rest of the 52-page issue was filled with the same Western true-crime stories that had been the meat of the preceding eight issues. *Black Diamond* was apparently a hit, and it stayed so through issue #60 (February–March 1956). By #10 (April 1949), the Diamond picked up a sidekick, a Russian circus strongman yclept Statistor Bumpinovitch. It was merciful that his handle was shortened to Bumper. He and Marshal Bonner stayed on as supporting cast members. So did Patricia, Bob Vale's half-sister and love interest. After all, Black Diamond needed someone besides his horse to talk to.

The series kept up the Lev Gleason brand of quality in art and story—especially story. By issue #15 (September 1949), the Diamond's horse finally got a name: Reliapon. (Giggle, and these two shootin' irons'll make you dance.) The next issue (November 1949), besides containing two Black Diamond stories and getting Bumper a horse in one of them, was notable for something new: Basil Wolverton's own *Bingbang Buster and his horse, Hedy!*

Basil "Westwart" Wolverton blasts out one of his inimitable characters, Bingbang Buster and his horse, Hedy! © 1949 Lev Gleason Publications.

Wolverton, possibly the most unique artist in all of Golden Age comics, added some welcome humor to *Black Diamond Western*. Bingbang Buster was a sagebrush saga riff on his dimwitted but gold-hearted super-strongman, *Powerhouse Pepper*. In this case, Bingbang could indeed perform feats of strength, but his horse, Hedy, was so eager to protect him he usually didn't have to.

The tale, credited to Basil Westwart Wolverton, commenced with Bingbang and Hedy watching a horde of townspeople and horses fleeing past places like Shorty's Shindig Shack and Mulligan's Stew Saloon at top speed. "Bulletbean McBlast, the bandit, is headed this way!" Informed that Bulletbean shot everyone he saw on sight, Bingbang decided to hang around and see for himself.

He and Hedy had to jump out of the way of four shots in quick succession. Enter the huge, bearded gunman, Bulletbean McBlast, and his own steed. While the horses gave each other wicked looks, Bingbang protested, "Hey! You might have hit us!"

To which Bulletbean replied, "Yuh've gotta lotta nerve presumin' to stay alive around me, Bulletbean McBlast, the baddest bandit in the badlands!" To demonstrate his power, McBlast destroyed an entire gambling house ("Feverish Freddy's Fun House") with a single blow.

"You shouldn't have done that!" Bingbang replied, sensibly. "Don't try it again!" Unmoved, McBlast announced he was about to plug Bingbang. But he hadn't reckoned with Hedy, who promptly bit him on the rear, making him shout and throw his gun. Bingbang recovered the hogleg, marched McBlast past Frank's Flealess Flophouse, and told him to leave town.

But Western baddies are sneakier than that. Bulletbean brandished a second weapon and fired twice at Bingbang. Bingbang returned the fire, and the men's bullets collided and fused with each other. Reasonably frustrated, McBlast lunged at Bingbang. Wisely, our hero stepped aside and let Hedy kick him almost into orbit.

That should have been the end of it, but Bingbang realized the flying felon had stolen his hat. He mounted Hedy and gave chase, keeping the skybound outlaw in sight. It took a fairly long time. Bulletbean came down head-first on the North Pole (a literal wooden pole, right next to the Gallup Pole), and Bingbang treaded over the tundra, asking for his hat back. Bulletbean refused.

So Bingbang did the only thing a reasonable man could be expected to do: he hauled off and smacked his foe with a punch that was mostly a bunch of speed lines. Then he recovered his hat from Bulletbean, who was resting in a man-sized hole in the snow. After that, since Hedy complained about carrying him such a long way, Bingbang loaded her on his own back and started on the long journey home.

That took all of three pages. To fill a whole issue with such a saga, Wolverton would have had to exhaust entire dictionaries for alliterative puns. But, no doubt he could do it. Bingbang and Hedy livened up the back pages of *Black Diamond* in issues #16, 17, and 20–28 (November 1949–November 1951) and were probably worth the whole 10 cents for the comic.

Black Diamond himself continued with scripts a notch or two above the then-current comic Westerns, and Overgard's art improved. One story featured a bandito with a rifle concealed in his guitar, a gimmick the movies didn't pick up on till Roy Orbison's *The Fastest Guitar Alive* in 1967. In the same tale, both Black

Diamond and his foe were struck down, leaving Reliapon and the villain's mount to fight a death duel. The likes of Cochise and Billy the Kid filtered through the stories. The Diamond and Bumper took on every Western cliché there was and did 'em right.

Overgard scripted at least some of the stories he drew, finishing up with issue #23 (February 1951). After that, he was spelled quite ably by Al Luster and Dick Rockwell. Carl Wessler was among his scripters, and Pete Morisi and Bob Globerman joined the ranks of his artists later on. But time and, probably, rising production costs were taking their toll. *Black Diamond Western* started as a monthly 52-page comic. With issue #29 (December 1951), it shrank to 36 pages. By #36 (February–March 1953), it became a bimonthly. The stories were still good.

Like Crimebuster and the Little Wise Guys, Black Diamond held on all the way to 1956. In the third story of issue #60 (February–March 1956), a bully named Big Bill Laramee challenged him, saying, "It'll be Black Diamond's last fight!" Though Laramee lost the battle, the saying was prophetic: Black Diamond and Bumper had one last adventure, and then faded away. So did Lev Gleason's comics line. The Diamond made a blink-and-you'll-miss-it cameo in *Femforce* #7 (May 1987). As far as we know, that's the last anyone's seen of him.

Prize Comics, which had been around since 1939, took their time about getting into the Western saddle. But when they did, converting their flagship title *Prize Comics* into *Prize Comics Western* with issue #69 (May–June 1948), they showed just about everybody how to do it.

The star strip of the early issues was *Dusty Ballew*, a competent oater drawn well by Al Carreno of Captain Marvel, Jr., fame. He lassoed a gun-toting outlaw by the foot on the cover, remarking, "I've roped lots of steers, but this is the first time I ever caught a coyote!" The first page showed Ballew and his sidekick, Gumption Jones, knuckle-dusting a

Dusty Ballew ropes a ranny on the first cover of *Prize Comics Western*. © 1948 Feature Publications, Inc.

bunch of toughs in a bar in Tombstone, Arizona, in the early 1880s. Dusty wasn't a marshal, but he was a free-roving do-gooder. He and Gumption soon met up with a bunch of nesters who had been driven from their land by a bad guy who wanted it to sell to the railroad when they came through. Within 13 pages, Dusty and Gumption, the latter of whom would reminisce about an historic incident or yell "Remember the Alamo!" at the drop of a hat—or maybe without even that—had beaten Blackie Powers fair and square, and forced him out of town. Dusty rode through two more sagas in that issue. Irving Werstein wrote his stories and what wasn't drawn by Carreno was probably done by George Gregg or Dick Ayers. Joe Simon and Jack Kirby stepped in for the cover of issue #75 (May–June 1949). Dusty lasted through issue #89 (September–October 1951).

The Lazo Kid shared space with him in issue #69, introduced as "that singing, guitar playing Mexican cowboy" who stood atop a boulder in the first panel and lassoed two crooks, pulling them over a cactus patch, while the gun in his other hand emitted smoke. In his debut story, he foiled some murderous rustlers and saved a family of sheepherders while strumming tunes almost all the way through. The sheepman's son, Pedro Montez, ended up being Lazo's sidekick. George Gregg, Bill Elder, John Severin, and Mort Meskin were among his artists. The colorful caballero crusaded through the last issue, #119 (November–December 1956), with a sole AC reprint in *Best of the West* #26 (2002).

Also in that first *Prize Comics Western* issue, *Rod Roper* raised a ruckus, as the not-entirely-serious creation of Dick Briefer of *Frankenstein* fame. Rod was another generic cowboy with another generic old-coot pardner, Hominy Fife, but the semi-humorous way Briefer handled the art and scripting made it a welcome comic relief. He was a one-shot character. So was *Gadge Anderson*, who took his place in the next issue (#70, July–August 1948). So were *Rocky Dawn and Windy Smith*, who appeared in the same issue.

Prize Comics Western finally plugged the hole in their early lineup with *the Black Bull*, birthed by Briefer, in issue #71 (September–October 1948). The Black Bull, another Western vigilante, was dressed all in black with a head mask that sported two horns. He fought outlaws when he wasn't being Dale Darcy, the supposedly dudelike ne'er-do-well son of cattle baron Cornelius Darcy. (He even called his dad "pater." In the old West, that'd practically be a hanging offense.) The tale also introduced rival cattleman Abner Sprague and his pretty daughter Libby, who soon became Dale's sweetums. A villain stirred up a range war between Darcy and Sprague, but Dale donned the duds of the Black Bull, took down the bad guy with some gunplay and fistic massage, and finally brought the fracas to an end. Then, like Clark Kent or Zorro's Don Diego, the Bull went back to his wimpish secret identity until duty called again. Soon enough, Egbert, the family's British butler, learned the Bull's secret and played Alfred to his Batman. Libby was replaced by or renamed Ellen Martin. Whatever the case, she didn't appear again after that. The succeeding stories weren't as fun as Briefer's, but they were still entertaining.

Briefer did a mighty fun job on the first tale, but he was immediately supplanted by other hands. Considering those hands belonged to Severin, Gregg, Elder, Harvey Kurtzman, Mort Meskin, and Marvin Stein, it worked out pretty well. Briefer bounced back for "The Black Bull Bulldogs a Bandit" in issue #77 (September–October 1949), in which, by golly, a real live bulldog helped the Bull blitz a baddie. The horn-headed hero righted wrongs until issue #85 (January–February 1951). Ages later, the inevitable AC reprints occurred, in *Best of the West* #18, 60, and 67 (2001–2008).

Issue #75 offered up *Prize Western*'s first photo cover, featuring Randolph Scott. The lead story was a 14-page adaptation of Scott's movie *Canadian Pacific,* drawn by Mart Bailey. Movie adaptations always seemed to work for kid readers in that day (if you missed a movie, that was *it*—you might be lucky enough to catch it on TV in years to come), so the insert wasn't surprising. The next issue did an interpretation of *Streets of Laredo* with William Holden, also by Bailey. The book was lessening its dependence on Dusty Ballew, which was probably a smart move. A multi-featured book had more of a chance of having something for everybody. The other features were coming up in quality, too. The movie adaptations continued for a while. So did generic Western stories, all of them well done by the likes of Elder and Severin.

The Preacher took the pulpit with issue #82 (July–August 1950). He was one Lance Brent, a former owlhoot who had three slugs pumped into his belly one day. He was found and nursed back to health by an Indian tribe. After that, he decided to turn his back on crime and told his old boss, Clay Durkin, that he was going straight. Durkin scornfully called him "Preacher," and a bar fight ensured. Brent was aided in the fracas by a Gabby Hayes figure called Cyclone Sims, who soon became—you guessed it—his sidekick. After that, Brent specialized in speaking out—or "preaching"—against Durkin, and, after saving a wounded Indian youth, closed in battle with the badmen's boss and brought him down. Then, with a grateful town at his back, the Preacher and Cyclone moved on. They kept moving through issue #90 (November–December 1951). Mart Bailey did the art.

Finally, in issue #85 (January–February 1951), *Prize Comics Western* presented the feature that would be the lead till the end, and a great one it was indeed. The cover showed us a fort being stormed by Shoshone Indians, and U.S. Army soldiers trying to hold them off. In the main stage, an Army captain argued with a huge, bare-chested, headdress-wearing Indian who had a bow and arrow in his hands. The captain argued it was suicide for him to try and break through the line of attackers to get help. The brave said he had to try, or the Shoshones would annihilate them.

And thus, *Prize* introduced *American Eagle.*

John Severin and Bill Elder of the EC bullpen provided the art, and what art it was. The first page showed us the Eagle, in full war-whoop as he raised his tomahawk toward us. Though he was a warrior, he was friends to both Indians and whites, and neither one was shown as total bad guys. The opening caption set the scene at "Wyoming territory around 1860." American Eagle's tribe, the Crows, was listed as friend to both red and white men, conveniently, and living around Yellowstone. The text also acknowledged that Indians were not a united people, but composed of various usually warring tribes. But the Eagle was a big enough man to stand for the right among all.

And, unlike Straight Arrow, the Apache Kid, and a few others, he wasn't a white man posing as an Indian. The American Eagle was the real deal.

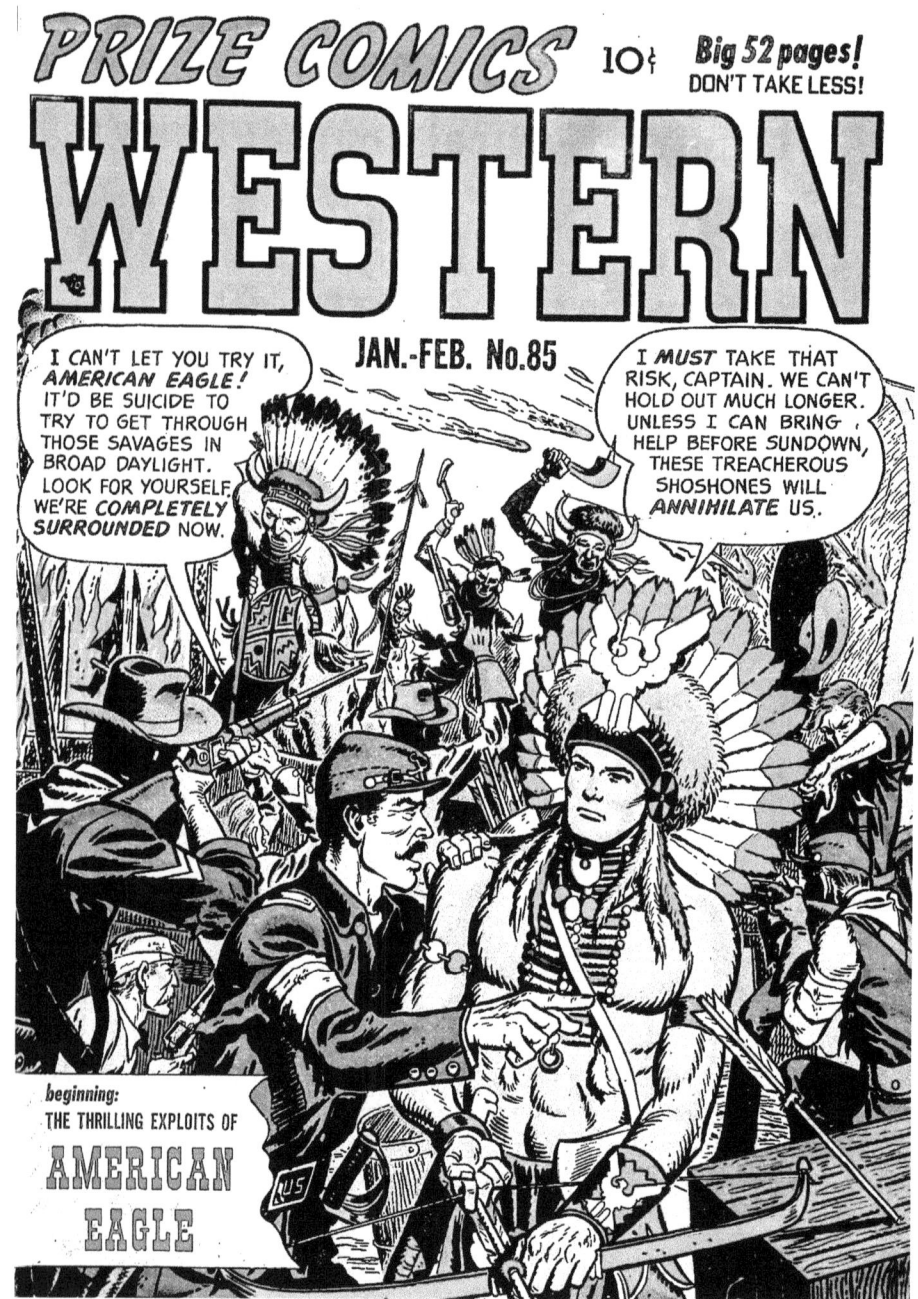

The start of one of the greatest Western heroes in comics: the American Eagle. © 1951 Feature Publications, Inc.

Anyway, here's how the story went: on their way back from an arrowhead-material-finding expedition, the Eagle and his comrades discovered that a village of Crows had been massacred by the Shoshone. Learning the truth from a dying man's last words, the Eagle headed out to warn his own tribe. On the way, he crossed paths with some white men besieged by the bad guys. With a "Hoka hey!" the Eagle set into his foes, downing many with his arrows and others with his tomahawk. But in the end, he got mugged from behind and was left for dead.

When the Indian hero awoke, he saw a scout's rifle pointed at his face. The Shoshone had done their killing with Crow weapons, and the Eagle found himself framed and a prisoner. After he was taken to the U.S. Cavalry fort, he was told, not kindly, that the Crows would be blamed for the attack and the Eagle himself would be forced to ride in the forefront when the soldiers attacked. His protests did about as much good as any Indian's protest did.

However, when the good and semi-good guys were trapped by the Shoshones, another Gabby Hayes figure turned up, one Kansas Hawk, an old scout. He gave us as much of an origin story as American Eagle ever had: "I was with Cap'n Hurry-Up Black when the lad was born! His pappy was so thankful for our help in driving off a band of Sioux that attacked him at that time, that he named the lad *American Eagle* after the *emblem of the United States Cavalry!* The lad's a powerful good friend of ours!"

With that, the Cavalry's captain changed his mind. He allowed the Eagle to sneak past the attacking Shoshone, whereupon he single-handedly overpowered a trio of enemies who had captured the scout who had captured *him*, met a war party of Crow led by his dad, and joined them in raining death and destruction onto the Shoshone. In the end, the Cavalry captain and the scout owned up to their mistakes, apologized to the Eagle, and allowed he was a good guy. "The red man and the white man must work side by side!" proclaimed the Eagle. "Together we can build a mighty nation ... a prosperous nation ... one that will provide generously for all men ... red and white alike!"

We're still working on it, Eagle.

The story and dialogue, by persons unknown, was a cut above the average. But what really made it a standout was John Severin's action-packed and realistic art. Severin was always best at Westerns and war, and he never did a Western that was better than *American Eagle*.

Bill Elder did inking, and possibly more. Both of them, and others like Jerry DeFuccio and Colin Dawkins (who wrote it) and Al Williamson (who later drew it), had worked or would work for EC Comics, most notably in *Mad, Two-Fisted Tales*, and *Frontline Combat*. Others who continued the feature through 1956 included Ted Galindo, Joe Gevanter, Rocco Mastroserio, and Marvin Stein. Altogether, it was one of Prize's greatest. Considering that output included Briefer's *Frankenstein* and Simon and Kirby's *Black Magic* and pioneering romance stories, that was saying a lot.

Latter-day America has often had a problem with its history of Native Americans. At the time of conflict, "the red man" was seen as a threat that had to be mastered. Since then, often out of guilt, the Indian has been romanticized. By the Fifties, he was often depicted as a noble warrior, willing to cooperate with the white man. *American Eagle* followed this pattern.

Whitey didn't always come out heroically in these stories. In the second Eagle tale, an ignorant and authoritarian cavalry commander (one of *those* again) refused to believe Indians would bring one of their tribe to justice, disregarded a treaty, and shot an innocent. War ensued. The officer was killed, the tribe moved against the whites, and only trickery on the Eagle's part stopped the bloodshed.

The American Eagle's position as peacemaker between Indians and whites almost always put him on the spot. The whites accused him of crimes he didn't commit. Other Indians considered him a traitor. Only his wits and his strong right arm—and, of course, his tomahawk and arrows—saved his life, issue after issue. Buck Dolan, the young scout from his first story, was often his only ally. White men saw the light time and again, but only at the end of the story, and only after many of Severin's exquisite battle scenes. And there were problems with greedy, power-hungry tribesmen as well. The Eagle didn't have much job security.

But, somehow, he always prevailed.

Laughing Dog, a big, fat, lantern-jawed Sioux warrior, soon became American Eagle's ally and comic relief, starting with issue #93 (May–June 1952). The Indian avenger continued his battle against bad men both red and white, and finally ended it in issue #119 (November–December 1956), with a story and a cover that had nothing to do with each other.

For the Eagle, that was it. He got the usual reprint treatment from AC Comics, in seven issues of *Best of the West* from #13 to 43 (2000–2004) and once in *The Al Williamson Reader* (2008), but as far as most fans today know, he might as well have been the Vanishing American. *Prize Comics Western* died with him. A few years later, so did *Prize*.

Charlton Comics, which picked up a double handful of titles from publishers who went under in the Forties and Fifties, had a few Westerns of their own. Since they were a notoriously cheap outfit, the quality varied, but hey—if you needed work and you were an artist or writer, you could usually find it at Charlton. *Cowboy Western* was their first sagebrush-saga offering, and it started with #17 and ran to #39 (July 1948–July–August 1952).

Cowboy Western mostly offered fictionalized versions of real Western historical figures, and led off with *Jesse James*, with interesting art by Tex Blaisdell. The first story portrayed him as the victim of a frameup for a bank robbery he probably didn't pull. Jesse, just out of a sickbed, shot a couple of bounty hunters and rode off into outlaw status. His tales were featured in *Cowboy Western* #17–25, 31, 32, 34, and 38 (July 1948–April–May 1952), *Space Western* #40 (October 1952—don't ask us about that one!), the later *Cowboy Western* #50–58 (July–August 1954–January 1956), *Six-Gun Heroes* #47 and 48 (July–September 1958), *Outlaws of the West* #58 (April–May 1966), and a reprint in *Gunfighters* #55 (September 1979). So much for that.

Annie Oakley, in a different version than Marvel's, debuted right after him with art by Joe Orlando. In this series, she was an attractive brunette gal who could sharpshoot with the best of them. Her daddy was killed by outlaws and she swore to avenge him. Buffalo Bill Cody showed up in town, saw her shoot a cigarette out of his mouth, and decided to hire her on the spot for his Wild West show. Annie declined on the grounds she was 17 years old and had to get Unger, the man who killed her pa. While looking at herself in the mirror on a hill one day, she saw Unger behind her, aimed while looking in the mirror, and wasted him. Then she told the town sheriff to write Buffalo Bill and tell him she could join his show immediately.

Annie's series ran in *Cowboy Western* #17–24, 31–34, 38, 39, 51–65 (July 1948–November 1957), and *Six-Gun Heroes* #46–61, 63–83 (May 1958–March-April 1965), with a batch of reprints in *Gunfighters* #53–58 and 70–74 (June 1979–September 1982).

Texas Trail, which was the actual name of the character, came next. Since I can't find anything good to say about this strip, I'll just note he appeared in *Cowboy Western* #17 (July 1948) and leave it at that.

Legends of Paul Bunyan came after that. It was a fun little series that featured an old-timer telling a kid about Paul Bunyan's legendary exploits, with art by Clinton Harmon. Paul was depicted as a white-haired, white-bearded fellow with his big ox, Babe, and a friend named Billy Pilgrim. We have no information as to whether or not Kurt Vonnegut ever read this comic. The strip ran in *Cowboy Western* #17–39 (July 1948–July-August 1952).

Wild Bill Hickok, the next offering, was a crude but competent strip by William Allison depicting Bill's battle with the McCanles brothers. He initially ran in *Cowboy Western* #17–33 (July 1948–June-July 1951). Then he appeared in the second series of *Cowboy Western* #50–67 (July-August 1954–March 1958), acquiring his sidekick Jingles from the then-current TV show in issue #62, and was in *Lash LaRue Western* #62 and 77 (December 1956–March 1960), *Six-Gun Heroes* #40–43, 46–56, 58, 60, 63, and 64 (February 1957–August 1961), *Wild Bill Hickok and Jingles* #68–75 (August 1958–December 1959), *Texas Rangers in Action* #20 and 22 (February-June 1960), *Cheyenne Kid* #23 (July 1960), and *Masked Raider* #27 and 28 (December 1960–February 1961). His reprints ran in *Gunfighters* #53–78 (June 1979–April 1983) and *Billy the Kid* #132 (November 1979).

A tale of the Texas Rangers finished off *Cowboy Western* #17. Issue #19 (November 1948) gave us "The Adventures of *Wyatt Earp*, Fighting Marshal." The feature was drawn by Mario DeMarco and hopefully he lived it down. Thankfully, it was a one-shot. Charlton did do a *Wyatt Earp* comic in the Fifties and we'll cover that in a future volume, by which time we may have recovered from this story.

Well, let's see... issue #21 (March 1949) gave us *The Vigilantes*, which somehow managed to ooze into issues #23, 24, and 26 (July 1949–February 1950). There was also a solo tale of *Buffalo Bill* in #21. Issue #22 (May 1949) gave us *Buck Evins*, a hero who was drawn to look like Roy Rogers, and we gave it back. Issue #24 (September 1949) had a photo-cover of Joel McCrea and a short adaptation of his movie *Four Faces West*. Issue #25 (December 1949) had another photo-cover and another movie adaptation (*Northwest Stampede*). That covers the book up to 1950, and we beat a hasty retreat.

Tim McCoy was another Charlton offering (#16–21, October 1948–August 1949). The real McCoy was a movie cowboy who starred in films from 1925 to 1965, and Charlton signed him up for his own comic. Somehow, one feels sympathy for him. The comic was up to the usual early Charlton standards and that, of course, is what you could expect. The book adapted a batch of Monogram and Republic pictures, and was probably turned into landfill afterward.

Thankfully, that's all we have to cover from Charlton. In later years, they improved. There was nowhere to go but up.

St. John Comics got into the act with *The Texan* #1 (August 1948). The comic didn't originally house a character called the Texan, but it did offer up some reprints from Chesler comics and a couple of original features, *Buckskin Belle* and *Mustang Jack*.

Buckskin Belle Landers was the owner of the Circle "S" Ranch and, like all such ranchers, was dealing with rustlers in her own inimitable way, shooting them with a rifle beside her aged right-hand man, Cactus. All of her crewmen absconded rather than face more gunplay, but Belle's kid brother Billy pitched in and angled his way into wearing a gun. Together, the three of them managed to ward off the desperadoes. Artist Tex Blaisdell seemed as much interested in doing glamour portraits of Belle as he was in the action. Others who handled her included Matt Baker. She ran through issues #1–4 (August 1948–May 1949) and had all four stories reprinted in *The Hawk* #9–12 (November 1954–May 1955).

Then came Mustang Jack Clarke. He was drawn initially by Ken Battefield and was a down-on-his-luck cowboy who had to hock his saddle when the cash ran low. In the first story, he was framed for murder by stagecoach robbers. Luckily he had a pretty girlfriend, Linda Hale, who helped him prove his innocence and bring in the real culprits. He also got his saddle back and, thankfully, Linda's dad had a place for a new wrangler. Mustang Jack rode on through *The Texan* #1–3 and 5 (August 1948–August 1949) and *Fightin' Texan* #17 (December 1952). Walter Johnson, Howard Larsen, and Rudy Palais took their turns on the art.

Matt Baker's Buckskin Belle introduces herself—with a gun. © 1949 St. John Publishing Co.

The Texan, aka Roaring Jory Braden, turned up fashionably late in issue #2 (October 1948). He got the cover shot, drawn by Bob Lubbers, who also did the story inside. The cover showed Jory riding in and whirling a lasso intended for a dance hall gal who was showing a lot of stocking and holding a gun. An older guy was lurching away from a gambling table, with cards and chips going everywhere. It had nothing to do with the story, but it gave Lubbers, a Fiction House alumnus, a chance to draw a girl.

Roaring Jory, who was a Texas Ranger in a black hat and shirt, had a brown horse named Fury and a Hispanic partner named Lopez. They came too late to save an assayer from phony Indians (that trope again), but brought some of the bad guys in. It developed that Bart Hodges, the local gold claim registrar, was behind the assayer's killing, duped the victim's daughter into believing him, and framed Jory for the killing. Lopez managed to save our hero from a hangman's noose with a thrown knife. As it was, Hodges was trying to convince all claim holders that their claim was a phony, which he did, and bought up their claims himself. But the two-fisted Texan walloped him smartly, made him confess and give up the claims to the girl, and saw him fall to his death while escaping. Altogether, it wasn't a bad little intro.

The Texan skipped the next issue, though he made the cover. When he came back in #4 (May 1949), Howard Larsen was the artist, Lopez was more Zorro than Pancho, and the story was improved. But after Larsen, Lopez was re-stereotyped, though still heroic. Be that as it may, the Texan continued through issue #9 (August 1950), drawn well by Matt Baker. He picked up again in #11 (December 1950), then sat it out for the rest of the run. When the book was renamed *The Fightin' Texan* for issues #16 and 17 (September–December 1952), he at least showed up for reprints. All in all, the Texan was an absentee landlord in his own book. Outside of more reprints, that was the last we saw of him.

An inset panel on the cover of *The Texan* #6 (November 1949) showed us an Indian chief in full headdress, with the legend, "WAKANDA, custodian of the Mystic White Bear Claws!" Actually, the bear claws weren't the *only* things white in this strip.

Fade in on a bunch of attacking Indians (hey, Indians were either attacked or attacking in these strips—probably not enough story value in peaceful life) who were bent on warring with the Sioux. But they pulled up short at the sight of a half-naked, Indianly dressed, heroically posed man. "What dread manner or shape is possessed by this bizarre creature known as Wakanda? He is … *a white man!*"

Yep, *that* trope again. Comic book Indians spent more of their time raising whites than they did their own kids.

Standing up to the warriors, Wakanda said, "Did you think you could scheme to destroy your brothers without my knowing?" As proof, Wakanda held up a squirrel in his hand. The squirrel said, in squirrelish, "Oh yes, great one, I heard it all!" No judge could overrule such a testimony. Nonetheless, the bounders were about to attack him. It was probably to get our minds off wondering where the squirrel came up with a Berlitz course in humanish.

Wakanda grabbed one of the seven mystic claws he had around his neck and said, "I'll need the … claw of strength!" Thus empowered, he lifted two horses and their riders from the ground, one pair in each hand. A couple of braves shot arrows at him. He took hold of the claw of speed, jumped over the shafts, and plowed his foes down with his fists. Then Wakanda tied up the whole war party and asked them why they were on the warpath.

It turned out that they were in dispute over water rights with the Sioux. To sort things out, Wakanda twisted his central claw, and as all the tribesmen gasped in awe and knelt, he summoned ... *the Great Spirit!*

Manitou, somewhat displeased at being interrupted in his thoughts, towered over everybody (Wakanda was about as big as his hand) and asked what was going on. Wakanda explained that the Blackfeet and Sioux were having a water problem. The Great Spirit said, "The waters of the lake must be divided ... *cut in half!* And ... now ... I ... go...." He went. That left the mortals the problem of figuring out what that meant.

Wakanda explained it all: just as the waters could not be divided, neither could the blood ties of the two tribes. A message had to be sent to the Sioux, and the Indian / white man / superhero used the claw of birds and beasts to summon a great stag for him to ride. On the way, Wakanda got on his claw-radio, contacted the animals of the forest, and had them herd the stunned Sioux tribe toward the Blackfeet for a powwow. The two chieftains shook hands and vowed peace. Wakanda proclaimed, "No tribe can boast a particular guiding spirit. There is only ... *the Great Spirit!*"

Who was Wakanda? How did he get adopted by the Indians? How did he get the necklace of the White Bear Claws? No answers. This was his only appearance. It would be anything but Wakanda forever.

There was a five-month gap between that issue and the next (April 1950), so we'll save the rest of *The Texan*'s features for another day.

We now proceed to Novelty Comics, whose first comic, *Target Comics* V. 1 #1 (February 1940) had a Western hero on the cover: *Bull's-Eye Bill*. And it was drawn by Bill Everett.

Everett, who gave Marvel the Sub-Mariner, Centaur Amazing-Man, and *Reg'lar Fellers* Hydroman, set his sights on dry land this time. "Bull's-Eye" Bill Target showed up on the first page of his first story getting onto or off of his

Bill Everett's Bull's-Eye Bill leads off the first issue of *Target Comics*. © 1940 Novelty Press, Inc.

white horse and a caption informed us this was "Wenton, Arizona ... one of the last of the old frontier outposts." Bill was "talented in the gifts of gunslinging, hard-riding, and cowpunching," and he'd need them all in the episode that followed.

In quick order we were introduced to Bill; his stereotypical Chinese cook, Quing; his foreman, Steve Casey; Sheriff Bob; and a woman named Dee Parsons. The first episode went something like this: Steve rode up and needed hiding, since he'd shot a guy (and claimed the other guy shot first—right!). Bill hid him, got braced by the Sheriff, and was arrested as an accomplice. Dee rode up and told everyone that Travis Trent's gang had attacked and burned the Peters ranch and barn, shot Mr. Peters, killed his two sons, and left Mrs. Peters crying. The Sheriff un-arrested Bill so he could help against the bad guys.

As soon as they left, Travis and his men approached Bill's ranch, and, most importantly, approached Dee. When they did, Quing approached Travis with a pot of hot coffee and scalded his face. Dee escaped, mounted her horse, and was trailed by Flint, Travis's fellow thug, trading shots with her. She led him right into the arms of the Sheriff's posse. All concerned put daylight through Flint.

Dee, still on horseback, let Bill know that Trent was held prisoner by Quing back at the ranch, and the guy that Steve had shot survived and wasn't going to press charges. They overlooked such things in the West. Bill rode out, met Steve, and joined with him in opposing Trent, who had escaped from Quing. Bill roped his foe on horseback and Steve bashed Trent a good one. "It's high time someone hogtied you for a spell!" Bill remarked, and that was the end of the story. It took eight pages. After that, everyone caught their breath.

In the next issue, Trent escaped from Bill and Steve, a Mexican bandit approached Dee, Bill approached the bandit with a cry of "Why, you dirty greaser!" and shot him, and had another running fight with Trent's bunch. By issue #3 (April 1940), Dee's little sister, Dawn, sent Bill a letter saying she'd been kidnapped by a bunch of ruffians, and Bill and the Sheriff got into a battle with a bunch of plug-uglies who'd just ridden into town. Actually, Dawn, who was hiding out with Happy, a stereotypical black cook from her dad's ranch, had cooked the entire ruse up to horn in on Bill and get him to pay some attention to her. He did, chasing an escaping bad guy to her hiding place, but she made amends in part by lassoing the bad guy. Dawn admitted her guilt, saying, "Yuh don't think th' sheriff will punish me too bad, do yuh?" We'd have to wait till the next issue to see.

The next Bull's-Eye Bill tale opened with a big cowhand fighting and knocking out first Steve, then Bill. In the meantime, a huge black-bearded guy approached and grabbed Dawn, who looked no older than 11 in this story. Quing saved the day by shooting the bearded one to death with a rifle. The cowhand escaped and lit out for the tall timber, but that didn't stop Dawn from saying, "But wasn't he wunnerful?" That took three pages. In the next five, we found out the cowhand was one Ted Cameron, who was out for revenge against Parsons, father of Dee and Dawn. The elder Parsons had killed Ted's dad years ago for stealing cash from him, so Ted concocted a plan to steal Parsons's will and forge his name onto it as the recipient. Quing got shot again. This one moved so fast, as usual, that the soles of Bill's boots must have burned off from friction.

With that issue, Bill Everett departed, busy with putting the Sub-Mariner through his paces. We never found out what happened to Cameron. But, since Dee Parsons continued in the strip and didn't seem too discomfited, odds are Bill gave him his comeuppance behind the scenes. The reins were taken up by writer Doug Allen and artist L. Kennerly. They kept the saga going well, if much more simply. Elton Fax, Bernie Krigstein, and Joe Certa also lent their talents to the feature. It went on.

Bull's-Eye Bill made it through *Target Comics* V. 9 #10 (December 1948). He also showed up in *Dick Cole* #2 and 6–8 (February–March 1949–February–March 1950) and got reprints in *White Rider* #5 and 6 (1958), *Indian Warriors* (1958), and *Dick Cole* #7 (1958), the latter three from Accepted Publications. Bill had himself a respectable ride at the *Target* ranch.

In Novelty's *Blue Bolt* V. 1 #1–11 (June 1940–April 1941), Jack A. Warren contributed the funny Western *Pony Tracks*. We've already covered *Bolt*'s other Western, *White Rider and Super Horse*, in our previous volume. Novelty was a relatively smaller publisher, and that was the extent of their cowboy stuff.

On to Hillman Comics. The publishers of *Airboy* started out with a short-lived title, *Miracle Comics*. In the last two issues of its four-issue run (#3 and 4, April 1940–March 1941), they offered up *Bill Colt, the Ghost Rider*. Despite the name, he had nothing in common with the white-clad characters from Magazine Enterprises and Marvel, or the skull-head cycle rider of the '70s. He had an "uncanny ability for turning up when trouble brews," and that was the only uncanny thing about him.

In 1948, when comics in general seemed to agree it was time for Westerns, Hillman delivered two volleys: *Western Fighters* and *Dead-Eye Western Comics*. They had no continuing characters, but they did feature some fine stories and art. *Western Fighters* lasted 43 issues (April–May 1948–March–April 1953), *Dead-Eye Western* 25 issues (November–December 1948–April–May 1953).

Street & Smith, the publisher of *The Shadow* and *Doc Savage*, really knew what to do with pulps, but they seemed to have a hard time figuring out what to do with comic books. Anyway, their first Western hero was *Captain Death*, who made three appearances in three different titles. The first one was in *Doc Savage Comics* V. 1 #1 (1940). He was Steve Kenny, a Texas cowboy. The first caption explained, "So many of his adventures have wound up with the individual he goes after dying, that he became known by this gruesome name." The first panel showed Death riding along on his horse, with the shadow of a skull and crossbones on the grass behind him. At least we *think* it was a shadow. Its closeness to the horse's behind made us think it might be something else.

Anyhow, Steve's first adventure saw him tangling with a Mexican rebel known as "L'Liberator," and bringing him in. As he rode away, we saw a white skull and crossbones on the back of his vest. Better there than on the ground. Captain Death and his horse, Charon, also appeared in *Shadow Comics* V. 1 #9 (March 1941) and *Super-Magician Comics* V. 2 #2 (June 1943) and, in comics, nowhere else.

Sheriff Pete Rice, by Jack Farr, showed up in the next feature of *Doc Savage Comics* #1, all five pages of it. *Billy the Kid* brought up the back of the book and was presented as a hero. The third issue (February 1941) featured a generic Western story, and that was it.

Sonny Tabor, a fairly well-done strip despite a hero whose name probably wouldn't strike fear into the heart of a five-year-old kid, featured a cowboy hero in modern Arizona who was supposedly an outlaw. In reality, he was an undercover agent for the governor. (In reality, of course, he didn't exist, but let's not belabor the point.) He had a faithful Chinese sidekick, Sing Lo, who at least once saved him from the gallows. With a price on his head in six states, Sonny nonetheless prevailed and brought in real crooks on the sly. He was written by someone named Semeroff and drawn by Pete Riss, and did his stint in *Bill Barnes, America's Air Ace Comics* #3–6 (June 1941–April 1942).

Shadow Comics V. 7 #2–4 and 6 (May–September 1947) offered *Parson Pete*, "who rode the trails with a Bible on one hip and a .45 on the other," and we hope he didn't confuse which one he reached for when he confronted a baddie. In his first tale, he got justice for a boy whose father had been frightened into a heart attack by a bartender and a tough guy playing a joke. The Parson slapped the bad guy, who challenged him to a duel. The duel consisted of the Parson lighting a fuse to a powder keg and seeing which of them ran for cover first. The bad guy fled first. Grinning, the Parson explained to the kid that there was no powder in the keg. He rode on for a total of four stories.

Finally, Street & Smith came up with a memorable Western, even though it only went two issues. *Buffalo Bill Picture Stories* #1 and 2 (June–July–August–September 1949) corralled some very notable artists, though a couple were in their beginning stage.

Bill himself led off the book with "The Name in the Snow," a 24-pager drawn by Doug Wildey. This was one of Doug's very first comics sagas, and he'd soon make himself known for his Western work throughout

Street & Smith didn't do many Westerns, but with Buffalo Bill, they did it right. © 2022 Street and Smith Publications, Inc.

1950s comics, his creation of *Jonny Quest*, and a masterful cowboy strip called *Rio* in the Eighties starting with Eclipse. That being said, it must also be noted that Doug's work on this story was pretty rough-hewn. The lousy lettering didn't help it much, either. Regardless, Wildey put together an engaging tale of Buffalo Bill and his pard Shaggy trying to clear a man who had been framed for murder when his supposed victim wrote his name in the snow. There was much more to it than that, but on page 24, Bill and Shaggy were victorious, the mystery was solved, and the real culprits were found. Doug did another Buffalo Bill adventure, "The Pool of Mystery," in the second issue, and the series ended.

Dick Rockwell drew the next feature in issue #1, *Cal Colt*. The title hero was a kid whose daddy had been killed by a bad 'un named Grouty in a gunfight. His mama made him promise never to hold a gun in his hand. But she didn't say anything about a whip, and Cal mastered the weapon. He got beaten up by Grouty's punk son and degraded by Grouty himself, but that stuff only goes so far. By the end of the story, Cal had faced off with Grouty fils, whipped a gun out of his hand, then whipped the punk with his fists. After that, he whipped Grouty about the face, saved a sheriff's life, and saw the bad man brought to justice. He was in the second issue, too.

Finally, we got *Don Quickshot*, a fun and funny strip written and drawn by Bob Powell, and it was really the star of the book. A tenderfoot from back east who read too many Western pulps got on a train one day, went West, showed up in a dime store cowboy outfit, and, predictably, made a fool of himself. But wait! With the help of his Sancho Panza–like sidekick, Slim (who was anything but), Don Quickshot exposed a rancher as the rustler who had secretly been pirating cattle all over the land. When he brought the desperadoes in, Don Quickshot was immediately made a deputy. He blundered and bobbled his way through a second story in the second issue, but did it with style. And, regrettably, as stated before, that was the end of *Buffalo Bill Picture Stories*.

Moving on to Holyoke, we shall note one Western feature. *Cat-Man Comics* #1–6 (May 1941–January 1942) contained *Hurricane Harrigan*. This was a very well-drawn strip by Charles M. Quinlan, concerning an American cowboy who came from a small Texas town and went to India to see if it was all Rudyard Kipling made it out to be. "Shux, looks kinda dead to me," he declared. In the next panel, a whole bunch of natives rushed by, knocked him off his feet, and stole his wallet. Harrigan leaped up, caught up with the brigands, clobbered them all with his bare fists, and got his wallet back. He was lured into another trap in which a beautiful villainess tried to have the "infidel" slain by a bunch of scimitar-wielding geeks, but with the help of an Indian kid (an *Indian* Indian kid, not an American Indian), he walloped them all and won free. Hurricane blew up a storm for the next five issues, and that's the best pun we can make at the time. Unless we call him the original turban cowboy.

Aaron A. Wyn's Ace Magazines included *Buck Steele, Robin Hood of the Range* in *Sure-Fire Comics* V. 1 #1 and 2 (June–August 1940). He was a generic cowboy hero in two generic cowboy stories, and that's all we need say of him.

But in 1948, Ace drew out *Western Adventures* #1–6 (October 1948–August–September 1949). On the cover of the first issue, a gunslinger in a white hat, red shirt, and green pants holstered one of his two six-guns into his left holster with his right hand, and used the gun in his left hand to shoot a hogleg out of the hand (and that's all we saw, just a hand) of his adversary. He was billed as *The Cross-Draw Kid*.

On the first page of his saga, we learned that "when he was only a boy, he saw his father drilled in the back by some desperate bushwhacker … and, strapping on his father's guns, he took a vow to rid the West of all killers!" It would take a while for that, hopefully long enough to get through a series. The Cross-Draw Kid's real name was Bud Steele, and he was drawn reasonably well by Max Elkan. In his first story, he was provoked by a local gangster named Patch-Eye, whom he proceeded to outfight, outshoot, and foil the plans of, freeing a town from his dominance. Along the way he rescued the pretty (but of course!) daughter of a judge. The Cross-Draw Kid carried on through every issue of *Western Adventures*.

Duke Buckland, the next feature in the issue, was another innocent-but-framed outlaw who rode the range and dealt out justice with his pal Kit McCane. Rudy Palais was the artist on this one, but he only lasted two issues. The third character in the book was *Sheriff Sal*, another long-legged, busty, sure-shootin', pistol-packin' mama who got elected sheriff of the town, in this case Red Dog. Sally Starr got the job because the town was so peaceful no man wanted the job. Sure as you're born, a gang of villains rode into town, because a place with a lady sheriff was bound to be easy pickin's. They robbed a bank. Sally proceeded to recover the money, turned a plot of her foes against them, and brought 'em all in, shooting the guns out of their hands. King Ward drew her, and Sheriff Sal showed her skills in all six issues.

O. Henry's famed *Cisco Kid* character, known to most baby boomers from the TV show featuring Duncan Renaldo (and from a hit song by the funk-rock group War in the Seventies), hit the comics first in

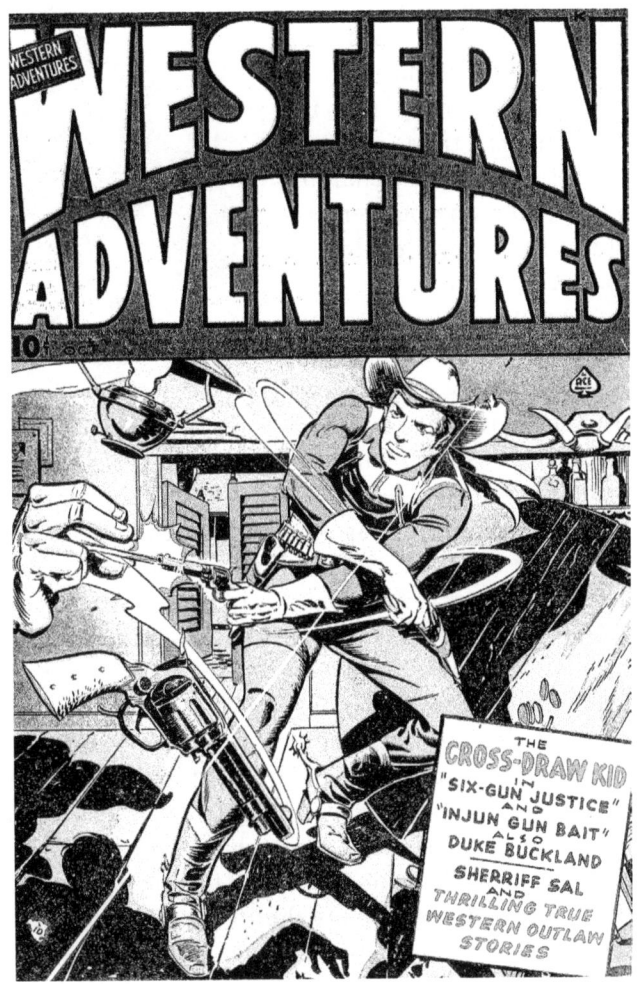

Ace's Cross-Draw Kid shows his style. © 1948 A.A. Wyn.

1944. Bernard Baily was the publisher. John Giunta did the cover, featuring Cisco as a dashing caballero, gun in hand, posed on a rearing black horse, with his partner Pancho and a mule in the background. Originally a ruthless killer in O. Henry's story "The Caballero's Way" from 1907, the Kid's personality and backstory had been totally reformed to make him a hero. He appeared in a ton of films all the way back to the silent era, portrayed by the likes of Warner Baxter, Cesar Romero, Gilbert Roland, Jimmy Smits in more modern times, and, of course, by Duncan Renaldo. Thanks to numerous reruns of the TV series, Renaldo is "our" Cisco Kid.

Anyway, Cisco was shown on the splash page serenading a bevy of beautiful senoritas with a guitar (actually, it was so small it could've been a ukulele). The

The Cisco Kid may not have been a friend of mine, but his first comic appeared in 1944. © 1944 Swappers Quarterly.

first caption read: "Drag out your spurs and your ten gallon sombrero, neighbors! Hitch yore nag to the rail! Sit down and take a load offen your feet! Take a chaw offen a plug o' terbacky! Pull yore belt in real tight, 'cause ... the Cisco Kid is comin', and he ain't got no time to mess with no small-fry, small-change! Whar thar's trouble ... thar's Cisco ... whar thar's a pretty senorita ... thar's Cisco! An' whar thar's Cisco ... thar's that ever-lovin', torilla-eatin', fat an' lazy Pancho!"

Hey, don't blame me for it. I only wrote it down!

In the one and only Cisco Kid story in the book, a sheriff and his posse were gaining on our heroes. Specifically, they were gaining on Pancho, whose hoss was much slower than Cisco's. Or, perhaps, Pancho didn't know how to get his cayuse up to speed. With Pancho's promise to fix him hot tortillas if he was saved, the Kid leapt up to a tree and lassoed the sheriff and his deputy as they came by. With them tied around their chests and swinging from a tree, Cisco had a chance to ask why he was being pursued. The sheriff said it was because he'd broken the heart of every girl in town. He and the deputy agreed not to pursue him if he'd let them down. Cisco got on his horse, rode a distance away, and shot the rope in two from said distance. Then he and Pancho rode on.

After Pancho had a chance to eat and Cisco played some guitar, both went to sleep and woke up to the sight of two beautiful women. The ladies begged Cisco to stop their grandfathers from gunfighting over a gal named Conchita. The dashing caballero made peace between the two men, but Pancho let slip the fact that his pal was the Cisco Kid. Immediately the girls made for Cisco and fawned at level 11 over him. He tried to leave, but the granddads threatened to shoot him if he did. They insisted he go to Conchita and have her make a choice between them. Conchita, who was a tad overweight, chose ... Pancho. He hit the dusty trail, and Cisco, who was being hit on by the two senoritas, was close behind. So ended the first Cisco Kid comic story. The issue also featured a text story of the Kid and Pancho, but that was it.

But in 1950, Dell offered a Cisco Kid book in *Four Color Comics* #292 (September 1950), and one was all it took. *The Cisco Kid* was off and running with issue #2 and stayed through #41 (January 1951–October 1958). The Kid was drawn straight, with Pancho as a human cartoon. The tales were more action-packed than the 1944 one-shot, with Paul S. Newman and Rod Reed as writers and Bob Jenney, Ray Bailey, Alberto Giolitti, and Al McWilliams on the art.

The TV show got canceled, but reruns kept it going through the Sixties. In March 1973, Street Enterprises, publisher of *The Comic Reader*, issued a volume of *Cisco Kid* strip reprints. Ken Pierce Books did the same in 1983. And in 2005, Moonstone Books published *The Cisco Kid: Gunfire and Brimstone* #1–3. It may take a while, but we have a hunch Cisco and Pancho will be back someday. They wouldn't want to disappoint the senoritas.

Harry "A" Chesler's comics came next, and we will ignore their comedic Jewish *Cowboy Jake* to see what else they had to offer. *Red Seal Comics* #14–18 and 20–22 (October 1945–December 1947) had *The Gay Desperado* among its features. The Desperado, not "gay" as the current term would have it, was supposed to be gay as in dashing–Zorro style, though he was an Anglo. He was Jim Collins, "hunted by the law for other men's crimes" (said other men probably being responsible for the same crimes other outlaw-heroes were supposed to have done), out to prove his innocence with the help of his kid sidekick, Patsy. (Patsy was a boy.) George Tuska drew the strip, which meant it was pretty decent. The Gay Desperado showed up years later in a few IW-Super reprints, and that was all she wrote, except for some Chesler reprints in which, for some reason, he was renamed *The Bold Buckaroo*.

Hi-Lite Comics #1 (Fall 1945) offered a middling-fair story called "Rodeo" which, fittingly, was about a rodeo. It was five pages long. That's all we need to say.

EC Comics, which began in 1945 and, in the Fifties, would produce some of the most famous (and notorious) comics ever, offered *Saddle Justice*, *Gunfighter*, and *Saddle Romances* in the late Forties. Cowboy romance comics were definitely a thing back in the day, but until (and unless) we cover romances, *Saddle Romances* will have to wait. We'll round up *Saddle Justice* first.

Continuing its numbering from *The Happy Houlihans*, *Saddle Justice* #3 (Spring 1948) was billed as "True and Terrific" on the cover. While it didn't have any continuing characters, it did have Bill Gaines as editor, taking over from his father, the late M.C. Gaines, and trying to make a go of things. It was the highest-quality Western anthology this side of Biro's *Desperado* and gave us some dang-good stories in its six issues. Henry Kiefer, Al Feldstein, Stan Asch, Graham Ingels, Johnny Craig, Ed Waldman, and Ed Schwartz drew them. Issue #8 (September–October 1949) was the last before it converted to *Saddle Romances*, which ran a whole three issues before becoming *Weird Science*. That was weird enough.

Gunfighter took over the numbering of *Fat and Slat* and started with issue #5 (Summer 1948). The book was named for its lead hero, Gunfighter. Or maybe he was named for the book. Whatever. Graham Ingels drew the strip and Gunfighter himself was a mystery man, riding the West on his horse, Ranny, which is our favorite name for a comic book horse. The first story saw him framed for murder, but, as one might expect, he showed up the real killers and delivered them unto the law. In later days, he got a Hispanic guitar-strumming pardner named Pancho Don Carlo. Fred Peters and Wally Wood also drew the trail that Gunfighter followed. It was a good enough strip for its time, and Gunny appeared through issue #14 (March–April 1950), the last one.

The Buckskin Kid followed him up in *Gunfighter* #5, with scripting by Gardner Fox and art by Johnny Craig. The story opened with an Indian massacre on a train of Conestoga wagons. The Sumners, a married couple, were killed and scalped, but Chief Red Arrow took a shine to their baby and raised it as his own. Under the name of White Raven, the kid grew to manhood among the Indians, as was the case with a bunch of other cowboy heroes. He was fleet of foot, great with a bow and arrow, and outstanding in stealing horses from other tribes. But while he was out doing the last, his tribe was massacred. Kit Carson came upon him and adopted him, teaching him how to be a mountain man and shoot like the proverbial Western ace. His given name became Johnny Raven and his nickname, as you might have guessed, was the Buckskin Kid. Whilst guiding another wagon train through Indian territory, the Kid discovered his tribe's betrayer was in the group, clobbered him, and had him taken prisoner. The Buckskin Kid rode the dusty trail through *Gunfighter*'s last issue. Henry Kiefer arted the strip.

Saddle Justice, a Western anthology strip, followed up. Then, of all things, the book ended with a tale of *Moon Girl*, EC's lone superheroine, in a fracas out West. She turned up in the next issue, too, but since she cross-pollinated into most of their titles at the time, that wasn't too unusual.

For the last couple of issues (#13–14, January–February 1950 and March–April 1950), the Six-Gun Sisters, a couple of masked fillies named Tess and Belle Parker, inherited a newspaper in the town of Gunsight and, when necessary, donned masks, hats, Western outfits, and, most importantly, guns, to mete out justice to those who threatened it. Gardner Fox wrote the strip, Harry Harrison penciled it, and Wally Wood inked it. *Six-Gun Sisters* should have gone on longer, but EC was about to pull off its New Trend transformation, and *Gunfighter* was turned into *The Haunt of Fear*. The book made more money that way, anyhow.

Magazine Enterprises, aka ME, was poised in 1948 to become one of the greatest Western comics publishers of all. The one that spearheaded their westward drive was *Tim Holt* #1 (1948), and, though based on a movie cowboy actor, it soon

The Buckskin Kid gives an enemy the whiplash. © 1948 Fables Publishing Co. © 2022 E.C. Publications

morphed into something else entirely. And in that form, it showed ME the path to follow.

Born Charles John Holt III in 1919 in Beverly Hills, Tim Holt was the son of an actor and was schooled in a military academy, where he made a habit of practicing his quick draw and affirming he would be a Western movie star someday. He made

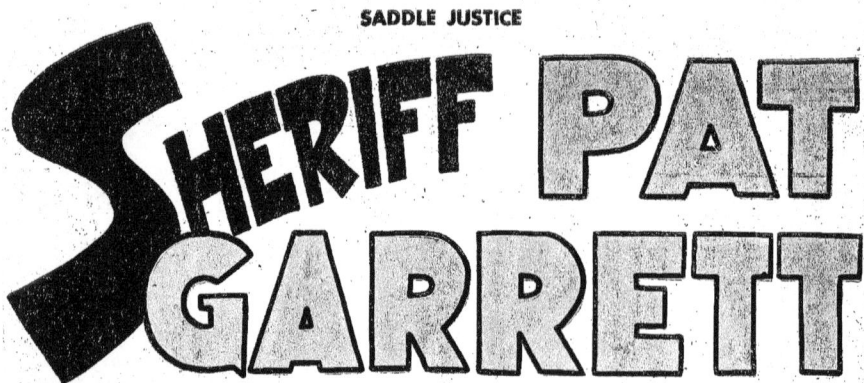

It wasn't exactly *Tales from the Crypt,* but EC did try Western titles in the pre–Trend days. © 1948 Fables Publishing Co. © 2022 E.C. Publications

his first picture in 1937 and his first Western in 1938. Though he did a ton of oaters, Holt's most famous roles were probably in Orson Welles's *The Magnificent Ambersons* (1942) and John Huston's *The Treasure of the Sierra Madre* alongside Humphrey Bogart (1948). In between, he served in the Army Air Force as a bombardier in the Pacific. In the movies, he had a sidekick named Chito Jose Gonzales Bustamante

Rafferty, played by Richard Martin. Chito carried over into the early ME comics. The movies eventually dried up for Holt, but he excelled in other occupations. His death in 1973 was from bone cancer, and he was inducted into the Western Performers Hall of Fame in 1991 and got the Golden Boot Award a year later.

In the first issue of his comic, Tim and Chito made it to the T-Bar-H Ranch in Bullet, Arizona, which he had recently bought, sight unseen. On the way down there, he solved the mystery of a cursed stagecoach, got the living hell beaten out of him by outlaws, found out he was falsely accused of wanting to cut off water to other settlers in the area, got a horse called Lightning, was almost burned to death in a flaming house, and finally punched his way to victory. The story was probably written by Gardner Fox and definitely arted by Frank Bolle, who would do just about all of the Holt stories in comics.

Fox and Bolle churned out issue after issue of Tim Holt tales, buoyed up by Fox's superior plotting ability and Bolle's distinctive art. But after a while, a change seemed necessary. Even in the late Forties, there were a lot of cowboys crowding the comic racks. (Also, Holt's movie career was starting to sag.) So, by issue #20 (November 1950), a major change was in the wind.

Enter Redmask.

A great Bolle cover depicted Tim Holt in a red Stetson, a red bandanna mask over his face, red shirt and gloves, reddish-brown pants and boots, fighting off three outlaws while hanging onto a huge church bell. The logo proclaimed, "TIM HOLT *as Red-Mask*," and that was all the info we needed. A new masked cowboy hero had been born!

In the story, Tim saved a girl who had been tied to a tree trunk and sent over surging waters. She told him she had been victimized by El Terror, a bandit king who was trying to worm out the secret location of a treasure hidden in the house of her father, Don Vincente Gomez. While

Tim Holt rings the bell for Western justice as Redmask!
© 1950 Magazine Enterprises, Inc.

guesting at Gomez's hacienda, Tim heard the story of the legendary Redmask, who obviously had stolen Zorro's playbook. He lived over 100 years before the time of the story, wearing a scarlet mask and bringing justice to the oppressed with his lightning-fast rapier and his well-aimed guns. In the room Don Vincente gave him to sleep in, Tim Holt found a chest with—surprise!—a red mask, an outfit of red, a rapier, and a gunbelt. He didn't need an anvil to fall on his head before he figured out his next move.

Hours later, El Terror and his men invaded Don Vincente's house and threatened to burn his daughter's face with a brand if he didn't fess up the treasure's location. Since he didn't know it, things looked pretty grim. And then ... WHAM! A hurled epee struck the head of one of Terror's goons.

"Look here, El Terror!" said a red-clad figure in an upper windowsill. "Ah, your eyes grow wide with fright, with amazement! Si—si, El Terror, I am *Redmask!*"

So saying, the masked hero leaped for a chandelier, swung down to a table below, double-kicked El Terror in the face, and helped Don Vincente and his daughter, Donna Mercedes, escape. Then he went back to work on the bad guys. The battle on the great bell ensued, and when it crashed down, it went through the floor and revealed the great treasure of the Don's ancestor ... who, coincidentally, was named *Don Diego* Gomez. Hmmm…

At the end of the story, Redmask came down on a falling ladder, knocked El Terror off his horse, and captured him. And in the last panel, in his room, we saw Tim Holt unmasking and preparing to stow his outfit in the chest. "Something tells me I'll be using this outfit a lot in the future! If I know this side of the Rio, there'll be plenty more work for—Redmask of the Rio Grande!"

Count on it, Holt!

From there on in, Tim appeared as Redmask at least once in every issue. On such occasions, when he rode Lightning, he put a big red mask on the horse. That, we can be assured, was enough to conceal the nag's identity. It was apparently a shot in the arm for *Tim Holt*, as the comic continued through issue #41 and then, as *Red Mask*, went on to issue #54 (September 1957). Redmask also rode into *Best of the West* #2-12 (1951–April–June 1954). ME had found a gimmick that worked.

And it did work. So well, indeed, that Redmask got some "name" villains: The Cape (#22, February–March 1951, and *Best of the West* #12, April–June 1954), a sort of anti-Zorro; Strawman (#27, December 1951–January 1952), who wore the garb and mask of a scarecrow; Lady Doom (#30, June–July 1952), who foretold men's deaths with a wheel of fortune; and Iron Mask (#32, October–November 1952), who had to be the inspiration for Kid Colt's greatest enemy 10 years later. *Tim Holt* had been converted from a simple Western to a cowboy superhero comic.

But that wasn't all. Issue #25 (August–September 1951) opened with a cover shot of Redmask defending himself against a masked blonde beauty with a gun in one hand and a knife in the other, and a bald, bare-chested oaf with a whip. *The Black Phantom* had arrived!

Though soon to become a heroine, the Black Phantom was an outlaw in her debut story. About all we got of her origin came from a later AC Comics story, which said she "fell in with a bad crowd." She was still with them when the story opened.

With a Johnny Craig cover and a Graham Ingels interior, Gunfighter makes the scene! © 1948 Fables Publishing Co. © 2022 E.C. Publications

The Phantom wore a black mask, black gloves, black boots and black pants in this story, but had a green shirt, opened darn near to the waist. In later tales, she'd sport an all-black outfit. Apparently she took fashion tips from *Airboy*'s Valkyrie.

Anyway, Black Phantom and her gang (which included the bald-headed Beast from the cover) robbed a train in the first couple of pages. Then she decided to take a break, so she rode into town, surprised her identical twin sister, Jicilla—who, by the way, was a bar singer and as hot as the Phantom herself—and switched places with her. Tim's aide Chito snuck in, hoping to pitch some woo to Jicilla, and got judo-tossed by the unmasked Phantom. Confusion ensued.

Chito was unlucky enough to try his luck again, got clobbered by the Phantom and her gang, and was fated to be thrown in the "Whirlpool Well" and drowned for seeing the unmasked lady bandit. But Tim Holt saw the crew carrying him away, deduced the blonde bad girl was Jicilla's twin sister, and went after them as Redmask. As it transpired, Redmask performed a last-desperate-chance rescue of Chito, and the Black Phantom leaped to her apparent death rather than risk capture. Probably, that's how it was supposed to end.

As you might expect, it didn't.

The Black Phantom didn't return for over two years. But when she did, in *Tim Holt* #38 (October–November 1953), she was practically welded into the series. Her next *chronological* appearance, however, was in *Red Mask* #49 (May–June 1955), where, in a flashback story that filled in some important plot points, we learned that when she apparently jumped to her death, she'd actually fallen into a deep enough stream to save her life. The Phantom tried to make the Mexican border, but ended up exhausting herself and falling into the hands of two disgruntled members of her old gang. Redmask stopped them from killing her. Then he convinced the masked maiden to give herself up and do her time, and emerge from jail as a heroine. Redmask had to nurse her back to health, until she declared she couldn't take any more of his cooking and tackled the job herself. Then she did indeed accompany him to jail, after helping him fight off some renegade Indians. "When I get out, I'm going to join you in your fight against crime! Maybe two of us will be better than one of you!"

And so she did, emerging from the hoosegow in *Tim Holt* #38. From then on, the Black Phantom appeared in most issues of the comic and continued when the book was renamed *Red Mask*. Sometimes she got her own feature, but mostly she backed up Redmask in his stories with her considerable gun skill and fighting ways. Tim Holt had become a deputy sheriff by this time, and she followed up as a deputy's deputy. She didn't know his double identity. At least, they said she didn't.

The Phantom proved so popular that she got her own one-shot title, *Black Phantom* #1 (1954). A second issue was planned—some ME comics showed its cover in ads—but it was scrapped and at least one of the stories was recycled into a *Red Mask* backup. Her last ME appearance was in *Red Mask* #54 (September 1957), which was Redmask's swan song as well.

Did things end there? Not quite!

AC Comics, which revived everything not nailed down and probably a lot that was, brought the Black Phantom out of mothballs for a spoof Western in *Bizarre Thrills* #1 (1977), with a Redmask cameo as well. Then she reappeared in a two-parter in *Sentinels of Justice* #6 (1987) and *Femforce* #8 (July 1987), both tales set in the Old West. Next came *The 3-D Zone* #9 (October 1987), which reprinted a Redmask story in which she co-starred and featured several pin-up illoes of her, all in 3-D. In *Latigo Kid Western* #1 (Summer 1988), Black Phantom, Redmask, and the Durango Kid teamed up with the titular Kid for a new adventure by Bill Black. (Another original team-up tale in *Best of the West* #6 [1999] brought her together with Redmask, the Durango Kid, and the Presto Kid, of which more later.) Things were brewing.

Next, AC came out with a three-issue *Black Phantom* mini (#1–3, 1989–1990) with reprints from ME, plus two retellings of early Black Phantom stories, adding a lot of bathing and semi-nude scenes as well. Finally, in *Femforce* #64–69, 71, and 73 (1993–1994), the Phantom went through a quasi-mystical adventure which saw her die, go to Hell, get revived, get transferred to the modern day, hook up with Darkshade, AC's ghost character, and interact with the Femforce. She's appeared in several more stories set in the present, but, as always, your mileage may vary on this one. And of course, there were tons of reprints of Redmask and Black Phantom stories in *Best of the West* and other AC Comics.

Kicking things off, the Black Phantom heads up her own comic. © 1954 Magazine Enterprises.

And that should be all to cover for *Tim Holt* and *Red Mask* comics, right?

Right?

Not exactly. Let's go back to *Tim Holt* #6 (May 1949), turn to the back, and look into a story featuring another character: *The Calico Kid*. This will build into something, believe us.

The Calico Kid was the star of a string of five-page stories in the middle of *Tim Holt*. Initially, he didn't even have a given name. He was just the owner of a trade wagon with the banner "California Calico Company" on its side, and he wore Clark Kent spectacles and was about as timid as the aforementioned alter ego. But when trouble struck, he snuck off, doffed his black outfit, and stood revealed in cowboy gear and Stetson as a powerful, lasso-throwing, straight-shooting cowboy who only went by the handle of "Stranger." As such, he shot said trouble, often literally. In his first appearance, he saved a Chinese man by the name of Sing Song (remember, folks, I didn't write these stories) from a lynch mob of prejudiced citizens. He was blamed for the murder of a marshal, but the Kid unearthed the real culprits. Sing Song became his sidekick from that day forward.

Things continued as such until issue #11 (November 1949). Evidently it was felt that the Calico Kid wasn't enough of a draw, so a small picture on the cover clued us in to a change. It depicted a cowboy, all in white, astride a white horse against a dark background. The cutline read: "Introducing ... the GHOST RIDER!"

The inspiration for the character was obviously the country song, "Riders in the Sky," later titled "Ghost Riders in the Sky," first recorded in 1948 by Stan Jones. Just about everybody covered it in 1949: Vaughn Monroe, Burl Ives, Gene Autry, Bing Crosby, Peggy Lee, the Sons of the Pioneers, and, not to be forgotten, Spike Jones. The song told of a young cowboy who saw a bunch of spectral riders in the sky, warning him to change his ways or he might end up like them, "trying to catch the Devil's herd." From that day to this, "Ghost Riders in the Sky" has been a perennial, and everybody from Lawrence Welk to metal bands have tried their hands at it sometime or another.

The first Ghost Rider tale was written by Ray Krank and illustrated by Dick Ayers. It opened with the Calico Kid and Sing Song in their wagon, being stormed by a tribe of attacking Indians. The Indians were led by a white outlaw in disguise, one Bart Lasher. They overcame the Kid and his pal, and the bloodied hero recognized their foe. He recognized the Kid, too: "And I know you, calico-peddlar! Roving marshal Rex Fury! ... But you're turning in your badge now, Fury—with your boots on!"

So saying, Lasher and his men threw Fury, née the Calico Kid, and Sing Song into the Devil's Sink, a place where a small river vanished "into the bowels of the Earth!" The Chinese man said goodbye to his friend, but Fury bade him never give up hope.

Evidently, Fury had the right idea: both of them were swept into an underground cave, with a bunch of human bones and busted-up wagons for company. They finally found their way above ground, at which point Rex Fury said, "You know, Sing Song, I've got a pretty tricky idea!" Since we'd already seen the cover and the splash panel, we had an idea of what that idea would be.

Fury eavesdropped on Lasher and found out his next target. When the renegade and his Indian soldiers descended on a widow's ranch, they were confronted by a new, fearful apparition: a glowing white rider on a glowing white horse. The hero didn't have a mask yet, and he was easily recognized by Lasher, who recoiled in fear: "It's R-R–Rex F-F-F-Fury! His g-*ghost!*"

"Bart Lasher, I want you!" yelled the wrathful rider. Lasher broke in fear, and Rex Fury gave chase. Eventually, Lasher's mount threw him, and he was impaled on a broken spoke of the Calico Kid's wagon. Obligingly, he died. A final caption promised, "The Ghost Rider will ride again! Watch for him!" You bet we would!

By the next issue (#12, December 1949), the Ghost Rider had his mask, a white handkerchief-mask over his face with holes for eyes. He was also spooking the hell out of his enemies and concealing his body with the reversible black side of his cape, making it seem as though his head was floating in mid-air. In his second adventure, the Rider stopped a lynching and terrified the real murderer into confessing his guilt, with the help of a dummy he rigged up to look like the killer's victim.

His dialogue seemed in the tone of the Shadow's: "Men call me the Ghost Rider, Manders! I came for the letter you stole from Larry Rutledge!" The resemblance had to be intentional. Dick Ayers drew all of the Rider's stories, with Gardner Fox installed as the new scripter with the second story.

The Ghost Rider quickly dropped his hanky-mask for a full-face covering and played his dead-man identity to the hilt. Losing either his body or his head to opponents' eyes when he used his black cloak, the Rider also used mirrors, voice-throwing gimmicks, and his great horse Spectre to unnerve the outlaws he faced. Even the Indians he encountered feared him as a revenant from the grave. Almost every *Tim Holt* cover let us know the Ghost Rider was inside, by word or by picture. Holt was getting competition in his own comic.

Tim Holt #17 (May 1950) came out with a fabulous and fearsome Frank Frazetta cover, featuring the Ghost Rider and Spectre interrupting three crooks from planting a red-hot branding iron on a victim's bare chest. A cover blurb read, "In this issue, 2 thrilling tales of the Ghost Rider!" Tim Holt was nowhere to be seen, except in a photo beside the title logo.

At about the same time, *Ghost Rider* #1 (1950) appeared, with an impressive cover by Dick Ayers and stories just as impressive inside. The first offering expanded on the Ghost Rider origin from *Tim Holt* #11. The story was replayed up to the time when Rex Fury pulled Sing Song from the waters of the Devil's Sink. Sing was unconscious and Rex himself was exhausted and near death. In that state between this world and the next, a *real* apparition appeared: a long-haired man in Western dress. "Rex Fury! Open your eyes!" it said.

Awakened, Rex gaped at his host. "You're Wild Bill Hickok! But you're dead! *Dead!*" If so, he hadn't been *long* dead; Bill passed on in 1876. But there he was, big as ... well, maybe not as big as *life*, but still there.

The unforgettable Frazetta rendition of the Ghost Rider! © 1950 Magazine Enterprises, Inc.

"What makes you think you're alive, Rex Fury?" said Hickok. "You are on the very borderland … where life and death walk freely. That is why I can come to you…." The ghostly gunman led Fury on to meet his brethren: Pat Garrett, Kit Carson, and Calamity Jane. "Many of the men and women who tried to make the West safe for the home-makers are dead. But banditry and outlawry still flourish! We want to help in the only way we can—by passing on our knowledge to one who can do what we cannot…."

The aforementioned gunpeople, along with Marshal Billy Tilghman of Dodge City, taught Rex Fury unerring aim, a quick draw, mastery of the rifle and the knife, and the skills of tracking, all in the next world. It probably took a good while, but we can guess that time in the ghost world and in the world of the living don't exactly coordinate. Finally, Wild Bill told his charge that he needed a horse. Reasonably, Rex asked where he could find one.

On cue, Rex caught sight of a giant silver stallion. He raced after the horse on, well, horseback, and finally caught and roped him. Then Hickok handed Rex the famed white costume, cape, and mask, and bade him farewell. "Good luck, *Ghost Rider!*" said Wild Bill.

Riding off on the great white horse he named Spectre, the Rider stopped a fight between two prospectors and then went back to the cavern to recover Sing Song. He went into a dream, woke up, and found himself garbed as Rex Fury, helping Sing Song back to life. Had it really been a dream? The two of them left the cavern and found Spectre waiting for them. That argued against it.

With an improved origin, the Ghost Rider rode again.

In the next story, Sing Song rigged up a magic lantern to project an image of the sagebrush spook anywhere he wanted. Gunnies could empty their weapons into the Rider's image and only hit a wall, or they could ride a horse right through the ghostly being without touching him. It added to the Rider's mystique, and proved Sing Song was more than a stereotypical sidekick.

The series used the trappings of the supernatural but, for the most part, eschewed ghost stuff after the origin. Frazetta contributed more top-notch covers and Fox and Ayers kept the story quality high. By *Ghost Rider* #7 (1952), a new series, "Tales of the Ghost Rider," featured the phantom paladin hosting stories of really horrific doings in the Old West. Also, an ad featured a Ghost Rider mask kids could get by mailing in a dollar. The weirdest hero in the West was proving his selling power.

The longer the Ghost Rider went on, the more horrific the trappings became. After all, horror comics were becoming the thing in the early Fifties (in the case of Charlton's *The Thing!*, quite literally), and even characters like Captain Marvel, Plastic Man, and Doll Man flirted with the occult to try and draw in readers. But a counter-reaction to crime and horror books was brewing, thanks mainly to the efforts of Dr. Fredric Wertham's crusading—and, it must be allowed, to the comics themselves, which were competing to show more gore-galore than they were able to get away with. The fact that *Ghost Rider* stories weren't really supernatural, just mummery, wasn't going to cut much ice. When the axe fell on horror comics, it took *Ghost Rider* with them—sadly.

The Ghost Rider ended with issue #14 (1954). The title character continued in *Tim Holt* through issue #41 (April–May 1954), and, after it turned into *Red Mask*, took his last bow in #50 (July–August 1955). Similarly, he appeared in *Best of the West* #2–12 (1951–April–June 1954), *Bobby Benson's B-Bar-B Riders* #13–15 (February–July–August 1952), *Great Western* #9 (April–June 1954), and *Black Phantom* #1 (1954). Undoubtedly, it was his success that spurred ME to spawn more costumed and masked cowboy heroes. With the final tale in *Red Mask* #50, in which he brought in three identical triplet outlaws, the Ghost Rider rode away.

But—you guessed it—not quite forever.

In 1958, IW-Super published *Great Western* #8 (1958 series), reprinting the Rider's origin from *Tim Holt* #11, along with the rest of that issue. For about nine years, that was his only appearance.

Then in 1967, Marvel Comics published *Ghost Rider* #1 (February 1967).

Dick Ayers, now a Marvel stalwart, was again the artist; Roy Thomas, a fan of the original character, and Gary Friedrich were the writers; and the cover shot of the Ghost Rider would make one think the ME character had—wait for it—come back from the grave. But that wasn't quite the case. The Mark II Ghost Rider, though his story was set in the Old West, was a schoolteacher from back East named Carter Slade. He got shot while trying to save settlers from phony Indians, was saved from death by an Indian shaman, and was given the costume, horse, and glowing, phosphoric dust to make himself "He who rides the Night Winds"... aka the Ghost Rider. The series was pretty good, but only lasted to issue #7 (November 1967). The new Ghost Rider continued a few years later in *Western Gunfighters* and made several more appearances over the years.

In *Marvel Spotlight* #5 (August 1972), a cycle-riding Ghost Rider was delivered up by Gary Friedrich and artist Mike Ploog. This Rider, one Johnny Blaze, was a stunt-riding daredevil who sold his soul to the Devil to save the life of his mentor (who ended up dying anyway) and became the flaming-skulled Spirit of Vengeance. This version continued for a long time and spun off a movie in 2007 starring Nic Cage as the spectral cyclist. But more relevant was the appearance of Sam Elliott, who played the Western Ghost Rider and rode a flaming steed beside his successor's burning cycle. (Fittingly, "Ghost Riders in the Sky" was played over the end credits.) The Johnny Blaze Ghost Rider was then replaced by another version, who is still apparently around.

As for the original Ghost Rider, he wasn't quite finished yet.

In the same year that Marvel's Mark III Ghost Rider debuted, AC Comics (as you might have guessed!) published *Macabre Western* #1 (1972), with reprints from the ME series. The Ghost Rider was renamed *The Haunted Horseman* to avoid legal problems. (He'd already appeared under that name in a pin-up in AC's *Paragon Presents* #2 [1970]). In the second issue, another Ayers-drawn story was reprinted with modifiers from Bill Black. The Haunter, as he was called, appeared in a passel of reprints and new stories from AC, continuing over the decades. In a few stories, Dick Ayers returned to draw him.

Guess you just can't keep a good Ghost Rider buried.

In the same year as Tim Holt's comic debut, ME hatched another Western hero in the middle of *Manhunt*, an anthology comic. *Trail Colt, U.S. Marshal* (ME overflowed with U.S. Marshals) first appeared in *Manhunt* #8 (May 1948). Fred Guardineer did a bang-up job on the cover, showing Colt smashing through a window with pistols drawn, and did a pretty fair job on the story inside. Guardineer did the next story as well. The third (*Manhunt* #10, July 1948) was done even better by Paul Parker and Dan Loprino. And the fourth (#11, August–September 1948) was drawn by—hot ziggety!—Frank Frazetta, who signed his name "Fritz." Colt faced his first "name" villain, the Rainbow Robber, therein. (He shot the guy to death.)

Trail Colt got his own comic in 1949, with Frazetta drawing the only story in the issue to feature him. (The rest were holdovers from *Manhunt*.) In *Trail Colt* #2, which looked even more like a renamed *Manhunt*, Dick Ayers drew the last original Colt story. There were two reprints in *Manhunt* #13 (1952) and *Great Western* #8 (1953). Occasionally the two Frazetta stories get reprinted, but that's about it.

The year after *Tim Holt* appeared, ME tried their luck on another Western movie hero. This one came with his own alter ego, his own costume, and his own heroic name. It was issue #1 (August–September 1949) of *Charles Starrett as the DURANGO KID*.

Once again, a little background: Charles Starrett, born in 1903, got hired to play an extra in a football film in 1924, liked the experience, and became an actor. By 1930 he started in *Fast and Loose*, a romantic comedy, and went on to other roles and other movies. In 1935, he made his first Western, *Gallant Defender*. Then he went on to make more such movies. By 1940, Starrett appeared in *The Durango Kid*, as a mysterious, black-clad, masked vigilante who worked against outlaws in the Old West. In his civilian identity, Durango was a guy named Steve. After five more years and a whole bunch more oaters, we got *The Return of the Durango Kid*. The masked maverick

The man in black is the dauntless Durango Kid. © 1949 Magazine Enterprises, Inc.

was popular enough to sustain a whole series, ending up with 1952's *The Kid from Broken Gun*. Starrett subsequently retired from filmmaking, lived quite well on his investments, and passed on in 1986.

The writer, possibly Fox or Krank, gave his secret identity Steve the last name of Brand. Eventually he was revealed as—heavens to Betsy!—another federal marshal. They created a new sidekick for him, one Muley Pike. In the first story, Durango and Muley were doing their drifting cowboy bit near a town called Gun Hammer Gulch when they stumbled upon a gang of masked owlhoots robbing a payroll from a stagecoach. The bandits fled in fear from the sight of the masked man in black. Durango switched to Steve Brand to investigate. Over the course of the story, he exposed a banker as the one who was robbing his own bank and brought him to justice. At story's end, Brand was elected sheriff. But by issue's end, Durango found a better choice for sheriff, or one who would allow him to quit the job, anyway. He and Muley rode off into the sunset.

Durango Kid #17 (June–July 1952) finally gave us his origin. During the Civil War, in which Steve Brand, his brother Pete, and Muley fought together on the Union side, Pete Brand pegged fellow soldier Tex Danbar as a spy. During a subsequent battle, Danbar shot Pete Brand—in the back. Holding his brother's body, Steve Brand swore to find Tex Danbar and kill him.

Steve and Muley searched the West for Danbar, ending up in Durango, Colorado. But Muley pointed out that if Steve did kill his foe, he'd be a hunted outlaw. In response, Steve said that he'd make a disguise, "a black mask, a black uniform. I'll find a white horse and train him.… I'll become the *Durango Kid!* I'll devote my life to fighting crime, catching owlhoots. Someday, Tex Danbar will run afoul of the law—and that's when I'll catch up to him!"

He did catch up to him, too. In a final fight, Durango said he wouldn't kill Danbar, but would bring him in for two murders—one of Pete Brand, the other more recent. Danbar, weakened from desert dehydration, drew a knife and tried to finish the hero, but stumbled and fell on his own weapon. Before Danbar died, Durango unmasked and showed his identity, not unlike the Lone Ranger unmasking before Butch Cavendish.

Muley figured that Steve could give up his double identity after that. Steve demurred. "The Durango Kid will keep on riding, as long as the people need me!" Which, for the rest of the series, they did.

The first years of *The Durango Kid* were drawn quite competently by Joe Certa. Each issue featured Durango and Muley in a new locale, with three action-packed stories per book. Somehow nobody figured out that Steve Brand and the Durango Kid were the same, even though Muley Pike assisted both of them. Still, ME figured that the series needed even more oomph, and in issue #7 (October–November 1950), a character called "the Boss," visually based, probably, on Sydney Greenstreet, developed a disintegrator ray (yes!), and Durango had to stop him. The Boss committed suicide, and Durango threw the ray gun into a quicksand bog. Hopefully, it's still there.

With *Durango Kid* #19 (October–November 1952), Joe Certa was out and Fred Guardineer was in. There was still plenty of action, with Muley Pike helming a subset of stories in which he played both the hero and the clown. In the next issue (#20, December 1952–January 1953), Steve and Muley bought a spread, the Lazy-X Ranch, and settled down to raising cattle when they weren't battling bad guys. Jenny Jasmine, owner of the ranch next door and Steve Brand's potential romantic interest, was introduced in the same issue. It didn't cut down on Durango's bad-guy busting much.

Issue #23 (June–July 1953) gave us the *Red Scorpion*, Durango's first real competition. He was an outlaw who could, the text told us, "ride like the wind, run like a deer, [and] shoot with fantastic accuracy…." The Scorpion, astride his horse, Flame, was tailor-made for an encounter with the Durango Kid. He was masked on the cover but bare-faced in the interior, and terrorized the people of Dead Man Dam, so much so that the local sheriff left town. The citizens summoned Durango, and Durango came, but couldn't catch him. Accordingly, the masked man challenged the Scorpion to a duel atop a dam, and appeared to lose when he lost his footing and fell into the waters below. But our hero survived, made it back into town, and beat the Red Scorpion in a hand-to-hand fight. However, that wouldn't do if ME wanted to bring him back for a return match, and they did. The villain escaped, plunging with his horse into the waters below the dam, and made Durango secretly hope he survived.

In issue #31 (September–October 1954), the Red Scorpion returned, in a red eye mask, hat, and outfit that might make you think he was Redmask. This time he met up with a gang of outlaws, was injured in an avalanche, and unwillingly gave up his costume to the crooks. They masqueraded as him, one at a time, and terrorized folks into giving up their cash during robberies, leaving corpses, unlike the real Scorpion. Naturally, Durango got involved, and the Red Scorpion broke free and helped him nab the bad guys. Durango let his enemy go, remarking that he detected a streak of decency in him.

But we never found out, one way or the other. With issue #41 (October–November 1955), the Durango Kid was gone. He made side ventures into *Best of the West* #1-12 (1951–April–June 1954) and was reprinted in *Great Western* #8–11 (1953–October–December 1954). As far as ME was concerned, that was it.

In 1971, Skywald reprinted various Durango Kid stories in *Wild Western Action* #1–3 (March–June 1971), *Sundance Kid* #1–3 (June–September 1971), and *The Bravados* #1 (August 1971). Then, as one might expect, AC Comics took over. They did an illo of him in *Americomics Special* #1 (August 1983) and finally brought him back with a horde of other Western characters in *Femforce* #7-8 (May–July 1987). In *Latigo Kid Western* #1 (1988), he appeared on one page with Latigo, Redmask, and the Black Phantom. Durango got his own reprint series from AC, *Durango Kid* #1–3 (1990–2000). He showed up in another original story, teamed up with Redmask, Black Phantom, and the Presto Kid in AC's *Best of the West* #6 (1999), in which tale Muley Pike returned. And, of course, AC did scads of reprints. The last of them, to our knowledge, was in *Western Treasury* #3 (2019). Will he show up again in a new story? As with all the rest, it's possible.

But there was a feature within *Durango Kid* that still makes comics fans search out old back issues. Its formal name was *Dan Brand and Tipi*, but most know it by its later name: *White Indian*.

Frazetta leaps in again with *White Indian*. © 1949 Magazine Enterprises, Inc.

The reason they seek it out is the first artist on the feature: Frank Frazetta. Frazetta, one of the most talented comics artists and fantasy illustrators of all time, doesn't need an introduction to anyone but newbies, but we'll do it anyway. He was a Brooklyn-born artist who, like all good artists, was drawing from an early age (two, to be exact), went to art school by age eight, and started drawing comics when he was 16. Presumably, he got some rest sometime in between. He started out inking John Giunta's pencil drawings in 1944 and did a whole big batch of comics subsequently for about as many companies as had sense to hire him. We've already noted him for *Thun'da* and *Tomahawk*, so we'll mention his Buck Rogers covers for *Famous Funnies*, his work with Al Capp on *Li'l Abner*, his Conan paperback covers for Lancer, his cover work (and one comic story) for Warren, and all the other famous work he did up to his death, and leave it at that.

Uh, we were talking about comics, weren't we? Right. Let's get back to *White Indian*.

The first page of the first story (*Durango Kid* #1, August–September 1949) offered up a splash panel of a black-haired white man in Indian dress, bare-chested, leaping at an enemy with his knife in hand. Behind him, an Indian boy, Tipi, stood with bow drawn and ready to use. The bad guy wasn't about to get out of this one easy, to be sure.

The caption clued us in that Dan Brand, the White Indian, was an "ancestor of Steve Brand." Editor Ray Krank wrote the story and probably most if not all of the text. We faded in flashback to the wedding of Dan, suitably dressed in colonial attire, and his white-dressed bride, Lucy Wharton, on their wedding day. Suddenly, Peter Bradford, Dan's rival for Lucy's hand, appeared on a balcony, and swore that if he couldn't have the girl, nobody would. He drew a pistol and shot. Lucy, trying to protect her husband, threw herself in the way of the shot and died.

Brand cradled his wife as she perished and demanded Bradford be brought to him, but the killer had escaped. At her funeral, Dan Brand swore vengeance, if it took the rest of his life. The trail led him westward, out past the colonized part of the United States. But his town-bred muscles sometimes gave him trouble, and never more than when he encountered a grizzly bear. The bruin slashed his shoulder and broke his arm. Brand managed to kill the bear with his knife, but fell unconscious, and looked like a goner.

Two days later, he awoke in an Indian village, with the Catawba chief Great Deer and his son Tipi before him. They told him they'd found him in the forest and nursed him back to health. His arm in a sling, Brand thanked them, but found he could hardly get up. Tipi caught him as he fell. Great Deer cautioned the white man, "Stay with us a while and recover your health. We will teach you the ways of the forest, the Indian lore, and then you will conquer both the wilderness and your enemy." Dan agreed to stay and be taught.

And taught he was: how to shoot and bring down game with a bow and arrow, how to strengthen himself until he could bring down the strongest brave hand-to-hand, and how to be an Indian in everything but heritage. Dan Brand wore no shirt, donned leather pants and moccasins, and kept his long hair back with a headband. He had become, as one might have guessed, a white Indian.

Then tragedy came again when a tribe of Chippewa, maddened by booze and stirred to war by the white renegade who sold them the liquor, went against Great Deer's tribe. In the battle, Dan Brand saw a familiar figure ride up, shoot, and take it on the lam—Bradford. His shot brought down Great Deer. With his dying breath, the chieftain asked Brand to avenge him and take care of his son Tipi. Then Brand set out for vengeance, and nobody could draw a vengeful expression better than Frazetta.

Dan Brand used his newly hewn tracking skills to find Bradford, engaged him in combat, and was about to be shot when Tipi appeared and disarmed the villain with his bow and arrow. Brand gave him two powerful punches, one for his wife and one for Great Deer, and Bradford fell to his death.

Tipi, in tears, declared they had together slain their greatest foe, that they were blood brothers, and that he would never leave Dan's side. "I have no one else in the world to love." Dan admitted he didn't, either. "I think I have found my home and my future here—in the wilds!" And so he had. The saga of Dan Brand and Tipi had begun.

They continued, in issue after issue, excellently drawn by Frazetta through *Durango Kid* #16 (April–May 1952). His command of Colonial-era Western scenes, of battle, and of character were unchallenged. Dan and Tipi walked a line as fine as that of American Eagle, trying to keep red and white men away from each other's throats ... even when they didn't deserve it. When Dan Brand's well-defined, mighty fist connected with a bad man's face, that was *it*. You didn't get up from a White Indian punch.

The stories began circa the 1750s, but toward the end were set in the time of the Revolutionary War, some twenty years later. Tipi didn't seem to age. For that matter, neither did Dan. George Washington, whom they often aided, did, though that may have just been his wig.

Frazetta did have to leave, but that didn't mean Dan Brand was doomed to bad art. Fred Meagher, one of ME's best (and regular artist on *Straight Arrow*), picked up the baton and ran with it through issue #41 (October–November 1955). His stories were excellent and don't deserve to be forgotten because of Frazetta's. Other writers, including Gardner Fox, and other artists, such as Sid Check and Angelo Torres, contributed to the original-material issues of *White Indian*, #14 and 15 (July–September–October–November 1954). The first three issues of *White Indian,* #11–13 (1953–April–June 1954) contained Frazetta reprints. Pure Imagination reprinted some Frazetta tales in 1980's *The Comic Strip Frazetta*, and Vanguard reprinted them all in *The Complete Frazetta White Indian* in 2011. There have been other assorted reprints before and after, but nobody has revived the White Indian and his sidekick. Perhaps it's just as well.

The Westerner was a title published by an outfit known either as Wanted Comics or Orbit Comics, depending on what they put out, but it's usually referred to now as Orbit-Wanted. Without questioning who wanted that particular orbit, we shall delve into its history. *Westerner* ran from issues #14 to 41 (June 1948–December 1951), and nobody seems to know what they continued the numbering from. Like its partner, *Wanted Comics*, most covers of *The Westerner* featured a "Wanted" poster-style bit under the logo, featuring a front and side view of an Old West outlaw like Jack McCall. Hopefully, no kids tried hunting them up for the reward. Initially, the book was a Western variant of *Wanted*, with true-West stories leading off, done excellently by the likes of writer Bill Woolfolk and artists such as Mort Leav, Maurice Del Bourgo, Bernie Krigstein, and Syd Shores.

The star of *The Westerner* was one *Wild Bill Pecos*, who debuted in the first issue and kept going through the last. His first story, drawn possibly by Mort Lawrence, introduced the wandering cowboy and his sidekick, Nuggets Nugent, another Gabby Hayes figure, sans origin. All we knew is that he came from down Pecos way, he and Nuggets were headed for prospecting territory, and he already had a fearsome rep as a gunfighter. In those days, that was origin enough.

A bunch of rustlers killed a man on the first page, and the local sheriff and his posse nailed Bill (who was scrubbing himself in a tub) and Nuggets for the crime. Judy Carlson, the murdered party's daughter, couldn't ID either Wild Bill or Nuggets as the killer, and Bill shot the guns out of the posse's hands before they owned up that he probably wasn't the murderer. To make up for the loss of Judy's dad, Bill and Nuggets went to work for her—Bill rounding up cattle, and Nuggets churning up butter. It turned out the chief suspect was the richest man in town, the tyrannic Jerald Blaze, who had dammed up the local river to run the homesteaders out of town. As you might expect, Bill ended up shooting down a lot of Blaze's men, blowing up the dam, and setting fire to an oil tank on Blaze's property. He casually watched Blaze burn to death. Nuggets and Judy figured Bill for a goner too, but on the penultimate panel, he bobbed up out of a water well. While Judy kissed Bill, Nuggets opined, "I knew all th' time that Bill Pecos was too ornery a varmint to go an' die like a decent hoomin being!" That ended the first story.

The second one (*Westerner* #15, August 1948) may have chronologically been the first one in the series. It was set in 1865 in Abilene, Texas, and Nuggets shot off his mouth in a bar about being a Union supporter. They strung him up right there. Bill, passing by, entered the bar, shot the rope in two, and saved Nuggets. From there they got into a gunfight, Bill was framed as a damn-Yankee murderer for defending himself, and things took a while to sort out. Wild Bill Hickok guest starred.

Mort Leav drew a bunch more stories in the series; Mort Lawrence, Mort Meskin, and Syd Shores (who didn't even change his name to Mort) drew others; and Woolfolk wrote a number of them. Wild Bill Pecos was a cut above the average, and that helped keep the book alive.

Wildfire, the story of an outlaw horse who was broken by a boy he befriended, ran in issues #14 and 15 and were drawn by Del Bourgo. The rest of the book, up to issue #19 (March 1949), was filled by well-done Western one-shots. With #20 (April 1949), Bill Pecos got the whole danged book. By #21 (May 1949), he was back to a single story. He gradually increased to two stories per issue and sometimes, again, took over the whole blamed book. Nuggets Nugent got his own strip in *Westerner* #22 (August 1949) and kept it in most issues through #41 (December 1951). It was drawn mostly by Bernie Krigstein, and sometimes by John Buscema, Mort Lawrence, and Pete Tumlinson.

By *Westerner* #26 (April 1950), in a story titled "Wild Bill Pecos Meets Calamity Kate," Wild Bill Pecos, well, met *Calamity Kate*. Kate was a sexy masked female gunslinger who was as quick and sure on the draw as Bill himself. She also appeared to be a bandit, and when Bill, newly appointed a sheriff and riding with a load of silver on a stagecoach, met her, he was just too much of a gentleman to shoot her. But it turned out that the gorgeous girl outlaw was really working against a band of bandits who had killed her dad, and stole the silver to keep it out of the real thieves' hands. Bill deduced her identity as one Patricia Layne, saved her life, and helped her bring in her father's killers. Kate took off her mask near story's end, thinking she could now give up her double identity. But Bill convinced her to keep riding for justice, and Pat Layne smiled and said, "Call me Kate!" We did, too, and Calamity Kate got her own feature, probably drawn by Krigstein, in the next issue. Patricia's last name was changed to Wentworth in that story, but they came back to their senses after that and called her Layne again. She was still hot. Soon enough, she got a recurring villain, the romantic Gaucho Kid. John Rosenberger and Bill Everett shared art duties on her strip. She appeared in *Westerner* #27, 28, 30, and 31 (June–December 1950).

Calamity Kate teams with Wild Bill Pecos for a shoot-'em-up with sex appeal. © 1950 Patches Publications, Inc.

Lobo the Wolf Boy (*Westerner* #32, January 1951) was the next addition to the Pecos cast. His origin, written by Woolfolk and drawn by Lawrence, was a familiar one: an Indian raid massacred a wagon train, save for one bawling baby. This time, he was rescued by a mother wolf. She had lost her own cub (shades of Tarzan!) and adopted the babe for her own. He grew to be a swift, sure hunter, the leader of the pack, and wore a fur loincloth for some reason. Soon enough, the youth's path crossed that of Bill and Nuggets, and when Lobo and Bill got into a fight, the cowboy had to knock him cold. Lobo wound up being held in jail. The wolf pack didn't like that a bit, and killed the town deputy to let everybody know. But Bill saved Lobo from a lynching, gained his trust, and taught him human language and customs. Lobo got his own strip, initially by Woolfolk and Buscema, in issues #37–41 (June–December 1951).

That was the end of *The Westerner*, though, as always, AC Comics dipped into the well for a slew of reprints from 1989 to 2006, and Fantagraphics published a Mort Meskin reprint volume in 2012 and a Krigstein one in 2013. One suspects that, if revived, Will Bill, Nuggets, Calamity Kate, and Lobo would make a heckuva fun team.

But wait! Calamity Kate *was* revived, kinda, in a semi-satirical story in AC's *Bizarre Thrills* #1 (1977). And Wild Bill Pecos *was* revived, in cameo, in *Femforce* #7 (May 1987), with the heroine Ms. Victory disguised as Calamity Kate. So, perhaps, there is still hope. Or maybe not.

The American Comics Group, usually known as ACG and usually known for titles like *Adventures into the Unknown* and *Forbidden Worlds*, hitched up with *Blazing West* #1 (Fall 1948). The cover showed a cowboy on horseback shooting an enemy's hand through the wrist, making him drop his gun. Inside, the book introduced four new characters, and the first of them was *Injun Jones*.

Injun Jones indulges in horse-hopping in *Blazing West*. © 1951 American Comics Group/ACG.

By now a familiar trope, *Injun Jones* was the white man who was raised by Indians. As the story went, in Arizona circa 1850, a bunch of outlaws dry-gulched (as in: looted) a wagon train, and a 10-year-old named Bob Jones saw his father shot dead by a masked outlaw with a skull tattooed on his wrist. He was found days later by Indians, who raised him as their own. The boy hated all white men for his father's murder, and he became known as Injun Jones, as one might expect from the feature title. But by 1863, a white girl was in danger of being burned at the stake by a chieftain wanting revenge for his dead daughter, slain by a white. Injun Jones burst in, noted that killing the girl wouldn't bring the chief's daughter back nor catch her killer, and cut her free as the flames were licking her feet. The tribe didn't appreciate this, but Injun fought back and got himself and Vickie, the girl, to safety.

Later, Jones washed his face and stood revealed to Vickie as a white man. As it turned out, he learned that townie Hoss Withers was his dad's killer and that he intended to loot Vickie's wagon train for a gold shipment. Injun returned to the tribe who had almost killed the girl, convinced them that Withers and his men had killed their chief's daughter, and led them in battle against the baddies. Jones killed Withers with a hurled tomahawk. In the end, Vickie and Injun got together. "When I look at yuh, I forget the Injun part of my life, Vickie!" Injun proclaimed. "I'm all white man!" Regardless, Injun Jones ran through *Blazing West* #20 (November–December 1951), and then, when it title-changed to *The Hooded Horseman*, in issues #21–27 (January–February 1952–January–February 1953). Richard Hughes probably wrote the stories, and Ed Moritz drew them.

The next story in *Blazing West* #1 featured *Buffalo Belle*, another hard-riding beauty, who shot the gun out of a hoodlum's hand in the splash panel while on horseback, twirling a lasso which encircled her horse's head. (We will *not* try to explain that!) Belle Trent was a redheaded hellion who, when she was told to take cover as a dangerous outlaw approached, snapped back, "Why? I'm not afraid of anythin'!" Said outlaw burst into town and wounded the sheriff. He deputized Belle and she brought in the outlaw and his men. Afterward, the sheriff opted to keep her on as deputy. Buffalo Belle blazed her way through issue #20 (November–December 1951). Hughes and Max Elkan were responsible for the story.

Up next was *The Tenderfoot*, an Eastern dude who was dancing to avoid bullets shot at his feet on the splash panel. His name was Horace Eddington Brentwood, and he was deeded half the Carter Ranch by the late owner, the other half going to Carter's daughter, Margie. Brentwood would have made Caspar Milquetoast look like a macho man. Or at least it seemed so, at first. Margie's ranch foreman was a bad 'un who planned to take over the spread any way he could. When the timid Brentwood came in by train, the foreman tricked him into a quicksand pool and went back to force Margie to sign over the ranch to him. The Tenderfoot, who had been faking his ineptitude, threw off his glasses, freed himself from the bog, broke a wild horse, and rode back to clobber the fiendish foreman. At the end, he told Margie his nickname back home was "Spike." Tenderfoot picked his way through most of the issues from #1–13 (Fall 1948–September–October 1950). Hughes, again, wrote the story and Paul Cooper drew it.

Powder River Pete was the fourth feature in the first issue, a comical Western that wouldn't have been out of place in ACG's *Giggle* or *Ha-Ha* except that it was about funny people rather than animals. Pete signed off with issue #3 (January–February 1949). After him in issue #3 came *Texas Tim, Ranger*, a Texas Ranger who needed excitement and found it fighting cattle rustlers. Hughes probably wrote it and Edmond Good and A.C. Hollingsworth drew it. Tim Brennan made it through *Blazing West* #13 (September–October 1950).

In issue #4 (March–April 1949), Powder River Pete was replaced by *Little Lobo*, a bantam buckeroo who was still a boy. Leonard Starr was the artist, and the tale was told of how Lobo's prospector daddy was killed by a gang of outlaws who left Lobo himself for dead. The boy was picked up and raised by a farmer named Mike, who found his new charge could ride, rope, and shoot with the best of 'em. (How else would he get his own strip?) To stop a bad apple from foreclosing on Mike's ranch, Lobo won every event in a rodeo and gave the prize money to the mortgage man. But a chance remark revealed the man to Lobo as his father's murderer. The small saddleman rounded up a bunch of vigilantes, took down the murderer's mob, and brought down the killer himself. With issue #6 (July–August 1949), Lobo's strip was indeed retitled *The Bantam Buckaroo*. The compact cowboy went on through issue #20 (November–December 1951) and in *Hooded Horseman* #21–25 (January–February–September–October 1952).

The Hooded Horseman was the lead feature from issue #14 (November–December 1950) on, but since he started after January 1950 we'll have to hold off on him till a future volume. That'll give us all something to look forward to.

And in *Four Color Comics* #228 (May 1949), we all received *The Mark of Zorro*.

Once again, the necessary history dump: Zorro, the masked, cloaked, and hatted swashbuckling vigilante, came from a 1919 novel by Johnston McCulley, *The Curse of Capistrano*. In a trope that would be copied by comics creators for ages, the wimpish, fop-like Don Diego de la Vega would transform himself in secret to the black-masked, black-cloaked, black-hatted and black-dressed Zorro, Spanish for "Fox," and lend his sword, his strength, his acrobatic talents, and his not-inconsiderable luck to the aid of the poor peasantry. His setting was the Pueblo of Los Angeles sometime between 1769 and 1821 and, thanks to prose, movies, radio, television (especially the Guy Williams series of 1957–1959), and, yes, comics, Zorro has become a true pop culture icon. Fittingly, Bob Kane, later the creator of Batman, was in a kid gang called the Zorros in his youth.

Believe it or not, Zorro debuted in comics a year before his *Four Color* appearance. Kid Eternity, the boy who could summon dead men from the past to aid him, brought back Zorro in *Hit Comics* #55 (November 1948). Quality Comics scribes fudged the line between fictitious characters from the past and real people frequently, as Kid Eternity revived Sherlock Holmes and Dracula, among others. So there was precedent for Zorro, indeed. The Curse of Capistrano showed up on the cover and in the story, minus his mask and costume but with his whip, fighting off a crook called the Brute. Sadly, though he made a great showing, Zorro was kayoed by the Brute. The Kid sent him back to Eternity, and this version of Zorro never surfaced again.

The first *Four Color* Zorro story was drawn by Bill Ely and adapted from

McCulley's *The Mark of Zorro* by Steve and Mick Dubin. On the cover, the Fox, minus the mustache that would be his trademark thereafter, matched swords with Captain Ramon, one of the major villains of the series. In 32 pages, Zorro showed his mettle, starting off with a shot of him standing over the fallen Sgt. Gonzales, whose forehead bore a "Z"–shaped wound. The Fox warned Gonzales against mistreating Indians and rode off. The real foe was Captain Ramon, who was a rival of Don Diego's for the hand of the lovely Lolita, a young woman of high standing. Lolita disdained the weak Don Diego, but lusted for the dashing Zorro, who wooed her while masked. Ramon challenged the masked man and ended up with a Z on his forehead and a wounded arm. Ramon vowed vengeance on Zorro and the girl, having the governor imprison Lolita and her family. But Zorro rallied a group of nobles, including his father, against the corrupt politician and broke them free. Ramon got a sword point in the gut for his troubles. The governor came across with a pardon for Zorro, and the hero unmasked before Lolita. Their engagement was subsequently announced.

That was the way both the comic and the novel ended. But sequels both in prose and comics ignored the ending. Zorro had more buckles to swash, and nobody except his few trusted allies would know the face behind his mask.

Four Color #425 (September 1952), titled *The Return of Zorro*, was scripted by Gaylord DuBois and drawn by an unidentified artist, but Zorro had his mustache back, at least. In this, it was revealed that Lolita had wed Don Diego and subsequently died of a fever. The unmasking sequence was apparently retconned and Don Alejandro, Diego's daddy, was back to ragging his son for being unmanly after her death. In *this* version, at least, Don Alejandro remembered that his son had been Zorro. Then a lady got word to them through Zorro's aide, Bernardo, that she needed the Fox's help. She got it. It transpired that her brother had been running up some gambling debts and, to get out from under, was trying to convince her to marry his debtor. Also, he was induced to sign lousy business deals with a corrupt trader. The masked man heard the lady's story and got to work. In 34 pages (the story finished on the inside back and back covers), Zorro set things to rights, dealt out another "Z" mark or two, revealed his identity again, and got the girl. There was going to have to be another retcon.

A year later, *The Sword of Zorro* (*Four Color* #497, September 1953) appeared, with art by the always excellent Everett Raymond Kinstler. This time, Zorro faced masked foes: the Night Riders, a gang of terrorists and thieves who were looting and laying waste to rancheros all over the place. Once again, Don Alejandro saw his son become Zorro and take after the bad guys. Swords flashed, Z-marks were gouged, and Zorro stopped the head villain from taking over Alta California. Panchita, the girl from the last adventure, had gotten fed up with Diego putting off her wedding and called it off herself. But she reconsidered at the end, and revealed that she knew about Diego's double identity.

Kinstler was back for *FC* #535 (March 1954), *The Mask of Zorro*. Russian fur traders were raising hell in Alta California—appropriate villains, as this was at the peak of America's anti–Communist stance. Panchita was back, the governor knew Zorro's identity (who didn't, at this point?), and the masked man stopped the Russkies from taking over the state. Along the way, a traitor who had been romancing Panchita fell to his death. It was another quite decent tale.

The Hand of Zorro (FC #574, August 1954), scripted by Paul S. Newman and illustrated, again, by Kinstler, found a band of highwaymen stealing tax money, with its leader being the head tax collector himself. (This was way, *way* before the IRS.) Diego put off his wedding again, Panchita got captured again, Zorro rescued her again, and he carved his mark in the villain's forehead—again. It was still a good story.

Also, it was the last American Zorro comic for three years. The books must have sold, but not enough to cause Dell to commit to a regular series.

Naturally, things did not end there. In 1957, Walt Disney, whose works Dell had been adapting for almost two decades, premiered the *Zorro* TV program, starring Guy Williams as the man in the mask and mustache. He was born to the part, and kids all over America dug his adventures. Nobody had to give Dell a wakeup call.

Walt Disney Presents Zorro (FC #882, 1958) premiered with a photo-cover of Guy Williams in the role and two new stories, both done by Alex Toth, whose tour of duty on the feature would be rightfully famed. It's not certain who wrote the stories, but he did an excellent job. Chronologically, the series either predated the previous *Four Color* stories or took place in an alternate continuity. Whatever the case, "Presenting Senor Zorro" served as an origin story. It was adapted from the first *Zorro* TV episode, and was done excellently.

Don Diego de la Vega was summoned from Spain to the Alta California estate of Don Alejandro, finding time for a spiffy sword-duel along the way. As he soon learned, the state had been placed under martial law by the evil, corrupt, tyrannical, and definitely bad Captain Monasterio, and Don Alejandro needed his son to help resist the tyrant. But, wisely, Don Diego knew that a frontal assault against their powerful foe wouldn't work.

Accordingly, with the help of his servant Bernardo, Diego fashioned, as we've seen, the foppish role of himself and the dashing identity of Zorro. "When you cannot clothe yourself in a lion's skin, put on that of a fox!" he declared. To help things along, Bernardo, a mute, pretended to be deaf as well. A friend of the family, one Nacho Torres, was arrested and imprisoned as a traitor. His crime was writing a letter of complaint to the governor. Zorro revealed to Bernardo his great black horse, Tornado, and a Batcave of sorts, hidden behind a sliding piano. Thus equipped, the hero of Jurassic-era Los Angeles crushed Monasterio's plot to have Torres shot while escaping, broke the man out of jail, and delivered him into the hands of Padre Felipe, a sympathetic monk. That was after he beat Monasterio in a sword duel and made jerks out of Sgt. Garcia and his soldiers. The stage was set for high adventure, and Zorro did not disappoint.

Five more *Four Color* Zorros followed (#920, 933, 976, 1003, and 1037, June 1958–September–November 1959) before Dell broke down and gave the Fox his own comic. Toth did the art for all the *Four Color* issues except #1037, which was illoed by Warren Tufts. Disney diva Annette Funicello appeared on that issue's cover, though not, alas, in a bikini. *Walt Disney's Zorro* took its numbering from the TV episodes and ran for issues #8–15 (December 1959–February 1960 to September–November

1961), with art by Tufts and John Uhler. Then, with Zorro's TV show ended and the two one-hour Disney specials about Zorro having aired, the series was canceled.

In 1962, most of Dell's licensed features moved to the brand-new Gold Key Comics. Zorro was given another tryout in *Walt Disney's Comics and Stories* #275–278 (August–November 1963). The masked man shared cover space with Donald Duck and company, appearing in five-page stories drawn by Nat Edson. The feature apparently didn't catch fire. Three years later, Gold Key tried it again with *Walt Disney's Zorro* #1–9 (January 1966–March 1968). These were all Dell reprints and probably didn't make enough of a noise for them to consider doing original stories.

That, of course, didn't stop other countries from doing their own comic versions of Zorro, licensed by Disney, and they did. Zorro tales, many of them very short, showed up in France's *Le Journal de Mickey*, Germany's *Mickeyvision*, and Britain's *Walt Disney's Weekly*, among others. Some of these foreign comics were quite competent indeed and saw reprinting decades later in the States. But Zorro had to wait a long time for a return to original American comics. A few stories were reprinted once again in *Walt Disney's Comics Digest* and *Walt Disney Showcase*, but without a TV show or movie to support him, Zorro's episodes fell on stony ground.

Zorro cameoed in Marvel's *Tomb of Dracula* #49 (October 1976) as one of a small army of fictional characters mentally conjured up by a girl to battle the vampire king. Dracula proved quite capable of matching swords with the Fox, but the fake Zorro soon vanished. It wasn't until 1986 that Zorro returned in comics stories unseen by most U.S. readers. Eclipse Comics published the collection *Zorro in Old California*, with translated tales from *Le Journal de Mickey*, and they were a welcome feast for Zorro buffs. This was followed two years later by their *Zorro: The Complete Classic Adventures by Alex Toth* #1–2 (June–July 1988), which recollected all the Dell Toth stories.

And two years after that, Marvel got into the game.

The Family Channel on TV was running a new *Zorro* series, and Marvel jumped in with an adaptation. *Zorro* #1 (December 1990) was written by Ian Rimmer and illustrated by Mario Capaldi, with a cover shot of the classic pose, Zorro astride a rearing Tornado. Inside, while escaping from pursuers, Zorro was thrown almost to his death when his steed slipped. Half-amnesiac, he remembered his own origin in some detail. The story added a silent boy sidekick, Felipe, and a new romantic interest, Victoria. The Alcalde, a new tyrant, was the uber-villain of the series. It was about average quality for Marvel at the time—but Zorro was *back!* The series lasted through issue #12 (November 1991).

Two years later, he was back again, in one of his best comics incarnations ever. Topps Comics, a short-lived imprint created by the famed gum card company, got into the adaptation market big time in 1993. Guess what was one of the properties they licensed?

Except for a little preview book, *Dracula vs. Zorro* #1–2 (October–November 1993) was the first sight of a new Zorro. This one wasn't restrained by Disney or Family Channel standards. Marvel and Eclipse scribe Don McGregor, who hero-worshipped Zorro, wrote it, Tom Yeates drew it, and on the cover (at least one of them), Zorro swung down on a rope, sword in his other hand, toward the figure of Dracula in the act of draining a woman dry. This time, it was all business.

Briefly, Zorro went to Spain to have a new sword crafted by a supremely skilled maker and fought off a mob of locals who thought the savant was a sorcerer, while Dracula had his coffin shipped to France. Don Diego was on the very ship that Dracula was on, and that's the way things started. When they finished, Zorro slew—for a time—Dracula with a religious artifact reputed to be Christ's crown of thorns. He jammed it on Dracula's head. Unlike Marvel's Dracula, Topps's had no interest in matching swords with him.

Zorro #0 (don't question the number, folks) premiered on November 1993, at least by cover date. In this abnormally short preview comic, written by McGregor and drawn by Mike Mayhew and John Nyberg, the Fox encountered a crazy mountain man who laid more traps than you'd find in an average James Bond movie, and Zorro bled a lot (he did that through the whole series), but won in the end. Things were set up for the series to follow.

In short order, Captain Monasterio, Sgt. Garcia, and Don Alejandro were back, and so were new characters like Machete and Moonstalker. But in issue #3 (March 1994), we met a character who was to survive the end of Zorro's own book: *Lady Rawhide*.

The lady in question was a masked vigilante like Zorro, though her red leather duds and red-dyed hair would never have been tolerated or even thought of in the era depicted. Lady Rawhide (aka Anita Santiago) was a sexy heroine, usually more undressed than dressed, and she wielded a whip and performed acrobatic stunts as well as Zorro. She didn't like him much more than Monasterio, blaming him for the accidental blinding of her brother. Thus, Anita created her own secret identity and ended up collaborating with Zorro, though she affirmed that she wanted to kill him. The introductory issue sold out.

McGregor wrote the entire series in his customary highfalutin style. The series ended with issue #11 (November 1994). In an editorial note, McGregor said he was working on a new series called *Zorro: Matanzas*, but that could wait, and it would— for several years, in fact. Lady Rawhide was a hotter property, and she appeared in a couple of mini-series and small specials of her own before Topps's comic division was shuttered.

McGregor, Ron Wagner, and Rick Magyar had done a fine adaptation of the popular movie *The Mask of Zorro* for Image (#1–4, August 1998–January 1999). And shortly after that series, McGregor and Tom Yeates crafted a fine Zorro strip for the newspapers, starting on April 12, 1999. Image collected the first year of it in *Zorro: The Dailies* #1 (October 2001). An omnibus of the second and last year was planned but not published.

McGregor returned to the character again with Papercutz's *Zorro* #1–4 (May– August 2005), drawn by Sidney Lima. The adventure took Zorro and a girl he rescued from Monasterio to Yellowstone in Colorado, where they met new allies and new foes. The art was manga-influenced. The fourth issue began another unfinished arc, proving there is probably a small industry in uncompleted McGregor stories. It wasn't until 2010 that the story of McGregor's Zorro continued, in a four-parter from

Dynamite Comics called *Zorro: Matanzas*. In it, Zorro encountered Machete again, and Don Alejandro was graphically gored by a bull and almost killed. The story was unresolved at the end. And, sadly, that was McGregor's last turn with the character, since *Matanzas* had been done earlier.

It wasn't the end of Zorro in comics, naturally.

Besides a couple of AC Comics reprints, the character fell to the hands of Dynamite in 2008, as did Lady Rawhide. Matt Wagner was the scribe and Francesco Francavilla the artist on *Zorro* #1–20 (February 2008–March 2010). *Lone Ranger and Zorro: The Death of Zorro* (#1–5, March–June 2011) and *Zorro Rides Again* (#1–12, August 2011–October 2012) followed up the next year, both series written by Wagner. He continued his tour on the character with *Django / Zorro* #1–7 (November 2014–May 2015), teaming the Fox with a movie antihero. A newly coined Lady Zorro fought side by side with Lady Rawhide in *Lady Rawhide / Lady Zorro* #1–4 (March–July 2015) and then went off to a career of her own. A new incarnation of Zorro teamed up with the Green Hornet, Kato, the Shadow, the Spider, the Black Bat, the Green Lama, Miss Fury, the Black Terror, and any other pulp heroes that weren't nailed down in *Masks* V. 1 (#1–8, 2012–2013), by Chris Robertson, Dennis Calero, and Alex Ross.

Zorro took a few years off and then signed up with American Mythology Productions. *Zorro: Swords of Hell* #1–4 (2018–2019), by David Avallone and Roy Allan Martinez, was his first series. Then came *Zorro: The Legendary Adventures* (V. 1 #1–4, 2018–2019, and V. 2 #1–4, 2019), translated reprints of stories from *Le Journal de Mickey*. *Zorro: Rise of the Old Gods* #1–4 (2019) and *Zorro: Sacrilege* #1–4 (2019) followed. Odds are there will be more such series, and more reprints of the Toth stories, in years to come. Zorro still rides!

Gunsmoke, which came before both the 1952–1961

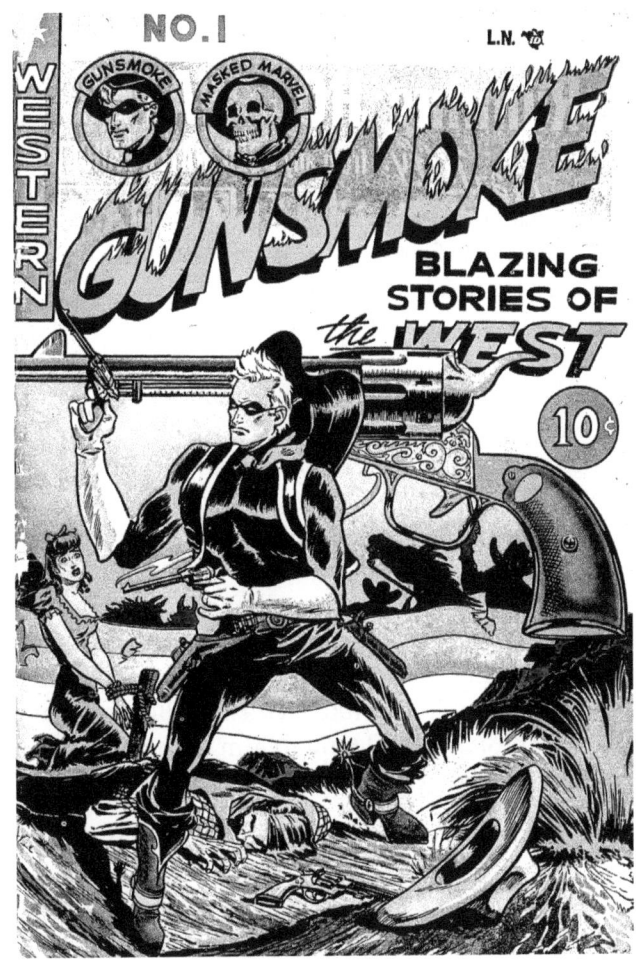

Long before Matt Dillon appeared on TV, *Gunsmoke* was there in comics. © 1949 Western Comics.

radio show and the 1955–1975 TV program, was published by Youthful but looked an awful lot like an EC Western. That was probably due to Graham Ingels doing the cover and two stories inside. *Gunsmoke* was the name of the featured hero, a masked, black-clad, gun-slinging mystery man of the West. He had no origin, and his secret ID was never revealed. When a kid named Pedro sent him a smoke signal, he rode into town to keep a crooked rancher from swindling an honest one, and did so, shooting down a batch of bad guys in the process. Then Gunsmoke rode away.

By the next issue, Gunsmoke had dropped his mask and Pedro was his sidekick. They roamed the West, seeking justice (and maybe a job, while they were at it), doing so for the entire run (#1–16, April–May 1949–January 1952). Besides Ingels, Manny Stallman and Doug Wildey lent their artistic talents to the strip.

The Comanche Kid was *Gunsmoke* #1's next feature. He was without an origin and wasn't particularly original, either. Clad in buckskin, the Comanche Kid tried to lead a wagon train to safety, got fired for getting too close to the boss's daughter, tried overseeing them from afar when he learned of an outlaw's plot to waylay and rob the wagons, and got shot for his trouble. He recovered and gave the bandits some shots of his own, from which they did not recover. The Kid was not particularly well-drawn or -written, and he was only in the first two issues.

The third feature, *The Masked Marvel*, had much more potential. His secret ID was that of Chet Fairchild, a bespectacled playboy who lived at the spread of his millionaire oilman father. But when danger threatened, he threw on a green skull mask, a black hat and cape, a yellow shirt, regular pants, red gloves, and a pair of six-guns, and became the fearsome Masked Marvel. He began his career by clearing the name of a man framed for the killing of a rancher. Ingels drew the first story. Bill Fraccio, Tony Tallarico, and Al Liederman succeeded him. The Masked Marvel appeared in all 16 issues.

The 16th issue (January 1952) bore a cover with Gunsmoke on horseback, fighting an Indian skeleton mounted on another horse. The Indian's horse had a skull and crossbones branded on it, and the blurb "Beasts of Horror" was on the cover. Evidently the publisher was trying to hook into horror fandom, but it didn't work or else it came too late. *Gunsmoke* had emptied its weapon. Youthful put out other Westerns, but they started after 1950.

And that may be the lot of American Western comics heroes from the Forties. The genre would really flourish in the Fifties and peter out in the Sixties and Seventies, though European markets would love and romanticize the Old West cowboy for years to come in series like *Lieutenant Blueberry* and *Lucky Luke*, and comic strips like *Rick O'Shay* would tend to him in the newspapers. But as we've seen, the Western hero in American comics never truly dies. We doff our Stetsons to him, and then pass on.

Conclusion

So here we come to the end of our present journey. History, even pop history, doesn't deserve to die. In *Secondary Superheroes*, we told the stories of the neglected superheroes of the 1940s. There were still a batch of famous Golden Age heroes in other genres, and we've tried to cover them here.

Sheena, Tarzan, John Carter, the Lone Ranger, Zorro, and a number of others are perennials, so appealing to fans and creators (and, thankfully, available for licensing) that they'll probably always be around. Others in the public domain, like Spacehawk, Kaanga, and Dr. Drew, are up for grabs, and nostalgia-influenced publishers are grabbing them. They're always around for rediscovery, and as long as comics are around, we'll be rediscovering them.

Many of these heroes bossed adventure comics in the Fifties, though the jungle queens were neutralized by the Comics Code. Time and sales providing, we may cover the characters of that decade as well. But for now, we hope you've enjoyed our venture into the wilds of Africa, the chasms of space, the battlefields of World War II and after, and the plains of the Old West.

Heroes are made for action, and comics' action heroes usually did it best.

Bibliography

As usual, a ton and a half of research went into this one, and I loved it. Here are some of the sources I used in writing the book.

Andreychuk, Ed. *The Lone Ranger on Radio, Film, and Television*. McFarland, 2018. Good history of the Masked Man. Besides, the publisher would probably smash me if I didn't include this one.
The Autry Museum (https://www.geneautry.com/museum/). Cofounded by Gene and Monte Hale.
Digital Comic Museum (http://digitalcomicmuseum.com/) and Comic Book Plus (https://comicbookplus.com/). Scanned versions of many of the books covered can be found here.
Ellington, Richard. "Me To Your Leader Take." *All in Color for a Dime*. Ed. Dick Lupoff and Don Thompson. Krause Publications, 1970. Great article on *Planet Comics*.
George-Warren, Holly. *Public Cowboy No. 1: The Life and Times of Gene Autry*. Oxford University Press, 2007. The lowdown on Gene Autry.
Grand Comics Database (https://www.comics.org/). Index of darn near every comic published (that's an exaggeration, but we're working on it). Invaluable tool for research.
Harmon, Jim. *The Great Radio Heroes*. Ace Publications, 1967; expanded ed. McFarland, 2001. You haven't lived until you read Jim's coverage of the radio adventures of Tom Mix, the Lone Ranger, and all the rest. Grab it while you can.
Harmon, Jim, and Donald F. Glut. *The Great Movie Serials: Their Sound and Fury*. Woburn Press, 1973. Coverage of a number of great serials, including *Perils of Nyoka*, *King of the Congo*, and a bunch of others.
Horn, Maurice. *Comics of the American West*. Winchester Press, 1977. Pretty much the ur-history of Western comic books and comic strips.
Maglio, Mitch. *Fiction House: From Pulps to Panels, From Jungle to Space*. IDW Publishing, 2017. All you ever needed to know about Fiction House.
Movie, Radio, and TV Cowboy Comics (https://sites.google.com/site/bwesterncowboycomics/). Another great comics download site.
Nevins, Francis M. *Hopalong Cassidy: On the Page, On the Screen*. Museum of Western Film History, 2016. Good study of Hoppy.
The Old Corral (https://www.b-westerns.com/). A ton and a half of stuff on B-movie cowboys and cowgirls. Great source of info.
Rainey, Buck. *The Life and Films of Buck Jones: The Sound Era*. The World of Yesterday, 1991. The bio of Buck Jones.
Rothel, David. *Tim Holt*. 2014. Riverwood Press. Covering Tim Holt, but not Redmask or Black Phantom!
Rothel, David. *Who Was That Masked Man? The Story of the Lone Ranger*. Riverwood Press, 1981. My fave history of the Ranger.
Roy Rogers Museum (https://royrogersfestival.com/museum.php). Tell 'em we sent you.
Savage, William W., Jr. *Comic Books and America, 1945–1954*. University of Oklahoma Press, 1990. Compact history of the postwar decade, useful for Westerns and jungle comics.
Schelly, Bill. *American Comic Book Chronicles: The 1950s*. TwoMorrows Publishing, 2013. Excellently researched and written tome about Fifties comics.
Thornton, Chuck, and David Rothel. *Lash LaRue, King of the Bullwhip*. Empire Publishing, 2003. The Man in Black who whipped things into shape.
Tom Mix Museum (https://www.tommixmuseum.com/home). Great online site about Tom Mix.
White, Raymond E. *King of the Cowboys, Queen of the West: Roy Rogers and Dale Evans*. University of Wisconsin Press, 2005. The bio of Roy and Dale, just for you.

Index

Numbers in ***bold italics*** indicate pages with illustrations

Abel, Jack 25
AC Comics 14, 19, 25, 35, 38, 43, 44, 47, 53, 74, 77, 83, 108, 1245, 140, 163, 185, 210–212, 219–220, 222–224, 230, 266, 274, 282, 284, 285, 289, 292, 298, 305
Adams, Kellog 212, 217
All-Top Comics 43, 44, 45, 46
Allison, William (W.M.) 205, 246, 267
Americomics 35, 40, 292
Anderson, Murphy 75, 76, 77, 87
Antartic Comics 14, 38, 40, 43
Archie Comics 28, 32, 209
Ashe, Edd 157, 160, 161
Astarita, Rafael 14, 28, 38, 89
Atlas 53, 55, 59, 231, 232, 236, 237, 238, 246; *see also* Timely, Marvel
Autry, Gene 200, 209, 210, 211, 219, 286, 309
Ayers, Dick 234, 240, 262, 286, 287, 288, 289, 290

Bailey, Mart 263
Bailey, Ray 178, 277
Baker, Matt 25, 36, 42, 47, 48, 83, 119, 136, 164, 234, 268, 269
Barry, Sy 199, 200, 203
Battefield, Ken 157, 268
Beck, C.C. 178, ***178***, 217
Binder, Jack 153, 220
Binder, Otto 30, 107, 161, 220, 223
Biro, Charles (Charlie) 81 108, 182, 256, ***256***, 258, 278
Black, Bill 35, 125, 185, 284, 289
Blackthorne Comics 10, 14, 88
Blacton, Bill 12–13
Blaisdell, Tex 266, 268
Blue Ribbon Comics 28, 92, 246
Blum, Alex 7, 12, 71, 129, 164, 234
Bolle, Frank 165, 215, 281
Bourgo, Del 295, 296

Boyd, Bill 207, 208
Briefer, Dick 6, 64, 66, 100, 102, 103, 116, 117, 262
Brodie-Mack, Edward 26
Brodsky, Sol 10, 241
Broome, John 193, 199, 200, 203
Brown, Bob 203, 204
Buck Rogers 76
Buck Rogers v, 62, 67, 91, 107, 111, 294
Burroughs, Edgar Rice 59, 60, 62, 105
Buscema, John 212, 238, 296, 298

Calkins, Dick 64, 92, 99, 217
Cameron, Don 194, 203
Campbell, Stan 223, 225
Captain Terry Thunder and the Congo Lancers 19
Cardy, Nick 28, 67, 87, 123, 124, 203
Carreno, Al 261, 262
Celardo, John 14, 77, 116, 249
Centaur (Comics) 91, 92, 185, 187, 204, 205, ***205***, 270
Certa, Joe 272, 291
Charlton (Comics) 34, 35, 46, 60, 163, 179, 209, 219, 220, 222, 223, 224, 255, 266, 267, 288
Cole, L.B. 156, 157, 162, 173
Congo Bill 26–27
Congorilla 27
Craig, Johnny 278, ***283***
Crandall, Reed 14, 28, 166, 225, 228, 229, 240
Crown Comics 36, 164, 165

Dale, Jon 16, 19
Dale, Kathy 226–227
Dale, Mary 80
DC Comics 6, 7, 26, 27, 60, 76, 90, 100, 111, 112, 157, 173, 180, 184–185, 188–189, 191–198, 200–201, 203–205, 209, 212, 213, 219, 234, 240, 253, 253, 256

Dell Comics 59, 60, 105, 111, 160, 179, 180, 181, 182, 187, ***187***, 206, 207, 210, ***211***, 212, 213, 214, 215, 216, 217, 277, 302, 303
Devil's Due Publishing 10, 23
Doolin, Joe 75, 78, 83
Doyle, Frank 223, 224
Drake, Christian 10
Drucker, Mort 196, 200
DuBois, Gaylord 59, 60, 181, 210, 211, 212, 217, 301
Dynamite (Comics) 11, 19, 21, 23, 53, 60, 215, 305

EC Comics 46, 87, 90, 120, 165, 175, ***176***, 199, 230, 263, 265, 277, 278, ***280***, 306
Eclipse Comics 144, 156, 274, 303
Eisner, Will 5, 6, 64, 71, 113–116, 118, 125, 126, 143, 144, 185, 186, 229
Elder, Bill 262, 263, 265
Elias, Lee 73, 75, 138, 140
Elkan, Max 212, 213, 275, 299
Ely, Bill 203, 300
Englehart, Steve 244, 245
Evans, George 88, 223
Evans, Phil 200, 207, 217
Everett, Bill 55, 92, 270, ***270***, 272, 297
Exciting Comics 36, 38, 107, 246

Fantagraphics 53, 223, 298
Fantomah 21, 23, 205
Fawcett Comics 7, 29, 30, 33–35, 109, 160–163, 178, 184–185, 207–210, 217–222, 224, 225
Fawcette, Gene 38, 39, 47, 71, 108
Feldstein, Al 165, 230, 278
Fiction House 1, 4, 7, 8, 9, 11, 12, 17, 20, 21, 26, 30, 32, 36, 53, 60, 62, 63, 68, 75, 77, 81, 87, 90, 91, 92, 113, 116, 118, 121, 125, 128, 129, 136, 138, 140, 144, 145, 164, 269

311

Index

Fight Comics 1, 23, 113, 117, 188, 120, 122, 124–126, 128–129, 141
Filchock, George 205
Filchock, Martin 205
Fine, Lou 64, 101, 117
Firfires, Nicholas 207, 210
Fitch, Ken 223, 224
The Flash 209
Flash Comics 194
Flash Gordon v, 21, 62, 63, 91, 111, 117, 196
Flash Gordon 29, 30, 89, 111
Fletcher, Henry *see* Hanks, Fletcher
Forte, John 44, 49, 252
Foster, Hal 30, 59
Four Color Comics 59, 111, 160, 207, 210, 212, 213, 214, 216, 217, 277, 300, 301, 302
Fox, Gardner 49, 112, 171, 173, 175, 193, 194, 199, 200, 278, 281, 287, 295
Fox Comics 40, 41, 42, 43, 46, 103, 104, 105, 165, 172, 222, 229
Frank, Leonard 220, 221
Frazetta, Frank 39, 49, 50, 51, 111, 112, 201, 203, 287, **287**, 288, 290, **293**, 293, 295
Friedrich, Gary 241, 289
Froehlich, August 30, 140

Giacoia, Frank 198, 200, 201
Gill, Joe 60, 234, 240
Gill, Ray 152
Gill, Tom 214, 215
Giolitti, Alberto 214, 277
Giordano, Dick 197, 223
Giunta, John 199, 276, 294
Glanzman, Sam 60, 203
Gleason, Lev 81, 108, 109, 157, 182, 255, **256**, 257, **257**, 259, **259**
Gold Key Comics 59, 60, 183, 211, 212, 215, 217, 303
Good, Edmond 46, 201, 221, 255, 300
Goodan, Till 210
Goodman, Martin 27, 55, 231, 245
Grandenetti, Jerry 144, 203
Guardineer, Fred 91, 112, 173, 257, 290, 291

Hampton, John 28, 30, 217
Haney, Bob 196, 203
Hanks, Fletcher 20, 21, 71, 103, 120
Harman, Fred 216
Hart, Ernie 223, 224, 240
Hartley, Al 232, 241
Hasen, Irwin 198, 199, 200, 201
Hastings, Dan 91, 92, 107
Hayes, Gabby 207, 219, 220, 263, 265, 296

Heath, Russ 55, 240, 245
Heck, Don 58, 215
Herron, France (Ed) 194, 199, 203
Hillman Comics 30, 106, **168**, 169, 272
Hing, Chu 234, 238, 240
Hollingsworth, A.C. 230, 300
Hopper, Fran 19, 75, 78, 83
Hughes, Richard 177, 206, 299, 300

Iger, Jerry 5, 6, 64
Infantino, Carmine 194, 196, 199, 201
Ingels, Graham 87, 107, 253, **254**, 278, **283**, 306
Isip, Rey 76, 87, 135
IW-Super 43, 44, 47, 77, 140, 144, 152, 156, 157, 168, 255, 277, 289

Jan of the Jungle 26
Jordan, John 162, 184
Jumbo 1, 3–9, 11, 77, 91, 113–118

Ka-Zar 14, 27
Kaanga (Ka'a'nga) 11, 12, 14, 23, 25, 43, 61, 307
Kamen, Jack 25, 42, 44, 120, 125, 127, 133, 157, 165, 178–179, 230, 252
Kane, Bob 6, 113, 300
Kane, Gil 194, 196, 197, 198, 199, 200, 201, 209
Kanigher, Bob 105, 194, 195, 196, 203, 204, 256
Kazanda, Queen of the Lost Continent 26
Keller, Jack 239, 241
Kida, Fred 234
Kiefer, Henry 71, 106, 278
Kinstler, Raymond (Everett) 46, 254, 255, 301, 302
Kirby, Jack 6, 27, 80, 116, 117, 147, 199, 200, 233, 234, 241, 244, 262, 265
Krank, Ray 51, 286, 291, 294
Krigstein, Bernie 199, 228, 272, 295, 296, 297, 298
Kubert, Joe 199, 200, 201, 240, 250
Kurtzman, Harvey 201, 262

Lane, Rocky 222, 223
Larsen, H.L. (Howard) 142, 169, 252, 254, 255, 268, 269
LaRue, Alfred (Al, Lash) 223, 224, 267, 309
Lawrence, Mort 296, 298
Leav, Mort 295, 296
Lee, Stan 27, 53, 232, 233, 234, 237, 239, 240, 241
Lesser, Sol 9

Lev Gleason (Publications) 81, 108, 157, 182, 255, **256**, 257, **257**, 259, **259**
Lieber, Larry 237, 241
The Lost World 83, 84, 87
Lubbers, Bob 132, 140, 268, 269

Magazine Enterprises (ME) 278, 279, 281, 282, 284, 285, 289, 290, 291, 292
Magyar, Rick 215, 304
Maneely, Joe 55, 58, 234, 240, 244
Manning, Russ 60, 213
Marsh, Jesse 59, 60, 207, 210
Marshall, John (aka John Starr) 138, 140
Martin, Archie 26
Marvel Comics (Timely, Atlas) 10, 27, **54**, 55, **56**, **57**, **58**, 59, 60, 100, 231, 232, 234, **235**, **236**, 237, 238, **238**, 240, 241, 242, **243**, 245, 246, 270, 272, 289, 303, 306
Master Comics 7, 30, 34, 109, 185, 206, 207, 208
Mastroserio, Rocco 225, 265
Mayo, Ralph 19, 38, 39, 194
McCalla, Irish 9, 10
McGregor, Don 303, 304, 305
Meagher, Fred 182, 295
Meskin, Mort 6, 29, 188, **189**, 262, 296, 298
Millard, Joe 168, 193, 227
MLJ (Comics) 91, 92, 107, 246
Moldoff, Sheldon (Shelly) 39, 40, 162, 175, 255
Moore, Alan 38, 83, 165, 196
Moreira, Ruben 14, 83, 194, 247, 249
Mystery Comics 27, 107, 157, 231

Nedor (Publications) 36, 38, 107, 108, 246, 247, 249
Newman, Paul S. 200, 214, 215, 217, 221, 224, 234, 240, 254, 277, 302
Nolin, Gena Lee 10
Novelty Comics (Press) 96, **98**, 117, 145, **148**, 151, **151**, **153**, 155, 270, **270**, 272

Oran of the Jungle 25
Overgard, William 258, 261

Paddock, Munson 107, 229
Palais, Rudy 87, 132, 268, 275
Paris, Charles 193, 194
Parker, Paul 171, 290
Parkhurst, Harry 28, 208
Pathfinder: Worldscape 19, 21, 23, 53
Peddy, Art 67, 230, 254
Peters, Fred 278

Index

Pfeufer, Carl 162, 184, 221
Pike, Jay Scott 55, 57
Planet Comics v, 62, **63**, 63, 64, 66, 67, 68, 71, 72, 74, 75, 77, **78**, 79, 80, 81, 83, 84, 85, 87, 88, 89, 90, 91, 99, 106, 113, 309
Popular Comics 59, 160, 181, 182, 210
Powell, Bob 7, 8, 51, 52, 66, 73, 165, 173, 224, 230, 274
Premiani, Bruno 194, 203
Prize Comics 30, 117, 261
Prize Comics Western 261, **261**, 262, 263, 266
Purcell, Howard 173, 199

Quality Comics 28, 105, 106, 184, 225, 226, 228, 229, 300
Quinlan, Charles M. 74, 165, 274

Raboy, Mac 29, 30
Rangers Comics 26, 113, 129, 132–136, 138–141, 143–145
Ray, Fred 27, 203, 204
Raymond, Alex 30, 64, 92, 99, 111
The Red Panther 21
Reed, Rod 161, 220, 277
Renée, Lily 75, 78, 88, 124, 125
Reynolds, Bob 3, 5–8
Reynolds, Marcia 89, 90
Rice, Pierce 230, 238
Rico, Don 57, 58, 104, 234
Riss, Pete 221, 273
Roberts, Pistol 39
Roberts, Tanya 10
Rockwell, Dick 261, 274
Rocky Hall, Jungle Stalker 26
Rogers, Marshall 244, 245
Rogers, Roy 210, 211, **211**, 212, **212**, 213, 219, 267, 309
Rosenberger, John 77, 297
Roy Lance 21
Ryder, Robert 217

Saaf, Art 14, 38, 39, 40, 67, 73, 116, 134
Sarrett, Joan
Savitt, Sam 210, 217
Schoffman, Irwin 220, 221, 223, 224

Schomburg, Alex 38, 39, 107, 108
Schwartz, Alvin 199, 200, 203
Schwartz, Julius 209
Scott, Randolph 219, 228, 263
Seduction of the Innocent 42
Sekowsky, Mike 199, 240
Severin, John 203, 223, 233, 234, 262, 263, 265
Shadow Comics 30, 32, 109, 153, 272, 273
She 6
Sheena, Queen of the Jungle iv, 8, 11
Sherman, Howard 192, 203
Shores, Syd 58, 223, 231, 232, 234, 244, 245, 295, 296
Simba, King of the Beasts 21
Simon, Joe 147, 262, 265
Skywald Comics 10, 43, 44, 47, 255, 292
Slam-Bang Comics 30, 109, 219
Small, Jon 214, 252
Snyder, Marcia 14, 19, 38
Spacehawk (Spacehawk) 1, 93, 94, 95, 96, **96**, 97, 98, 99, 100, 307
Speed Comics 107, 230
Spiegle, Dan 208, 212
Starr, Leonard 75, 77, 165, 194, 198, 300
Startling Comics 39, 40, 107, 246
Stein, Marvin 179, 262, 265
Stokes, Manning (Lee) 42, 44, 49
Stone, Chic 27
Street & Smith 30, **31**, 109, 153, **154**, **155**, 173, 272, 273
Striker, Fran 213, 214
Sultan, Charles 28, 71, 83, 117, 177, 227

Tabu, Wizard of the Jungle 20
Target Comics 93, 96, 99, 152, 270, **270**, 272
Taylor, Stuart 117, 118
Temson, Zack 25
Thomas, Roy 87, 191, 203, 241, 289
Thompson, Ben 27

Thompson, Jimmy 253, 254
Thorne, Frank 203, 204
Thrilling Comics 36, 108, 246, 247
Tiger Girl 23, 25
Tip Top Comics 59, 247
Toth, Alex 185, 194, 195, 196, 200, 212, 302, 303, 305
Tufts, Warren 302, 303
Tumlinson, Pete 240, 296
Tuska, George 7, 13, 19, 28, 58, 72, 74, 75, 76, 92, 104, 117, 119, 121, 132, 136, 138, 224, 234, 277

Ulmer, Al 169, 250

Wags 5, 6, 26, 113, 115, 117
Walsh, Bill 238, 240
Wambi 19
Webb, Robert 8, 25, 28, 116
Webb, Steve 252
Weisinger, Mort 188, **189**, 191
Werstein, Irving (Irv) 199, 262
Wertham, Fredric 42, 60, 288
Wessler, Carl 203, 240, 261
Whitman, Maurice 14, 75, 77, 83, **91**, 216, 225
Whitney, Ogden 58, 171, 172, 173
Whiz Comics 29, 30, 163, 217, 218, 219
Wildey, Doug 60, 225, 273, 274, 306
Williamson, Al 57, 237, 265
Wings Comics 1, 72, 78, 91, 129, 144, 145
Winter, Chuck (Charles) 14, 83, 168
Wolverton, Basil 92, 93, 96, 97, 99, 100, **259**, 260
Wood, David 194, 199, 203
Wood, Wally 44, 46, 278
Woolfolk, Bill 221, 223, 295, 296, 298

Yeates, Tom 303, 304

Zolnerowich, Dan 14, 75, 115, 129
Zoot Comics 41, 42, 43, 105

www.ingramcontent.com/pod-product-compliance
Ingram Content Group UK Ltd.
Pitfield, Milton Keynes, MK11 3LW, UK
UKHW051850210426
5322IPUK00025B/649